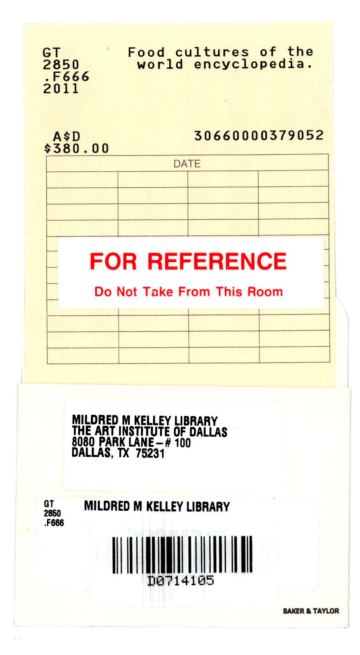

Food Cultures of the World
Encyclopedia

Food Cultures of the World Encyclopedia

AFRICA AND THE MIDDLE EAST

Volume 1

KEN ALBALA, EDITOR

GREENWOOD

AN IMPRINT OF ABC-CLIO, LLC
Santa Barbara, California • Denver, Colorado • Oxford, England

Library of Congress Cataloging-in-Publication Data

Food cultures of the world encyclopedia / Ken Albala, editor.
     v. cm.
   Includes bibliographical references and index.
   ISBN 978-0-313-37626-9 (hard copy : alk. paper) — ISBN 978-0-313-37627-6
(ebook)   1. Food habits—Encyclopedias.   2. Food preferences—
Encyclopedias.   I. Albala, Ken, 1964–
   GT2850.F666   2011
   394.1'2003—dc22   2010042700

ISBN: 978-0-313-37626-9
EISBN: 978-0-313-37627-6

15 14 13 12 11   1 2 3 4 5

This book is also available on the World Wide Web as an eBook.
Visit www.abc-clio.com for details.

Greenwood
An Imprint of ABC-CLIO, LLC

ABC-CLIO, LLC
130 Cremona Drive, P.O. Box 1911
Santa Barbara, California 93116-1911

This book is printed on acid-free paper ∞

Manufactured in the United States of America

The publisher has done its best to make sure the instructions and/or recipes in this book
are correct. However, users should apply judgment and experience when preparing
recipes, especially parents and teachers working with young people. The publisher
accepts no responsibility for the outcome of any recipe included in this volume.

Contents

List of Abbreviations

c = cup

fl oz = fluid ounce

gal = gallon

in. = inch

lb = pound

mL = milliliter

oz = ounce

pt = pint

qt = quart

tbsp = tablespoon

tsp = teaspoon

Preface

This encyclopedia is the culmination of nearly a decade's work on the *Food Culture around the World* series. As that project expanded to 20 volumes, we realized that many peoples and places, fascinating and important in their own right, had not been covered. Considering that the cultural study of food has become more sophisticated and comprehensive over the past decade, that food has become a legitimate academic topic in curricula at every level of education, and that we seem to become more obsessed with food every day, we recognized that we simply could not leave out much of the planet. The only way to satisfy this growing demand is the set you see before you, which includes material covered in the series plus new articles that span the globe. We have gathered food scholars from around the world—people whose passion and expertise have given them deep insight into the ingredients, cooking methods, and ways of eating and thinking about food in their respective countries.

A number of questions regarding breadth and depth naturally arose in planning this work, particularly about the level of analysis for each article. Could we do justice to the vast array of distinct cuisines on earth? Could we include regional coverage for well-recognized food cultures? That is, rather than the nation-state as the criterion for inclusion, why not add Alsace, Provence, and Burgundy with France, or Sichuan, Hunan, and Canton with China? It became apparent that we would need another 20 volumes or risk very brisk, superficial coverage and that as arbitrary as the construction of nation-states has been historically, in particular the way minority cultures have tended to be obscured, the best way to organize this encyclopedia was by nation. Regional variations and minority groups can, of course, be discussed within the framework of nation-based articles. On the other hand, some groups frankly demanded separate entries—those who stood out as unique and distinct from the majority culture in which they happen politically to be included, or in some cases those people who either transcend national boundaries or even those very small places, whose great diversity demanded separate coverage as truly different from the culture around them. Thus we include the Basques separate from Spain and France, and the Hmong. We have not, however, included every single people merely on the basis of national status. This should not be taken to suggest that these cultures are unimportant but merely that many places share a common culture with those around them, though divided by national borders. In such cases we have provided cross-references. This seemed a preferable solution to suffering repetitiveness or unmanageable size.

The format for each entry also raised many questions. "Eating Out," for example, is simply not relevant in some places on earth. Would forcing each article into a common structure ultimately do injustice to the uniqueness of each culture? In the end it seemed that the ability to conduct cross-cultural analysis proved one of the most valuable assets of this set, so that one could easily compare what's for lunch in Brazil or Brunei. Moreover, tracing the various global currents of influence has been made possible since a shared set of parameters places each article on a common footing. We can trace, for example, the culinary influence of various peoples as they spread around the world. In this respect this work is unique. There are several excellent food encyclopedias on the market, all of which cover individual ingredients, topical themes, cooking methods, and sometimes recipes. None, however, treats individual food cultures as discrete units of analysis, and for students hoping to find an in-depth but succinct description of places, or for those hoping to compare a single food topic across cultures, this is the only source to which they can turn. We anticipate that this work will be invaluable for students, scholars, food writers, as well as that indomitable horde popularly known as foodies.

The other major question in designing this encyclopedia was how to define what exactly constitutes a *food culture.* This term should be distinguished from *cuisine,* which refers only to the cooking, serving, and appreciation of food. Naturally we include this within each entry and in doing so have taken the broadest possible definition of the term *cuisine.* That is, if a people cooks and recognizes a common set of recipes and discusses them with a common vocabulary, then it should be deemed a cuisine. Thus there is no place on earth without a cuisine. A nation, continent, region, and even a small group may share a common cuisine. This encyclopedia, however, covers much more. It explores the social context of consumption, the shared values and symbolic meanings that inform food choices, and the rituals and daily routine—indeed everything that constitutes a food culture. Thus we include religion, health, mealtimes, and special occasions, as well as the way certain foods confer status or have meanings beyond simple sensory gratification. Nor have we neglected the gastronomic angle, as recipes are an essential expression of what people think is good to eat, and their popularity is the outcome of decisions made at every level of society, from the farmer who grows food, and the environment and material resources that make it possible, to the government policy that promotes certain ingredients, to the retailers who market them, to the technologies by which they are transformed, and to the individual preference of family members at the level of the household. To this end we have added food culture snapshots to each entry, which puts a human face on the broader topics under discussion.

As with the series that preceded this encyclopedia, our aim is to present the panoply of human experience through the lens of food in an effort to better understand and appreciate our differences. We will find remarkably common experiences among us, especially as the world increasingly falls under the sway of corporate multinational food industries, but we will also find deep, profound, and persistent distinctions, ones that should and must be preserved because they are essential to who were are and how we define ourselves. These are differences that should not be effaced nor lost as our tastes become increasingly cosmopolitan. I hope that in reading these articles you find, like me, that the world is a marvelously diverse place and what people eat tells us about them in such an immediate and palpable way that in a certain sense you feel you know the people at some level. This, of course, is the first step toward understanding, appreciating, and living with each other peacefully on this small lump of turf we call earth.

Ken Albala
University of the Pacific

Africa

Algeria

Overview

The People's Democratic Republic of Algeria is situated between the North African countries of Morocco and Tunisia. It is the largest country bordering the Mediterranean Sea and the second-largest African country, with a total landmass as large as the whole of Western Europe. Algeria is divided into 48 *wilayas,* or provinces. More than 90 percent of the population lives in the most fertile and smallest region, called the Tell, which runs the entire length of Algeria's Mediterranean coastline. The remainder of the country can be divided into three parallel geographic bands that run east–west. South of the Tell is the Tell Atlas mountain range, followed by the Saharan Atlas mountain range, and finally the Sahara desert. Algeria's Sahara comprises more than 90 percent of the country and is bordered by Western Sahara, Mauritania, Mali, Niger, and Libya.

Most Algerians are of Arab-Berber heritage; identification with either or both can depend on cultural ties or political beliefs. Arabic has been the official national language since independence from French colonial rule, as written in the constitution of Algeria in 1963. *Tamazight* (the Berber language) was recognized as a national language in 2002 by constitutional amendment. Although French is widely used in government, media, and education, it has no official status. In recent years, there has been a popular movement to emphasize a national Algerian identity, rather than regional ones.

Islam is the official religion of Algeria. The vast majority of Algerians are Sunni Muslims; Christians and Jews comprise less than 1 percent of the population. Pork and any food products derived from pork are forbidden from the diet in accordance with Islamic dietary laws.

Algerian cuisine represents a historically unique mix of Mediterranean and African peoples. Thousands of years of immigration and conquest by, and trade with, Phoenicians, Arabs, Jews, Romans, *Moriscos* (Muslims from Spain), Ottomans, Italians, French, and Spanish have left their mark on the basic Berber foundation of Algerian cuisine. However, like Morocco and Tunisia, the single largest influence was medieval Islamic cooking. Algeria, Tunisia, and Morocco are collectively known as *Al-Maghrib* ("the West" in Arabic) to geographically and culturally distinguish the region from the Middle Eastern part of the Arab world, called *Al-Mashriq* ("the East").

🍽 Food Culture Snapshot

Geographic location and social class play key roles in determining what Algerians eat. Lyesse and Chaima Chenna live in a middle-class neighborhood in Algiers, the capital of Algeria. Lyesse, originally from the Kabylie, is an architect; his wife, Chaima, originally from Tlemcen near the Moroccan border, is an attorney. Their lifestyle and diet are representative of educated urbanites living in a large cosmopolitan city, whose diet includes dishes from different parts of Algeria, France, Spain, Italy, and the Middle East.

Lyesse and Chaima begin their day at 7 A.M. with homemade *baghrir* (semolina pancakes) served with honey, or baguette bread, purchased from a bakery, served with jam and coffee. The Chennas eat lunch with coworkers at a diner that serves simple dishes such

Algeria, city and the main marketplace. (Corel)

as composed salads, *karantika* (chickpea pie), or lentil soup. Later in the afternoon, around four o'clock, the Chennas go to a tearoom to have traditional Algerian pastries or Ottoman-influenced baklava with mint tea or coffee. Dinner is around 8 P.M. and is the largest meal of the day. The main dish is roasted or grilled lamb or chicken (served with bread) or a *tagine,* a braised stew of lamb or chicken with vegetables served with couscous. Side dishes include salad, pan-sautéed or stewed vegetables, and lentil or chickpea dips. Dessert is typically fresh fruit.

Urbanization and globalization have brought rapid changes to Algeria. City dwellers tend to live in smaller family units away from large extended families, and urban women are more likely to work outside the home than their rural counterparts. The growing number of supermarkets in big cities not only has made shopping for meals more convenient but also provides access to a range of prepared and packaged foods that considerably reduce meal-preparation times. However, shopping in *souks* (outdoor markets) and small shops is still very much a part of daily life in Algeria. Chicken drumsticks purchased at a supermarket are seasoned with spice blends purchased at a small shop and served with vegetables purchased from a sidewalk stall.

Lyesse and Chaima have an increasing variety of restaurants to choose from when they dine out. Besides enjoying traditional Algerian dishes at small restaurants, street-food bazaars, and fast-food outlets, they go to French-style cafés for simple bistro fare and

Italian restaurants for pasta or pizza. When entertaining foreign clients for business, they go to hotel restaurants where a range of international dishes are available, even Chinese specialties.

Major Foodstuffs

Despite having an impressive share of the Mediterranean coastline, fishing in Algeria is an underdeveloped industry. Sardines, anchovies, squid, shrimp, and mussels are the most commonly available seafood. Algeria has very little fertile land; only 3.17 percent of the total land area is arable. Crop cultivation is heavily concentrated in the northernmost part of the country in the Tell region near the coast and in mountainous areas with high plateaus such as Setif and Constantine in northeastern Algeria. Major crops are wheat, barley, and potatoes. The remainder of the country is arid or semiarid and largely unsuitable for farming. The exceptions are oasis towns where dates thrive. Vast tracts of date palms in the desert create microclimates where apricot, orange, and olive trees also grow and smaller plant foods such as onions, tomatoes, and cabbages thrive.

The Algerian Sahara isn't entirely barren outside of oases; it is rich in petroleum and natural gas reserves. For the past several decades, the country's economic growth has been heavily dependent on high gasoline prices, making it one of the wealthiest African countries. Investment in the gas industry was at the detriment of other industries including agriculture, livestock, and fishing. The former breadbasket of ancient Rome has become one of the world's largest grain importers. By 2008, more than 60 percent of all foods were imported to meet demand. With falling gasoline prices, the Algerian government has recently taken measures to boost agricultural productivity.

Dietary staples are wheat in the form of couscous, bread, or pasta and chickpeas or lentils in dips or soups. Almost all Algerians eat a combination of grains and legumes daily. Common vegetables include zucchini, carrots, eggplant, cardoons, artichokes, okra, turnips, cabbage, spinach, tomatoes, and peppers. It's difficult to imagine contemporary Algerian cooking without ingredients from the Americas such as tomatoes, peppers, and potatoes. Tomatoes were probably introduced to Algeria in two stages: first by the Spanish, who captured Algerian ports shortly after setting sail for the Americas in 1492, and then by the Italian immigrants who came almost 350 years later with French colonial rule. Evidence suggests three possible points of entry for chili peppers into Algeria: through the Mediterranean coast via the Spanish, through West Africa via Portuguese Atlantic trade, or through eastern Mediterranean land trade routes. Spanish or Italian settlers possibly introduced potatoes into Algeria.

Watermelon and other melons are valued for their high water content. Fresh grapes, apricots, apples, oranges, tangerines, lemons, kumquats, quince, and bananas are available seasonally. Fruit is dried or preserved in sugar for storage. Citrus fruits, lemons in particular, are preserved in salt and used to flavor tagines and sauces. Olives are brined or oil cured.

Algeria's growing dairy industry has failed to meet the even more rapidly increasing demand; in 2008, about 17 percent of all food imports were dairy products. The demand for powdered milk is especially high. Powdered milk is used by manufacturers in various products or reconstituted with water for drinking. Fresh milk is drunk plain, churned into butter, fermented into kefir or yogurt, or made into soft cheese. Gruyère, Parmesan, mozzarella, and spreadable processed cheeses are purchased in stores.

Lamb is the preferred meat. Beef is increasingly available because of globalization and a growing dairy industry. Chicken and eggs are relatively inexpensive sources of protein; Algerians have an astonishing array of chicken and egg dishes.

Since butter is highly perishable, it is often clarified or fermented to extend its shelf life. Clarified butter is used for cooking, and fermented butter is used as a flavoring agent. Margarine is increasingly popular as a relatively inexpensive alternative to butter. Olive oil is the most preferred cooking medium and is also highly valued for its purported medicinal properties. It is also used to flavor marinades, dressings, and dips.

Water is served with meals. Syrup-flavored water and carbonated beverages are drunk with light snacks. Coffee and tea are served at breakfast, with afternoon pastries, and after dinner. Mint tea is the national drink of Algeria.

Cooking

Algerian kitchens are simple by North American standards. Most cooking is done on stovetops or propane-fueled burners using just a few pots and pans. Pressure cookers were introduced into Algeria in the 1970s and are used frequently for their time- and energy-saving benefits. Tagines that once took hours to cook in clay vessels now take about an hour in a pressure cooker. However, even in urban areas, tagines are still sometimes cooked in clay *tagines*— the dish and the cooking vessel are both called *tagine*—outdoors over braziers.

Tagines are simply stews or soups of meat, poultry, or seafood with vegetables. There are no codified rules as to how they should be prepared. Cooking techniques and ingredients vary from region to region and family to family within regions. Some cooks add ingredients in layers: a layer of sliced onions at the bottom, followed by lamb sprinkled with spices, and then vegetables such as celery, carrots, and zucchini. Other cooks place everything into the pot at once. Tagines with thick sauces are often eaten with bread, which is used to scoop up food. Soupy tagines are usually served with couscous. Every Algerian household owns a *couscoussier* (a large pot with a steamer insert) for steaming couscous over a pot of simmering soup or stew of meat, chicken, or seafood with vegetables.

Flatbreads and *warka* pastry sheets are made at home using a flat, round griddle called a *farrah*. Since many households do not have ovens, round leavened breads known as *khobz eddar* (house bread) are cooked in deep pans on the stovetop or purchased from a bakery. Leavened breads are also baked in a *taboun* (a large outdoor oven). In rural areas, tabouns are often community owned. Small bakeries in cities charge a baking fee to patrons who bring homemade dough.

Men are typically in charge of outdoor grilling. Grills for kebabs and sausages are simple metal grates placed on top of a metal box or clay brazier filled with burning charcoal or wood. Roasting a whole lamb is a bit more complicated: The lamb is rubbed with spices and cooked on a rotisserie spit over a large fire. The lamb is frequently basted with clarified butter or olive oil to keep the meat moist and to create a crispy skin. The spit is turned every 20 minutes to ensure even cooking.

Preparing Algerian food can be labor-intensive. Middle-class to affluent families often have cooks, called *dadas.* In rural areas, where several generations of a family live in one household complex, the older women supervise food preparation while their daughters and daughters-in-law do most of the actual cooking. Nuclear families living in cities often use packaged food products and convenience items to reduce cooking times and kitchen labor needs.

Spices are purchased ground or whole from spice vendors who also sell proprietary blends called *ras el hanout* ("top of the shop") consisting of a dozen or more spices. Whole spices are ground at home using a mortar and pestle or an electric grinder. The most widely used everyday spices are cumin, paprika, and turmeric. The use of other spices such as coriander, cinnamon, fennel, anise seeds, cardamom, and nigella seeds tends to have many regional variations. Expensive spices, for example, saffron, are usually reserved for special-occasion dishes.

Algerian cooks rarely dry-roast spices. Spices are usually added to soups and stews in several stages throughout the cooking process to create depth of flavor. Lemon juice or vinegar is sometimes added to finished soups and stews for acidity. Spice pastes and marinades are made with a mixture of spices, pounded garlic, grated onion, olive oil, chopped herbs, and citrus juice or vinegar. In wealthier kitchens saffron is used for color; sugar, honey, and dried fruits for sweetness; fresh citrus and vinegar for acidity; and nuts as thickening agents.

Tomatoes became widely used in Algerian cooking because they provided the culinary functions of quite a few ingredients, especially many that are beyond the budgets of humbler households: Chopped fresh tomatoes, fresh tomato juice, sun-dried tomatoes, sweet tomato jam, tomato puree, and tomato sauces are used to add color, sweetness, and acidity and to thicken sauces. Sweet bell peppers are used almost as much as tomatoes. However, the use of hot peppers tends to be more localized. *Harissa,* a hot chili sauce, is more commonly used in eastern Algeria near Tunisia than in other regions of the country. Overall, Algerian foods are not hot and spicy.

Tomatoes and peppers are also stewed, grilled, or stuffed, as are most other vegetables. Algerians have a fondness for vegetables stuffed with ground lamb or rice. A range of vegetables such as cabbage, zucchini, cardoons, artichokes, and eggplant are prepared similarly. Stuffed vegetables are called by Arabic and Turkish names, *mashi* or *dolmas,* respectively.

Potatoes are ubiquitous in Algerian cooking. They are a readily available and inexpensive starch that helps compensate for grain and cereal shortages. French fries are stuffed into baguette bread with spicy lamb sausages (*sandwich aux merguez*); sautéed potato wedges are used to garnish tagines; raw potatoes are hollowed out and stuffed with ground lamb; pureed potatoes are served as an accompaniment to roasted meats; and leftover mashed potatoes are shaped and fried into croquettes.

Deep-fried foods such as beignets, a kind of doughnut, and pastries are usually purchased from

Tagine, a braised stew of lamb or chicken with vegetables, served with couscous. (Laurent Renault | Dreamstime.com)

street vendors or at restaurants as snacks. Pickling and canning is still done at home in rural areas. Tomatoes are canned or sun-dried; citrus is preserved in salt or sugar; meat is preserved in fat or dried for jerky; fruits are preserved whole in sugar syrup, cooked into jam, dried, or coated with sugar; and peppers, turnips, and cabbages are pickled in vinegar.

Typical Meals

Algerian meals vary depending on region, socioeconomic status, and urban or rural location. National economic growth during the past few decades has resulted in a growing middle class. However, Algerian society still tends to be economically stratified into two groups: the rich and the poor. Middle-class to wealthy Algerians often eat four times a day: three light meals of breakfast, lunch, and a late afternoon snack with tea, followed by a main dinner meal. Poor Algerians, particularly in rural areas, subsist on coarse grains and cereals supplemented with small portions of legumes and dates.

Couscous is the staff of life and the iconic dish for all Algerians. Couscous is often referred to simply as *ta'am* (Arabic for "food"). Couscous is the traditional meal after *salaat-ul-jumu'ah,* a congregational prayer held at mosques every Friday immediately after noon. There is no special occasion or holiday without couscous.

Traditionally, Algerians sit on the floor for meals, sometimes on a carpet or cushions. Most dishes are served at room temperature; tagines, soups, and meat dishes are served hot. A small selection of *mezze,* or appetizers, is served for guests or on special occasions. Main dishes may be served all at once or in courses. Food is eaten only with the right hand in accordance with Islamic tradition. The left hand is used for personal hygiene and thus considered unclean for eating. Couscous is eaten with the first three fingers of the right hand or a spoon, never with a fork.

The following are examples of typical meals in middle-class families in three regions of Algeria. The food of Setif in the mountains of northeastern Algeria is simple and rustic. Spices are used sparingly, if at all. The region has a long history as a center of grain production and trade going back to ancient Rome. Farming is done on the rain-inducing plateaus, and livestock graze in hilly pastures. The diet is based on whole grains such as barley, bulgur, and millet, which are all steamed for couscous. Lamb and chicken tend to be more abundant here than in many other regions.

Agrarian families rise at dawn to a breakfast of *kesra* (Berber flatbread made with semolina flour) and buttermilk. Fresh or dried fruit is packed for snacking while working in the fields. Lunch consists of couscous with buttermilk or kesra with a small piece of grilled meat and a salad of fresh herbs and wild greens. Mint tea is served late in the afternoon with semolina butter cookies or biscuits.

The main meal, dinner, is eaten around sunset. Dinner consists of couscous made from bulgur. The steamed bulgur is served on a large platter surrounded by the meat and vegetables from the tagine; the tagine broth is strained and served separately in a tureen or large bowl. Other dishes are soup with chickpeas and barley, grilled or braised lamb, and several vegetable preparations. Dessert is fresh fruit, followed by a selection of fried sweets soaked in syrup.

In the Mediterranean port city of Annaba, near the Tunisian border, the foods are hot and spicy; harissa and hot peppers are ubiquitous. Breakfast is eggs poached in a spicy tomato sauce with chickpeas. Italian settlers came with the French occupation of Algeria, and their culinary influence is very apparent in Annaba. Lunch is pizza topped with spiced lamb or pasta in a tomato sauce with seafood.

Dinner, typically served at 7 P.M., is the largest meal of the day. Couscous is served with seafood in tomato broth. The presentation for couscous is similar to Tunisian and Sicilian couscous: The broth is spooned over a large platter of couscous, and the seafood is placed on top. Fruit is served for dessert, followed by semolina cake drizzled with honey syrup.

The port city of Oran has a different meal structure. From Oran, it takes only nine hours by ferry to reach Alicante, Spain. The city provided a refuge for Moriscos after the Christian reconquest of Andalusia. In 1509 the Spanish captured the port of Oran. For the next 300 years Oran would change hands back and forth between the Spanish, Barbary pirates, and the Ottomans. Oran was also where Spanish settlers came with the French invasion of Algeria. They brought with them rice dishes such as arroz con pollo (chicken and saffron rice) and paella (rice with seafood, vegetables, and/or meats). Oran is still famous in Algeria for exceptional rice preparations.

Breakfast in Oran is a scrambled egg dish called *shakshuka,* an Ottoman-influenced dish of sautéed bell peppers and onions with eggs stirred in. Lunch consists of Spanish-influenced *cocas* (puff pastry stuffed with sautéed vegetables) or *frita,* a pizza-like baked dish topped with olives, peppers, and tomatoes. Dinner is served at 8 P.M. The main dish is arroz con pollo made with long-grain rice or basmati rice, which is a new "foreign" ingredient sold in supermarkets. Dessert is baklava, a flaky pastry with nuts, drizzled with Seville orange syrup, served with cardamom-infused coffee.

Eating Out

Algerian restaurants tend to be categorized according to specialties or type of cuisine. The capital city of Algiers, in particular, offers diners a range of Mediterranean dishes and cuisines. Restaurants serving non-Mediterranean foods are rare, although Algiers has a handful of Indian, Vietnamese, and Chinese restaurants. International dishes beyond Mediterranean cuisines are usually available in hotel restaurants.

Street food is very popular in Algeria. Vendors usually specialize in a single dish. Fried donuts called *sfenj* or *beignets* and *briks* (warka pastry stuffed with egg) are common breakfast items. Kebabs, merguez sausage sandwiches stuffed with French fries (*merguez frites*), and sandwiches of thinly sliced rotisserie-cooked lamb in baguettes are popular lunchtime fare. In the evening entire town squares are turned into street-food bazaars with vendors serving more extravagant dishes such as paella and *bastila* (a pie of chicken, eggs, and almonds in many layers of flaky phyllo-like dough). Roving mint tea and coffee vendors walk the streets throughout the day.

Fast-food restaurants in Algeria are similar to casual North African and Middle Eastern places found in Europe and America. They serve vertical rotisserie-grilled meats (called either Turkish-influenced *doner* or Arab-influenced *shawerma*); falafels stuffed into pita bread; and French fries. In recent years, globalization has brought in a Belgian fast-food chain, Quick. A McDonald's opened in Algiers in 2008.

Traditional Algerian restaurants tend to focus on a small group of related dishes such as couscous served with a choice of several tagines or soups; kebabs and *mechoui* (roasted or grilled dishes); or seafood preparations. The former European colonial presence is still very much alive in the restaurant world. French-style cafés serve simple bistro fare like *steak frites* (steak with a side of French fries) and *moules ail et persil* (mussels steamed in garlic and parsley). Italian diners serve pizzas and pastas.

Small Algerian bakeries and pastry shops typically specialize in only traditional Algerian breads and sweets. Larger bakeries in cities integrate French goods. Baguettes are ubiquitous in Algeria; croissants, éclairs, and European-style cakes are also fairly common.

Harira, a hearty soup made with lamb, legumes, grains, and spices. (iStockPhoto)

Special Occasions

Algeria is predominantly a Sunni Muslim country. A small minority of Mozabites (a Berber group) in central Algeria are Ibadi Muslims. The most important holidays for Sunni Muslims are the holy month of Ramadan and Eid al-Adha. Ramadan falls on the ninth month of the Islamic lunar calendar every year. Fasting is one of the five pillars of Islam essential to Sunni Islam. During Ramadan, Muslims do not eat or drink from dawn to dusk. The fast is broken with *iftar* ("breaking the fast") immediately after sunset with a date and a glass of milk or *lben* (a thin yogurt drink). This is followed a large feast featuring many extravagant dishes such as *harira,* a hearty soup made with lamb, legumes, grains, and spices, or a sweet lamb tagine with dried fruits, nuts, and honey. Rich sweets such as *makroud* (a fried pastry stuffed with fig paste) and *zalabiya* (deep-fried fritters drenched with honey syrup) are common Ramadan treats. The second meal for Ramadan, *suhoor,* is eaten before dawn and morning prayers. Suhoor dishes often contain little or no salt, since salt induces thirst.

Harsha (Quick Semolina Bread for Ramadan)

1 c fine semolina flour

1 c unbleached all-purpose flour

¼ c sugar

1 tbsp baking powder

¼ tsp salt

1 c buttermilk

½ c water (or more as needed)

1 large egg

5 tbsp unsalted butter, melted and cooled slightly

Preheat oven to 400°F.

Sift flours, sugar, baking powder, and salt into a medium bowl. Whisk the buttermilk, water, and egg in another medium bowl; whisk in the melted butter. Add buttermilk mixture to dry ingredients; stir just until incorporated (do not overmix).

Bake for 20–30 minutes or until golden. Serve with butter and honey.

Zakah al-fitr is a form of charitable giving at the end of Ramadan. Muslims are expected donate food to the poor at this time so that all Muslims, regardless of their means, can celebrate Eid al-Fitr, the festival of breaking the fast, a three-day celebration beginning on the first day of the month after Ramadan. On the morning of Eid, Muslims gather for morning prayer at a mosque or in large public spaces. After Eid, people visit family and friends with platters of sweets and pastries and to exchange presents.

Eid al-Adha (the Festival of Sacrifice) is celebrated in the last month of the Islamic lunar calendar after the hajj (the annual pilgrimage to Mecca), to honor the prophet Abraham's willingness to obey and sacrifice for Allah. Muslims commemorate this day by sacrificing a lamb. Organ meats are cooked and consumed on the day of the sacrifice; the rest of the lamb is cut into portions, and much of the meat is donated to the poor. Platters of sweets, cookies, and pastries are also served.

In Algeria, sacrificing a lamb also commemorates the birth of a child, circumcision, and marriage. Traditional Algerian weddings can last three days or more, depending on the region and the family's wealth. Algerian weddings are comprised of several events celebrated on successive days or nights: the engagement party; the henna-painting ritual; the recitation of the *Fatiha,* the first chapter of the Quran, and *durud* (blessings); and the wedding celebration. Guests are served food every day. Contemporary Algerian weddings can be as short as a single day and take place in a banquet facility or hotel.

Diet and Health

In some regions of Algeria, olive oil is highly prized for its purported medicinal value as a cure-all for minor ailments such as indigestion, headaches, and irritated skin. Gently heated olive oil is rubbed directly onto the skin to treat problem areas. Folk remedies also include herbal infusions. For example, in the Kabylie, water infused with fresh mint is believed to be a digestive aid with antispasmodic and antinausea properties. Proper digestion is considered very important; certain foods are eaten or avoided to prevent upset stomach.

Islamic culture places great emphasis on maintaining good health through proper personal hygiene and dietary habits. Ablution (ritual cleansing) is performed before each of the five daily prayers of Islam, and food is eaten with the right hand only; the left hand is reserved for matters of personal hygiene. Foods are either *haram* (prohibited) or *halal* (permitted). Haram foods include alcohol and other intoxicants; pork and products derived from pork such as gelatin; and blood, including meat that has not been completely drained of blood. Animals must be slaughtered according to *zabiha*, the prescribed Islamic methods for ritual slaughter, to be considered halal. All plant-based foods are halal.

Susan Ji-Young Park

Further Reading

Çelik, Zeynep, Julia Clancy-Smith, and Frances Terpak. *Walls of Algiers: Narratives of the City through Text and Images.* Seattle: University of Washington Press, 2009.

Gitlitz, David M., and Linda Kay Davidson. *A Drizzle of Honey: The Lives and Recipes of Spain's Secret Jews.* New York: Saint Martin's Press, 1999.

Rodinson, Maxime, A. J. Arberry, and Charles Perry. *Medieval Arab Cookery.* Devon, UK: Prospect Books, 2001.

Stora, Benjamin. *Algeria, 1830–2000: A Short History.* Translated by Jane Marie Todd. Ithaca, NY: Cornell University Press, 2001.

Wright, Clifford. *A Mediterranean Feast: The Story of the Birth of the Celebrated Cuisines of the Mediterranean from the Merchants of Venice to the Barbary Corsairs.* New York: William Morrow, 1999.

Zaouali, Lilia. *Medieval Cuisine of the Islamic World: A Concise History with 174 Recipes.* Translated by M. B. DeBevoise. Berkeley: University of California Press, 2007.

Angola

Overview

The Republic of Angola is the seventh-largest country in Africa and the largest of the five countries in Africa where Portuguese is the official language. It covers about 482,625 square miles and is situated south of the equator on the southwestern coast of the continent. There are great variations in the climate and geography, including rain forests in the north, fertile central highlands, deserts in the Kunene and Kuando provinces in the south, drier coastal lands, and sandy soils in the east. The climate is characterized by both dry and rainy seasons that occur at different times in the various regions. Angola is bordered by the Democratic Republic of the Congo on the north, Zambia on the east, Namibia on the south, and the Atlantic Ocean on the west. Cabinda, an enclave that lies north of the Zaire River, is surrounded by the Democratic Republic of the Congo and the Republic of the Congo. Six major rivers flow westward cutting through the coastal lowlands and providing fertile lands for extensive agriculture. They are the Congo (formerly Zaire), Cuanza (Kuanza), Cunene (Kunene), Cubango (Kubango), Zambezi, and Kuando.

The country currently known as Angola was discovered by the Portuguese navigator Diogo Cão during his first voyage of exploration in 1482–1483. The Portuguese were the first Europeans to penetrate Africa south of the Sahara. The word *Angola* comes from the title used by the rulers of the Ngongo state. The title *ngola* was first mentioned in Portuguese writings in the 16th century. Before the arrival of the Portuguese, Angola was inhabited by the peoples of a number of ethnic groups in small kingdoms in the area known as Rio Kuanza (the Kuanza River region) from the 13th century until 1520, when the Portuguese began to impose rule over these people. At that time there were over 100 languages and dialects in Angola. Today, the three dominant ethnic groups are the Ovimbundu, Mbundu, and the Bakongo. The Ovimbundu, the largest ethnolinguistic group, are located mainly in the west-central part of Angola. Their language is Umbundu. The Mbundu comprise the second-largest group. They speak Kimbundu, and they have lived mostly in the plateau region north of the Ovimbundu. The Bakongo are concentrated in the Uíge and Cabinda provinces of the northeast, and even though their capital was Mbanza Congo in the Northwest of Angola, some members of their ethnic group are found in the present-day Democratic Republic of the Congo (formerly Zaire) and the Republic of the Congo (formerly Congo Brazzaville).

The official language of Angola is Portuguese, but many people are bilingual or even multilingual. The six most commonly spoken Bantu languages are considered national languages: Chokwe, Kikongo, Kimbundu, Mbunda, Oxikuanyama, and Umbundu. In total 40 languages are spoken in Angola. Though there is a sense of Angolan identity, the people are divided among various ethnicities, regions, and religious and racial groups, among other factors. In the 1970s there was a movement to discourage tribal identity. Out of that movement came the following, heard throughout Angola: *De Cabinda ao Cunene, um so povo, uma so nação* ("From Cabinda to Kunene, one people, one nation"). The Portuguese language has set Angola apart from its neighbors and created ties not only with Portugal but also with Brazil,

Fishing boats at sunset in Luanda, Angola. Luanda is the capital and largest port in Angola. (Corel)

Mozambique, and the other Portuguese-speaking countries in Africa and Indonesia.

🍽 Food Culture Snapshot

Sara and José Santos live in a middle-class neighborhood of Luanda, and they own their home. José is a notary for a local bank, and Sara is a housewife. Their lifestyle and eating habits are typical of the middle class. They enjoy both traditional Angolan food and Portuguese-influenced dishes. They begin their day with a breakfast of bread (soft white rolls similar to the Portuguese *pão*) with butter, coffee, fruit, eggs, and cheese. Sometimes breakfast includes sausages or leftover fish or meat. The bread is purchased at a nearby bakery, and fruit, eggs, butter, and cheese come from the local open-air market or grocery store.

Lunch is usually the largest meal of the day and can consist of grilled fish, boiled manioc root, rice, seafood, chicken, or pork. Some of the most popular dishes are rice with fish or other seafood, meat stew, and *muamba de galinha* (Angolan-style chicken). Lunch usually ends with coffee and a dessert. Dessert can consist of cakes made with grated coconut, pineapple, chocolate, sweet potato, or bananas. Puddings are also common and are made with egg yolks, coconut, or tapioca. The egg sweets are a Portuguese influence. Coffee is prepared by placing the grounds in a muslin bag and placing the bag over an enameled coffeepot. Freshly boiled water is poured slowly into the strainer over the ground coffee. If the coffee is not strong enough, it can be poured back through the muslin strainer once again. Fish is purchased at the local fish market or the open-air market. Meat and poultry come from local farmers, small grocery stores, or supermarkets. Manioc flour and manioc root are purchased at open-air markets, supermarkets, or corner stores.

The evening meal is usually served around 7 P.M. and consists of soup and bread or leftovers from lunch. The soup is sometimes made with rice mixed with pieces of stew beef, pumpkin, and beans, or fresh fish, dried fish, sweet potato, and spinach, all served with *funji* (a manioc puree).

Meals in many of the rural areas and small villages are quite different from those found in the urban areas. Many of the rural residents are farmers, and some of their meals are prepared with milk and curds and whey. Many dishes also consist of boiled green vegetables, beans, cereals, manioc, yams, and sweet potatoes. Most of the food is locally grown, and the milk comes from cows and goats owned by the farmers. Churned into butter in gourds, the milk of cows and goats remains part of the basic diet today. A typical menu for families of fishermen along the coast might include, for breakfast (*mata-bicho,* meaning "to kill the bug of hunger"), bread, coffee or tea, and sugar. For lunch, there would be a stew of potatoes and squid, and for dinner a beef soup.

In the interior of the southern province of Benguela, which borders the desert, breakfast for many is usually the largest meal of the day. It could consist of leftovers from the night before or a combination of the following: cereals, sweet potatoes, cassava, beans, peas, or boiled green vegetables. The more affluent enjoy a breakfast similar to that eaten in larger cities, like Luanda and Moçâmedes.

Major Foodstuffs

Until the late 15th century the principal work of the indigenous peoples of these small kingdoms was agriculture. They cultivated cereals, such as sorghum, and grew corn. Legumes and vegetables, including beans, okra, and various types of pumpkins, were also part of their diet. These crops were grown on large farms. When the fields had been overworked and could produce no more crops, farmers simply moved to another area and planted again. This method of agriculture is called itinerant farming. Both men and women worked in the fields, but the men cleared the forests and the women did the planting. The instruments used to harvest these crops were the hoe and

hatchet, both made of iron. The technique of casting iron for tools was utilized in West Africa since around 300 B.C. by the early inhabitants, who were known as Bushmen, Khosian, or San. It is believed that they came from present-day Cameroon through the old commerce routes that crossed the Sahara. They also fished and hunted to supplement their diet. This diet included wild animals and birds, insects, and domesticated animals such as chickens, goats, and cattle. The skins from the hunt were used for clothing.

In 1490, seven years after Diogo Cão "discovered" Angola, Portuguese ships arrived bringing presents from the king of Portugal to the king of the Congo, including a brick builder to construct a church. The first contact was friendly, and the king of the Congo was happy to receive the arms the Portuguese brought them. The ships then returned to Portugal with ivory, beautiful Congolese fabrics made by local artisans, and, sadly, some slaves.

In 1575, Paulo Dias de Novais arrived in the Bay of Luanda and landed on the Ilha do Cabo, which he named São Paulo de Loanda. He brought 400 soldiers and 100 Portuguese families, who came to cultivate sugar and tobacco and extract salt and palm oil for export. The salt was used as a product to trade for other necessities. European cattle, pigs, and goats were brought, which were raised in the central and southern regions. The locals drank the goat milk and also used it to make cheese. The goatskins were used for clothing, rugs, pocketbooks, and bags.

Various cereals were grown, including wheat, which was also used to make alcoholic beverages. In 1576 the Portuguese settlement moved to the mainland. Their influence in Angola was pervasive and in some cases subtle. To the African cuisine they brought the European sense of flavoring with spices and roasting and marinating techniques. The Portuguese also brought products from their gardens and orchards, some of which were influenced by Arabic culture and exotic plants from Asia and the Americas. These contributions, some more valuable than others, changed the cultural and economic face of the indigenous peoples and altered the nutrition of their population. The root from the cassava tree was one of the first plants to be brought to Angola from the New World at the end of the 16th century. One of the advantages of this exceptional plant for many of the indigenous peoples was that the roots were able to remain in the soil as if they were in storage, without spoiling, and the by-products from these tubers—flour, tapioca, and starch—could be kept for a long time without spoiling. Corn, which originates in North America, was another food that was well received in Angola.

The Portuguese also brought the avocado, rich in fat and protein, peanuts, papayas, guavas, pineapples, and mango trees, which eventually spread throughout sub-Saharan Africa. From Asia they brought and planted lime, lemon, and orange groves along the Atlantic coast and introduced pawpaws and groundnuts into the Gambia region. They also introduced the domestic pig. It is interesting that the names of many of these foodstuffs that were brought to Africa are derived from the Portuguese language. Portuguese mariners also brought many fruits and vegetables from Brazil. Once the crops that were introduced from the New World became staples of the Angolan diet, land was developed for farming those crops, and settlements began to spring up in the forests.

Angola is one of the African territories that contributed significantly to the cuisine of the New World, especially Brazil. By 1667, Brazil, already a Portuguese colony in 1530, was also an important player in the culture and cuisine of Angola. Angola enriched Brazil with palm oil, salt, peanut oil, and coffee. Brazil supplied Angola with sugar, *aguardente* (a rumlike spirit distilled from sugar), rice, flour, dried beef, bacon, manioc flour, coffee, and beans. And both of these then-colonies supplied Portugal with these products. Slaves from the Congo-Angola region brought to Brazil such traditional Angolan dishes as *caruru* (shrimp and okra stew) and *vatapá* (shrimp and bread pudding) and condiments like *jindungo* (hot chili pepper). By 1796, most of the food products originally imported from Brazil were being produced in Angola. Angola has made contributions not only in the culinary area but also with regard to social and cultural customs in Brazil, including vocabulary such as *moleque* (street urchin), *samba,* and *macambúzio* (melancholic). As the saying goes, Angola is truly the "mother of Brazil."

Cooking

Cooking techniques in Angolan cuisine vary throughout the country. In Luanda and all the larger cities, relatively affluent families have their meals prepared by cooks. Those meals are mainly Portuguese influenced and reflect Angola's prolonged contact with the former colonialist regime. Most Angolan kitchens are not as elaborate as Western kitchens. Food is prepared on a gas stove fueled by a propane tank that usually lasts about a month. Many households also have a charcoal grill on which meat and seafood are cooked. A large pot is a necessity for stews and soups, and large frying pans are used for sautéing and frying. A meat grinder is needed for meat, peanuts, and onions, as well as a grater for coconut, a mortar and pestle to crush spices, and a muslin strainer to make coffee. A clay water jug with a filter for purifying water is found in almost every Angolan kitchen along with a strainer (*paneira*) for washing rice and a set of wooden spoons for stirring stews. Some cooks even own electric blenders and grinders. Aluminum pots and pans have replaced the clay pots (*panelas de barro*), including clay dishes, because it is currently difficult to obtain them. In rural areas, however, many cooks still use clay pots. The use of the clay pots gives a special flavor to certain dishes, especially beans cooked in palm oil. The clay pots also hold the heat longer than aluminum ones.

The Angolan coast is very rich with fish and other seafood. Some of the crustaceans found in the waters are lobsters, shrimp, scallops, clams, mussels, oysters, crab, prawns, and crayfish. Not only does Angola have quality seafood, but the method of preparation results in succulent and most delicious meals. Lobsters and other shellfish are often cooked in seawater. The water is brought to a boil and seasoned with lard or butter, hot peppers (jindungo), and salt. The lobster is dropped into the boiling water, and when the water returns to a boil, it is reduced to a simmer and the lobster is cooked for about 10 minutes, depending on its size. Meats are prepared in stews, sautéed with vegetables, or grilled over open coals. Chicken is either grilled or stewed (*guisado*) with vegetables. A sauce called *refogado,* very popular in many of the Portuguese-speaking countries, is the basis for many stews and soups. It is made with onions, tomatoes, and garlic sautéed in olive oil.

Rice is usually served as a side dish at each meal and is cooked with a *refogado* to which parsley or cilantro is sometimes added. Rice as a main dish is cooked with beans, fish, chicken, salt cod, sausages, or cabbage. Macaroni is also very common and is usually cooked with sausage (*chouriço*), beans, or meat. Potatoes are most often boiled and served with meat, fish, or salt cod. Potatoes are also stewed with fish, sausage, macaroni, or cabbage. Peanuts are added to many cooked vegetables such as greens, as well as to fish, chicken, and desserts such as *doce de amendoim* (peanut dessert). Most homes have stoves with ovens, so baking is common. Cakes, pies, tortes, and appetizers similar to *empanadas* are all a part of the Angolan diet. Deep-frying is not very common in Angolan cooking. Most appetizers are baked, although French fries and appetizers such as empanadas and certain pastries are cooked in about two inches of oil. Olive oil, peanut oil, safflower oil, and palm oil are used for cooking. Palm oil is used mostly in traditional Angolan dishes such as *muamba de peixe* (fish ragout), *calulu* (fish with okra), *muzongue* (hangover soup), and *funji e pirão* (manioc puree).

Calulu, which is known as *caruru* in Brazil, was brought to Africa by slaves aboard Portuguese ships returning to Angola to pick up more merchandise and slaves. Calulu was later introduced to São Tomé and Princípe by Angolan workers who went to work on plantations. The dish later became a part of the local cuisine. Although of African influence, calulu was first concocted in Brazil and then taken to Angola, where it became known as *kalulu,* today usually spelled *calulu,* but it is essentially an African dish. A prime ingredient in Brazilian caruru, as well as the Angolan and Santomean varieties, is okra. This vegetable pod originated in West Africa and was introduced into the Western Hemisphere in the 17th century. The word *okra* comes from Nigeria's Ibo language, and the Portuguese equivalent, *quiabo,* is a creolization of a word from Angola's Kimbundu language. Another ingredient of caruru and calulu that is of African origin is palm oil (*azeite de dendê*).

The important spices and herbs commonly found in Angolan cuisine are parsley, mint, cloves, bay leaves, garlic, nutmeg, ginger, cinnamon, cumin, oregano, paprika, cilantro, and hot chili peppers. Every kitchen has a supply of hot chili peppers (jindungo) hanging from a hook. These spicy peppers are essential to Angolan cooking and are usually prepared in a sauce served as a condiment with meats, fish, or other seafood or are added directly to certain dishes. Fruit preserves are also common in Angola. Preserves are made from pumpkins, papayas, mangoes, apples, and bananas and are served as desserts or with bread for breakfast. Bananas are also very popular as desserts. There are many types of bananas, but the most common for desserts is the *banana pão* (bread banana). It is usually cooked after it is very ripe and the skin is dark. Banana pão can also be served with manioc flour or mashed and served with meats. Most Angolan desserts consist of simple fruits, but there are also puddings like *cocada amarela* (yellow coconut dessert), an example of Portuguese influence. Its main ingredients are sugar, water, cloves, coconut, and egg yolks.

Many dishes are characteristic of the Angolan cuisine, and muamba is one of them. A similar dish is found in many cuisines of southwestern Africa, especially Namibia. The main ingredients are chicken, okra, pumpkin, onions, and palm oil. Palm oil is made from the red fruit of the African palm tree. Some cooks also add white potatoes to this dish. When this dish is made with fish instead of chicken, it is called muamba de peixe.

Muamba de Galinha (Angolan-Style Chicken)

Serves 8

Ingredients

- 4 lb boneless chicken thighs
- 2 large onions, minced
- ¾ c vegetable oil
- 2 large cloves garlic, chopped
- 1 bay leaf

½ to ¾ c palm oil, or half palm oil and half vegetable oil

4 fresh chili peppers (jindungo), chopped and seeded

1 lb pumpkin or butternut squash, peeled and cubed

1 lb okra, trimmed and cut in half if large

3 tbsp lemon juice

1 tsp salt

Cut the chicken thighs in half, and place them in a large pot with the onions, vegetable oil, garlic, and bay leaf over medium heat. Stir to mix the ingredients well. Cook for 20 minutes, or until the chicken is tender and the vegetables have formed a sauce, adding a little water from time to time to keep the dish from drying out.

Add the palm oil, peppers, pumpkin, okra, lemon juice, and salt. Cook over low heat for 15 minutes to allow seasonings to permeate the sauce. Serve hot in a large serving dish accompanied by manioc puree.

Funji (Manioc Puree)

Purees are served with stews, soups, or any meat, fish, or poultry dish that has a little sauce or liquid to make the puree.

Ingredients

4 c chicken broth

1 c finely ground manioc meal

Bring the broth to a boil. Slowly pour the manioc flour into the boiling broth, stirring with a whisk to avoid lumps. Continue stirring for 3 minutes, or until the puree is the consistency of cooked cereal. Serve with muamba.

Typical Meals

Angola, with its 18 provinces, has many regional flavors and ethnic food cultures. There are some differences between the cuisine along the coast and that found in the interior of the country. However, there are many meals that are typically Angolan and enjoyed throughout the country. The Portuguese influence is evident in dishes such as *arroz de mariscos* (rice with seafood), made with shrimp, lobster, clams, or cockles and red chili peppers (jindungu or jindongo); *caldeirada de peixe* (fish stew), prepared with thick fish steaks, potatoes, onions, tomatoes, green peppers, chili peppers, and olive oil; *guisado de bacalhau* (salt cod stew), made with salt cod, okra, jindungo, onion, tomato, and palm oil; and *rissóis Angolanos* (creamy shrimp turnovers), whose filling is prepared with shrimp, onions, tomato, garlic, and hot sauce in a white sauce. Most of the stews are served with white rice.

Dishes that are typical of Angolan cuisine include *muzongue com pirão* (hangover soup with puree), made with fresh fish, dried fish, spinach, and sweet potatoes and served with a manioc-flour puree; *couves cozidas com oleo-de-palma e amendoim* (collards cooked in palm oil and ground peanut sauce); *mariscos cozidos com jindungo* (shellfish in hot sauce), including clams, oysters, prawns, and lobsters; muamba de peixe (fish ragout), made with fish, potatoes, okra, and palm oil; muamba de galinha (Angolan-style chicken), made with chicken thighs, onions, palm oil, jindungo, pumpkin, and okra; *caldeirada de cabrito* (goat-meat stew), usually served

Caldeirada de cabrito, a goat meat stew, is typical of the Angolan cuisine. (iStockPhoto)

on Independence Day, which includes goat meat, onions, potatoes, bell peppers, port wine, and cognac; *calulu de carne seca* (dried beef stew); *galinha de cabidela* (chicken stew with blood sauce); and, for dessert, *cocada Angolana* (Angolan coconut candy), *bolo de maracujá* (passion fruit cake), and *bananas assadas* (baked bananas). A puree made with manioc flour or corn flour accompanies many meals.

The meat dishes in the Angolan cuisine are varied. The most common meats used are beef, pork, chicken, fish and other seafood, and, in some rural areas, game and goat. Soups are very common and often served as the main course of a meal. They include chicken or beef and are served with rice or funji (manioc puree). Snacks are usually eaten in the afternoon and can consist of fruit, fried manioc, fritters, sugared nuts, or pastry.

Eating Out

Eating out is a luxury for most Angolans. Many of the restaurants, including those in hotels, cater mainly to foreigners and serve mostly Continental fare but also include a few local dishes. Breakfast in most restaurants includes cereal, yogurt, scrambled eggs, bacon, tomato wedges, sausages, toast, and exotic fruits. For lunch they will serve dishes like cabbage soup with white beans, rice with vegetables, grilled meats and fish, boiled potatoes, French fries, and salt cod croquettes. For dinner the choices might include seafood soup, grilled grouper or other fish, stewed chicken, cold shrimp and crab, and grilled lobster. Usually one or two of the following local dishes will appear on the menu each day: *cabidela e galinha* (chicken stew with blood sauce), caldeirada de cabrito (goat-meat stew), muamba de peixe (fish ragout), muamba de galinha (Angolan-style chicken), funji (manioc puree), *galinha com jingub* (chicken with hot sauce), *lulas guisada* (squid sautéed with potatoes), arroz de mariscos (rice with seafood), rissóis Angolanos (creamy shrimp turnovers), muzongue com pirão (hangover soup with puree), *doce de amendoim com cocada* (peanut dessert with coconut), *doce de banana* (banana dessert), cocada Angolana (Angolan coconut candy), and *banana frita* (fried bananas).

Many small restaurants, street stalls (*barracas*), and cafés where the food is relatively inexpensive are frequented by workers during breakfast and lunch. For breakfast these places might serve rolls, coffee, cheese, or fruit. For lunch they usually serve local fare including fried fish, grilled meat and chicken, French fries, hamburgers, meat patties, and other items such as ice cream, other desserts, and pastries. The barracas on the beaches do a lively business selling snacks and drinks to beachgoers. Drinks at all restaurants include cola, local beer, other alcoholic drinks, and local fruit drinks with and without sparkling water. The most popular fresh fruit drinks are made with banana, pineapple, and tamarind. There are also drinks that are fermented. The process usually takes about 80 hours before the beverage can be bottled. Two popular fermented drinks are *kisangua* and *kitoto*. The former is made with corn flour and sugar, and the latter is made with corn. There are also beers made from corn: *quimbombo, quissângua,* and *quitoto,* each in a different province of Angola.

Special Occasions

Angola gained its independence in 1975, and the country then had a civil war that ended only in 2002. Because the majority of the population lives in poverty, many of the festivals formerly celebrated throughout the country have disappeared, are held infrequently, or now occur only in the larger cities. The public holidays are New Year's Day (January 1), National Holy Day (February 4), Victory Day (March 27), Workers Day (May 1), Independence Day (November 11), and MPLA (People's Movement for the Liberation of Angola) Foundation Day and Family Day (December 25).

Other special occasions are the end-of-term parties for students, when arroz de mariscos (rice with seafood) is a necessity. Mariscos cozidos com jindungo (shellfish in hot sauce), rissóis Angolanas (Angolan-style creamy shrimp turnovers), and cocada Angolana (Angolan coconut candy) are specialties served at weddings, parties, holidays, and special dinners. At these occasions local beverages such as maize beer and palm wine are served, along with soft drinks and other alcoholic beverages.

Angolans celebrate Independence Day with the traditional dish of caldeirada de cabrito (goat-meat stew). It is a wonderful stew made with goat meat, onions, potatoes, tomatoes, and bell peppers, enhanced with port and cognac. The stew is quite easy to prepare, and delicious.

Caldeirado de Cabrito (Goat-Meat Stew)

Serves 10–12

Ingredients

8 lb goat meat, cubed

Boiling water to cover goat meat

¾ c vegetable oil

2 lb onions, thinly sliced

6 lb white potatoes, peeled and sliced

4 lb tomatoes, peeled and thinly sliced

6 green bell peppers, seeded and sliced into strips

Salt and black pepper to taste

2 tbsp red pepper flakes

½ c chopped fresh parsley leaves

½ c chopped fresh cilantro leaves

2 bay leaves

2 c port or sweet red wine

1 c cognac

Wash the pieces of goat meat well, and place in a large pot of boiling water. Return the pot to a boil and remove the goat meat. Set aside.

In a large skillet, heat the oil and first sauté the onions, then the potatoes, goat meat, tomatoes, and bell peppers. Sprinkle with salt, pepper, and the red pepper flakes.

Sprinkle the parsley and cilantro over the ingredients. Add the bay leaves and cover with the port or red wine, 2 cups water, and the cognac. Cover tightly and cook over low heat for 30 to 40 minutes, or until the goat meat is tender. Do not remove the cover and do not stir. Just shake the pan occasionally to prevent sticking. This will keep the potatoes from breaking up. Serve hot with white rice.

Note: If you cannot find goat, most butchers will bone a shoulder or leg of lamb for this dish.

Diet and Health

The foods that are the mainstays of the traditional Angolan diet are manioc prepared in many ways (including the leaves of the plant), palm oil, peanuts, beans, rice, okra, hot chili peppers, sweet potatoes, bananas, corn, cashews, coconut, dried or fresh fish, dried or fresh beef, pork, and chicken. A majority of the Angolan population is considered to be underfed. So it is rare to find obesity. Given that 70 percent of the population lives in poverty and over half are unemployed, hunger is a serious problem. People living in the coastal areas eat a lot of seafood, in the southwest herders live primarily on dairy products and meat, and farmers consume their produce of maize, sorghum, cassava, and other crops. Gathering firewood and water in some rural areas requires a great deal of energy.

Medical care is not available everywhere despite government efforts. In rural areas clinics lack staff and basic equipment, and thus most people rely on traditional healers whose practice depends largely on herbal remedies. In the larger cities Angolans have better access to public health care at hospitals and clinics. There are also hospitals specifically to treat women's and children's illnesses. Angola recently appointed a regional director to the World Health Organization to oversee the fight against HIV/AIDS and other infectious diseases. The director will also work to provide better-quality health care to all citizens and to ensure better coordination of tracking diseases. Doctors of traditional medicine are also working with government approval to broaden their reach to people in the interior and introduce the use of medicinal plants as cures for some sicknesses.

Cherie Y. Hamilton

Further Reading

Hamilton, Cherie Y. *Cuisines of Portuguese Encounters.* New York: Hippocrene Books, 2008.

Hamilton, Russell G., and Cherie Y. Hamilton. "Caruru and Calulu, Etymologically and Sociogastronomically." *Callaloo: A Journal of African Diaspora Arts and Letters* 30, No. 1 (2007): 338–42.

Benin

Overview

Formerly known as Dahomey, the Republic of Benin is located on the southern coast of the West African bulge. It shares borders with Togo to the west, Nigeria to the east, and Burkina Faso and Niger to the north. Its southern coastline leads to the Bight of Benin. The country covers 112,622 square kilometers (44,484 square miles) and can be divided into four distinct geographic areas between south and north: a marshy coastal plain, the Guinean savanna, flatlands and rocky hills, and the Atacora range of mountains in the northwest along the Togolese border. The climate is hot and humid with two rainy seasons and two dry seasons a year. There are 42 different ethnic groups in the country, including the Yoruba, the Fulbe (or Fulani), and the Bariba in the northeast, the Dendi in the north-central area, the Somba in the mountainous northwest, the Fon in the south-central area and around Abomey, and the Mind and Aja on the coast. In the south there is also a sizable creolized Afro-Brazilian community descended from Africans, Europeans, and former slaves returned from Brazil. The capital is in the Yoruba city of Porto Novo, but the seat of government is located in the Fon city of Cotonou. Coastal Benin had early contact with Europeans, which led to it being one of the seats of the slave trade for more than 300 years; during this time, it was also known as the Slave Coast.

The majority of the population of 6.5 million lives in the south of the country, which, like many other countries on the West African bulge, experiences a distinction between the more westernized southern segments of the country and those to the north. In the 2002 census 42.8 percent of the population were Christian, 22.4 percent were Muslim, and 17.3 percent practiced the indigenous religion of Vodun or Orisa worship. The remaining people practice other religions or claim no religious affiliation. More than half of the population speaks Fon, but French is the national language, and English is taught in secondary schools.

🍽 Food Culture Snapshot

Théodora and Théophile Grimaud are retirees. His career was in the airline industry, and she was a teacher and housewife. His career postings took them to various areas of western Africa and the world, and they are members of the westernized elite. Their diet combines Western dishes with traditional Beninese specialties, especially dishes from their Fon ethnicity. They may dine with friends either in their homes or in local restaurants. On special occasions or when guests are in town, they may dine in one of the larger restaurants in town. The family eats three meals a day. Breakfast is usually in the European mode—a Continental breakfast of some sort with French bread, coffee or tea, and fruit juice or fresh fruit. Théodora does the shopping, going to local and neighborhood markets where she knows the vendors based on ethnic identity or the quality of their goods. She also shops in the local French-style supermarkets and often at the larger city market in Cotonou known as the Dan Topka. Foods may be supplemented by specialties like agouti (bush rat) or land crabs that are sometimes sold on the side of the roads by young children. Local delicacies are purchased from special purveyors at local street stalls.

Major Foodstuffs

As in much of West Africa, the basic meal consists of a starch prepared as a thick mush and eaten with a soupy stew that contains vegetables along with either meat or fish. The stews are prepared from a variety of ingredients, including okra, leafy greens, eggplant, tomatoes, onions, pumpkin seeds, and chilies. Meats include goat and lamb. In the south smoked, dried, or fresh fish is often a part of the meal; beef is more commonly found in the north. Christians raise and eat pigs. Seafood includes crustaceans such as crab and shrimp as well as Atlantic and river fish. Dried smoked shrimp are ground and used to season dishes, as are chilies. Okra, squash and pumpkin seeds, and peanuts are used to thicken some of the sauces. Cubebs, referred to as *piment pays* (pepper of the country), are ground and used to season traditional dishes like *kpete*, a savory goat stew.

Moyau (Chicken Stew)

1 smoked chicken, skinned (about 3½ lb)

5 large ripe tomatoes, peeled, seeded, and coarsely chopped

1 large onion, thinly sliced

1 tbsp peanut oil

1 cube Maggi or beef bouillon

1 habanero chili, pricked with a fork

Wash the chicken and cut it into serving pieces. Pat it dry. Place the chicken and the remaining ingredients in a Dutch oven, bring to a boil, and then reduce the heat and allow to simmer uncovered for 20 minutes, stirring occasionally. When the dish has reached the desired spiciness, remove the pricked chili. Serve hot over white rice.

In the south corn, rice, and manioc are the primary starches, while sorghum, millet, and yams have preeminence in the central and northern communities. Fruits are eaten and include tropical fruits such as soursop and mangoes as well as several varieties of citrus, pineapples, and papayas.

Traditionally millet beer called *choukachou* or *chouk* is consumed in the north, while palm wine and *sodabi* (a stronger version of palm wine) are consumed in the south. French wines and brandies are drunk by the westernized elite, and gin is often used in ceremonies.

Cooking

Throughout western Africa in general the main culinary techniques are boiling, steaming, stewing, frying, roasting, grilling, and baking. All of these methods are the basis for the traditional dishes of the country that were based on the use of the traditional cookstove. In rural areas the traditional three-rock wood stoves remain the standard, and many households still cook over wood or charcoal fires. In villages communal cooking is common. In the urban areas, the Western stove is used, but many Beninese cooks still prefer to cook outdoors over a small brazier called a *feu malgache*. Pressure cookers are used to tenderize tougher cuts of meat. Refrigerators are also the norm among those with sufficient funds and access to electricity.

Many urban households have some kind of household help. It may be a relative from the country looking for employment in the city and working in exchange for lodging, or a professional paid for services. Cooking therefore is often done by another person, overseen by the lady of the house. Cooking is considered women's work. Cooking, however, remains a family activity for festive foods. Extended families combine to prepare dishes at times of feasting, with the matriarch directing the kitchen. The myriad cultures of Benin are oral cultures, and this is the manner by which the youngsters of the household learn to prepare the traditional foods. Microwaves, freezers, food processors, and the full range of other Western culinary conveniences are de rigueur among the elite. French influence prevails among the elite as well, and in their households the full European *baterie de cuisine* may be found among those with means; there, adepts at the preparation of French *cuisine bourgeois* and/or *cuisine classique* can be found in many households.

Typical Meals

Breakfast may be leftovers from the previous day's meals or something purchased from a street vendor. Alternately, in urban areas, it may be a French-influenced small meal of a hot beverage and a form of bread. The basic main meals consist of a soupy stew served with a starch that is then dipped into the stew. There is no major distinction between lunch and dinner. Alternately, the main meal may be grilled chicken or a grilled fish seasoned with chili or served in a sauce of tomatoes and onions. The Afro-Brazilian segment of the population eats dishes that hark back to Brazil, such as their own form of *feijoada,* a stew of beans and meat. In urban areas where men have traveled in search of employment, the meal may be taken at a small outdoor restaurant or in a local market. There are also night markets called *marché de nuit* that offer traditional foods that can be served in a bowl and taken for consumption elsewhere.

Eating Out

Cotonou and Porto Novo have a number of small establishments in the style of the *maquis* (a small local restaurant of the Côte d'Ivoire). They are owned by women and specialize in serving *poisson braisé* and *poulet braisé* (grilled fish and grilled chicken) accompanied by a local starch or French fries. There are also restaurants in large and small hotels serving Beninese and European fare as well as a few French-style restaurants run by French

Chickens are wheeled around on the back of a bike in an open market in Cotonou, Benin. (AFP | Getty Images)

colonials who have remained in the country. American and West African fast-food chains are found in the major cities as well as marchés de nuit that sell local foods for takeout.

Special Occasions

Like many in western Africa, the Beninese have a well-developed sense of ceremony, and religious holidays are celebrated with feasting by Christians and Muslims alike. Religious ceremonies in both Vodun and Orisa worship call for their own ritual meals as well. Weddings, and especially funerals, always involve a feast of some sort. Traditional funerals may require several days of feasting.

Diet and Health

During the Socialist period (1972–1991) the government encouraged rural development and favored agricultural initiatives, and the country is self-sufficient in food production. Almost half of the population is involved in some form of agriculture. An internal system of trade still functions and has the ability to ensure food distribution from one area to another. However, the lack of rural infrastructure means that intermittent food shortages are faced by about 900,000 people, mostly in the hard-to-reach northern parts of the country.

Jessica B. Harris

Further Reading

Bay, Edna G. *Wives of the Leopard: Gender, Politics, and Culture in the Kingdom of Dahomey.* Charlottesville: University of Virginia Press, 1998.

"Benin." http://www.everyculture.com/A-Bo/Benin.html.

Harris, Jessica B. *The Africa Cookbook: Tastes of a Continent.* New York: Simon and Schuster, 1998.

Burkina Faso

Overview

Burkina Faso, formerly known as Upper Volta (Le Haute Volta), is a landlocked country in West Africa, with an area of 105,869 square miles (274,200 square kilometers), which is about the size of the U.S. state of Colorado. The population of the country is about 15 million and steadily rising. As a former French colony, Burkina Faso's official language is French, but 3 of its more than 60 local languages are recognized as national languages: Moore, Jula, and Fulfulde. There are 63 ethnic groups living in the country, of which the most numerous are the Mossi, who make up almost half of the population and inhabit the central plateau. The country has a Sahelian climate with distinct dry and rainy seasons.

The Burkinabe are predominantly Muslim (55%); about 25 percent of the population is Christian, and the rest, around 20 percent, practice traditional African religions also referred to as animism. Religion, geography, and, to a lesser extent, also ethnic origin play a role in determining what Burkinabe eat. Muslims do not eat pork or drink alcohol, and they fast from dawn till dusk during the holy month of Ramadan. Discounting this difference, the diets of Muslim, Christian, and animist Burkinabe are very similar, with a typical meal consisting of a starchy staple served with a sauce that ideally contains a mixture of meat or fish and vegetables. Burkina Faso remains one of the least developed countries in the world, classified as a low-income, food-deficient country. The United Nations Development Program's 2006 *Human Development Report* ranked Burkina Faso 174th out of 177 countries. Over 45 percent of the population lives below the poverty line. This means that meat and fish, both expensive foodstuffs, are not consumed regularly.

Food Culture Snapshot

The Bationo are a middle-class family, consisting of four generations living together in one compound. The first meal of the day is breakfast. At around 7 A.M., those adults in the family who have a job will have coffee or tea and bread; those who are less fortunate will either have leftovers from their previous meal, that is, dinner, or buy some millet gruel from a neighbor, or occasionally even go hungry. Children, who start school at seven o'clock, have already left and will have their first bite only during the first snack time at school, at around 10 A.M., provided they were given food money by their parents.

Lunch is the main meal, and the ingredients for it are provided by Mama Bationo, a widow in her sixties. Those of her adult children who have jobs also contribute some money for the meal, but she is the main provider. Lunch is ready at 12:30 or 1:00 P.M. at the latest, and the food is divided into several eating groups. Family hierarchy, linked to age, gender, and the individual's financial contribution to the family budget, is reflected in the portion a person receives. The portion one is served is expected to include dinner as well.

In the afternoon, those who are not at work and can afford to do so may send a child to get a snack from one of the street vendors. These foods are only occasionally shared with other members of the family. Dinner is usually the leftovers from lunch, but Mama's unmarried daughters, who both have well-paying jobs, will often prepare extra food and, depending on the amount prepared, also share it with other people in the compound.

Major Foodstuffs

Burkina Faso is predominantly rural, and much of the food is produced locally. Most meals are made from scratch, as there is little processed food. The only processed foods used on a daily basis are tomato concentrate and stock cubes, a ubiquitous ingredient in every Burkinabe dish.

In the north and northeast of Burkina Faso, where a dry, almost desert-like climate dominates, food is less varied than in the southern and southwestern parts of the country, where the climate is subtropical and the rich soil produces a wide variety of vegetables. Foods consumed also vary greatly according to the season, there being distinct rainy and dry seasons. After the rainy season, the markets offer a great variety of vegetables. Burkina Faso has a large production of green beans, which are grown throughout the year and are mainly exported to Europe, but the main harvest is in the winter months, when the price is also affordable for the local population.

The main grains are millet, sorghum, maize, *fonio* (*Digitaria genus*), and rice. Millet, maize, and rice are the ingredients eaten by most Burkinabe on a daily basis, with rice being more a town folk's food because of its cost. Rice is grown locally, but generally people prefer the imported varieties of Thai and Indonesian rice. Sweet potatoes, yams, and potatoes are also grown locally and used as everyday food, but of these, potatoes are the most expensive and therefore are not eaten on an everyday basis.

Groundnuts (peanuts), which were introduced to West Africa as a cash crop in the colonial period, are also an important ingredient. The Bissa people are particularly well known for their taste for peanuts. Various pulses, such as beans, chickpeas, lentils, and bambara groundnut (*Vigna subterranea*), are also part of the everyday diet. The Mossi people are known as great eaters of beans (*benga*). Beans are eaten boiled and served with salt and oil.

Vegetables that are grown locally are tomatoes, zucchini, carrots, leeks, onions, beets, okra, pumpkins,

An African woman selling groundnuts (peanuts) by the roadside. (iStockPhoto)

cucumbers, and various types of lettuce. They are mostly used in sauces, apart from lettuce, which is an expensive ingredient and is eaten only at festive meals or in wealthier families. Greens—spinach, sorrel, and cabbage, among others—are important vegetables that are used in sauces that accompany the main staple food of millet or maize porridge.

Foods are seasoned using salt, stock cubes, and/or *sumbala* (African locust bean tree seeds—*Parkia biglobosa*). Hot peppers are added to sauces, but food is only mildly hot. A paste made of hot peppers can be added to the meal, especially when eating fried foods or meat. Traditional cooking fats such as shea butter and palm nut oil have largely been replaced by groundnut oil. Sunflower oil is used only in upper-class families.

Fruits are consumed as snacks and are sometimes used for making juices. Their availability depends on the seasons—mango season is from March to May or June. Water is served with meals. Milk is a drink that is popular among the Fulbe (Fulani) nomads, who also sell it at the markets. Locally produced juices made of hibiscus flowers, ginger, lemon, and baobab fruit (which looks like a coconut and contains a sour powdery white pulp) are also popular, particularly at parties. Chinese tea prepared over several hours on small charcoal stoves, with large quantities of sugar, is very popular with men, many of whom belong to a regular tea group that meets on a daily or weekly basis.

Cooking

Food preparation in Burkina Faso is rather labor-intensive, in both rural and urban areas, although in towns and cities, the task is made easier by the fact that most compounds have access to water through a water tap or a nearby public well. While women in the countryside often have to walk far into the bush to fetch firewood for cooking food and heating water, in urban environments this can be bought from ambulant sellers. Because of the hot climate, foods for cooking need to be bought on a daily basis (very few families have refrigerators, and those who do mostly use them to store cold water and ice), which means that the women in urban areas have to go to the market to buy ingredients for the daily meal every day. In rural areas, the market takes place every five days. Most Burkinabe families are large and include several generations living within one compound, which makes the task of cooking a demanding one; it is usually overseen by the eldest woman in the family, who is aided by her daughters, nieces, daughters-in-law, and/or a live-in maid. While child maids are common in Burkina Faso, they are often not entrusted with cooking the main family meal but are instead assigned the more menial tasks of washing the dishes, sweeping the kitchen floors as well as the compound, and doing the laundry.

As Burkina Faso has a hot climate, cooking is often done outdoors in the yard, except when the weather (rain, dust, wind) prevents this. The kitchen is a small room with walls blackened from smoke. It has no furnishings other than a small stool for the cook, a stove composed of three stones used for balancing the pot (in town this would be a metal stove with a hole on one side for firewood), and sometimes pots and pans piled up in the corner. Upper-middle-class families will have a kitchen inside the house, with a sink and a stove with two or more burners

fueled by bottled gas. However, gas is expensive and thus always used frugally. When cooking for large numbers of people, wood remains the preferred fuel.

When cooking lunch, women usually use two pots, one for the staple food and one for the sauce. One of the staple foods, the millet or maize porridge known locally as *tô*, requires particular skill and strength on the part of the cook, as the flour requires vigorous stirring while being heated over the stove and the cook needs to sit close to the fire to prevent the pot from moving. The irritation from the smoke, which gets into the eyes, is something the women get used to over the years of performing this demanding task.

Preparation of rice as a staple dish is less demanding, but the rice must be carefully cleaned before cooking. Dust, stones, and other dirt must be removed and the rice carefully washed. The Burkinabe like their food well cooked, so the rice will cook for well over an hour. Similarly, when pasta is prepared it must be totally tender to be considered edible. The Western style of cooking rice or pasta al dente is not appreciated by the Burkinabe.

The sauce for the main meal is cooked in the following way: First, oil is heated in the pan, and then once the oil is very hot, meat or fish is added and fried well. After that the cook adds the onions and then the rest of the vegetables; water is added, and then the sauce has to simmer until all the ingredients are well cooked. In case of *ris gras* or *spaghetti gras,* rice or pasta is added to the sauce and then cooked until all the water has evaporated and the rice or pasta is well cooked. Frying is common for fish and meat especially when these are purchased outside the house or served as a side dish; otherwise, it is first fried and then cooked in sauce.

The local specialties of fonio couscous and *attiéké* (fermented manioc couscous, which originates from Côte d'Ivoire but is very popular in Burkina Faso) are prepared by steaming, and so are some other cereal-based dumplings and pancakes. Other pancakes and doughnuts are either deep-fried or fried with a small amount of fat (oil or shea butter, depending on the region and the type of flour used). As oil is an expensive foodstuff, it is often used several times, as there is no belief or knowledge that

Cooking doughnuts over a wood fire in Africa. (iStock-Photo)

would forbid reheating used oil among the average Burkinabe. Oil that was used for frying meat can later also be used for seasoning salads.

Typical Meals

Breakfast is not an important meal for the majority of the population, and it is mostly eaten by those who can afford it. Breakfast can consist of either leftover food from the day before or specially prepared or purchased foods, such as bread and coffee or tea, millet gruel, or fried eggs.

For the average Burkinabe, lunch is the main meal and is based on a staple food such as millet or maize porridge or rice, always served with a sauce. Meat is a favored food item, and ideally all sauces should contain at least a small quantity of meat or fish. However, due to poverty many people cannot afford to buy meat or fish on a daily basis, so small amounts of dried fish are used to give a meaty taste to the meal. In the most hard-off families, this will be replaced by a meat stock cube. Wealthier urban families may occasionally prepare macaroni with sauce as the main dish, or a yam ragout, but rice and porridge (made of millet in the rural and maize in the urban areas) remain the dominant staple foods. Some of the more popular sauces are *sauce oseille* (sorrel sauce), *sauce feuilles de baobab* (sauce made with baobab leaves), *sauce claire* (a light sauce made with grated onion and zucchini), *sauce arachide* (groundnut sauce), and *sauce gombo* (sticky sauce made with fresh okra), which is usually eaten together with *la soupe* (a meat-based sauce).

Lunch is eaten between 12:30 and 1:30 P.M. In rural settings, the tradition of women and men eating from separate dishes, using the right hand, is maintained, with women often eating after men. In urban areas, people often eat from individual plates, using a spoon or a fork. A full set of cutlery is used only in upper-class families. People in lower- and middle-class families don't eat sitting together at the table, nor do people in the villages. They either sit on the floor around the dish, eating together as a group, or on stools, holding their own plate. Dinner can be either a separately cooked meal or, as is often the case, the same dish as lunch, heated up on a charcoal or gas stove. It is eaten at 8 P.M. or later.

Eating Out

Street food is typical of the urban areas of the country. Ready-to-eat foods can be bought immediately outside one's house, as there are many small stands selling foods in front of people's compounds. These mostly sell fried foods. Places around town cater for every taste. Food is available at virtually any time of the day, although certain parts of town, especially the central area around the markets, cater only to lunch customers.

Early in the morning makeshift breakfast places appear on the side streets of urban Burkina Faso. These are made up of a couple of benches and a table. On a small wood or charcoal stove the vendor boils water for coffee and tea, and a large cardboard box serves as a bread bin. The more prosperous cafés are built like a small bar with a roof and bar stools around the bar. These can be locked up at night and might even have a fridge and a gas stove inside. As a rule, they are run by men serving coffee or tea alongside buttered bread. The more enterprising vendors will also prepare fried eggs or omelets, and if they posses an icebox, or even a refrigerator, they might also serve yogurt and/or cold drinks. Customers are almost exclusively male; women rarely venture into one of these places. It would be inappropriate for an unaccompanied woman to be sitting in the street in the company of unknown men. Men, in contrast, are free to sit at the café and chat with the vendor and other customers. Breakfast places often open in the wee hours of the day, at about 4 or 5 A.M. Some of them open at dusk and stay open until the early morning hours.

As breakfast is not one of the meals provided by the head of the family, the men who go out to work often allow themselves the luxury of eating breakfast at a café instead of just having a small bowl of *la bouillie* (millet or rice gruel) bought from a neighbor, as most of their family members do. Most people will have some gruel or a cup of coffee for breakfast at home. Some families prepare la bouillie themselves, or they may buy it from a neighbor who prepares it for sale every morning. This is the cheapest breakfast food available. It is mostly prepared with millet flour, which is slightly sour and therefore requires sweetening, so that most people end up spending more money on the sugar than on the gruel itself.

In Ouagadougou and Bobo Dioulasso, the capital and the second-largest city respectively, there are also patisseries and bakeries that serve breakfast. Apart from bread, coffee, and omelets, they also have croissants and other pastries, yogurt, juices, and sodas, and they serve the tea and coffee in pots and cups. These places are not within the reach of the average Burkinabe, and most customers are businessmen, tourists, and higher-ranking civil servants from another part of the country who are in town on an official mission.

Most breakfast places start packing up between 10 and 11 A.M. That is the time when stands selling lunch will start appearing. They offer the usual home fare and sell it by the plate to regular customers and passersby. As the lunchtime meal is something one should normally get from one's family, these places are most often frequented by people who are visitors or passersby and have no family in town whatsoever. If people are visiting a town where distant relatives live, ones with whom their own immediate family is on good terms, they will be fed once a day at least for a few days, unless the relatives live in extreme poverty and have trouble providing even for themselves. The many people who work for one of

the numerous local and regional transport companies and travel back and forth on buses and trucks usually eat at one of the lunch places around the train station. Also, with the capital Ouagadougou growing significantly in size, people may work a long way away from their house and therefore have no choice but to eat outside, to save the money for the transport home and back to work again after the two-and-a-half-hour designated lunch break.

In the eyes of an average Burkinabe, lunch should consist of one of the staple dishes, such as maize or millet porridge or rice accompanied by a sauce, the value of which is determined by the amount of meat it contains. The types of foods that are offered at street stalls during lunch hours reflect this local concept of a proper meal. Since the types of foods sold are much like the main meal prepared by every Bobolese housewife, it is the women who prepare and sell lunchtime food in the streets. The women who sell these meals, sometimes alone, sometimes in pairs, prepare the food early every morning in their kitchens at home and then, with either a donkey cart or a taxi, transport the large pots to their vending spot. Some women have set up proper small restaurants, often linked to their own backyard, with a metal roof over some wooden tables and benches for customers to sit on and enjoy their meal. Most street stalls consist of a table on which the food is placed in large buckets, and there are a few benches for customers to sit down on while eating. A man will sit on a small wooden bench and eat from his plastic plate, usually using a fork. Women eat lunch in places like these only if they are accompanied by their husband or if they are clearly visiting from another town or village and do not have relatives who could provide for them.

Similarly to breakfast, lunch can also be eaten in restaurants that cater to a wealthier clientele. There is a great variety of restaurants around, from those serving the lower-ranking civil servants to those that are frequented only by the expatriate population and wealthy local businessmen and -women. The cheaper restaurants serve both Burkinabe and Western dishes, while the upmarket ones usually specialize in a particular cuisine. In the capital several restaurants serve Italian, French, Lebanese, or another foreign cuisine. These places are open for lunch and dinner.

If the lunchtime foods are mostly the same as one would get at home, the evenings and nights on the streets of Bobo provide one with a true culinary experience. From the late afternoon, little street stalls selling ready-to-eat foods begin to appear. Most food stalls immediately outside compounds sell fried foods. These can include yam, sweet potato, and plantain chips; bean and sweet banana fritters; and doughnuts made from millet, corn, or wheat flour. For those who do not have the time or inclination to stop and sit down, the food is wrapped in pages of old newspaper or pieces of large paper flour bags. Those with more time to spare may decide to sit down on a bench next to the vendor and eat food off a plate and perhaps engage in some small talk with the vendor.

Since in the evening many single, and also married Burkinabe men, go out to bars with their girlfriends, or more rarely with their wives, the pavements outside these bars and clubs are packed with little food stands. At night the vendors tend to be men, but they never sell the types of foods associated with women's cooking. While women, some of whom also have stands in the street at night, sell mostly rice and sauce, tô and sauce, pasta, attiéké, or sandwiches, men specialize in barbecued meat and poultry and in omelets or fried egg sandwiches. The typical location for the stands is outside popular nightclubs, so that customers can get a bite to eat.

Sometimes people leave their compounds and drive to a particular part of town in order to buy a dish that will satisfy their craving. Others walk onto the street outside their compound and buy a small plate of beans or rice with sauce if they have run out of food at home. Eating in restaurants is not a common practice for most Burkinabe, who cannot afford the expense, and even if they could, many of them prefer home cooking. People are generally very careful about where they buy the food they eat and do not trust that the restaurant food is prepared as carefully as a home-cooked meal. However, with westernization, one can now see more Burkinabe couples and families eating in restaurants than a decade ago.

Special Occasions

Feasting in Burkina Faso is mostly linked to religious holidays or celebrations—Ramadan, Tabaski (Eid al-Adha), and Mouloud for the Muslims; Christmas and Easter for the Christians; days of sacrifice among the animists—and celebrations of life-cycle milestones (christenings and naming ceremonies, weddings, and funerals). As there are few specific festive dishes, on such events what matters is the quantity of food and the quality of the ingredients, but the recipes mainly stay the same. In rural areas the dish served would still be tô, but for a feast the male head of the family usually slaughters an animal (if not a sheep or lamb, then a chicken), since meat is regarded as a particularly important ingredient of a festive meal.

In urban areas a dish that is served at every feast and celebration is *malo zaamen* (Jula), *moui nado* (Moore), or riz gras, a rice-based dish now synonymous with parties in urban Burkina Faso. Its origins may be traced back to the Senegalese rice-based dish *tiebou djen,* which is prepared with copious amounts of meat and fish. While the Burkinabe version is less elaborate than its Senegalese counterpart, it still contains large amounts of meat and vegetables (instead of fish) and is considered a rich man's dish. Good riz gras is made from top-quality ingredients and numerous stock cubes. The meat and vegetables are served on a bed of rice that has been cooked in the meat and vegetable stock.

Riz Gras

4 c rice

I large onion, chopped

Parsley

Garlic

18 oz lamb or beef

I *goyo*, cubed (African eggplant)

18 oz ripe tomatoes (or a16-oz can of tomatoes)

I green bell pepper, chopped and seeded

2 carrots, halved

Half a cabbage, cut into large pieces

2 Maggi meat or vegetable stock cubes

1 tbsp tomato concentrate

Salt

Oil

Heat the oil, and add the meat, cut in small pieces. While frying the meat, add salt, and as the meat turns brown, add the chopped onion, tomatoes, and pepper and stir well. Then add tomato concentrate, chopped garlic, and parsley and stir again. After sautéing the ingredients for about 10 minutes, fill up the pot with water. Add the cabbage, carrots, eggplant, and stock cubes. Allow to simmer until the vegetables are tender and cooked. Once the meat and vegetables are well cooked, use a spoon to take them out. Keep them warm. Pour the rice into the sauce in which the meat and vegetables were cooked and check for salt. If needed, add some salt and stir the rice. Continue cooking over a low fire and stir occasionally. Once all the water has evaporated, the rice should be cooked. Serve it with the meat and vegetables piled on top.

No feast would be complete without drinks. Among the Christian and animist populations the festive drink of choice is beer, traditionally made of millet or sorghum, and in the southwest of the country also palm wine. In towns bottled beer is the drink of choice for adults and soda for children, although among the Bobo ethnic group, children are given millet beer at an early age. Muslims drink soft drinks, both homemade juices from the hibiscus flower, ginger, or lemons and bottled sodas. Some less pious Muslim men drink alcohol but never inside their home.

With Western influences particularly in the urban areas, some new foods are finding their way onto the festive menus of the Burkinabe. These foods are often referred to as "white man's food" and are served at civil wedding receptions and in smaller quantities to a select few special guests at traditional feasts. White man's foods can be locally grown, but when prepared in an untraditional manner, they become foreign. Salads of raw vegetables or *crudités,* popcorn, Chinese crab crackers, and vermicelli pasta are some of the foods served on such occasions. These foods are not meant to feed but to be seen, as they are expensive and will be served only in small quantities.

During the holy month of Ramadan, when Muslims fast from dawn till dusk, special foods are prepared for breaking the fast. The fast is usually broken by first taking some liquid, water, or specially prepared herbal tea. Then one drinks millet or rice gruel, followed by millet doughnuts, called *les gallettes du mil* in French. The food consumed after breaking the fast is usually a richer version of the daily staple. There are two main meals after breaking the fast, one around 8 or 9 in the evening and one at about 3:30 A.M. before beginning the fast. On the day that celebrates the end of Ramadan, Eid al-Fitr, additional festive foods, such as riz gras, are prepared in quantities large enough to be shared with relatives, neighbors, and friends. A sheep will be slaughtered by the head of the family, and the meat is used for the festive meal and distributed to relatives and friends. The same happens on another major Islamic holiday Eid al-Adha, locally called le Tabaski. Sending gifts of food to relatives, neighbors, and friends is an important part of everyday sociality in Burkina Faso and helps people maintain important support networks.

Diet and Health

African ideas of healthy eating are very different from Western ones. Possibly due to food shortages in the past, people eat as much as they can. Fatness equals good health, life force, and wealth and is an appreciated feature. People who become rich will initially start eating larger quantities of fattening foods. They will add extra foods to the communal meal and go for particularly rich breakfasts and several daytime snacks. With time, the same people might become more health conscious and start buying better-quality ingredients instead of simply doubling the quantity of their intake. In urban areas people are becoming more weight conscious, and some women talk about reducing fat in their food intake. However, since oil is a cherished ingredient and communal cooking does not consider special needs, those who wish to follow a special diet need to prepare their food themselves. This requires both time and money and is thus often not an option for many people. When people are unwell, meat soup and tô are considered as strength-giving foods. Tô is believed to be more easily digested than rice and thus more suitable for someone who is frail and ailing.

Liza Debevec

Further Reading

Debevec, Liza. "Family Meals, Sharing and Hierarchy in a West-African Town." In *Nurture: The Proceedings of Symposium on Food and Cookery,* edited by Richard Hosking, 66–77. Bristol, UK: Footwork Press, 2003.

Debevec, Liza. "The Meaning of African and 'White Man's' Food at Muslim and Civil Wedding Celebrations in Urban Burkina Faso." *Anthropology of Food,* S3| (December 2007), http://aof.revues.org/index2572.html.

Freidberg, Susanne. "French Beans of the Masses: A Modern Historical Geography of Food in Burkina Faso." *Journal of Historical Geography* 29, No. 3 (2003): 445–63.

Osseo-Asare, Fran. *Food Culture in Sub-Saharan Africa.* Westport, CT: Greenwood Press, 2005.

Ouédraogo, Joséphine. "Les femmes chefs de ménage en zone rurale du Burkina Faso." In *Femmes du Sud, chefs de famille,* edited by Jeanne Bisilliat, 99–107. Paris: Karthala, 1996.

Roget-Petitjean, Myriam. *Soins et nutrition des enfants en mileu urbain africain.* Paris: L'Harmattan, 1997.

Central Africa

Overview

The countries considered here as part of Central Africa are the Democratic Republic of the Congo (DRC), the Republic of the Congo, Gabon, Equatorial Guinea, Cameroon, and the Central African Republic (CAR). They all border the equatorial rain forest, home to a highly diversified fauna and flora and crisscrossed by numerous waterways. The Congo River, the fifth-longest river in the world, forms with its many tributaries the world's second-largest drainage basin. The navigable parts of these rivers often offer the best way to access the region. In the north and south of Central Africa, the rain forest gives way to grasslands, whereas in the east of the DRC the mountains indicate the transition to the Great Lakes region. In contrast to the rain forest, these areas are suitable for the cultivation of cereals and cattle rearing. The western border of Central Africa is formed by the Atlantic Ocean. At the equator there are two rainy seasons and two dry seasons, while further north and south there is only one distinctive rainy and one dry season.

Central Africa is home to a high number of ethnic groups, each with its specific food habits and taboos. The national borders do not reflect ethnic boundaries. Some groups are present in two or even more countries, such as the Fang, who live in Cameroon, Equatorial Guinea, Gabon, and the Republic of the Congo. Most people in Central Africa speak Bantu or Ubangi languages, both language groups that belong to the Niger-Congo language family. In the north of the region, other Niger-Congo, Nilo-Saharan, and Afro-Asiatic languages are spoken as well. Even if these language groupings are sometimes used as

ethnic labels, this does not reflect by any means a cultural, and certainly not a racial, reality. The hunter-gatherers of the rain forest, for instance, known as *pygmies,* a derogatory term, speak Bantu or Ubangi languages but are considered culturally distinct from peoples speaking the same or closely related languages.

In the DRC the hunter-gatherers are sometimes called *autochthons.* They are considered to be the first peoples present in Central Africa. Bantu-speaking communities, who now constitute by far the majority in this region, left the Nigerian-Cameroonian borderland only some 4,000 to 5,000 years ago, from where they spread toward eastern and southern Africa. These Bantu-speaking peoples developed an agricultural system combined with the procurement of wild resources. Some of the hunter-gatherers adopted the languages of these newcomers. The Aka of the CAR, for instance, are hunter-gatherers who speak a Bantu language.

The first Europeans to arrive in the region were the Portuguese, who were exploring the coasts of the Atlantic Ocean at the end of the 15th century. They introduced some plants they had acquired in the Americas, notably Brazil. The Columbian Exchange (the exchange of foodstuffs between the New and the Old World) resulted for Central Africa in the adoption of cassava, corn, sweet potatoes, the new cocoyam, peanuts, peppers, tomatoes, pumpkins, and several fruits. During the colonial period more foodstuffs were introduced and, more important, a whole array of European food customs, such as the three-meal day. The legacy of the French colonial past in the CAR, Cameroon, Gabon, and Congo involves,

Preparing beignets in Lieki, Orientale Province, Democratic Republic of the Congo. (Courtesy of Birgit Ricquier)

among other things, the consumption of baguettes at breakfast, whereas the Belgian ex-colonizer left beer breweries in the major cities of the DRC. Globalization combined with a strong urbanization tendency ensures that the Western influence is only getting stronger. Other legacies of the colonial period are the national boundaries and the official languages, that is, French in all countries, Spanish as the first official language in Equatorial Guinea, and English as the second language in Cameroon. As a consequence, French names are used for several food items and dishes. Finally, the Europeans also brought a new religion, Christianity. Even if traditional elements have often been incorporated into the new faith, others have been lost, and this also has repercussions on food culture, such as the loss of specific food taboos.

🍽 Food Culture Snapshot

Mengue M'obiang Geneviève lives with her husband, Ndong Essone Jean-Baptiste, in Libreville, the capital of Gabon. They have three children of their own and take care of two children of Jean-Baptiste's brother. When Geneviève goes to the market, she must make sure to get the required starch foods, proteins, condiments, and vegetables. In the first category she purchases a package of 10 cassava sticks (chikwangue, bâtons de manioc) or two to three kilograms (4.4–8.8 pounds) of plantains, a quantity sufficient for a few days. Once a month she buys a bag of 50 kilograms (more than 100 pounds) of rice. The protein intake is ensured by approximately two kilograms (4.4 pounds) of meat, such as chicken, and two kilograms (4.4 pounds) of smoked, salted, or fresh fish. Sometimes she opts for bush meat, but this is rare and quite expensive. As condiments she purchases peppers, onions, garlic, and Maggi bouillon cubes in various flavors. Geneviève takes particular care with respect to the vegetable choice since vegetables make the difference between one dish or another. This time she chooses to prepare beans, of which she buys approximately one kilogram, but she could as well have purchased three or four bundles of greens. Occasionally she may add some seasonal fruit, such as mangoes or *safou* plums. Geneviève now has enough groceries to prepare the main meal of the day, which is served at noon. The leftovers will be served in the evening.

For breakfast the family has bread, the French-style baguette, with butter or condensed milk, coffee, and cocoa prepared with powdered milk and sugar. The kids sometimes get cornflakes and occasionally baguette with chocolate spread, which is purchased as *pain chocolaté* at the corner shop. All breakfast items can be found at the market or in small quantities at the corner shop. However, middle-class families often prefer to get these groceries from the supermarket.

When Geneviève, Jean-Baptiste, and the children visit the family in the village, both the meals and the grocery shopping are quite different. Instead of three meals, they'll have only breakfast and dinner, with snacks appeasing their stomachs during the day. The fare is much simpler. Maggi cubes, for instance, are rarely used. In the rural areas people grow foodstuffs in their fields and gather them in the forest. Hardly any food is purchased, meat, fish, and rice being the main exceptions.

Major Foodstuffs

In large parts of Central Africa starchy food consists mainly of tubers and plantains. Without any doubt the most important tuber is cassava (*Manihot esculenta*). There are "sweet" and "bitter" varieties, referring to the amount of cyanogenic glycosides. The bitter varieties require soaking in water for a few days to remove the toxins. Before the Columbian Exchange true yams (*Dioscorea*) were the most important root crops, and they still are consumed in a large variety. Some are cultivated, such as the aerial yam (*D. bulbifera*) and the yellow yam (*D. cayenensis*). Others are simply found in the rain forest, for example, *D. burkilliana.* Some of these yams attain a weight of several kilograms, *D. mangenotiana* being one of the champions, with a possible weight of over 200 kilograms (441 pounds), but it is no longer harvested when more than 5 kilograms (11 pounds). Some yam varieties are toxic and require soaking like cassava. Two tubers of Asian origin were introduced fairly early into Central Africa: the water or purple yam (*D. alata*) and taro (*Colocasia esculenta*). Other root crops are the new cocoyam (*Xanthosoma*), the sweet potato (*Ipomoea batatas*), and several species of African origin that today have only minor importance, such as the Hausa potato (*Solenostemon rotundifolius*), the Livingstone potato (*Plectranthus esculentus*), and several wild tubers. Another important starch food is actually a fruit, that is, the plantain (*Musa paradisiaca*) in the banana family. This originally Asian plant must have been present in the area for some millennia, but scholars disagree on the time and place of its introduction. Plantains are often considered as the food of the ancestors and play an important role in festivities.

Pulverizing and sieving soaked cassava tubers in preparation of making Chikangue in the Matombi, Kouilou Province, Republic of Congo. (Courtesy of Birgit Ricquier)

The largest part of Central Africa is not favorable to the cultivation of cereals. Corn (*Zea mays*) forms the exception and is widely grown. On the fringes of the forest, however, three cereals of African origin are found: sorghum (*Sorghum bicolor*), pearl millet (*Pennisetum glaucum*), and finger millet (*Eleusine coracana*). Finally, rice (*Oryza sativa*) is cultivated in some areas, but it can be purchased at markets all over the region. These tubers, plantains, and cereals are used to prepare the starch constituent of the meal, snacks, and alcoholic beverages.

People in Central Africa grow and gather an amazing variety of greens, such as various species of amaranth (*Amaranthus*), the leaves of *Gnetum africanum,* bitterleaf (*Vernonia amygdalina*), the shoots and leaves of various *Dioscorea* and *Solanum* species, and so on. Also, the leaves of plants primarily grown for their tubers or fruits are consumed, for example, the shoots and/or leaves of cassava, sweet potatoes, taro, the new cocoyam, various legumes, and gourds. Some of these greens require extensive cooking to remove toxins.

Other vegetables include various legumes, cucurbits, eggplant, and okra. Legumes of African origins are, for instance, the cowpea (*Vigna unguiculata*), the bambara groundnut (*Vigna subterranea*), and the yambean (*Sphenostylis stenocarpa*), which also provides edible tubers. The bambara groundnut has been largely replaced by the peanut (*Arachis hypogea*), the name for the first now being used in many languages for its American successor. A recently introduced legume is, for instance, the common bean (*Phaseolus vulgaris*). In addition, the cultivated cucurbits include species from both African and American origins. A famous African gourd is the bottle gourd or calabash (*Lagenaria siceraria*), used for spoons and containers. Another example is the *egusi* melon (*Citrullus lanatus*), which is grown for its seeds. The African eggplant or garden egg (*Solanum aethiopicum* and related species) comes in many bright colors. It is somewhat smaller than its purple Asian counterpart, and its shape resembles an egg more closely. Some species can be eaten raw, and as already mentioned, the leaves are used as greens. Okra (*Hibiscus esculentus*) is one of the originally African food items that took part in the Columbian Exchange and is now also a favorite in New Orleans.

Fruits of certain trees have the same function as vegetables. This includes the safou plum (*Dacryodes edulis*), breadfruit (*Artocarpus communis*), and the African black olive (*Canarium schweinfurthii*). The same holds for the newcomers the avocado (*Persea americana*), green mango (*Mangifera indica*), and diverse citruses. Many of these can, however, also be eaten raw. Another important foodstuff is mushrooms. A high number of edible species are gathered, many of which are found on trees.

There are two main types of condiments in Central Africa: seeds and palm products. With respect to the first, the use of several cucurbit seeds as well as peanuts has already been mentioned. Other seeds are, for instance, those of the wild mango (*Irvingia gabonensis*) and sesame (*Sesamum indicum*). Seeds are usually pounded into a paste, which is added to the broth of various preparations. Two products of the oil palm (*Elaeis guineensis*) are common condiments: palm oil and palm butter. Both are extracted from the boiled palm fruits, which are pounded in a mortar, mixed with water, and filtered to remove the kernels and fruit skins. The resulting sauce is palm butter, better known as *moambe,* and from this substance the palm oil can be strained. It is also possible to extract palm oil from the kernels, but the resulting oil is rarely used in cooking (instead, it is used in medicine or cosmetics). It should be mentioned that the palm tree also provides palm wine.

A condiment that is present in almost every preparation is salt. In Central Africa salt is traditionally derived from plants. Herbs or greens are dried and burnt to ashes. These ashes are mixed with water and used as such, or boiled until the water evaporates. There is also salt from mines and sea salt, both available in the markets. Other condiments are peppers, tomatoes (often canned), onions, and garlic. In Central African cities it is common to cook with Maggi cubes.

Meat is available from domestic animals, such as goats, sheep, guinea fowl, chickens, and, to a minor extent, cattle and pigs. However, in the rural areas it is quite common to hunt or trap game: various mammals such as antelopes and monkeys, birds such as pigeons and herons, and reptiles such as crocodiles and snakes. This bush meat is a sought-after product for those who procure it at markets at the side of the main roads. The trade in bush meat has become such a lucrative business that it threatens wildlife in some areas. Apart from the meat, also the entrails and sometimes the skins of these wild animals are prepared for food, and for antelopes and buffalo the contents of the second stomach. Thanks to the many rivers and the Atlantic Ocean, there is also a large variety of fish, as well as some shellfish like crab and prawns. People also gather caterpillars, beetles, and termites. The fat and nutritious larvae of the palm weevil (*Rynchophorus* sp.) are particularly popular, and the adult beetles are also eaten. Dairy products are not commonly consumed. Eggs occasionally appear on the menu, but the consumption of milk products is restricted to the grassland regions where cattle can be kept. It must be observed, however, that powdered milk is currently available all over the region. A final animal product is honey. This highly valued resource is, among others, used to prepare *hydromel,* a fermented alcoholic drink like mead.

Finally, several products are eaten raw as a snack. Those include various wild fruits, for example, the African star apple (*Chrysophyllum* sp.), gumvines (*Landolphia* sp.; a sour fruit about the size of an orange with seeds in a stringy pulp), monkey oranges (*Strychnos* sp.), and junglesop (*Anonidium mannii;* an odd light green fruit that looks something like a segmented artichoke). Many cultivated fruits have also been introduced, for example, the sweet or dessert banana (*Musa* sp.), pineapple (*Ananas comosus*), and papaya (*Carica papaya*). The stalks of several cereals and grasses, like sorghum, corn, sugarcane (*Saccharum*), and elephant grass (*Pennisetum purpureum*), are chewed for the sweet sap, especially by children. Cola nuts are another popular snack, reputed to have stimulating and aphrodisiac qualities.

Cooking

Whereas the labor to procure food (cultivating, hunting, trapping, fishing, and gathering) is divided between men and women, cooking is foremost a female activity. Some foods, however, can be eaten only by men, and they often prepare these themselves on a separate fireplace in separate pots. In addition, some preparatory activities like butchering are men's tasks,

but the remaining cooking activities are performed by women.

The organization of the cooking area in Central Africa is different from one ethnic group to another. Some kitchens are a separate building, for example, among the Yassa and Mvae of southern Cameroon. Others, such as the Songola (central DRC), prepare food under a veranda that also serves as the living room, whereas the kitchen of the Shi (eastern DRC) is situated in the hut, next to the bed. In all cases, the cooking area consists of one or a few fireplaces, a smoking shelf, and shelves to store food and cooking utensils. The fireplace is made up of three stones placed in a triangle with firewood in between. Cooking equipment consists of wooden mortars and pestles in various sizes, a wooden board for kneading cassava, aluminum pots (rather than the traditional ceramics), a long stirring stick or spatula used in making *fufu* (a thick starchy porridge), knives, and so on. In most villages all over the region a large number of preparatory activities are performed in the courtyard, where a large drying shelf is usually also placed. City dwellers have Western-style kitchens, but these often contain Central African elements as well, such as a wooden mortar, and urban cooks equally perform certain cooking activities outside, such as roasting meat on a fire placed under the veranda.

Chikwangue, or cassava sticks (bâtons de manioc), ready for steaming in Malemba, Kouilou Province, Republic of Congo. (Courtesy of Birgit Ricquier)

Few food items are stored. In the case of cassava, plantains, and wild yams storage isn't necessary, since these plants can be harvested year-round. Cultivated yams and taro, in contrast, have a harvest season and are sometimes stored in granaries. Meat and fish are often smoked to be preserved. Other items with a long storage time are the dried pastes of seeds and vegetable salt. Most food items are simply procured seasonally. Shorter-term storage does occur more often, in order to better organize the work. Women will, for instance, make an amount of chikwangue or flour that will suffice for several days. These are then stored in baskets. Of course, city kitchens usually have a refrigerator, thus expanding storage possibilities.

In rural areas meals are made from scratch. This implies that cooking is a time-consuming and labor-intensive task. Instead of simply purchasing cassava flour at the market, women in the countryside first need to harvest the tubers, peel them and leave them in water for several days, and then put the soaked tubers on a shelf to dry, after which these can be pounded into flour and sieved. Only then can the flour be used to prepare the staple food of the region, called fufu. Fufu, also called *nshima, bidya,* or *bukari,* is a sticky porridge made by stirring flour into boiling water with a long spatula or stirring stick. It is usually prepared with cassava or corn flour, but flour from plantains, rice, and millet can be used as well. This is the same dish as the East African *ugali* or Zimbabwean *sadza.*

Fufu

This version of fufu is made with cassava flour. You can replace it with another type of flour, but then the amount of water has to be modified. Some brands give indications for the quantities on the package.

5 c water

5 c cassava flour

Bring 5 cups water to a boil. When large bubbles appear, take 1 cup of the boiling water and set aside. Add the flour, and stir well with a long wooden spatula. To have better control of the kneading, remove the pot from the fire, sit down, place the pot between your feet, and stir with two hands. Add the remaining water as necessary. Scrape the sides and bottom of the pot while kneading. Keep on turning the porridge until it gets sticky and translucent and no lumps remain.

Fufu can also be made by mashing boiled plantains or tubers, such as yams. Another elaborate starch preparation made of cassava is chikwangue or bâton de manioc. In the south of Congo, it takes one to two weeks to prepare this staple. After several days of soaking, the tubers are pulverized by hand in water, passed through a sieve, and the fibers removed with a knife. Next, the water is drained off, and the remaining cassava paste is poured into a bag to drip for one or two days. The paste is kneaded on a wooden board, by hand and with a wooden roller. It can be left to rest for another day but often is immediately steamed, kneaded for the second time, and shaped into sticks, which are then wrapped in leaves, and finally these are steamed again. Chikwangue can be stored for several days and thus makes an ideal travel supply. Other, though less popular, starch foods take little time, for instance, boiled taro or fried plantains.

The foodstuffs served with fufu or chikwangue, be they vegetables or animal products, are usually

A libóké of fish baking on the ashes in Kimbonga-Louamba, Bouenza Province, Republic of Congo. (Courtesy of Birgit Ricquier)

boiled with diverse seasonings and in various combinations, for example, meat with eggplant, salt, and peppers. The most popular side dish, *saka-saka,* or cassava leaves, is again a time-consuming preparation, involving pounding and several hours of boiling. Another preparation method is to wrap a mixture, for instance, fish with salt and peppers, in banana or other leaves and steam, boil, or roast the package. The choice of the leaves used for wrapping is very important because of the flavor they add to the preparation. Other methods include frying and several ways of roasting, for example, on skewers or on the warm ashes of the fire.

Typical Meals

As already mentioned, people have three meals a day, with a European-style breakfast, a main meal at noon, and leftovers in the evening. In villages, people have a small breakfast, snacks during the day, and the main meal in the evening, with breakfast often consisting of the leftovers of the meal they had the previous day. Beignets also make a popular breakfast food, especially among children. The main meal consists of a starch served with a stew or relish. For some ethnic groups, such as the Gbaya (CAR), there is no meal without the flour-based fufu. Elsewhere, the starch served can also be chikwangue, boiled or roasted plantains and root crops, or rice. With the starch a large variety of stews or relishes may be served. A popular dish known in Congo and the DRC as *moambe* consists of meat, fish, and/or greens prepared in a sauce made of pounded palm nuts.

Poulet à la Moambe (Chicken with Palm Butter)

Like all recipes, *poulet à la moambe* exists in many variations. You can replace the cassava leaves with other greens, okra, eggplant, and so on, or the chicken with salted or smoked fish. The palm oil, canned moambe (palm butter), and saka-saka can be found in African stores. Of course, this is an expatriate version. In Central Africa, the moambe and saka-saka are made from scratch.

1 chicken, cut in bite-size pieces

Palm oil, for frying

2 onions, finely chopped

2 chili peppers (to taste), finely chopped

5 ripe tomatoes, chopped

1 large can of moambe (approximately 28 oz)

1 can saka-saka (approximately 14 oz), drained

1 or 2 Maggi cubes, chicken flavor (or cubes of another brand)

Salt

Fry the chicken in some palm oil until brown but not done. Heat some more palm oil in a large pot, add the onion, peppers, and tomatoes, and cook for about 5 minutes. Add the meat and 1 cup of water. Then pour in the canned moambe and dilute the sauce with an equal amount (1 can) of water. Finally, stir in the drained saka-saka and season with salt and Maggi cubes. Cover the pot and let simmer for 30 to 40 minutes. The moambe is ready when oil appears on the surface. Serve with fufu, chikwangue, plantains, or rice.

Another popular Central African dish is chicken or fish in peanut sauce, often with tomatoes and onion. Fish, shrimp, or greens can also be prepared *à la pépé-soupe,* the name pointing to the addition of peppers. In Cameroon one might be served *ndolé* soup, which consists of bitterleaf, shrimp, fish and/or meat, peanuts, and various spices. A particular dish from Equatorial Guinea is *pangolín con chocolate,* pangolin meat stewed with onion, garlic, and "chocolate." *Chocolate* refers to the grated nut of the wild mango, and this sauce is also used to prepare fish and other meat in Equatorial Guinea, Cameroon, and Gabon. A final example is *libóké,* which is a Lingála word meaning "package" that refers along the Congo River to the preparation of fish or meat in broad leaves. All these dishes come in a high number of variations.

In rural areas men and women usually eat separately. The small children eat with their mothers, but older children form a third group. Each group shares the served starch foods and relishes. Sometimes children have their own plates, just like the sick and the elderly, who eat alone. It is not considered polite to watch visitors eating, so they too eat alone. Children often have the liberty to prepare their own meals, and they gather, trap, or even hunt (for small animals) the necessary foodstuffs themselves. In the cities, as well as among certain ethnic groups, such as the Aka (hunter-gatherers from the CAR), the social organization is entirely different, the meals being shared by the nuclear family. A simple matter of hygiene is washing the hands before eating. Often a bowl of water is passed around, and every person has to offer the bowl, the towel, and soap (if present) to the next person. This is all the more important since the meal is eaten with the hands. People will take a bit of fufu and use it as a spoon to scoop up the relish. Nowadays, forks and spoons are used as well.

The snacks eaten during the day can be simply fresh fruits. When preparation is necessary, most often one cooking technique is involved and no seasoning. As such, tubers, plantains, corn on the cob, vegetables like gourds, various seeds, and legumes are either boiled or roasted. More elaborate snacks are, for instance, diluted porridges, sweet or savory, and preparations in leaves. A Cameroonian favorite is *koki,* a "pudding" made of ground beans, palm oil, pepper, and the tender inner cocoyam leaves that is mixed, wrapped in the outer cocoyam leaves, and boiled or steamed. In the south of Congo *mbwaata,* a diluted cassava porridge commonly served with roasted peanuts, is quite popular.

In many places, it is not the custom that drinks accompany the meal. However, especially in the cities, European habits have set in. Coffee and cocoa accompany breakfast, for instance. Traditional drinks include various juices (e.g., from monkey oranges), infusions (e.g., from lemongrass or ginger), soups (e.g., from peppers and eggplant), and several alcoholic beverages. Hydromel is made by dissolving honey in water and leaving the mixture to ferment for several days. It is a seasonal product, depending on the blossoms and flowers. Palm wine is the fermented sap of a palm tree (oil palm, raffia palm, etc.). It can be collected by two methods: tapping the sap from the inflorescence in the top of the tree or

Palm nuts boiling to extract palm oil in Bomane, Orientale Province, Democratic Republic of the Congo. (Courtesy of Birgit Ricquier)

felling the tree. Fermentation of the sap takes only a few hours and is accomplished by exposure to the sun or by the addition of various plants or types of bark. Palm wine has a low percentage of alcohol and stays fresh only a short while, about 30 hours. There are many types of traditional beers, brewed with finger millet, sorghum, corn, cassava, and bananas, sometimes in combinations. The cereal beers are very different from European-style beers since they do not contain hops, which add bitterness and allow a longer shelf life. When fruits are in season people make wine of them, adding coloring, yeast, and sugar, for example, grapefruit wine. Wine can also be made of sugarcane. Spirits are distilled from various ingredients, such as corn and cassava (e.g., *lutuku*), palm wine, rice, pineapple, and sugarcane. Many European alcoholic beverages have become popular. Some are imported, such as red wine. There is, however, an important beer industry in Central Africa, especially in the DRC. Congolese beers include Primus, Skol, Tembo ("elephant" in Kiswahili), and Simba ("lion"). Finally, the omnipresent sodas like Coca-Cola and Fanta should be mentioned. In Lubumbashi these are called *sucrés* ("sugared" in French).

Eating Out

There is virtually no restaurant culture in Central Africa, but people still eat out. Eating out usually consists of visiting friends or relatives, and in the villages the men like to discuss the events of the day around some palm wine. These palm-wine gatherings are replaced by drinking (bottled) beer at the pub in the cities. A popular snack taken with the beer is roasted goat meat and onion served with chili powder and optionally slices of chikwangue. This snack is called *cabri* (French for "goat") in Kinshasa and *micopo* in Lubumbashi, the second-largest city of the DRC. Another way of eating out is buying a snack from a street vendor, which varies from roasted corn, sweet potatoes, and peanuts to cookies, candy, ice cream, and so on.

There are some restaurants in Central Africa. People like to eat there on special occasions, and they are also frequented by foreigners. Many restaurants serve exotic food, mostly European. One can have French-style croissants and milkshakes for

Pounding cassava leaves, or saka-saka, in Bomane, Orientale Province, Democratic Republic of the Congo. (Courtesy of Birgit Ricquier)

brunch in a patisserie or Italian pizza for dinner. Fast-food restaurants have made their entry, such as the Katanga Fried Chiken [sic] in Lubumbashi. In other restaurants local foods can be ordered.

Special Occasions

As anywhere in the world celebrations are paired with an abundance of food, especially rare and expensive products, such as bush meat and imported items like rice and red wine. Some preparations are indispensable at festivities, such as ndolé on the coasts of Cameroon. People celebrate many occasions, for example, the events of the Christian calendar year such as Christmas and New Year. Sometimes small things, like freshly prepared hydromel, are enough reason to throw a party. But it is the important moments in life—for example, birth, initiation, engagement, marriage—that require special attention. What foodstuffs are served depends largely on the ethnic group. The engagement ceremony of the Gbaya (CAR), for instance, involves preparations of chicken and smoked fish.

Other ceremonies are held for the ancestors. According to the Ambuun (western DRC), bananas are the food of the ancestors and hence are deposited at crossroads as an offering. And in the southern DRC people drink and offer sorghum beer during the commemoration of the famous 19th-century mwami M'Siri, king of the Yeke Kingdom.

Diet and Health

Variation in the menu is considered the key ingredient of good health. The seasonality of many foodstuffs (vegetables as well as insects) is the first step toward a balanced diet, and women will juggle the seasonal products to prepare a different dish every day. Starch dishes rarely vary; only the relish changes.

There are many food restrictions in the Central African diet, all depending on the ethnic group. Some are permanent, others only temporary. Permanent restrictions can be taboos linked to the clan. They usually concern certain types of game that are rare anyway, for example, lion, heron, or python. Sometimes the prohibition is only on the killing, and the

Soaking cassava tubers in a pond to remove the toxins in Musana, Pool Province, Republic of Congo. (Courtesy of Birgit Ricquier)

meat in question can be consumed if killed by another person. Women are prohibited certain foods, again usually scarce meat, such as baboon and crocodile. These items are linked to strength and masculinity. A taboo can also be linked to religion. Adherents of the Kimbanguist church, a Congolese branch of Christianity, don't eat pork or monkey and don't drink alcohol. Temporary restrictions are linked to pregnancy and giving birth, to initiation, and to mourning. In the case of pregnancy the prohibition is often linked to a characteristic of the food item. Pangolin, for instance, is a mammal covered with scales that moves slowly and rolls up in a ball as a defense mechanism. The Gbaya (CAR) fear that if the parents eat pangolin, the child will have skin problems and difficulty walking. In some places women who have their periods cannot prepare food for their family. Finally, food restrictions can be used as a remedy in case of illness.

Birgit Ricquier

Further Reading

Ankei, Takako. "Cookbook of the Songola: An Anthropological Study on the Technology of Food Preparation among a Bantu-Speaking People of the Zaïre Forest." *African Study Monographs,* Suppl. 13 (1990): 1–174.

Brain, Robert. "Cameroon Koki: A Bean Pudding from Bangwa." In *The Anthropologist's Cookbook,* edited by Jessica Kuper, 77–78. London: Kegan Paul International, 1997.

Cuypers, J. B. *L'alimentation chez les Shi.* Tervuren, Belgium: Musée Royal de l'Afrique Centrale, 1970.

Gibbon, Ed. *The Congo Cookbook.* http://www.congocookbook.com.

Gisaangi, Sona. *La cuisine de Bandundu (Rép. du Zaïre).* Bandundu, Zaire: CEEBA, 1980.

Hladik, Claude Marcel, Serge Bahuchet, and Igor de Garine. *Se nourrir en forêt équatoriale. Anthropologie alimentaire des populations des régions forestières humides d'Afrique.* Paris: United Nations Educational, Scientific and Cultural Organization, 1989.

Huetz de Lemps, Alain. *Boissons et civilisations en Afrique.* Pessac, France: Presses Universitaires de Bordeaux, 2001.

Munzele Munzimi, Jean-Macaire. *Les Pratiques de sociabilité en Afrique. Les mutations culinaires chez les Ambuun.* Paris: Publibook, 2005.

National Research Council, Board on Science and Technology for International Development. *Lost Crops of Africa.* 3 vols. Washington, DC: National Academy Press, 1996–2008.

Osseo-Asare, Fran. *Food Culture in Sub-Saharan Africa.* Westport, CT: Greenwood Press, 2005.

Petit, Pierre, ed. *Byakula. Approche socio-anthropologique de l'alimentation à Lubumbashi.* Brussels, Belgium: Académie Royale des Sciences d'Outre-Mer, 2004.

Roulon-Doko, Paulette. *Cuisine et nourriture chez les Gbaya de Centrafrique.* Paris: L'Harmattan, 2001.

Côte d'Ivoire

Overview

The Republic of Côte d'Ivoire (Ivory Coast) is located on the southern coast of the West African bulge. The country shares borders with Mali and Burkina Faso to the north, Guinea and Liberia to the east, and Ghana to the west. The country's southern coast is a long shoreline on the Gulf of Guinea. The greater part of the country is a vast plateau, but the Guinea Highlands in the northwest have peaks that rise over 3,280 feet (1,000 meters). Like many countries in western Africa, the country is divided geographically between north and south. The coastal areas have two rainy and two dry seasons: one short and one long. The coastal area was formerly rain forest, but much of that has been cut down to make way for increased exploitation of cash crops such as cacao and coffee.

In 2008, the population was estimated at 18,373,060. The capital city is Yamoussoukro near the country's center, but the largest city and former capital is coastal Abidjan, which with a population of over three million is the most populous city in French-speaking western Africa. Metropolitan Abidjan is, after Paris and Kinshasa, the third-largest French-speaking city in the world. While French is the country's lingua franca, 65 different languages are spoken among what are usually divided into five major ethnic groups: the Akan, Southern Mande, Northern Mande, Kru, and Senoufo/Lobi, with the Akan group comprising 42 percent of the population. The population is 40 percent Muslim and 30 percent Christian, with another 30 percent practicing indigenous religions. Since 1999 ongoing conflict and a civil war have transformed what was once the jewel of French-speaking western Africa into a country with an uncertain future.

🍽️ Food Culture Snapshot

Maurice and Simone Yaba are westernized Ivorians who live in Abidjan. They are a part of the country's developing middle class. Maurice works in upper management at a private enterprise, and Simone is a housewife. They live in the upper-class suburb of Cocody, and their lifestyle is influenced not only by the traditional customs but also by international trends. Their diet crosses ethnic and national boundaries. In European fashion, they eat three meals a day. Breakfast is usually influenced by French culture and consists of a cup of coffee or hot chocolate with French bread or toast with butter and jam. Other meals may range from Vietnamese takeout from one of the many small local restaurants to a traditional *sauce claire* (a tomato-based fish stew) served with *foufou* (a thick starchy mush). Occasionally the family will drive out to purchase a local delicacy like *aloko* (deep-fried plantains) from street stalls.

The ingredients for the meals come from the local supermarket, a neighborhood street market, or the Marché de Cocody—the traditional market area. Like Abidjan's largest market, which is located in Treicheville, the Marché de Cocody offers an array of products ranging from fresh produce to live poultry. Nearby shops sell imported and manufactured foods. Most Ivorian households of any means usually have a household servant of some sort, and the Yabas do as well. But Simone likes to cook, and so she usually does the shopping.

Abidjan market, Cote d'Ivoire. (Corel)

Aloko (Deep-Fried Plantains)

Serves 6

6 firm yellow plantains

Oil for frying (traditionally this is red palm oil, but any vegetable oil may be substituted)

Pour 4 inches of oil into the bottom of a heavy saucepan or a cast iron Dutch oven and heat it to 375°F. Cut the plantains lengthwise, then into ¾-inch pieces. Place half of the plantains into the oil and fry, turning if necessary, until they are golden brown. Remove and drain, then repeat with the second batch. Serve immediately. In the Côte d'Ivoire, they are usually served with a sprinkling of chili pepper and cooked onions as an accompaniment to grilled fish.

Major Foodstuffs

The diversity of the Côte D'Ivoire has led to many different diets throughout the country. In the more westernized southern section of the country, commercial agriculture is an important industry, and farmers grow cacao and coffee for the world market as well as vegetables and fruits such as avocados and pineapples, among others, for export to France. Throughout the country, Ivorians generally rely on grains and tubers as the basis of their diet. Yams, plantains, rice, millet, corn, and peanuts are staples throughout the country. Those living near the coast have a wide variety of seafood available, including tuna, sardines, bonito, and shrimp. Those more inland depend on local game like guinea hen, bush rat, or agouti, another ratlike rodent (although game is eschewed by most Muslims); chicken is the most popular animal protein. The amount of meat served at any given table indicates how affluent a family is (or how honored the guest is at a festive meal). Fermented cassava forms the basis for *attiéké,* a couscous-like starch that serves as the basis for many of the traditional sauces. Okra is much used, as are eggplant, tomatoes, onions, and leafy greens. Cayenne pepper, allspice, curry, garlic, caraway, cloves, ginger, and a range of chili peppers are used to season the dishes, as are traditional West African peppers like *melegueta* peppers and cubebs. Many homes use French *cubes Maggi* (Maggi bouillon cubes) to season stews and sauces. Fresh fruits such as mangoes, soursops, pineapple, mandarins and clementines, and pomegranates are typical snacks and may also serve as the basis for desserts in more westernized households where French culinary influence is felt. Flag beer (a West African brand) is consumed throughout the country by those who are not Muslim, as are manufactured local beverages, like white palm wine called *bangui.* There are also homemade beverages sold by street vendors like ginger beer or *nyamakoudji* (a drink prepared from pineapple peelings). Among the westernized, French wines are also consumed.

Cooking

Throughout western Africa in general the main culinary techniques are boiling, steaming, stewing, frying, roasting, grilling, and baking. All of these methods are the basis for the traditional dishes of the country that used the traditional cookstove. Even today, many households cook over wood or charcoal fires. Kerosene stoves have supplanted many of the wood-burning ones, but in the rural areas the traditional three-rock wood stoves remain the standard. In the urban areas, the Western stove is used, but for some dishes cooks still prefer to cook outdoors over a small brazier called a *feu malgache.* Pressure cookers are used to tenderize tougher cuts of meat. Refrigerators are also the norm among those with sufficient funds and access to electricity.

Most households have some kind of household help. It may be a relative from the country looking for employment in the city and working in exchange for lodging, or a professional paid for services. Cooking, therefore, is often done by another woman, overseen by the lady of the house. Cooking, however, remains a family activity for festive foods. Extended families will combine to prepare dishes at times of feasting, with the matriarch directing the kitchen. The myriad cultures of Côte d'Ivoire are oral cultures, and this is the manner by which the youngsters of the household learn to prepare the traditional foods. Microwaves, freezers, food processors, and the full range of the other Western culinary conveniences are de rigueur among the elite. French influence prevails among the elite as well, and in their households the full European *baterie de cuisine* may be found among those with means; there, adepts at the preparation of French *cuisine bourgeois* and/or *cuisine classique* can be found in many households.

Typical Meals

Given the regional diversity of the country, it is difficult to generalize about a typical meal. It can be said that in traditional rural households the typical heavier meals of the day consist of a soupy stew of some sort served over or accompanied by a starch such as the fermented cassava known as attiéké or the pounded cassava known as foufou. The starch may be dipped in the stew, or the stew may be scooped up with it. Rice is also an accompaniment for several dishes.

Foufou (Boiled Cassava)

Yields about three foufou balls

2½ c cassava, peeled, with the fibrous center removed

5 ripe plantains, peeled

Prepare the cassava and the plantain as directed, then cut them into chunks and place them in a large saucepan with water to cover. Bring to a boil, then lower the heat and simmer for 25 minutes or until the vegetables are tender. Drain them and return to the pan over very low heat. Then, with a potato masher, pound, mash, and stir the mixture for 15 minutes or until it becomes elastic and smooth. (You may need to sprinkle it with water from time to time to keep it from sticking.) Form the foufou into balls and serve immediately.

Eating for some traditional Ivorians is a ritual act that situates them within their community and within the universe. For that reason, in some rural villages, the community will still eat together in a common area. Seated on a mat on the ground they eat from a communal bowl using their right hands. It is considered rude to grab or act greedy. Women and girls eat as a group, men as another group, and young boys as a third group. The eldest are served first, and during the meal talking is discouraged. It is a time of commensalism thought to build community.

Alternately there may be the European paradigm of three meals a day, but traditionally it is often replaced with a different one that includes one or two meals plus a lighter meal or two to three meals with snacks. In urban areas, breakfast may follow the French mode and include French bread from a local bakery or toasted leftover bread with jam and butter. Coffee and hot chocolate are the usual drinks. In more traditional areas, alternately, the daily diet might include one of the more traditional breakfasts like the fried bean cakes known as *kosai* that are eaten by the Hausa in the north of the country.

Lunch and dinner for the westernized are often interchangeable and range between European fare or Ivorian favorites like grilled or roasted fish or chicken served with a piquant sauce and more traditional Ivorian dishes like *kédjenou* (a chicken stew).

Kédjenou de Poulet

Serves 4–6

1 frying chicken, cut into serving pieces

1 large onion, chopped

2 large tomatoes, quartered

1 tbsp red wine vinegar

¼ c red wine

½ c water

1 Maggi bouillon cube

1 pricked habanero chile, or to taste

Salt and freshly ground pepper to taste

Place all of the ingredients in a pot over a medium flame, cover, and cook for 1 hour, shaking the pot occasionally to make sure that the ingredients do not stick. Serve hot with white rice.

Eating Out

Unlike many of their West African neighbors, the Ivorians have a tradition of eating out in small local restaurants known as a *maquis*. Taking their name from the Corsican underbrush and the French resistance during World War II, these small restaurants often began as clandestine dining spots for the male migrant workers who flocked to the city. As their fame for various dishes grew, they became more public spots, and now no self-respecting Ivorian in any urban area would not know about at least a few of these small eateries where local specialties are served. They may be as simple as a terrace in someone's yard or can be a more commercial spot complete with a limited menu and a selection of beverages. The requirement for designation as a maquis seems to be that the food served is grilled over a low fire, so grilled chicken and grilled fish are the usual standbys; both are served with a sauce of onions and tomatoes and accompanied by rice, foufou, and attiéké. Meals are usually accompanied by beer, French wine, or bangui.

In the larger urban areas, there are white-tablecloth restaurants located in tourist hotels and the occasional colonial restaurant run by a homesick Frenchman where the clock seems stuck in the French provincial life of the 1950s. Sidewalk cafés exist in Abidjan's more European zones, while the more local areas have maquis and, in the evening, clubs where traditional grilled foods are served to the accompaniment of live music played by local bands. The influx of migrant workers means that surrounding most of the markets, bus depots, and taxi stands, women vendors hawk street foods that may range from plastic bags filled with beverages to entire meals that can be eaten while sitting on a stool or can be put in an enameled bowl and taken home. In the Abidjan suburb of Cocody, near the university, a night market exists where several vendors offer grilled fish or chicken and aloko to students.

Special Occasions

As is true for many of their West African compatriots, Ivorians have a highly developed sense of the ceremonial. Funerals call for shows of family solidarity and often end in a communal meal shared by all. Roman Catholics celebrate all of the Christian holidays with ceremony, and the cathedral at Yamoussoukro has been visited by the pope more than once. Muslims feast and fast during the period of Ramadan and thereafter, and those following traditional religions, as well as others who combine the traditional with their other beliefs, celebrate events like the Yam Festival (Fete des Ignames) in Agboville in the east of the country. Like the Akan festivals of neighboring Ghana, this festival celebrates the food that has traditionally been the community's mainstay with dancing, drumming, and feasting.

Diet and Health

The Côte d'Ivoire still suffers from the effects of its ongoing internal conflict. In 2006 the World Health Organization *Country Health System Fact Sheet* indicated that about 15 percent of the population was undernourished and added that 21.2 percent of the children under age five were underweight and more than 25 percent were considered short for their age, or "stunted." In March 2008 the country, along with others in western Africa, experienced food riots protesting the rising cost of staples. The country's north/south divide coupled with the urban/rural one means that rural dwellers in the northern part of the country are more subject to interrupted food supplies in the rainy seasons. The same happens in the dry season if drought occurs. The southern regions are closer to seaports and have more stable climactic conditions. The more developed economy means that there are methods of food storage, and most people can afford to purchase food from markets and other sources if their individual food supplies are destroyed.

Jessica B. Harris

Further Reading

Harris, Jessica. *The Africa Cookbook: Tastes of a Continent.* New York: Simon and Schuster, 1998.

Sheehan, Patricia, and Jacqueline Ong. *Côte d'Ivoire.* New York: Marshall Cavendish Benchmark, 2010.

Egypt

Overview

Egypt is geographically situated in northern Africa, bordering the Mediterranean Sea, between Libya and the Gaza Strip, and the Red Sea north of Sudan; it includes the Asian Sinai Peninsula. To the east of the Sahara desert, the Nile carves out a route to the sea. The river provides fertile silt and refuge from the arid land that surrounds the valley, and it was a welcoming environment to early populations. Egypt is comprised of 386,660 square miles of land. Natural resources include petroleum, natural gas, lime, phosphorous, manganese, potassium, zinc, iron ore, and more. Egypt is the most populous state in the Arab world, with over 80 million inhabitants. One out of every three Arabs is said to be Egyptian, and Cairo is Africa's most densely populated city. The median age of Egyptians is 24 years.

More than 43 percent of Egypt's inhabitants are urban dwellers living in the cities of Cairo, Alexandria, Port Said, Ismalia, Mansoura, Tanta, Luxor, Aswan, and other cities in the Nile Delta. Ninety percent of the population is Sunni Muslim, and 10 percent is Christian (a majority of whom are known as Copts). Most Egyptians are employed in the agriculture, manufacturing (textiles, pharmaceuticals, food products), and tourism sectors. Growing domestic sectors including technology, transportation, telecommunications, retail, and construction are also major sources of employment. Important agricultural crops include cotton, rice, corn, wheat, beans, fruit, vegetables, cattle, water buffalo, sheep, and goats. Sugarcane cultivation and fishing play important roles in rural and sea-side communities where subsistence agriculture is still important.

Egypt has the longest continuous history of any country. To this day, 99 percent of the population resides in the Nile Valley and the Delta. Ancient Egypt was powerful and gave rise to a great civilization with relatively little interference from the rest of the world. The ancient Egyptian empire once spanned from northern modern-day Sudan all the way to Lebanon. As Egypt became increasingly wealthy, it continued to gain increasing attention from the outside world, which became tempted to invade. Subsequently, Egypt lost her autonomy to a succession of powerful empires: the Persians, the Greeks, the Romans, the Copts, the Ottomans, the French, and the British. The interplay between the native population and those of the occupying forces enriched the nation's culture. Even the official language of Egypt, Arabic, has its own dialect that includes influences from various cultures.

Since the exploration and documentation of the archaeological remains during Napoleon's Egyptian Campaign (1798–1801), the Western world has been gripped by Egypto-mania, the fascination with ancient Egyptian culture and history. Egypt has had a significant impact on the cultural imagination of all Western cultures. Today, many aspects of Egypt's ancient culture exist in interaction with newer elements, including the influence of modern Western culture, itself with roots in ancient Egypt. Much as Egypt physically bridges the gap between Africa and Asia, she is culturally doing the same for the Western and Islamic worlds.

Market stall, Aswan, Egypt. (Corel)

🍴 Food Culture Snapshot

Soad El Tanbedawy is the mother of three children and a retired mathematics professor living in a town named Shiben El Khom in the province of El Menofia in northern Egypt. Her daughter, Asma' Khalifa, is a doctor, her son Ahmed Khalifa is an information technology specialist, and her son Ossama Khalifa is a senior in college. Since none of her children is married, they live at home with Soad and her husband. Before her two eldest children began working and her husband, Mohamed Khalifa, was promoted in his municipal position, it was easy for everyone to enjoy most meals together at home. With increasingly demanding schedules, Soad has made alterations to her schedule so that everyone can eat together. She begins and ends her day with breakfast preparations. Since the typical Egyptian breakfast consists of *fuul medammes,* or pureed fava beans, which require eight hours of slow cooking, she

soaks them the day before and puts them on a low fire before going to sleep at night. The next morning she arises, makes eggs, and sets out plates of tomatoes, watercress or arugula, carrots, cucumbers, and sheep-milk cheeses on her kitchen table to accompany the beans. Her husband buys fresh *aish baladi,* a healthful, bran-rich bread baked fresh in local bakeries, daily to accompany the breakfast. Prior to eating, everyone in the family washes their hands. After eating, they wash them again. Next, warm tea with milk is made and enjoyed only after the conclusion of breakfast. Since lunch is eaten at home and most members of her family can't return before 4 P.M., Soad often packs them light snacks such as cheese sandwiches and fruit.

Once everyone leaves the home, Soad begins her daily tasks of preparing her family's lunch. Since lunch is the main meal of the day, it is the one that most thought goes into. Most home meals begin with a soup, which can consist of a consommé and orzo or contain vegetables or lentils. The main course usually consists of a variety of different rice-based dishes with fish, beef, lamb, or poultry. Small salads are placed around the table to accompany the meal, as are pickles and bread. Little dishes full of a mixture of salt, cumin, and ground crushed red pepper are also placed on the table. It is common for the family members to dip each piece of food in this mixture, if they desire more seasoning. At the table, dishes are never passed; everyone simply helps themselves to whatever they would like more of. For larger gatherings, Soad puts multiple serving dishes of the same food at different ends of the table so that everything is within reach.

Sometimes Soad makes her specialty dishes liked *mahshi*—a combination of stuffed baby eggplant, zucchini, peppers, cabbage, and vine leaves that she serves with roasted meat and chicken. Another family favorite is *koushari*, which consists of rice, elbow macaroni, lentils, chickpeas, spicy tomato sauce, and fried onions. Koushari is so filling that it is served by itself. When Soad needs to make a dish that she can rely on to reheat well later, she makes *macarona béchamel*, layers of pasta with a thick broth-and-egg-infused béchamel sauce and savory minced beef that is an Egyptian home staple similar to Greek *pastitsou*. It can be made up to a day in advance and baked the day of serving. When she doesn't feel like cooking, Soad asks her husband to stop at the local falafel (*t'amaya* in Egyptian) stand and pick up fava falafel batter that she forms and fries at home. Most days, desserts consist of fresh seasonal fruit, which could be mangoes, guavas, oranges, bananas, strawberries, grapes, pears, pomegranates, or coconuts. On special occasions or for the weekly congregational prayer day, Friday, Soad usually prepares a sweet. She may make *k'nafeh* (a shredded phyllo pastry filled with nuts or cream pudding and topped with a simple syrup), rice pudding, or baklava. For the Eid al-Fitr, or Feast of the Fast Breaking, a three-day holiday that marks the end of Ramadan, Soad makes butter cookies known as *petits fours* in Egypt along with *Eid kahk*, a crunchy cookie that dates back to Pharaonic times and used to be stuffed with gold coins and distributed to the poor by the caliph during the Fatimid era. Her family greatly appreciates her cooking, which they see as directly linked to their good health, happiness, and close relationship with one another.

Soad's love of cooking and willingness to let the importance of communal meals dictate her daily life are increasingly uncommon in Egypt. Most young women do not learn to cook, because it is not viewed as an important part of their cultural identity. Long work schedules and difficult traffic in cities make it almost impossible for urban women to cook. There is also a bit of a cultural stigma (North America suffered the same attitude when women began working in the 1940s) that promotes the idea that "smart" and "upper-class" women shouldn't be bothered with cooking. As a result, many women employ maids or order out instead. The popularity of foreign food chains also makes preparing traditional cuisine less enticing to young people. Even those who do cook are constantly searching for foreign types of recipes to try. Egyptian émigrés, however, often use the cuisine as a link to their homeland and culture while they are abroad. They, and their families, will continue to spread traditional Egyptian foodways, along with tourists who return from their trips craving "a taste of the Nile" from abroad.

Major Foodstuffs

The main sources of the Egyptian diet are similar to others in the Mediterranean. Grains, bread, beans and other legumes, fruits and vegetables, dairy, and corn, olive, and other oils make up the majority of the diet. Seafood, meat, poultry and fowl, and nuts are also enjoyed. Both fresh herbs and dried spices are used in large quantities for daily cooking. Sweets consist of phyllo-based pastries, cookies, puddings, and European-style cakes and ice creams.

Grains

Popular grains and breads include wheat, rice, and barley. Wheat is usually used to make pita bread called aish baladi, which consists of whole wheat and the bran layer. Refined white flour is used to make small hotdog bun–shaped fresh breads called *aish fino*. Kaiser rolls and European breads and pastries are also made with wheat. White flour is also used to make sheets of phyllo dough for pastry and a delicious Egyptian specialty known as *fateer*. Fateer is a homemade puff pastry that is made in special shops similar to pizzerias. They can be made with

Egyptian bread at a market. Similar bread has been made in Egypt since ancient times. (Shutterstock)

multitudes of sweet or savory fillings, or served plain with black molasses and an Egyptian clotted cream called *ishta* and honey. They are traditionally made in wood-burning ovens.

Whole wheat berries are boiled and made into a cereal called *bileela* with milk, raisins, sugar, and nuts. Cracked whole wheat, bulgur, is used to make *kobeeba* (meat and cracked wheat croquettes), *taboola* (a salad of cracked wheat, herbs, tomato, and cucumber), and other dishes. Hulled grain is made from newly harvested wheat, which has a green color and smoky flavor. It is called *freekh* and is typically used to stuff chickens, pigeons, ducks, and turkey. The heart of the wheat grain (semolina) is used to make cookies and pastries. Egyptian rice is a short- to medium-grain starchy rice (sometimes called Calrose rice) used to stuff vegetables, made into pilaf-style dishes, and cooked with vermicelli and served as an accompaniment to roasts, stews, or kebabs. It is also used to make rice pudding or is made into rice flour, which is used as a thickener in other puddings. Barley is used to make cereals, soups, and stews. Egyptian rice was introduced into southern Spain in the 10th century and is the grandfather of modern Spanish paella and Italian risotto rices.

Beans and Legumes

Fuul medammes, a variety of fava bean known to be the world's oldest agricultural crop, is said to be Egypt's national dish. The dried beans are soaked in water overnight and then stewed for hours with cumin, coriander, oil, and additional spices. They are usually served for breakfast with accompaniments like chopped tomatoes, hard-boiled eggs, lemon juice, olive oil, tahini sauce (sesame puree), and other things. The skinned beans are also used to make Egyptian falafel (which is also eaten at breakfast—or any time).

Legumes including red, brown, and black lentils are used to make soups, stews, and dishes during the Christian fasting period. During antiquity, Egypt was the chief exporter of lentils in the world. One of the most popular Egyptian lentil dishes is called koushari. It consists of rice, pasta, lentils, chickpeas, a spicy tomato sauce, and fried onions. It is a typical street food that can be found anywhere. It is an inexpensive, delicious, vegan dish loved by locals and tourists alike.

The word *hommus* means "chickpeas" in Arabic. Chickpeas are widely used in soups and stews or as a puree. They are also roasted and spiced and served as a snack like nuts and popcorn. White beans are used in stews, soups, and easy purees as well.

Fruits

The history of Egyptian fruits is both ancient and modern. Dates are said to have been the first fruits grown in Egypt, with a 5,000-year history. Pomegranates, figs, and grapes also flourished in the desert heat. Strawberries, bananas, tamarinds, kiwis, apricots, coconuts, peaches, oranges, lemons, limes, apples, pears, and blackberries are all very popular. In the 19th century, mangoes and guavas were introduced from India. They adapted well to the Egyptian soil and have been important parts of the culinary landscape ever since. Egyptians prefer to eat their fruit fresh, while it is in season. Fruit is usually enjoyed as a snack or after dinner in place of or prior to dessert. The fresh, in-season fruits are also displayed at street-side fruit juice stands where fresh fruit "cocktails" are made to order. Grape, tamarind, pomegranate, and strawberry juices are boiled and reduced into syrups and molasses, which are used to make drinks and flavor pastries.

Vegetables

Leeks, cucumbers, lettuce, arugula, watercress, carrots, herbs, peas, okra, and green beans were all present in Egypt in ancient times. Depending on the season, eggplant, zucchini, peppers, artichokes, cauliflower, turnips, potatoes, rutabagas, spinach, cabbage, onions, and garlic are all integral parts of daily meals in Egypt.

Fats

The preferred traditional fat for cooking in Egypt is *samna,* a cultured, clarified butter similar to Indian ghee. Deeply rich and flavorful, samna can be made with sheep, cow, or water buffalo milk. There are also vegetable versions similar to shortening. In rural communities, some women still prepare samna at home. In urban areas, many people are opting to use olive oil for health reasons and corn oil for its convenience and economical price. Butter is used for pastries and for specific foreign recipes that call for it.

Seafood

Seafood was the first form of sustenance in ancient Egypt. In antiquity, festivals would be held in honor of the Nile god named Hapi. No one was allowed to fish from the Nile during the festival, which often lasted for weeks. Instead, they would place flowers, food offerings, and prayers into the Nile to honor the god who allowed the river to flood twice a year and provide adequate irrigation, and therefore sustenance. Only when the festivals were over were people allowed to eat the fish. Since then, fish has held a special place in the hearts and palates of Egyptians and other Mediterranean communities that were influenced by ancient Egypt. Even though not as expensive as meat, it is prized and appreciated. Nowadays, seafood from the Mediterranean, Nile, and Red Sea and imports from around the globe are all enjoyed in Egypt today. Shrimp, squid, sea bass, bream, red mullet, prawns, and Nile perch, known as *bulti,* are the most common. Famous Egyptian seafood recipes include kebabs, fried fish with cumin, and seafood soups and stews, as well as roasted fish. *Saadilaya,* or "the fisherman's wife," is a rice and fish skillet infused with spices like turmeric. The northern Mediterranean coastal towns are especially famous for their seafood dishes, and fish can be purchased fresh from the boats that come in to shore.

Meat

Ever since ancient times when nomadic tribes roamed the desert and meat was served only during important celebrations or to honor guests, it has held a special, ceremonial place at the Egyptian and Arab table as a whole. Beef, mutton, lamb, veal, and goat meat are all eaten in Egypt. Since meat is extremely expensive, many people cannot eat it every day. Traditional meat recipes include stews, roasts, kebabs, ground meat stuffing for vegetables, and meatballs. Serving meat to guests is a sign of respect and a way to honor them. Animals can be purchased live to custom slaughter, or meat can be purchased from butcher shops on the day of slaughter. Many butcher-shop owners also own and operate kebab shops. In Egypt, halal meat is available for purchase everywhere. *Halal* is an Arabic word that means "permissible." Permissible meat in the Islamic tradition comes from animals that have been treated kindly and killed in a way that minimizes the animal's suffering. The words *In the name of God, most beneficent, most merciful* must be uttered at the time of its death. All blood must be drained from the animal, and it must be cleansed before being eaten. Animals are not allowed to be killed for sport, and all parts of the animal are to be consumed. Sheep and cattle milk is used for dairy: milk, yogurt, and cheese making. Typical Egyptian cheeses have been made since at least 3200 B.C. and are similar to what we now refer to as Greek feta cheese and Spanish manchego cheese.

Poultry and Fowl

Chickens, quails, pigeons, and ducks are all part of the Egyptian table. Pigeons and quails have been served grilled and stuffed since Pharaonic times when they were served to brides and grooms at wedding ceremonies. Egyptian pigeons and quails are raised in special environs specifically for culinary purposes. Chicken is served grilled, as part of kebabs, stewed, roasted, and fried. Ducks are also eaten roasted, grilled, and fried. Ducks from the El Fayyoum Oasis are known for their delicious taste and there are special recipes just for them. Eggs are a popular breakfast dish.

Herbs and Spices

Most Mediterranean herbs such as cilantro, dill, mint, parsley, basil, thyme, chamomile, caraway, and oregano are used in Egypt. Multitudes of spices can be used. The most traditional are cinnamon, cumin, cloves, crushed red pepper, cardamom, paprika, black pepper, coriander, anise, turmeric, and nigella seeds. Hibiscus petals are sold at spice shops all across Egypt. Nubian in origin, these leaves are boiled and sweetened to make a delicious and nutritious drink that can be served hot or cold. Known as *karkade,* this drink is the best known of all Egyptian traditional medicinals. Rosemary, curry powder, allspice, and others are becoming increasingly popular in cooking. Egyptians drink herbal tisanes made from mint, anise, cinnamon, chamomile, and caraway for their health properties and taste.

Coffee and Tea

Egyptians drink Turkish coffee with cardamom made in stovetop filterless pots called *kanaka.* Coffee shops are also called *ahwa,* which is the Egyptian-dialect version of the Arabic word *coffee* itself. Coffee made its way to Egypt by the 16th century, where hundreds of coffeehouses existed long before Europeans ever tasted it. Nowadays, Nescafé and European-style espressos are also very popular in Egypt.

Tea is by far the most common drink in Egypt. Egyptians drink black tea that is served with mint. Both coffee and tea are sweetened while they are made, with one to three teaspoons of sugar per person. Tea and coffee are traditionally served without sugar only at funerals.

Nuts

Egyptians love to spend the late nights of Ramadan, visits with family and friends, and movie-watching nights with a variety of nuts. Peanuts, cashews, almonds, pistachios, and walnuts are all popular. Watermelon and sunflower seeds, popcorn, and spiced roasted chickpeas are all sold at street-side stores and vendors.

Cooking

Popular contemporary cooking methods in Egypt are baking, grilling, roasting, frying, stewing, and salt curing. Many of the methods were developed during antiquity. The ancient Egyptians began salt curing, smoking, and sun-drying foods to make them last longer. They also invented sieves, pestles, mortars, and knives to aid in food preparation. Tomb scenes from the Old Kingdom (2700–2600 B.C.) depict bread being shaped and produced in mass quantities. Clay pot cooking is also very traditional. The word *tajin* (sometimes spelled *tajine*) is used to describe a clay baking dish in the Arabic-speaking world. In Egyptian dialect, the "j" sound is pronounced like a hard "g" so the word is pronounced *TAH-gin*. Clay baking dishes are a traditional way of baking and serving stews. Families serve meals in large ones, while restaurants serve individual portions in small ones. Keep in mind that only the tajines of northwestern Africa (namely, Moroccan and Tunisian ones) have conical lids. Before air-conditioning and home ovens were commonplace in Egypt, housewives and cooks would have children take their stews to the bread baker to have them cooked in the cooler portions of the oven while the bread baked. On their way home from school, children would stop at the bread shop and pick up their bread and stew for lunch. This method was very cost and energy efficient. In a hot climate like Egypt, it would take a lot of air-conditioning to cool down a home after turning the oven on. Sometimes, in very densely populated urban areas in Egypt, one can still see children navigating their way through the labyrinthine maze of shops in the *souk* (marketplace) to bring their tagins to the bread baker.

T'amaya (Egyptian Fava Falafel)

Serves 4 (three falafel per person)

This recipe became popular after the fourth century A.D., when Egyptian Christians (Copts) had to fast for 55 days during Lent. The Coptic fasting period prohibits meat, dairy, and seafood, so vegan diets are required. Being a meat-loving culture, the

Egyptian Christians developed ingenious ways of using beans and legumes to make enticing, hearty dishes that rival their typical meaty mains.

Ingredients

1 c peeled dried fava beans (broad beans),* soaked overnight in water and drained

¼ c fresh dill leaves

¼ c fresh cilantro leaves

¼ c fresh parsley leaves

1 small yellow onion, diced

8 cloves garlic, chopped

1 tsp ground cumin

1 tsp ground coriander

Pinch of cayenne pepper

Salt

Freshly ground black pepper

1 tsp baking powder

Expeller-pressed corn oil, for frying

¼ c white sesame seeds

Variation

4 white pita breads

2 roma tomatoes, thinly sliced

1 cucumber, thinly sliced

¼ lb feta cheese, crumbled

Preparation

Place beans, dill, cilantro, parsley, onion, and garlic in a food processor and mix until a smooth paste forms. Mix in ½ cup water (or enough to make mixture wet and loose—it should resemble a thin paste). Add cumin, coriander, cayenne, and some salt and pepper to taste. Stir in baking powder and mix to incorporate. Spoon mixture into a bowl and let stand at room temperature for 1 hour.

Pour 3 inches of corn oil into a large frying pan over medium heat. When oil is hot enough to fry, a piece of bread dropped in it will turn golden and float to the top immediately. Using two teaspoons, gather a heaping teaspoonful of the paste in one spoon and

carefully push it off with the other spoon, forming a round patty in the oil. Repeat the process until the pan is full—leaving a ½-inch space between the falafel. While falafel are cooking, sprinkle a few sesame seeds on the uncooked sides. Fry until falafel are dark golden brown, approximately 5 minutes; turn over, and fry the other sides until they are the same color. Line a platter with paper towels. Using a slotted spoon, lift falafel out of oil and drain on paper towels. Repeat with remaining dough.

Shorbat Maloukhiya (Jew's Mallow Soup)

Serves 4

This soup is called Jew's Mallow in English because its main ingredient was the traditional bitter herb used on the Egyptian Jewish Seder plate. Jew's mallow, or *maloukhiya,* is a healthful green herb that grew in abundance in ancient Egypt. During the ninth century, when Caliph Al Muizz li Din Allah (a Fatimid ruler who founded Cairo) arrived in Egypt from Tunisia, he was very sick. The locals served him a bowl of maloukhiya, and he was instantly cured. He declared the soup a "royal broth." The name *maloukhiya* comes from the word *malook,* meaning "kings" in Arabic. Even though it is inexpensive, it is still coveted and beloved by Egyptians everywhere.

Ingredients

4 c homemade or good-quality chicken stock

1 (14-oz) package frozen maloukhiya*

Salt

Freshly ground black pepper

1 tbsp clarified butter (ghee)

6 cloves garlic, minced

1 tsp ground coriander

Preparation

Bring chicken stock to a boil in a medium saucepan. Add frozen maloukhiya and some salt and pepper to taste. Bring back to a boil, reduce heat to low, and simmer for 5 minutes.

In a small saucepan over medium heat, melt clarified butter. Add garlic and coriander and cook, uncovered, until garlic begins to turn color. Stir garlic mixture into maloukhiya soup, taste, and adjust salt and pepper, if necessary. Serve hot.

*Can be found in Middle Eastern specialty markets.

Typical Meals

Egyptian breakfasts consist of protein-packed staples. Pureed fava beans, eggs (usually in the form of an omelet), falafel, vegetables, and cheeses are usually followed by tea with mint. Many Egyptians like to eat a small sweet or pastry at the end of breakfast. Wheat-based cereals, toast, and sweet cakes served with Nescafé are increasingly popular. Breakfast is eaten early in the morning at home before work and school, or on the street or in a restaurant anytime before noon. Hotels offer seemingly endless buffet bars of sweet, savory, and traditional items and are usually open from 6 to 10 A.M.

Egyptian lunches are usually served between 2 and 6 P.M. This is the important meal of the day, and families like to gather together to eat it. Because of increasingly busy schedules, the lunch time continues to get later. This also reinforces the importance of a hearty breakfast. Typical lunches consist of a lentil soup or pasta and consommé-based soup to start, Egyptian rice with vermicelli and/or grilled or roasted meat or poultry, or a seafood and vegetable stew, stuffed vegetables, salads, and fruit. Desserts are usually reserved for special occasions.

Egyptian dinners can be served very late in the evening, typically from 10 P.M. to 2 A.M., although the time may be earlier when entertaining or during the month of Ramadan when the meal to break the fast is served at dusk. The same types of dishes as for lunch may be served and eaten outside of the home. At home, lighter meals, leftovers, sandwiches, or bread, cheeses, pickles, and salads may be served. There is usually no distinction made between lunch and dinner foods, but the time of lunch and the amount of food eaten then will determine what a person or family eats for dinner.

Eating Out

Dining options in Egyptian cities are endless. One can choose from street-side shops offering freshly squeezed fruit juices, falafel, koushari (lentils, rice, and pasta with a spicy tomato sauce), kebabs and *shwarma* (rotisserie-style shaved lamb served on a sandwich), fateer (homemade puff pastry filled with sweet or savory fillings like pizza), pastries, and much more. There is also a good selection of cafeteria-style restaurants, which are similar to American diners and offer endless menu options ranging from local and traditional dishes to burgers and fries.

In large cities, foreign fast-food, midrange, and upscale restaurants abound. French, Italian, Chinese, Turkish, Lebanese, and Japanese cuisine can also be found. Hotels and touristy restaurants serve endless buffets of "international" cuisine. In addition, many authentic restaurants serve grilled foods and traditional home-style Egyptian cuisine. These range in decor, price, and location from very inexpensive to five-star restaurants.

Special Occasions

Religion has always been an important aspect of Egyptian life. Egyptians have believed in monotheism since antiquity. The country's three major religions—Judaism, Christianity, and Islam—all have deep-rooted traditions and customs surrounding their holidays in Egypt. There are many monuments, tombs, and shrines dedicated to important religious figures in Egypt. Today, mosques, churches, and synagogues are an integral part of Egyptian life and constant reminders of the divine. Egyptian culture combines a spiritual zeal with a zest for life in its seasonal festivities. Christmas, Easter, Ramadan, Eid al-Fitr, Eid al-Adha, *moulids* (birthdays of important religious figures—Jewish, Christian, and Muslim), and national holidays like the "Smell of the Fresh Breeze" spring holiday are all part of the modern Egyptian scene. Marriages and birth celebrations are also extremely important community events in Egypt.

Egyptian Muslims break their day-long Ramadan fast during a group *Iftar* meal for the residents of a neighborhood in downtown Cairo, 2010. (AFP | Getty Images)

Diet and Health

The diet and health of all Egyptians cannot be easily categorized or explained. Personal tastes, lifestyles, religion, and socioeconomic factors determine what individual Egyptians eat on a daily basis. Farmers and fishermen have the healthiest diets, consisting of grains, produce, pulses, fish, and small amounts of meat. Their active lifestyles help them maintain healthy body weights, and they have low stress-related issues. Unfortunately, even though the traditional Egyptian diet is healthful and balanced, it is increasingly less popular due to working women's time constraints and the affluent's new taste preferences. Meat is the most prized item at the dinner table, and it is extremely expensive in Egypt, which deepens its image as a luxury item. Since it contains fat and cholesterol, it is not as healthy as whole grains, fruits, vegetables, and legumes. High cholesterol and heart

complications are on the rise in Egypt. Four or five pounds of meat in Egypt can cost the entire week's salary of a lower-class worker. For this reason, many people joke that the poorer people are healthier. Healthful traditional whole-grain breads are increasingly being replaced by white store-bought breads, and healthful herbal and flower-based drinks are being eschewed in favor of colas. Because the culture holds a strong respect for foreign (especially American and European) products, it is widely believed that American foods are better than Egyptian ones—even if they are of poor, mass-produced quality.

Amy Riolo

Further Reading

Amy Riolo. http://www.amyriolo.com.

Bey-Mardam, Farouk. *Ziryab: Authentic Arab Cuisine.* Woodbury, CT: Ici La Press, 2002.

Clark, Jacqueline, and Joanna Farrow. *Mediterranean: A Taste of the Sun in Over 150 Recipes.* London: Hermes House, 2001.

Davidson, Alan. *The Oxford Companion to Food.* New York: Oxford University Press, 1999.

Epstein, Morris. *All about Jewish Holidays and Customs.* Jersey City: Ktav, 1970.

Green, Gloria Kaufer. *The New Jewish Holiday Cookbook: An International Collection of Recipes and Customs.* New York: Times Books, 1985.

Halici, Nevin. *Sufi Cuisine.* London: Saqi Books, 2005.

Ilkin, Nur, and Sheilah Kaufman. *A Taste of Turkish Cuisine.* New York: Hippocrene Books, 2002.

Kaufman, Sheilah. *Sephardic Israeli Cuisine: A Mediterranean Mosaic.* New York: Hippocrene Books, 2002.

Marks, Gil. *The World of Jewish Desserts.* New York: Simon and Schuster, 2000.

Quinn, R. M. *Ancient Grain, New Cereal.* Alexandria, VA: ASHS Press, 1999.

Robertson, Carol. *Turkish Cooking: A Culinary Journey through Turkey.* Crandall, TX: Frog, 1996.

Segan, Francine. *The Philosopher's Kitchen: Recipes from Ancient Greece and Rome for the Modern Cook.* New York: Random House, 2004.

Toussaint-Samat, Maguelonne. *History of Food.* Cambridge, MA: Blackwell, 1992.

Zeidler, Judy. "Shavout Food: Turn Torah Fest into a Veggie Feast." *Jewish Journal of Greater Los Angeles,* June 10, 2005.

Ethiopia and Eritrea

Overview

Until 1993, Ethiopia and Eritrea were one national entity. Thus, in discussing food culture, it is useful to consider the two countries together. This is particularly true when considering historical and cross-cultural influences. Ethiopia (the Federal Democratic Republic of Ethiopia), located on the Horn of Africa, is an East African nation of about 437,600 square miles. The Great Rift Valley, running from southwest to northeast, divides a high central plateau into northern and southern lowlands. The largest river in Ethiopia is the Abay or Blue Nile. Ethiopia has three climate zones: cool, above 7,875 feet (freezing to 61 degrees Fahrenheit); temperate, at 4,920–7,875 feet (61–86 degrees Fahrenheit); and hot, below 4,920 feet (81–122 degrees Fahrenheit).

The population of Ethiopia was estimated to be more than 73.9 million in 2007. Most of the population is found in the highlands. The urbanized population makes up only about 15 percent of the total population. The government is attempting to relocate some highland farmers in an attempt to relieve population pressure on depleted lands.

Ethiopians are divided into at least 100 ethnic groups speaking 70 or more languages. Most of the languages spoken belong to the Semitic, Cushitic, or Omotic families of the Afro-Asiatic language family. A small number of Ethiopians speak languages belonging to the Nilo-Saharan family of languages.

The Amhara and Tigray are plow agriculturalists. Some of the Oromo are farmers, and some are pastoralists, while the Somali are pastoralists. The Sidama and the Gurage are hoe cultivators of *ensete* (a root crop in the banana family) and coffee. The distinctions between plow and hoe cultivation and pastoralism frame food culture.

Eritrea, on the northern and eastern borders of Ethiopia, has an area of about 46,774 square miles. Eritrea can be divided into three main areas: a north-central plateau region, plains in the western region bordering Sudan, and an arid coastal strip along the Red Sea. The only perennial river is the Setit River along the western border. There are other rivers, but they are seasonal. The highlands of Eritrea are cool, with temperatures averaging 60°F. The climate of the coast is semiarid, and temperatures average 86°F but can reach 122°F, while the Danakil Depression is one of the hottest places on earth. Eritrea also has 596 miles of coast along the Red Sea, which has fostered a long history of trade and interaction with other nations, particularly with Yemen, which lies only 20–80 miles across the Red Sea.

In 2004, the United Nations estimated the population of Eritrea at about 4.3 million. The urban population of Eritrea is about 20 percent. Nine major ethnic groups are recognized; however, as in Ethiopia, there is great ethnic and linguistic complexity. The ethnic breakdown is as follows: Tigrinya, 50 percent; Tigre and Kunama, 40 percent; Afar, 4 percent; Saho (Red Sea coast), 3 percent; and other, 3 percent.

Agriculturalists include the Tigray (central and southern plateaus), the Kunama (between the Gash and Setit rivers), and the Saho, who are agriculturalists or pastoralists depending on whether they live

Table 8.1   Ethnic Groups

	Ethnic Group	Language	Population (%)
Semitic			
	Amhara	Amharic	30.10
	Tigray	Tigrinya	6.20
	Gurage	Gurage	1.74
	Argobba		0.18
Cushitic			
	Oromo	Oromo	36.23
	Somali		6.31
	Afar or Denakil		1.89
	Sidama	Sidamo	4.55
	Agew (including Falasha)		1.20
Omotic			
	Welaita		2.29
Nilo-Saharan			
	Anuak		0.09
	Nuer		0.19
	Berta		0.28
	Gumuz		0.24

on the escarpment or the coastal plain. Pastoralists include the Afar (Red Sea coast), the Tigre speakers (northern hills and lowlands), and the Rasha'ida (Sudan border), who are Arabic speakers from the Arabian Peninsula.

Eritrea recognizes three official languages: Arabic, English, and Tigrinya. Arabic and Tigrinya are the most commonly spoken, though English is also widely known and is used as the language of instruction in middle and secondary schools and in higher education. As in Ethiopia, languages belong to three linguistic families: Semitic, Cushitic, and Nilo-Saharan.

Most of the people of Ethiopia and Eritrea are Orthodox Christians or Muslims. Protestants make up about 10 percent of the population. Smaller groups include Roman Catholics and Ethiopian Jews (Falasha), and those who practice traditional religions. Each religion has its own impact on dietary practices and food taboos.

Food Culture Snapshot

Makeda Abraha prepares breakfast (*qurs*) between 7 and 8 A.M. for her husband, Tefere, and their three children. Breakfast is often leftover *injera* (a fermented flatbread), shredded and mixed with spices (*berbere*) to make a dish called *fitfit*, accompanied by tea or coffee. Or they might have *kitta fitfit*, made with an unleavened flatbread (*kitta*) and berbere and served with yogurt. Lunch (*mesa*) is the most substantial meal of the day, eaten at midday. Lunch is typically injera served with a variety of stews (*wat*), followed by coffee. The family eats a smaller meal (*erat*) in the evening.

Makeda shops for the ingredients for their meals both at the traditional markets where produce, especially, is always fresh and at a neighborhood shop or one of the supermarkets springing up in Addis Ababa. At the supermarket Makeda can find not only traditional Ethiopian foods, some now prepared and packaged, but also a range of imported foods, especially canned goods, powdered whole milk, pasta, and cookies and sweets. Meat may be purchased from a butcher shop or at the supermarket.

In agricultural villages mealtimes follow the same pattern, although breakfast is likely to come earlier and be a very light meal. Much of what Louame uses to prepare meals for herself, her husband, Bekele, and their five children comes from her house garden or wild greens she has gathered. Grains and other foodstuffs are purchased at the weekly outdoor market. Louame and her family eat meat only infrequently, when she might slaughter a chicken or when there is a special occasion for which Bekele slaughters a goat.

Major Foodstuffs

The geography of Ethiopia has led to a wide diversity in agricultural production, practiced by peoples with equally diverse cultural systems. These range from people who practice intensive agriculture with ox-drawn plows (the Amhara and Argobba) to horticulturalists with hoes (the Gurage and Sidama) to pastoral nomads (the Rasha'ida). The staples of Ethiopia are dominated by cereals, pulses, and root crops. Although some crops are indigenous to Ethiopia, Ethiopian farmers have largely adopted

Oxen pull a plow in rural Ethopia. (Shargaljut | Dreamstime.com)

the Sudanic agricultural complex of sorghum, millet, and cowpeas. Ethiopian farmers have, however, improved the crops, introduced new varieties, and experimented with wild plants as new crops. Ethiopians were the first to cultivate teff, ensete, coffee, fenugreek, castor, safflower, *ch'at* (qat), and the oilseed *nug*. Until recently teff and ensete were not cultivated anywhere else in the world. Maize, potatoes, and cayenne pepper are the only New World crops added to Ethiopian agricultural production.

Among the cereals, teff is most important to the Amhara, though it is highly desirable in the cuisine of much of Ethiopia. Barley is foremost in Eritrea and Shoa, sorghum in the regions of the Harrar and Somali, and maize in the southwestern section of the country. All of the cereals are used to make porridge, fermented or unfermented flatbreads, raised breads, or hard bread balls carried by travelers.

Some of the cereals have other uses, for example, in the making of beer (*talla*).

Since it is unique to Ethiopia, teff (*Eragrostis teff*) requires special note. It is a grass with extremely tiny seeds, making it labor-intensive to harvest and process and, thus, expensive. Its value is in its high nutritional qualities, far superior to other grains. It contains 11 percent protein, 80 percent complex carbohydrates, and 3 percent fat, and it has more lysine than barley, millet, or wheat. It is also an excellent source of iron and fiber and has much more calcium, potassium, and other essential minerals than other grains. It is nearly gluten-free, so it cannot be used to make raised breads. However, the short fermentation period used to produce the yeast for flatbreads (injera) generates more vitamins.

Next to cereals, ensete (*Ensete edule*) monoculture provides an important dietary staple. Known as the "false banana," ensete is native to Ethiopia, some regions of Sudan, and the Great Lakes area of East Africa. Although it grows to a height of 43 feet, only the underground shoots and stem are utilized for food. Its banana-like fruit is inedible, though the seeds of the fruit are sometimes boiled and fed to children. Ensete is used for food only in Ethiopia, where it is cultivated by the Gurage and Sidama (Cushitic speakers) of the southern plateau. It is grown in huge plantations surrounding homes and villages. The nutritional value of ensete is not high nor balanced and is comparable to other starchy foods like manioc flour. In the areas of ensete cultivation, protein is derived from milk, meat, and legumes.

Pulses in the diet of Ethiopians include lentils (*Lens abyssinica;* Amharic *misir*), green peas (*Pisum abyssicum;* Amharic *ater*), chickpeas (*Cicer arietinum;* Amharic *shimbra*), horse (or fava) beans (*Vicia faba;* Amharic *bak'ella*), and haricot beans (*Phaseolus vulgaris;* Amharic *adanguarey*). Vegetables and fruits are grown but do not make up a large part of the traditional Ethiopian diet due to their high cost. Some of the vegetables included in the diet are the Galla potato (*Coleus edulis;* Amharic *dinitch*), squash (*Cucurbita pepo* and *C. maxima;* Amharic *dubba*), onions, shallots (*Allium ascalonicum;* Amharic *shinkurt*), Amharic cabbage or leaf mustard (*Brassica juncea;* Amharic *gomen*), peppers, carrots, tomatoes, spinach, radishes, eggplant, beets, taro (*Colocasia antiquorum*), yams (*Dioscorea*), and sweet potatoes (*Ipomoea batatas*). Wild greens are also gathered and incorporated in the diet as vegetables. Fruits include peaches (*Prunus persica;* Amharic *kwok*), oranges (*Citrus aurantium;* Amharic *burtikan*), lemons (*Citrus limonum*), citron (*Citrus medica*), pomelo (*Citrus decumana*), figs (*Ficus sycomorus*), and pomegranates (*Punica granatum*).

Spices are extremely important to Ethiopian cuisine. Among those used are cayenne pepper (*Capsicum frutenseus;* Amharic *berberi*), cone pepper (*Capsicum conoides;* Amharic *shirba*), Amharic cabbage seeds, black mustard (*Brassica nigra;* Amharic *sonafitch*), cardamom (*Aframomum coracima;* Amharic *kororima*), coriander (*Coriandrum sativum;* Amharic *dimbilal*), basil (*Ocymum basilicum;*

Amharic *zaccavi*), black pepper (*Piper nigrum;* Amharic *k'ondo berberei*), ginger (*Zingiber officinale;* Amharic *jinjibil*), black cumin (*Nigella sativa;* Amharic *azmud*), fenugreek (*Trigonella foenum graecum;* Amharic *avish*), and garlic (*Allium sativum;* Amharic *mech'shinkurt*). The leaves of the shrub *gesho* (*Rhamnus prinoides*) are used much like hops to give a bitter taste to beer, mead, and *arak'i,* a distilled liquor.

Several oilseeds are important in Ethiopian cuisine, both for their oil and as seeds. Oilseeds include nug (*Guizotia abyssinica;* Amharic *nug*), sesame (*Sesamum indicum;* Amharic *salit*), and safflower (*Carthamus inctorium;* Amharic *suf*). Flaxseed (*Linum usitatissimum;* Amharic *telba*) is also used in cooking.

Animal foods include cattle, sheep, goats, and chickens and their eggs. Some Ethiopians avoid eating eggs. A taboo on the eating of pork is observed by Muslims and the Falasha Jews. Pork is also not eaten by Amhara and Tigrean Christians or by some other groups like the Qemant, Galla, and Sidama. Another food most Ethiopians avoid eating is fish. Only those groups living on the Red Sea coast or around Lake Tana consume much fish.

Milk and milk products are also utilized in Ethiopian cuisine. Milk may be drunk fresh or as a sort of yogurt; the liquid part of the yogurt is separated for drinking. This drink is called *arera.* Yogurt (*irgo*) is also a part of the diet, as is a sort of cottage cheese called *ayib.* Butter is also made and used, though it is usually kept in the form of clarified butter for preservation. The pastoral nomadic peoples of Ethiopia depend much more on milk and milk products, in addition to grains.

Coffee (*Coffea arabica* L.) is another important part of Ethiopian cuisine and hospitality. It is said to have originated in the Kaffa region, whence its name. This is an important coffee-producing area. Several alcoholic drinks are made and drunk. Beer (talla), made from barley and flavored with leaves of the gesho shrub, is made by women. Mead (*tedj*), sometimes known to Westerners as honey wine, is made from honey and water fermented with the leaves and bitter roots of *saddo* (*Rhamnyus saddo*) or gesho (*Rhamnus gesho*). Mead is highly alcoholic. A distilled beverage, arak'i, begins as beer made from finger millet. The typical Ethiopian arak'i is a clear liquid that tastes like Italian *anice*. It is very strong and is drunk only in small amounts. Both mead and arak'i are also made by women.

Cooking

The hearth is central to Ethiopian home life. In addition to preparing food and cooking there, members of the family traditionally ate in the hearth area. It was the place for socializing within the family, and visitors also gathered there. The traditional stove is the well-known three stones, on which the cooking pot or the stone or metal griddle used to cook flatbreads is balanced. The fuel is wood or charcoal. A charcoal brazier might also be used, especially in the preparation of coffee. Urban homes have Western-style ranges, fueled by bottled gas.

Cooking is the responsibility of women, who prepare and serve the food. In villages it is also women's responsibility to gather fuel and fetch water. Although women should have food ready when their husbands come home, it is also the responsibility of the husband to be there to eat what his wife has prepared.

Meal preparation involves making a flatbread, usually injera made from a slightly fermented batter of teff flour, and the stews (wat) or other vegetable dishes that accompany the flatbreads. These foods are cooked in two different processes. Traditionally, flatbreads, fermented or unfermented, are baked on a stone slab or iron-sheet griddle (*mogogo*) supported by the stones of the hearth. Urban housewives now have an electric griddle (*mitad*) on which to bake injera. Stews are boiled or simmered.

Making injera requires advanced planning. The first step is to mix the flour, usually teff or sorghum, with water. This mixture is then put into a pottery jar and stored for three or four days to ferment. After it is fermented, more water is added to make a batter the consistency of pancake batter. The griddle, which has been heated to a high temperature, is greased. Then, to make the large, thin injera (about 20 inches in diameter), batter is poured and spread onto the griddle, which is over an open fire. It takes

Injera is a pancake-like bread made out of teff flour. It is traditionally eaten in Ethiopia, Eritrea, Somalia, Yemen, and Sudan. (iStockPhoto)

a great deal of skill to spread a thin layer of batter over the griddle without tearing the injera. The batter must also be spread completely before the first edge of the injera burns. When it is done, the injera is peeled off the griddle and stacked on a tray. The finished injera is thoroughly cooked but not crisp. It should be full of bubbles and spongy. Other flatbreads, called kitta, are prepared in much the same way, except that the batter is not fermented.

Injera
This recipe is adapted for Western cooks.

1½ c teff flour*

2 c lukewarm water

Salt

Vegetable oil for the griddle

1. Mix the teff flour with the water and let the mixture stand at room temperature (covered lightly)

until it ferments, 2–3 days. The mixture should be bubbly and the consistency of thick pancake batter. Set aside about ⅓ cup of the batter to make the starter for another batch of injera. The starter can be stored in the refrigerator for up to a month.

2. Add salt until you can just taste it.

3. If the batter is too thick, add more water until it is the consistency of thin pancake batter.

4. Heat a griddle or skillet, preferably an iron skillet, until a drop of water skips over the surface. Then, oil the griddle with a small amount of vegetable oil.

5. Pour about ¼ cup batter onto the griddle, quickly spreading it. It should be thicker than a crepe but thinner than a pancake.

6. Cook until the injera has bubble holes across the entire surface, about 2 minutes. It should be firm but not browned, and cooked on one side only.

7. Remove the injera from the griddle and stack it on a plate. A piece of plastic wrap or foil may be placed on each one to keep them from sticking together.

8. Continue until all the batter is used.

9. Serve by placing one injera on each plate and topping with the stews. Or serve Ethiopian style, with the injera on a pizza pan placed in the middle of the table, with the stews around the edge of the injera in front of each person. Makes about 10 eight-inch injera.

*If teff flour is unavailable, whole wheat or barley flour may be substituted. However, neither of those flours will ferment as teff does. In this case, in place of the fermentation step, add 1 tbsp baking powder, and substitute 2 cup club soda for the water, adding about ¼ cup lemon juice to approximate the sour taste of fermented teff. Sorghum flour will ferment like teff and is a good substitute, in which case you can proceed with the recipe as for teff. The result will be the Sudanese version of injera.

The next part of meal preparation is to make whatever stews are to accompany the injera. The stews, or wat, might be a combination of meat and vegetables or only vegetables or pulses. Typically these dishes are highly spiced, well beyond the endurance of the average Westerner. Onions or shallots are a typical ingredient in most stews, so these must be prepared and chopped. Vegetable ingredients must also be cleaned and chopped. If lentils or dried beans, such as cowpeas, are to be used, they must be sorted, examined for small stones, and washed.

If meat is to be an ingredient in the stew, it must also be prepared, with the amount of preparation depending on whether the cook is a villager or an urbanite. A village woman planning on adding chicken to her stew is likely to begin by slaughtering, cleaning, and butchering the chicken herself. Other animals would likely be slaughtered by her husband for her to butcher and further prepare. Townswomen would be able to purchase meat ready for them to cut up for their stews.

Some stews include hard-boiled eggs. If eggs are to be part of the stew, they must be prepared ahead, ready to be added when the stew is almost finished cooking. Other ingredients, especially spice combinations, are also prepared ahead, ready to be added during the cooking process. One such spice combination is *berbere,* an almost ubiquitous requirement for most stews.

Berbere

1 tsp ground ginger

2 tsp ground cumin

⅛ tsp ground cloves

⅛ tsp cinnamon

½ tsp ground cardamom

⅛ tsp ground allspice

¼ tsp ground nutmeg

1 tsp ground fenugreek

½ tsp ground coriander

⅓ tsp turmeric

2 tbsp onions, finely chopped

1 tbsp garlic, minced

2 tbsp ground cayenne pepper

2 c Hungarian paprika

½ tsp ground black pepper

1 tbsp salt

1½ c water

Toast the ginger, cumin, cloves, cinnamon, cardamom, allspice, nutmeg, fenugreek, coriander, and turmeric in a small frying pan (cast iron is good) over low heat for about 2 minutes, stirring constantly. Remove from heat and cool for about 5 minutes. Combine the spices, onion, garlic, and 3 tablespoons water in a blender and blend until smooth. Combine the cayenne pepper, paprika, black pepper, and salt in a skillet and toast over low heat for about 1 minute. Stir in water, ¼ cup at a time. Then stir in the blended mixture. Stirring vigorously, cook over the lowest possible heat for 10–15 minutes. Transfer berbere to a jar. Cool to room temperature, then cover with a film of oil. Store in the refrigerator in a tightly sealed jar.

Doro Wat, or Zegeni (Chicken in Red Pepper Paste)

Ethiopian National Dish

2½ lb chicken (a cut-up whole chicken, or use legs and thighs)

2 tbsp lemon juice

2 tsp salt

2 onions, finely chopped

¼ c *niter kibbeh* (spiced butter; recipe follows)

3 cloves garlic, minced

1 tsp fresh ginger, finely minced

¼ tsp ground fenugreek

¼ tsp ground cardamom

⅛ tsp ground nutmeg

¼ c berbere

2 tbsp paprika

1 c water

6–8 hard-boiled eggs

Freshly ground black pepper

Rinse and dry chicken pieces. Rub with lemon juice and salt, and let sit at room temperature for 30 min-

utes. In a heavy pot or Dutch oven, cook onions over moderate heat for about 5 minutes. Do not let brown or burn. Stir in the niter kibbeh. Then add garlic and spices. Stir well. Add berbere and paprika, and sauté for 3–4 minutes. Add water and bring to a boil. Cook briskly, uncovered, for about 5 minutes. Pat the chicken dry, and drop it into the simmering sauce, turning each piece until it is well covered. Reduce heat, cover, and simmer for 15 minutes. In the meantime, peel the hard-boiled eggs and pierce them with a fork. After the chicken has cooked, add the eggs, turning them gently in the sauce. Cover and cook for an additional 25 minutes. Add black pepper to taste. Serve a piece of chicken, an egg, and sauce to each person, placing them on top of the injera.

Niter Kibbeh (Spiced Butter)

2 lb unsalted butter, cut into small pieces

1 onion, coarsely chopped

3 tbsp minced garlic

4 tsp fresh ginger, finely minced

4 tsp ground turmeric

¼ tsp ground cardamom

1 cinnamon stick (1 in. long)

1 whole clove

⅛ tsp ground nutmeg

In a large saucepan, melt butter slowly over medium heat. Do not let it brown. Bring butter to a boil. Stir in remaining ingredients. Simmer uncovered and undisturbed for 45 minutes. The milk solids in the bottom of the pan should be brown, and the butter on top should be transparent. Slowly pour the clear liquid into a bowl, straining through a cheesecloth. No solids should be left in the niter kibbeh. Transfer niter kibbeh to a jar and store in the refrigerator.

Almost all stews, or *wat*, begin with lots of onions. But not all include berbere. Some, the *alecha wat*, are milder. Stews can be made with chicken, beef, fish, or lamb and a variety of vegetables. They may also be vegetarian, like *mesir wat,* which is a red lentil puree. Meat may also be sautéed to make *tibbs.* Tibbs can be "normal" or "special," the latter meaning it is served on a hot plate with a vegetable salad mixed in. Another favorite Ethiopian dish is *kitfo,* which is made with raw, minced beef marinated in *mitmita,* a spicy chili powder, and niter kibbeh. Other dishes include chickpea fritters made with chickpea flour, lentil salad, eggplant salad, *gomen sega* (mustard greens and beef), *sega wat* (Ethiopian lamb), *temiser w'et* (spicy lentil soup), *sambussa* (vegetable- or meat-filled pastries), *atkilt wat* (cabbage, carrots, and potatoes in sauce), or *inguday tibbs* (mushrooms sautéed with onions). The cooking techniques for all of these are similar, but there is great variation in the ingredients and the combinations of ingredients.

The cooking described so far focuses on cereals, pulses, and vegetables. The cuisine of the ensete complex requires some different techniques. The false stem and young shoots of the ensete plant are sometimes boiled and eaten as a vegetable. But the main consumption of ensete involves a long process. The mature ensete plant has a huge root (*wahta*) that is harvested, then scraped to extract the starchy pulp, which is edible. This starchy substance is buried in deep pits where it is left to ferment for at least two months and sometimes several years. The Gurage say that burying the ensete improves the taste, making it more highly favored than freshly harvested ensete. After fermentation the ensete is made into a heavy bread (*kocho*), about one inch thick. The bread is baked in an ensete leaf and tastes sour, rather like injera. This bread is eaten with kitfo, the raw meat dish already described, mixed with niter kibbeh and mitmita, a spiced chili powder made with the hottest of chilies. Fresh cottage cheese (*ayb*) is served with the kitfo. Another dish served with kocho is *gomen kitfo,* made by boiling collard greens, drying them, then serving the greens finely chopped and mixed with niter kibbeh. Ensete root is also powdered and prepared as a hot drink called *bulla.*

Ethiopians drink several types of beverages. Coffee is made in homes and in *buna bets,* or coffeehouses. Ethiopian coffee is made much like Turkish coffee, thick and prepared in a pottery pot (*jebena*). Sugar or sometimes honey may or may not be added to the brew. Coffee beans are typically roasted as a part of coffee preparation, pounded in a mortar (*mukecha*) with a pestle (*zenezena*), and then boiled in the jebena. Each person is served three rounds, known as *abol, tona,* and *baraka,* in small, handleless cups. Ethiopians say the first two cups transform the spirit, while the third gives a blessing (*baraka*) to the person drinking it. Sometimes the youngest child serves the first cup of coffee to the eldest guest.

The Majangir and Gurage, among others, serve coffee with niter kibbeh, clarified butter prepared with spices and onions. The Majangir prepare their coffee brew (*kari*) from the leaves of the coffee tree, which grows wild in the forests around their villages. Leaves of the coffee tree are infused in hot water, and niter kibbeh is added to the brew. Sharing is very important to the Majangir, and, interestingly, the sphere of sharing is delineated by the term *kari omong,* or "the same coffee," that is, the persons in the neighborhood close enough to share coffee drinking.

An Ethopian woman grinds coffee by hand. (Johan Bernspång | Dreamstime.com)

Other beverages include several types of *chilka,* each made from a different seed: nug, flax, sesame, or safflower. The recipe for chilka is 1 cup of seeds, 6 cups of water, and 1–2 tablespoons honey. First, the seeds are dry-roasted in a skillet for about 5–10 minutes and then, after cooling, ground to a powder. The powdered seeds are then added to the water and allowed to sit for about 20 minutes until the solids have settled out. Once the solids have settled, the liquid is strained into a pitcher, the honey is added, and it is chilled.

Chilkas are nonalcholic beverages, but as mentioned earlier, Ethiopians make and drink three main alcoholic drinks: mead (tedj), beer (talla), and arak'i. Mead is fairly simple to make. Honey is put into a pot with gesho (*Rhamnus pauciflorus*) leaves and water. The pot is covered and left to stand for 3–10 days, depending on the temperature. After the mixture has fermented the pot is opened, the gesho removed, and the liquid filtered, making it ready to drink. The process of making both beer and arak'i is more complicated and time-consuming. To make beer, first the leaves of gesho are dried, crushed, and soaked in a jug of water for three days. In the meantime, barley is used to make malt by soaking the grain in another jug for 24 hours. The water is then poured off the barley, and it is put between two layers of leaves and put into the house rafters until the sprouts reach 1½ inches. After it has sprouted, the barley is crushed until the grains are broken open. Then, the barley is placed in the sun on a metal sheet or a skin for a day, after which it is ground into flour. Flour from unsprouted barley is made into a paste, allowed to stand for three days, and then cooked on a metal griddle on an open fire. The resulting cake is broken into pieces, mixed with the sprouted barley, and added to the pot of gesho and water. The mixture is fermented for four days, then more water is added and the pot is allowed to stand for several days. The final step is to filter the beer from the fermentation pot into a freshly smoked clay pot. The resulting beer is a gray liquid with some grain floating in it and with a low alcohol content.

Making arak'i uses the same process as for making beer. But at the final dilution, only half the amount of water typically added to beer is added.

The thick brew is put into a large pot, and the top is sealed with a mixture of cow dung, mud, and straw. Next, a bamboo tube is inserted into a small hole near the top of the pot, sealed with mud. Then the pot is placed over a fire; as the liquid boils, steam escapes down the tube and condenses into a special copper or brass kettle set in water.

Typical Meals

Most Ethiopians eat three meals a day: breakfast (qurs) between 7 and 8 A.M., lunch (mesa) at noon, and supper (erat) after dark. They might also have a late afternoon snack with beer or coffee. Breakfast is usually a small meal and may consist of parched grain or porridge and coffee. Egg dishes may also be served. Lunch is the most substantial meal of the day, with injera, a main stew (wat), and perhaps several smaller accompanying dishes. Ethiopians may drink milk or beer with lunch and coffee after the meal is finished and cleared. Supper is a smaller meal, perhaps of leftover injera and stew.

Before meals are served a basin of water and soap are brought in for everyone to wash their hands and mouth. After the meal the hands and mouth are washed again. Meals are served on a low table (*mesob*) made from or topped with a flat basket, which also serves as the base for the injera. Injera serves as the plate, the utensil, and food. Several layers of injera are put on the mesob, and the various wats and other dishes are ladled onto the injera in front of each person. Small pieces of injera are broken off with the hands and used to scoop up the stews, vegetables, or salads. Only the right hand is used for eating. Food is scooped with two or three fingers. One should always chew with the mouth closed and along only one side of the jaw. Chewing on both sides is considered gluttony. A person eats slowly and with restraint in terms of how much is consumed. But others, particularly guests, are urged to eat. Women guests may show great reticence, claiming they have eaten already or are not hungry. During a meal with friends a person may tear off a piece of injera, dip it into the wat, then roll it up and put it into the mouth of a friend. This ritual is called *gorsha* and is an act of cementing the friendship. Sharing meals incorporates a great deal of symbolism, as in most cultures, with commensality reinforcing bonds with kin and forging bonds with neighbors and strangers. The practice of eating in a circle, from a common round "plate," is rife with social meaning. If the meal is a family one, husband and wife will eat together, then the children. If the people sharing the meal are outside the family circle, men and women eat separately.

Younger Ethiopians are making more use of processed or prepackaged foods that are becoming more readily available in urban markets. These foods include packaged berbere, bread, and cookies. "European" foods are also more readily available now, like pasta, macaroni, and rice. Partly prepared or processed foods have helped women save time in meal preparation. These foods not only help women who are joining the labor force but are also partly an outcome of wage labor.

Eating Out

Traditionally Ethiopians did not eat out, but meals outside the home were available. Until more recent times foods typically available in a market or street setting were mostly snacks (*maksas*). These street foods include boiled eggs or potatoes, boiled or roasted cereals, beans or peas, and breads. Street vendors might sell wats wrapped in a piece of injera. Drink stands serve a variety of fruit drinks, especially in larger towns and cities. In all cultures some accommodation must be made for travelers and other people unable to eat at home, so traditional market areas are likely to have clusters of open-air "restaurants."

These days a dining-out culture has been established in cities, where a range of restaurants from upscale to fast food can be found. Besides offering diners traditional Ethiopian fare, these establishments offer a variety of European cuisine. As with

A group of women cooking on the street in Ethopia, 2008. (Tiziano Casalta | Dreamstime.com)

globalization in all parts of the world, Western chains, like McDonald's, Pizza Hut, Kentucky Fried Chicken, and Dunkin Donuts, can be found. There are also Ethiopian versions of Western fast food, catering primarily to teenagers and young adults but also to families.

Special Occasions

The diversity of Ethiopian cultures means hundreds of celebrations and rituals celebrated with special foods, fasting, and feasting. The focus here is on the main festivals and holidays celebrated by the Ethiopian Orthodox Church and Ethiopia's Muslims. Practitioners of traditional religions also have their own rituals involving food practices.

Besides celebrating Christmas, Easter, and other familiar Christian holidays, the Ethiopian Orthodox Church practices fasting. The clergy of the Ethiopian Orthodox Church fast about 250 days per year, while the laity fast about 165 days per year. In addition to special fast days, fasting is observed every Wednesday and Friday. On fast days, observers have nothing to eat or drink until after 3 P.M. During Lent practitioners abstain from meat, eggs, and milk, eating fish instead. The Lenten fast is for 56 days. Christmas (celebrated on January 7) is also preceded by a fast of 40 days. Orthodox practitioners also observe many saints' days as well as a personal saint's day, on which they give small feasts. In addition, local voluntary associations (*maheber*) honor their patron saint with special services and feasts two or three times a year.

Muslims observe the Ramadan fast, during which practitioners refrain from eating from dawn to dusk. Since the Islamic calendar is based on a lunar calendar, Muslim holidays come earlier each subsequent year. At dusk on each day of the 28-day fast Muslims break the fast with special foods and drinks. At the end of Ramadan come the Eid al-Fitr and the Eid al-Adha holidays, both of which are celebrated by slaughtering a sheep or goat and feasting with family, friends, and neighbors.

Diet and Health

Even though the elements of the Ethiopian diet are quite nutritious, the food supply is not sufficient to meet the energy requirements of most of the population. Both man-made and environmental factors result in food insecurity. Food insecurity affects almost half the population. About 84 percent of the population is engaged in rain-fed agriculture; however, few households can produce all they need. There are few roads, and markets are not integrated, making the distribution of any surpluses across the country almost impossible.

Ethiopians do not eat much meat, eggs, or fish. Ethiopia has an abundant supply of fish, but the consumption of fish is low due to cultural taboos as well as inability to transport fish far from its original locale. Although the consumption of fruits and vegetables has increased over the past 10 years, it remains low. The per-capita supply of milk and eggs has also increased but remains low.

On the positive side, 96 percent of infants begin life being breast-fed. Most infants were found to be given the breast within one hour of birth, which is a crucial statistic because some cultures believe an infant will be harmed by the mother's first milk production. Interestingly, it has been found that Ethiopian mothers with no education were more likely to practice early initiation of breast-feeding. The median duration of breast-feeding is 26 months, though there is wide variation, and the duration of breast-feeding among urban mothers is much shorter.

Another dietary deficiency is the lack of iodine, particularly in mountain regions. Vitamin A deficiency is also a problem that affects young children and mothers. Anemia is another health problem due to the low consumption of animal foods. Anemia is also compounded by endemic malaria and other parasitic diseases. The consumption of teff protects against iron deficiency because the grain is high in iron. A Food and Agriculture Organization report (United Nations, 2008) suggests that food aid to Ethiopia, which primarily consisted of wheat, actually contributed to iron deficiency because wheat, low in iron, was substituted for the traditional inclusion of teff in the diet.

Barbara J. Michael

Further Reading

Asfaw, Zemede. "Conservation and Use of Traditional Vegetables in Ethiopia." In *Proceedings of the IPGRI International Workshop on Genetic Resources of Traditional Vegetables in Africa: Conservation and Use,* 29–31 August 1995, ICRAF-HQ, Nairobi Kenya.

Brandt, Steven A., Anita Spring, Clifton Hiebsch, J. Terrence McCabe, Endale Tabogie, Mulugeta Diro, Gizachew Wolde-Michael, Gebre Yntiso, Masayoshi Shigeta, and Shiferaw Tesfaye. "The Tree against Hunger: Enset-Based Agricultural Systems in Ethiopia." American Association for the Advancement of Science. 1997. http://www.aaas.org/international/africa/enset/eset.pdf.

Embassy of the Federal Democratic Republic of Ethiopia. "Festivals and Holidays." http://www.ethioembassy.org.uk/about_us/festivals_and_holidays.htm.

Embassy of the Federal Democratic Republic of Ethiopia. "Food and Drink." http://www.ethioembassy.org.uk/about_us/food_and_drink.htm.

Ethiopian Restaurant.com. http://www.ethiopianrestaurant.com/dishes.

Freeman, Dena. *Initiating Change in Highland Ethiopia: Causes and Consequences of Cultural Transformation.* Cambridge: Cambridge University Press, 2002.

Goodwin, Lindsey. "Ethiopian Coffee Ceremony." About.com, http://coffeetea.about.com/od/historyculture/a/ethiopiancoffee ceremony.htm.

Javins, Marie. "Eating and Drinking in Ethiopia." GoNOMAD.com. http://www.gonomad.com/features/0211/ethiopiafood.html.

Kifleyesus, Abbebe. "The Construction of Ethiopian National Cuisine." *Ethnorema* 3 (2006): 27–48.

Kifleyesus, Abbebe. "Muslims and Meals: The Social and Symbolic Function of Foods in Changing Socio-Economic Environments." *African Journal of the International African Institute* 72, No. 1 (2002): 245–76.

Kloman, Harry. "Tej Page." http://www.pitt.edu/~kloman/harry.html.

Levine, Donald N. *Greater Ethiopia: The Evolution of a Multi-Ethnic Society.* Chicago: University of Chicago Press, 1974.

Piccinin, Doris. "More about Ethiopian Food: Teff." 2002. http://ethnomed.org/clinical/nutrition/more-about-ethiopian-food-teff.

Shack, William A. "Hunger, Anxiety, and Ritual: Deprivation and Spirit Possession among the Gurage of Ethiopia." *Man,* n.s., 6, No. 1 (1971): 30–43.

Shack, William A. "Some Aspects of Ecology and Social Structure in the Ensete Complex of South-West Ethiopia." *Journal of the Royal Anthropological Institute of Great Britain and Ireland* 93, No. 1 (1963): 72–79.

Simoons, Frederick J. *Northwest Ethiopia: Peoples and Economy.* Madison: University of Wisconsin Press, 1960.

Stauder, Jack. *The Majangir: Ecology and Society of a Southwest Ethiopian People.* Cambridge: Cambridge University Press, 1971.

United Nations, Food and Agriculture Organization. *Nutrition Country Profile: Federal Democratic Republic of Ethiopia.* Rome, Italy: Food and Agriculture Organization, Nutritional and Consumer Protection Division, 2008. ftp://ftp.fao.org/ag/agn/nutrition/ncp/eth.pdf.

Ghana

Overview

Ghana is situated on the southern part of the western bulge of the African continent. It shares borders with neighbors Togo to the east, Côte d'Ivoire to the west, and Burkina Faso to the north, and it has a coastline on the Gulf of Guinea. The country has an area of 92,100 square miles (238,540 square kilometers). The country's population of over 22 million people is comprised of more than 60 different ethnic groups. Based on language and culture the people of Ghana are usually divided into five major groups: the Akan, the Ewe, the MoleDagbane, the Guan, and the Ga-Adangbe. Each has its own distinctive culture. No area of the country, however, is ethnically homogeneous, and no single group can be found in only one area. Ethnic groups are mixed in all urban areas. The Ghanaian government does not recognize any official national religion, but roughly 62 percent are Christians. The country has the largest percentage of Christians in West Africa. Fifteen percent are Muslim, and the remainder of the population practices various traditional forms of religion.

The main division of the country, as with many states on the Gulf of Guinea, is from north to south. The south, where Ghana's capital Accra is located, had the first contact with European culture, when the Portuguese arrived in 1471. Citizens of this region, therefore, are likely to have had a form of westernized education and are likely to be Christian. This is also true in the country's urban areas. Moving northward, the country becomes more rural, and Islam becomes the predominant cultural influence.

The climate is tropical with two rainy seasons: April through June and September through November. Northern Ghana has more extreme weather conditions than the south, which can lead to food shortages.

Food Culture Snapshot

Kofi and Grace Armah are westernized Ghanaians who live in the capital, Accra. He is in private industry, and she is a teacher. Their lifestyle is that of the urban elite, and they are influenced not only by the traditional customs of their ethnic group but also by international trends. Their diet crosses ethnic and national boundaries. Ghanaians traditionally eat three meals a day, and each meal generally is comprised of only one course. The ingredients for their meals come from the local supermarket, a local street market, or from Osu, the traditional shopping area, or Makola market, Accra's largest market, where fresh produce as well as imported and manufactured foods is available. Most Ghanaian households of any means usually have a household servant of some sort, and so do the Armahs. The shopping is frequently done by the houseboy based on consultation with Grace unless a special dish is to be prepared, in which case she will do the shopping for particular ingredients. Grace also supplements the larder daily with items seen in markets as she commutes to and from work. Local delicacies are also purchased from street stalls.

Major Foodstuffs

The cuisine in Ghana is a relatively simple one that depends on seasoning and preparation more than

Subsistence farmer stands behind palm nuts drying in the sun. (Corel)

as *egusi* or melon seeds, red palm oil, the palm nuts themselves, and a range of dried, smoked, and salted fish and mollusks are also used to season dishes.

Rice is a staple starch throughout the country, but there are regional as well as ethnic preferences. In the northern part of the country, millet, yams, and corn are more frequent, while the south shows a preference for plantains, cassava, and cocoyam (a tuber). Meat remains the food of the affluent and is relatively expensive, with beef, lamb, and goat predominating. Fish is readily available and may include sea bream, mackerel, sole, eel, herring, and more. Crustaceans such as crab, crayfish, and mollusks including mussels and oysters are also consumed. Snails are a particular delicacy, and Ghana boasts some of the world's largest. Fish and meat are often mixed in traditional dishes. Vegetables include tomatoes, avocados, green peppers, cucumbers, cabbage, and more. Fruits are widely available and include guavas, papayas, oranges, mangoes, pineapples, and bananas. Sorghum is used in the north and is the basis for a fermented beverage known as *pito*. In matters inebriating, the south shows a preference for palm wine, while the entire country (with the exception of the Islamic north) loves beer.

Cooking

The most common types of cooking in Ghana are boiling, steaming, stewing, frying, roasting, grilling, and baking. All of these methods are the basis for the traditional dishes of the country that used the traditional cookstove. In the 1950s, Ghanaian households cooked over wood or charcoal fires. Kerosene stoves supplanted many of the wood-burning ones, but in the rural areas the traditional three-rock wood stoves remain the standard. In the urban areas, the Western stove is used, as are pressure cookers, which are used to tenderize tougher cuts of meat. Refrigerators are also the norm among those with access to electricity and sufficient funds. Microwaves, freezers, food processors, and the full range of other Western culinary conveniences are de rigueur among the elite.

Most households have some kind of domestic help. It may be a relative from the country looking for

on a variety of foodstuffs. The culinary paradigm for the country is a well-seasoned soupy stew served with an accompanying starch. The stews are prepared from a variety of vegetables and meats including leafy greens of many sorts (the country boasts over 47 varieties of edible greens, each with its own distinctive flavor), peanuts, eggplant (called *garden eggs*), cocoyam, cassava, and the true yam, which is so popular that it plays an important role in many traditional Ghanaian religious observances. Ghanaian food gets its flavor complexity from a variety of spices, including cayenne pepper, allspice, curry, garlic, caraway, cloves, ginger, and a range of chili peppers that are used to season the dishes. There are also traditional West African peppers like the *melegueta* pepper and cubebs. Other ingredients such employment in the city and working in exchange for lodging, or a professional paid for services. Cooking, therefore, is often done by another woman and not the lady of the house. It is done, though, in full consultation with her and is often overseen by her. Cooking, however, remains a family activity for festive foods. Extended families will combine to prepare dishes at times of feasting, with the matriarch directing the kitchen. The myriad cultures of Ghana are oral ones, and this is the manner by which the youngsters of the household learn the traditional foods.

Typical Meals

Given the regional diversity of the country, it is difficult to generalize about a typical meal. In general, it can be said that the typical heavier meals of the day traditionally consist of a soupy stew of some sort served over or accompanied by a starch such as the fermented cornmeal known as *kenkey.* The starch may be dipped in the stew, or the stew may be scooped up with it. Rice is also an accompaniment for several dishes, as is the boiled, pounded yam known as *fufu.* There may be the European paradigm of three meals a day. That is often replaced with a different one that includes one or two heavy meals and a lighter meal or some snacking.

In urban areas, breakfast may follow the British mode and include a porridge of some sort like traditional European oatmeal, an omelet, or a sweet bread known as sugarbread, usually accompanied by the British legacy of tea with milk. Alternately, it might include one of the more traditional Ghanaian breakfast preparations like *ampesi,* a dish of cassava, yam, and plantain that is boiled with fish and onion and then pounded in a mortar and boiled again. Street breakfasts are also available around the country and usually consist of some form of an omelet and tea.

For the westernized, lunch and dinner are interchangeable and range between European and American fare like grilled or roasted chicken served with a piquant sauce and more traditional Ghanaian dishes like pepper soup or groundnut stew.

Groundnut Stew

3 tbsp vegetable oil

1 c chopped onion

½ c chopped carrots

Frying chicken, cut into serving pieces

½ lb fresh okra, topped, tailed, and cut into 1-in. rounds

1 large (28-oz) can tomatoes and their liquid

3 c chicken stock

3 c water

Salt to taste

1 habanero chili, pricked

1 c chunky peanut butter

Heat the oil in a large saucepan over medium heat. Add the onions, carrots, and chicken and sauté, stirring occasionally, until the vegetables have softened and the chicken has browned. Add the okra, and continue to cook for 5 minutes. Stir in the tomatoes and their liquid, the chicken stock, and the water. Salt to taste and add the pricked habanero chili. Then lower the heat, cover, and allow it to simmer for about 45 minutes or until the chicken is cooked through. Taste occasionally and, when desired piquancy is reached, remove the chili. Finally, stir in the peanut butter and continue to cook for 10 minutes. Serve hot accompanied by the starch of choice. Usually the starch is boiled yam, cassava, cocoyam, or sweet potato, called *ampesi* in Twi and Fanti, *nuko* in Ewe, or *agwao* in Ga. It can also be served with kenkey (fermented corn dough wrapped in leaves) or *banku* or fermented, boiled cornmeal that is the ancestor of the *coocoo* and *fungi* of the Caribbean.

Eating Out

Restaurants in the Western sense of the term are relatively new to Ghanaian culture. They are limited to the larger urban areas, and those that might be categorized as "white-tablecloth" restaurants are often located in the luxury hotels. Others are smaller and not as fancy, and they serve local specialties or dishes prepared by women who are known for certain dishes. Sundays in the Christianized south of the country are often times for eating out. There is a nascent fast-food culture, with American imports and also Mr. Bigg's, a Nigerian chain of fast-food restaurants boasting four Ghanaian locations. There are also Chinese restaurants run by Chinese who hark from Asian areas of the former British Empire. Here, fried rice is a staple and is often served with noodles as well as fried chicken. There may even be the particularly British touch of baked beans. Clubs featuring various local dishes and live Ghanaian music are fixtures of urban areas throughout the country. Finally, for eating out throughout the country, there is the country's street food, accessible to all except the poorest.

The street food is based on the local cuisine and includes spots such as street stalls and pedestrian and market vendors as well as lower-priced establishments called *chop houses* that are also places for the growing middle classes; they, too, specialize in local favorites and in dishes like grilled fish, fried chicken served with savory sauces, and beef kebabs dusted with peanut flour and hot pepper called *kyinkyinga,* which are also sold by ambulatory vendors. Fresh seafood predominates along the coast. Also notable in this country where the water is not always drinkable are the street beverages. Alcoholic drinks are sold only in licensed establishments, and carbonated drinks are sold only in permanent shops that can collect the bottles for recycling and refilling. Coconuts, therefore, are popular, as are small plastic bags filled with purified water or different flavored juices.

Special Occasions

Traditional life is extremely important to Ghanaians, and the country can boast that over 100 festivals take place annually. Many of them celebrate the harvest and pay tribute to ancestors. All festivals, even funerals, involve dancing, singing, and eating. Some of the most impressive festivals are the yam festivals like the Akan festival Odwira, the presentation of the new harvest of yams to the ancestors.

It is a weeklong festival in September or October that celebrates the harvest of yams, which are a traditional staple. The major Christian holidays of Christmas and Easter are national holidays, while in the northern sections of the country and in Muslim households, Ramadan is celebrated according to Islamic tradition.

Diet and Health

In 1995, the World Bank stated that 11 percent of the population was undernourished and added that 27 percent of the children under age five were underweight and more than 25 percent were considered short for their age, or "stunted." Between 1990 and 1995 one-third of all Ghanaian children had some form of goiter, which is indicative of thyroid disease. The country's north/south divide coupled with the urban/rural one meant that rural dwellers in the northern part of the country were more subject to interrupted food supplies in the rainy seasons when flooding might interrupt food sources. The same happened in the dry season if drought occurred. The southern regions are closer to seaports and have more stable climactic conditions. The more developed economy means that there are methods of food storage, and most people can afford to purchase food from markets and other sources if their individual food supplies are destroyed. The University of Ghana's Faculty of Science has a department of Nutrition and Food Science to address these issues, and the regional African office of the Food and Agriculture Organization of the United Nations is based in Accra, Ghana.

Jessica B. Harris

Further Reading

Harris, Jessica. *The Africa Cookbook: Tastes of a Continent.* New York: Simon and Schuster, 1998.

Osseo-Asare, Fran. *A Good Soup Attracts Chairs.* Baton Rouge, LA: Pelican, 1993.

Polgreen, Lydia. "A Taste of Ghana." *New York Times,* January 2, 2006. http://www.nytimes.com/2006/02/01/dining/01ghana.html.

Guinea

Overview

Guinea is a French-speaking country with a population of about 9.5 million people. The Republic of Guinea, or La République de Guinée in French, sits nestled between the Atlantic Ocean, Senegal, Côte d'Ivoire (Ivory Coast), Sierra Leone, Liberia, Guinea-Bissau, and Mali. It is sometimes called Guinea-Conakry to distinguish it from its neighbor to the north, Guinea-Bissau. Guinea has almost a quarter of the world's bauxite reserves and plentiful gold and diamond mines. There are four distinct geographic areas in Guinea—highlands in the interior, coastal plains and mangrove swamps, savanna, and rain forest. The capital, Conakry, is situated in the very wet, humid zone of southwestern West Africa located along the Atlantic coast. The area has a monsoonal climate and can easily receive over 157 inches of rain a year. The mountainous Fouta Djallon region also gets a lot of rain; the headwaters of three major rivers, the Niger, the Gambia, and the Senegal, are all located there.

The country has a young population—almost 50 percent of the people are 15 years old or younger—and it is quite ethnically diverse. The three largest ethnic groups are the Fulani (also known as the Peul or the Fula), the Susu, and the Malinké (also known as the Mandigo, Mande, or Maninke). Guinea is predominantly Muslim, with a smaller number practicing traditional religions and Christianity.

🍽 Food Culture Snapshot

Lamine and Salamata Bâ are Fulani. They live in Dalaba near the city of Mamou in the Fouta Djallon; they have a five-year-old daughter. Like many Fulani, Lamine raises cattle and Salamata is a homemaker who tends the family's garden plot and gathers what they need from the nearby mountains.

The couple usually eats two meals each day, usually at midday and in the evening. Should Lamine and Salamata start the day with breakfast, they eat bread with a cup of tea or instant coffee (usually Nescafé) sweetened with condensed milk or fresh fruit. Lunch is a much heartier dish of *maffe hacco,* a sauce of pureed leafy greens—most often cassava or sweet potato leaves—cooked with palm oil and a bit of meat, usually beef or chicken, and served over rice. The couple will eat leftovers for dinner if food remains, or they may eat steamed millet, sorghum, or *fonio* (a kind of millet, *Digitaria exilis*) with buttermilk or cream.

The climate and a lack of refrigeration or reliable electricity due to a crumbling infrastructure and the government's mismanagement of resources generally mean that people do without rather than make frequent trips to the market for ingredients. Only the wealthy, usually government workers or expatriates, may have refrigeration. Supermarkets are rare for the average person, but the markets carry just about everything a Guinean cook needs in the kitchen. On a typical trip to the market, Salamata would purchase meat and fish to prepare grilled *brochettes* (kebabs) or to add to the many leaf and vegetable sauces she prepares. People buy seafood directly from fishermen where access permits, but those like Salamata who live far from the coast buy dried fish to flavor their food while cooking. Maggi cubes (bouillon), salt, chilies, and dried shrimp are essential ingredients available in the market.

Major Foodstuffs

Most Guineans work in the agricultural sector in this predominantly rural country. The most important agricultural products are rice, cassava, oil palm fruit, plantains, and cattle. Meals in Guinea are generally higher in carbohydrates than protein, because typical starchy carbohydrates like rice, cassava, and plantains are cheaper than meat. The most common meal in Guinea is a vegetable-based sauce flavored with meat and seafood and always served with rice or cassava.

Rice is the most important staple crop, produced here in rice paddies in coastal areas where mangrove swamps have been cleared to accommodate them. Cassava is valued for the starchy tuber as well as the leaves of the plant, and Guineans also make a version of *fufu* from cooked cassava flour. (Fufu is a common West African dish that can be made from boiled, pounded tubers like yams, cocoyam, cassava, or plantains or from the flours of these products; it is eaten as an accompaniment to various soups, stews, and sauces.) The common potato, which is indigenous to South America and spread to the African continent through initial European contact, is known locally as the Irish potato and has made its way into sauces and other dishes. Sweet potatoes—the hard white variety and the softer orange one—are also grown for their flesh and their leaves, much like cassava. Millet and the indigenous West African grains sorghum and fonio are important as a bed for sauces or are eaten as porridges or, particularly by the Fulani, with thick, sweetened buttermilk. People tend to eat different grains or starchy staples at different times of the year.

Potato leaves are important ingredients and show up in dishes like maffe hacco, which can be translated from Fulani as "leaf sauce" and generally refers to cassava. Sweet potato leaves (*pouté* in Fulani), spinach, and jute leaves with their mucilaginous texture are also common in sauces. Okra, beloved throughout West Africa for the slippery texture and thickening properties it lends to dishes in which it is cooked, appears in Guinea in a pureed okra sauce. Onions and tomatoes are essential to preparing leaf sauces and the tomato-based sauce known in Fulani as *maffe soupou* (*soupou* means "tomato"). Fulani cooks use chilies sparingly, but they are essential to the fiery versions of leaf, peanut butter, and tomato sauces prepared in Malinké and Susu kitchens.

Maffe Hacco (Cassava-Leaf Sauce)

African food is really regional food; even within the vast region of West Africa where ingredients and techniques tend to be fairly similar, there are almost subregional differences. Leaf sauces are common in southwestern West Africa, particularly in Liberia, Sierra Leone, and, of course, Guinea. Here is the Guinean version of cassava-leaf sauce. The basic technique includes finely chopping or pounding leaves to puree them. Cassava leaves taste a bit like spinach with slightly tougher texture. Guineans may use any type of leafy greens as a substitute, often sweet potato leaves, which would make the dish *maffe pouté*. You can substitute collards, kale, mustard or turnip greens, spinach, or other preferred greens for the leaves in this recipe.

Ingredients

2 8-oz packages frozen, chopped cassava leaves or three medium bunches cassava leaves

1 large onion, finely chopped

1 tbsp red pepper flakes or chopped chilies to taste (optional)

1 c palm oil

1–1½ c water

2 tbsp dried, ground shrimp

1 bouillon cube

Thaw and drain frozen cassava leaves in a bowl and set aside. If using fresh leaves, wash, dry the excess water, and roll into a tight bundle. Using a sharp knife cut thin strips of the leaves to create very fine shreds. Finely mince onion while heating palm oil in a medium-large pot until it begins to smoke. Add minced onion and fry 1 minute. Add leaves and fry an additional minute. If using frozen leaves add liquid drained from leaves and 1 cup of water; if using fresh leaves use 1½ cups of water. Add dried shrimp and stir well. Add bouillon cube and red pepper, if using, then stir. Cover tightly, and reduce heat to medium low. Leave mixture simmering about 30 minutes or until liquid has cooked away and mixture is moist but dry on top, stirring occasionally. Serve with rice.

The tropical environment affords Guineans access to fresh fruits such as pineapple, papayas, mangoes, bananas, guavas, mangosteens, and sugarcane, all of which are grown commercially; people eat fresh fruits as snacks and prepare them as juices. Oil palm fruits, the source of both palm oil and palm butter, are another key crop. Palm oil is an important source of vitamins and perhaps the most important cooking oil. It is prized for the deep orange hue it imparts and the very distinctive flavor it adds to dishes.

Primary sources of protein are beans and meat, with one of the most regionally important being the peanut, called *l'arachide* or *le cacahuète* in French. Cowpeas (black-eyed peas), yambeans, and peanuts are important varieties of legumes in Guinea. Peanut butter is the key ingredient in a peanut butter–based sauce known as *maffe tegga* in Fulani. Beef, chicken, and goat and bush meat are sold in the market and eaten regularly by Guineans. Bush meat is wild game, usually from forested areas, and can include everything from snakes and rodents to wild pigs; it is an important and much-beloved addition to the Guinean table. Because Guinea is predominantly Muslim, most Guineans generally do not eat pork; however, bush pigs are a particular delicacy in the forest region. People tend to keep their own chickens in their yards; the breed tends to have tough flesh with a gamy flavor.

Seafood is an important part of Guinean cuisine. It may be purchased directly from a fishing boat on the coast and fried, grilled, or added to sauces, or it is consumed in dried, salted, or smoked forms by people living further inland where access to fresh seafood is limited or nonexistent due to a lack of refrigeration. Popular fish include tilapia, mackerel, black bass, and cod along with shrimp and crayfish. One very important seasoning that is a key flavoring in sauces is dried, ground shrimp or crayfish; it also appears across the Atlantic in the West African–influenced cuisine of northern Brazil.

Milk and milk products are important to the Guinean diet because the Fulani, one of the country's largest ethnic groups, are traditionally cattle herders. Newborns are generally given fresh milk while adults are more likely to eat products like butter, yogurt, buttermilk, and cream, usually eaten with grains. Sweetened buttermilk and thick cream are often eaten with steamed grains like millet and fonio.

Guineans drink coffee and tea throughout the day as well as soft drinks. Because Guinea is a Muslim country, alcohol is prohibited just about everywhere except in the forest region, which is predominantly Christian and animist. There, people may drink beer and locally produced palm wine.

Cooking

Ingredients and cooking techniques are similar throughout West Africa. Foods are primarily boiled, fried, roasted, or grilled and are generally made from scratch, as Guinea does not have a developed food-processing industry. Few prepared ingredients are available. Those that are include smoked, salted, or dried fish and meat; dried herbs; various flours; sugar; condensed milk; tea; and instant coffee. Most food preparation takes place outdoors over a fire or in a separate building adjacent to a family's living area. Most households don't have stoves or ovens. Families generally do not have cooks—the wives and daughters in a family prepare meals. In polygamous households, women may share cooking and other household duties. Spices and grains are crushed or ground in mortars and pestles; a household may have several in various sizes designated for specific purposes.

Typical Meals

Guineans typically eat from a communal bowl with spoons, exclusively with the right hand, because the left one is reserved for personal hygiene. Guineans, rich and poor, are very hospitable and welcome guests with food as budgets permit. Anyone visiting a family at or around mealtimes will be invited to

A woman cooks at a market in Gueckedou, Guinea. Gueckedou is a town in the south of Guinea, near the border with Sierra Leone. It has a large weekly market that attracts many traders, including those from across the border. (Travel Ink | Getty Images)

sit down and eat, and as a sign of hospitality they may also be given a kola nut to chew. It is polite for guests to leave a bit of food on their plates to show gratitude and satisfaction with the meal that has been provided.

While Guinea boasts a great deal of ethnic diversity, food and cooking are very similar among the groups, with the exception of flavor profiles. Of the three major ethnic groups, the Fulani tend to prefer less spicy dishes and may provide chili sauce on the side to add to taste. The food of the Malinké and the Susu is generally very spicy with chilies added directly to a particular dish while cooking. A traditional Susu dish is *achecké,* grated, fried cassava, which is usually used as a bed for grilled fish or meat, often served with chopped onions and tomatoes. A dessertlike porridge of steamed fonio is eaten with thick, sweetened buttermilk, much like the Senegalese dish *sow,* while fresh corn kernels are

sometimes eaten in bowls of fresh milk. The dairy in these dishes shows the influence of the cattle-herding Fulani.

Eating Out

There are plenty of restaurants in cities and towns throughout Guinea; however, dining in restaurants is not a common practice. At local *cookhouses,* people can find traditional sauces served with rice or cassava. One entrée commonly featured on the menus of these establishments is *riz gras,* a hearty dish of cooked rice fried in oil and piled with vegetables like carrots, cabbage, and squash. The dish is common throughout Senegal, Burkina Faso, Benin, and Guinea. It can sometimes contain meat and be cooked with tomato paste. There are also many Lebanese restaurants in larger cities and towns, where people can get Lebanese specialties.

Special Occasions

Guineans celebrate religious holidays according to their faith, although recently Muslims have begun to hold small Christmas celebrations. Tabaski, the Islamic holiday Eid al-Adha (known in English as the Festival of Sacrifice), is an important celebration for Muslims throughout the country. For this holiday in Guinea, livestock, usually a goat or a cow, is slaughtered for a feast that is shared among community members, particularly the poor. Milestones in life, like engagements, births, weddings, and funerals, are celebrated with parties, feasts, and music among family and friends.

Diet and Health

The Guinean diet is a healthy one with plenty of fresh fruit, seafood, and healthy palm oil. Minimal food processing and essentially no access to fast food have limited many diseases related to the overconsumption of highly processed, unhealthy foods. However, years of sporadic armed conflict along with governmental neglect and corruption have exacerbated poverty and accelerated the deterioration of the country's already-fragile infrastructure. Poverty has also caused ethnic tensions, while explosive population growth coupled with underdevelopment of the country's agricultural production systems has made malnutrition a real issue in Guinea, contributing to the problem of limited access to food even though a high percentage of the population works in the agricultural sector.

Overcrowding of the few hospitals and medical centers and a lack of doctors make treatment difficult even with large numbers of nongovernmental organizations running programs that target health. Only about half of all Guineans have access to clean water, and fewer than 20 percent have access to adequate sanitation. Poverty and corruption make maintaining adequate health programs a difficult task.

Rachel Finn

Further Reading

Celtnet Recipes. http://www.celtnet.org.uk/recipes/west-africa.php.

Ember, Melvin, and Carol R. Ember. "Guinea." In *Countries and Their Cultures,* 2:942–51. New York: MacMillan Reference USA, 2001.

Gibbon, Ed. The Congo Cookbook. http://www.congocookbook.com/.

Harris, Jessica. *The Africa Cookbook: Tastes of a Continent.* New York: Simon and Schuster, 1998.

Jackson, Elizabeth. African Chop. http://www.africanchop.com/.

Osseo-Asare, Fran. Betumi African Cuisine. http://www.betumi.com/.

Osseo-Asare, Fran. *Food Culture in Sub-Saharan Africa.* Westport, CT: Greenwood Press, 2005.

Smith, Ifeyironwa Francisca. *The Case for Indigenous West African Food Culture.* BREDA Series, no. 9. Dakar, Senegal: United Nations Educational, Scientific and Cultural Organization-Regional Bureau for Education in Africa, 1995.

Kenya

Overview

Kenya straddles the equator in East Africa, bordered on land by Ethiopia, Somalia, Sudan, Uganda, and Tanzania and by bodies of water: the Indian Ocean in the east, Lake Victoria to the west, and Lake Turkana to the north. A bit smaller than Texas, Kenya has several, varied types of terrain: central highlands that are relatively cool and well watered; Mount Kenya, the second-highest mountain in Africa; hot and arid lands in the east, north, and northeast; and in the west the Great Rift Valley, through which many migrants and invaders have passed. Another conduit of invasions and influences—Islam and Christianity, for example—is the hot, wet, tropical Indian Ocean coastal strip and adjacent islands.

Kenyans are renowned for their hospitality, kindness, and industriousness. Kenya has long been a popular tourist destination for game-viewing safaris and beautiful Indian Ocean beaches. Nairobi, the cosmopolitan capital, has served for years as the regional headquarters of organizations like the *New York Times,* the World Bank, and United Nations agencies. Kenya is a center of scientific interest on many fronts, including important archaeological sites such as Koobi Fora, where fossils of *Homo habilis,* possibly the first of the genus *Homo,* were found.

In Africa the population is drawn to the cities for economic reasons, yet 75 percent of the Kenyan population is still agricultural (2003 estimate). Literacy is upwards of 85 percent. However, there is an unemployment rate of 40 percent (2008 estimate), and fully 50 percent of the population is below the poverty line (2000 estimate).

Swahili (called Kiswahili when one is speaking the language) and English are both official languages. Each ethnic or cultural group also has its own language—indeed, much of the categorization into groups is done on a linguistic basis. The wide variety of Kenyan languages, coming as they do from an array of unrelated language families, speaks volumes about the numerous migrations that brought people to what would later be called Kenya.

Swahili is a much-misunderstood language. A simplified, stripped-down pidgin version became the lingua franca—a language of intergroup communication—when East African groups had no other common trading language. This pidgin variety gets little respect as it is inelegant and able to discuss only commerce and work, with limited grammar and vocabulary: It is no one's native language. This pidgin should not be confused with the "real" Swahili language, spoken as the native language of the Swahili people who live on the Indian Ocean coast, which is grammatically very complex and subtle. Swahili has had a rich, mostly poetic literature for several centuries; the language was first written in Arabic script, but for the past 100 years has been written almost entirely in the Roman alphabet.

The people of Kenya are diverse: Depending on the criteria used, there are some 40 to 70 different African linguistic or cultural groups, whom anthropologists have traditionally categorized as either hunter-gatherers, pastoralists, or agriculturalists. Since populations of hunter-gatherers have unfortunately been greatly reduced over the course of the last century, the focus will be on the other two groups in the discussion of traditional foods. These belong to the Bantu, Nilotic, Nilo-Hamitic, and Cushitic language groups.

Kenya's population in 2009 was almost 34 million, about 3 million of whom lived in the sprawling capital, Nairobi. The approximate breakdown of ethnic groups is Kikuyu, 22 percent; Luhya, 14 percent; Luo, 13 percent; Kalenjin, 12 percent; Kamba, 11 percent; Kisii, 6 percent; Meru, 6 percent; other African (Swahili, Maasai, Samburu, Gabbra, Okiek, and many more), 15 percent; and non-African (Asian, European, and Arab), 1 percent.

Kenya's culinary situation has come about from an amalgam of influences. The British, Kenya's colonial rulers for most of the 20th century, are important from a culinary standpoint. They tried to recreate English customs, dining rituals, and food anywhere they lived in the world. Colonial-age cookbooks attest to extensive experimentation with recreating their dishes using local ingredients—with widely differing degrees of success. British food is still popular in Kenya. Fish and chips, pasties, full English breakfasts, cheddar cheese, beef Wellington, and more can still be found.

Also of great importance are the people of the Indian subcontinent, referred to in East Africa as Asians. The effect of Indian cuisine on the food of East Africa cannot be overstated. The most popular gravy or sauce is curry; the national snack is the samosa; the favorite bread is a chapati; the most festive rice dish is *biryani,* showing pan-Islamic origins as well. Some of this is due to the influence of the British, too. The British Empire (the Raj) produced a pan-Raj set of standards, language, and, to a degree, food. Additionally there is Arab—or at least Muslim diaspora—influence, through Swahili food, and Italian influence, through the global ubiquity of pizza and a continually healthy number of Italian tourists, and also an influence of Somalis. Ethnic Somalis occupy a portion of northeastern Kenya that was previously part of the Italian colony of Somalia, which was taken from the Italians after World War II.

🍽 Food Culture Snapshot

Grace and Joseph Matheka, a mechanic, live on a farm in the rural Mua Hills outside of Machakos, the capital of Eastern Province, in a semiarid area. Grace rises before dawn, and she and her nine-year-old daughter, Rose, take their jerrycans and walk a mile to a stream where they draw water and then, using tumplines on their foreheads, carry the heavy jerrycans back to their homestead. They make a simple breakfast of tea for Joseph and the seven-year-old son, Wambua, who enjoy it with some *mandazi* (fried donuts) or leftover food from last night's dinner. The main meal of the day is the evening meal, which they have around 8 P.M. when Joseph returns.

To celebrate today's public holiday, the family will have a special dinner; Grace has had Wambua chase down one of their chickens that has stopped laying eggs. She cuts off its head, lets the blood drain off, plucks it, cuts it open, and cleans the carcass. She retains the liver and gizzard and gives the rest to the dogs that are quietly seated a yard from her watching with anticipation. Grace cooks a large pot of *ugali* (cornmeal porridge). To accompany it she makes *sukuma wiki* (kale) and a stew of the chicken, which she flavors with *dania* (cilantro leaves) and a packet of *bizari* (curry powder). They have grown the corn and paid the shop owner down the road to grind it into

Bananas growing wild in Kenya. (iStockPhoto)

meal with his gasoline-powered grinder. Grace grows her own greens and onions. She goes the six miles into Machakos town on market days with her cowife Maria, who lives in the house down the hill from her, and sells her extra produce, using some of the cash to buy sugar and tea.

With the meal the children usually drink water and the adults tea, but sometimes Joseph will buy Fanta for Grace and the children and three Tusker beers for himself. Grace sends Rose out to her father with a basin of cold water so that he can wash his hands before he starts on his dinner, which Grace brings to him in his favorite chair where he is listening to the evening news on BBC World Service. Joseph calls out for Rose to bring him some more water and soap to clean his fingers. Joseph insists that eating ugali with a spoon makes it tasteless and prefers the common method of eating with his hand. Afterward, he goes to a neighbor's house where the wife brews and sells *uki* (honey wine), and a group of men come to sit and talk for a couple of hours, drinking the illegal uki and smoking Sportsman, Rooster, and Embassy cigarettes, until it is time for them to return home.

Major Foodstuffs

The staple corn—the main source of calories for most Kenyans—as well as the tomato was originally from the Americas, brought to Africa. The rice in East Africa is *sativa*. Asian rice came via migrants from the Indonesian region through Madagascar perhaps 1,200 years ago. Other important carbohydrate staples of Kenyans, if not grains, are cassava (also called manioc or yucca), sweet potatoes, and potatoes, all three foods from the Americas.

Kenyans grow many types of bananas, both sweet and cooking types, as well as mangoes, passion fruit, pineapples, papayas, avocados, many types of legumes (including cowpeas, black beans, and kidney beans), millet, rice, cassava (manioc/tapioca), onions, garlic, and coriander. Fishing is an important food source as well as an export earner. Other main crops are wheat and dairy products. Kenya's colonial past resulted in a cheese-making tradition not shared by most other African countries. It produces, for example, superb Camembert.

Unlike the Western conception of what is the essence of a meal, usually a protein, Kenyans consider the grain (ugali, rice, or chapati) to be the main food of the meal, and the meat, fish, vegetable, or a stew of these to be the *kitoweo,* or accompaniment. Upcountry (away from the Swahili coast), the word *mboga,* literally "vegetable," but also "cabbage" (as the prototypical upcountry vegetable) or "pumpkin," is used in the same undifferentiated sense as kitoweo, as "something to accompany the main starch," even if the mboga be meat.

Important starches in addition to maize, rice, and breads are *viazi* (potatoes), *matoke* (plantain), and *muhogo* (manioc). Other main vegetables are *biringani* (eggplant), *saladi* (lettuce), *pilipili hoho* (hot peppers), *pilipili baridi* (sweet peppers), *ukwaju* (tamarind), *nyanya* (tomatoes), *karoti* (carrots), *kabichi* (cabbage), sukuma wiki (kale or collards), *mchicha* (spinach), *parachichi* (avocado), *vitunguu* (onions), and *vitunguu saumu* (garlic). Fruits (*matunda*) are varied and of high quality: *paipai* (papaya), *ndizi* (bananas), *tende* (dates), *pasheni* (passion fruit), *stafeli* (soursop), *madanzi* (grapefruit), *machungwa* (oranges), *mananasi* (pineapple), *ndimu* (limes), *dafu* (unripe coconut, for drinking), and *nazi* (ripe coconut, used for *tui,* or coconut cream). Also grown is *miwa* (sugarcane).

Mchuzi is the general word for sauce or gravy and sometimes, by extension, soup. *Supu* means only soup, a popular breakfast on the Indian Ocean coast (and many other places in the world). A common menu item in Mombasa restaurants is "special morning soup," usually made with goat. Mchuzi can also mean curry (sometimes called *kari*). Curries, for example, of *kuku* (chicken), *ng'ombe* (beef), *kima* (ground meat), *kofta* (meatballs), or *samaki* (fish), are probably the most popular type of mchuzi. *Masala,* or *mchuzi mzito* ("heavy mchuzi"), is masala, which in Kenya differs from curry most obviously in being heavier and drier. *Bizari* is the general term for curry powder, and premixed packets can be bought in any shop. A popular brand is Mchuzi Mix. However, at least on the coast, one can buy whole or ground spices, notably *pilipili manga* (black pepper; literally, "pepper of Oman"), *tangawizi* (ginger), *iliki* (cardamom), *jira* (cumin), *mdalasini* (cinnamon), *manjano* (turmeric), and *karafuu* (cloves). (The punishment in neighboring Zanzibar for smuggling cloves, so important was the spice to the local economy, was death, well into modern times.) Salt is *chumvi*.

Popular meats are *nyama ya ng'ombe* (beef), *nyama ya ndama* (veal), *nyama ya mbuzi* (goat meat), *nyama ya kondoo* (lamb or mutton), *kuku* (chicken), and in some places *nyama ya ngamia* (camel meat). *Karanga* is a menu term for beef stew, and *ng'ombe* ("beef") is the menu term for a beef stew with less beef than karanga. *Nyama choma* is roast meat, and *mishkaki* is roasted skewered meat.

Muthokoi (a Kamba word) is dehulled maize, usually served with legumes like *kunde* (cowpeas). Other important legumes are *maharagwe* (kidney beans), *pojo* (green gram, or mung beans), *dengu* (lentils), *njegere* (chickpeas), and *mbaazi* (pigeon peas). Popular nuts are *njugu karanga* (peanuts), much used in cooking, and *korosho* (cashews). The latter plant also bears the tart and refreshing fruit called *kanju* or *bibo,* the cashew apple.

Some Kenyans do not eat fish or seafood of any kind, though some groups that traditionally did not have now started eating these. Coastal people have always eaten from the sea. Popular foods from the Indian Ocean are *pweza* (octopus), *ngisi* (cuttlefish or squid), *kole kole* (pompano), *changu* (emperor's glory snapper), *tafi* (rabbit fish), *mkesi* (mullet), *tewa* (grouper), *papa* (shark), and *nguru* (kingfish), as well as *ng'onda* (semidried fermented fish). *Kamba* means either shrimp or lobster (if necessary, one distinguishes between *kamba mdogo,* "little kamba," for shrimp and *kamba mkubwa,* "big kamba," for lobster). Swahilis and other coastals eat shrimp, but, though called by the same name as shrimp, lobster is not eaten. Swahilis also do not eat *kaa* (crab) or *chaza* (oysters), all of which are, however, enjoyed by many *wageni,* the Swahili word

Locals buying fish on the beach in Mombassa, Kenya. (iStockPhoto)

for visitors, strangers, and guests. Tilapia, a fish, is raised in ponds and, like other freshwater fish, is taken from the inland lakes.

Beverages

Kenyan tea (*chai*) and coffee (*kahawa*) are famous and shipped worldwide. Kenya is now the third-largest global producer of tea, after China and India. Tea is the cornerstone of much Kenyan hospitality in the home and a common beverage in a restaurant. The normal chai one orders in a restaurant is made from tea leaves boiled with milk and sugar, sometimes with some spices like cardamom added. (To get black tea one orders *chai kavu,* literally "dry tea," and asking for *chai ya china,* literally "Chinese tea," will obtain a larger proportion of milk to water.) Also popular are bottled soda drinks such as Coke and Orange Fanta. Coca-Cola is an important and powerful industry. Soda can be found in the most rural, out-of-the-way places but is relatively expensive for much of the population, as is bottled beer. Kenya Breweries makes several varieties of pilsner-type beer (*bia*) much like those made worldwide. It can survive the long journey to the hinterlands that an unpasteurized beer never could. Also, some home brews are popular in Kenya, but they are technically illegal. Uki, *busaa,* and *muratina* are various (now-illegal) local brews, *cha'ngaa* is moonshine (illegal alcoholic spirits like gin or whiskey), and *mukoma* is tapped palm sap allowed to ferment into alcoholic palm wine. *Pombe* and *tembo* are the terms for alcoholic beverages in general. *Tembo* is also a word for elephant, and this play on words has resulted in Tusker (Elephant) brand beer (Tembo brand tembo). In a bar one orders bia either *baridi* (cold) or *moto* (hot, that is, room temperature). Many Kenyans never drink cold beverages, including soda.

Kenyan coffee is well known, though in the United States one often sees only "peaberry." A great deal of less expensive robusta (as opposed to arabica) coffee is grown and processed into instant coffee. A common restaurant drink is *kahawa maziwa* or *kofi,* instant coffee in hot milk. *Maji tamu,* literally "sweet fluid," is the term for fruit juice, of which there are *maji ya machungwa* (orange juice), *maji ya ndimu* (lime juice or lemonade), *maji ya nanasi* (pineapple juice), and *maji ya pasheni* (passion fruit juice). These are found fresh but often tinned. In addition, *maziwa* (milk) is also a popular beverage, most likely to be drunk in milk tea. Fermented foods are important and include locally fermented milk, *maziwa lala* (literally, "milk sleep"), beer, honey wine (uki), *uji* porridge (made from millet, corn, and/or sorghum flours), and distilled spirits, as well as European-style industrially produced yogurt, pilsner beer, spirits, and wine.

Cooking

In more traditional houses, food is cooked on a three-stone (*jiko*) hearth, in aluminum cooking pots with rims (*sufuria*) on a fire of wood or charcoal. The family might use an "improved jiko," an insulated sheet metal cooker that will use less fuel (but also throws off less heat into the living space). It is the women and children's job to supply water, and this may be a difficult task requiring hours of walking to a water source and back carrying heavy containers of water. Similarly firewood is the women's purview. More urban or middle-class families will use kerosene or gas cookers.

In cooking dania is the typical flavoring. In English the seed is called coriander and the leaves cilantro. Especially upcountry (away from the Swahili coast), dania leaves are often the only spice or herb used.

Food and drink in Africa are changing rapidly. Many traditional foods are disappearing because of change from ecological degradation, population pressure, westernized tastes, and other agricultural and cultural change. One such food, actually a drink, is uki (pronounced *oo-key*), honey wine made by the Kamba (Akamba in their language) people of Kenya. Its production and consumption were in the past subject to clearly defined rules that wove uki into the dense symbol structure of a highly organized community. The beverage still has much traditional meaning, but uki is on the wane. As an emblem of the old, tribal order, uki's decline was probably inevitable given the drastic upheavals of traditional society and the eagerness of young people worldwide for the new, the modern, the Western. But uki is a case where the demise of a traditional foodway was greatly expedited by the government, specifically, the hunger of a nation-state for tax revenue. Uki is hard to tax because its production is too hard to control. Beer and whiskey produced industrially are much more straightforward to tax.

In the past, pastoralists eschewed cultivated food and relied on food from their herds: milk, meat, and blood. Meat but especially milk, fresh or as a fermented product, provided the most nutrients and calories, with some essential nutrients provided by small additions of blood taken from live animals with a special arrow with a quite shallow half-moon arrowhead. This was shot at point-blank range into the vein of an animal and caused a shallow cut through which blood was collected in a gourd.

Settlement schemes, national borders, overgrazing, lack of water, encroachment on territory, and other influences have undercut the traditional culinary reliance on the herds and their milk. In the past, during famine Samburu would turn more to blood and to wild fruit. Nowadays, Samburu rely on store-bought food—cereals such as corn (or the more citified rice), beans, tea, and sugar. These they refer to as "gray food," which is cooked and eaten by the family domestic unit together. Morality, social distance, discipline, and respect were in the past bound up in separate eating. Milk could be taken at any time and not in a group—except a *moran* warrior's obligation to eat with an age-mate (another moran). Meat strongly showed appropriate separateness

Typical Meals

The prototypical Kenyan meal—and here Kenya is similar to much of the world—consists of a grain and a sauce. For many Kenyans the grain is rice, or wheat flatbreads, but, most commonly, a thick, stiff porridge of cornmeal (maize), served with a sauce of greens like collards or kale with the addition of onion and tomato and, if possible, fat and meat.

Sukuma Wiki

This is a popular and inexpensive staple dish of greens to accompany ugali, chapati, or another starch. It is made from any type of collards, kale, spinach, turnip leaves, or other edible greens.

One can read on many Web sites that *sukuma wiki* means "push the week," the idea being that this poor person's dish of greens can get one through the week. *Sukuma* does mean "push" and *wiki* does mean "week," but that fanciful origin is unlikely, among other reasons because pay is not weekly but monthly in Kenya—indeed, the term *mwisho wa mwezi* (end of the month) is a common phrase to explain why one is *waya* (broke). More likely is that *sukuma wiki* is close to the name for greens in some other language—there are over 40 languages in Kenya—and when Swahili speakers heard the word it sounded like *sukuma* and *wiki* to them. Whatever the history, it is a nutritious, inexpensive, and quite tasty dish.

1–2 lb greens
2 tbsp cooking oil or shortening
1 onion, sliced
1 hot chili, sliced (optional)
1 tomato or 2 tbsp tomato paste (optional)
1 tbsp curry powder or other seasoning powder (optional)
1 c any type of meat, raw or cooked, chopped (optional)
Salt

Wash a large bunch of greens well. Holding the cleaned bunch firmly in one hand on a cutting board, cut thin (½-inch) slices through the greens to produce shreds.

Sauté onion in oil till translucent. Add chili if using, and stir for a minute. Add meat (if raw), if using. Add tomato and curry, if using. Mix well and allow to heat through. Add greens, and mix well. Add meat (if already cooked), if using. If the mixture is dry and threatens to burn, add a half cup water. Cover and simmer for a few minutes till greens are tender. This time will vary considerably with the toughness of the greens used. Salt if necessary. Serve with ugali, chapati, bread, or rice.

Ugali, cornmeal (maize) porridge cooked till stiff, is the most common daily food. Typically a diner breaks off a piece, dimples it with a thumb, and uses it to scoop up the accompaniment of sauce, greens, or meat. On the Indian Ocean coast this corn porridge is called *sima* and *bodo,* cooked not as stiff as ugali but used essentially the same way for eating. Muslim coastal people and many others use only the right hand for eating. It is considered good form to use only the fingertips, though a very common technique is to roll the ugali or sima (or rice or other grain) using one's fingers and palm to form a ball (*kitonge*). *Wali* is (cooked) rice. Uncooked husked rice is *mchele,* while the rice plant and unhusked rice are called *mpunga*.

Eating Out

In cosmopolitan Nairobi there are many different types of restaurants. A standout among Nairobi restaurants has for decades been the superb French restaurant Alan Bobbé's Bistro. Two other popular restaurant cuisines are Italian and Indian. Nairobi has many superb Indian restaurants. The Carnivore is a well-known all-you-can-eat meat restaurant and

Ugali, a cornmeal (maize) porridge, cooked till stiff, is the most common daily food in Kenya. Here, it is served with sukuma, or kale. (iStockPhoto)

reflects the esteem in which Kenyans hold nyama choma, or roast meat. Their original logo was a man swallowing a whole live cow. The Carnivore's format appears to have come from the Churrascaria, a Brazilian cowboy restaurant. Format aside, the Carnivore caters to an important Kenyan tradition: A true feast involves eating quantities of meat, a highly desired food and a mark of status, sharing, and respect. Nyama choma, often washed down with beer or a local brew, is perhaps the most popular form of this. Many Kenyans are essentially vegetarian but not by choice. The economic situation of the vast majority—recall that half of Kenya is below the poverty line—places meat virtually out of their reach but makes it no less desirable. The Carnivore opened in 1980, to, as their ads say, "instant success." Indeed it is simply the most famous and upscale of the many nyama choma centers around the country.

The popular Nairobi Java House coffee shops provide a different angle on globalization. Their menu is indistinguishable—not virtually but literally indistinguishable—from that of similar coffee shop lunch places in any downtown in North America. The coffees on offer are house coffee, espresso, americano, macchiato, café au lait, cappuccino, café latté, mocha, and Malindi macchiato. The breakfast selections include cinnamon rolls, chocolate croissants, and Danish pastries; bagels toasted with cream cheese; guacamole and salsa; home fries; and a Denver omelet with ham, cheese, tomato, onion, and green chili. This is not a foreign food restaurant, as is a local Chinese or even an Ethiopian restaurant; it simply an urban Kenyan coffee shop.

An interesting contrast with the more upscale and middle-class restaurants is provided by local street foods sold in kiosks and other street-food outlets in lower-income neighborhoods in greater Nairobi. Few foods overlap with the upscale foods. Among cereals are chapati, the panfried unleavened bread made from wheat; mandazi, deep-fried, leavened buns like doughnuts made from wheat; *mahindi chemsha,* boiled corn on the cob; *mahindi choma,* corn on the cob grilled over charcoal; ugali; uji, a fermented porridge made from cereal flours; and *biskuti,* or cookies. Animal products include nyama (roasted, fried, or stewed meat) and samaki (fish), usually deep-fried. Mixed dishes are, for example, *githeri* (a Kikuyu word), made from a mixture of maize and beans. In street kiosks, tea is common as well as *irio* or *mokimo,* a mix of corn, potatoes, greens (such as kale, collards, or spinach), and sometimes beans, mashed together. This is served in almost all urban areas to go along with nyama choma. Also popular are samosas or *sambusas,* Indian-derived deep-fried triangular meat or vegetable patties with a pastry crust. On the coast they are served with lime, and diners often bite off a corner of the crust and squeeze the lime into the filling inside.

Special Occasions

Many Kenyans celebrate Christmas, and it is a period of travel and gathering of families in the ancestral home areas. Other important celebrations include naming ceremonies for children and weddings, and all have special food traditions attached. Food plays a central role in the important Muslim month of Ramadan. Devout Muslims fast during daylight hours. They are forbidden to eat food, chew *miraa* (a stimulant leaf, known elsewhere as khat), smoke cigarettes, or drink water. People rise before the morning prayer to eat a breakfast to sustain them throughout the day of fasting. The evening call to prayer signals each day that the fast is over. Restaurants in largely Muslim areas are closed during the day, as are many businesses. A special set of recipes are made and eaten at home during Ramadan. Eid al-Fitr is a festive holiday that ends the month.

Diet and Health

There are severe nutrition problems for much of the nation, made worse by the fact that 50 percent of the population is below the poverty line (2000 estimate). About 80 percent of Kenyan land gets very little rain. Less than 20 percent of the land is good for agriculture, and this 20 percent feeds 80 percent of the population. This land is overused and is being degraded. Kenya's food supply is limited, and

a third of the country is undernourished. Things are getting better but only slowly. Most people get their calories each day from cereals, sugar, and vegetable oil, but the availability of fruit, vegetables, and milk is increasing.

Young children are often malnourished. Although universal breast-feeding helps greatly, it is often mixed with nonbeneficial practices such as bottle-feeding, which are made more damaging by poverty. The Food and Agriculture Organization has concluded that long-term strategies are needed such as putting additives in common food to attempt to ensure that vitamins and other micronutrients get in the diet, promoting the consumption of more diverse foods such as fruit and vegetables, and in general educating the population about good nutrition.

Robert A. Leonard

Further Reading

Africa Safari Kenya. http://www.africanmeccasafaris.com/kenya/nairobi/excursions/carnivore.asp.

Burckhardt, Ann L. *The People of Africa and Their Food.* Mankato, MN: Capstone Press, 1996.

DeWitt, Dave, Melissa T. Stock, and Mary Jane Wilan. *Flavors of Africa Cookbook: Spicy African Cooking—from Indigenous Recipes to Those Influenced by Asian and European Settlers.* Rocklin, CA: Prima, 1998.

Essuman, Kofi Manso. *Fermented Fish in Africa: A Study on Processing, Marketing and Consumption.* Rome, Italy: Food and Agriculture Organization, 1992.

Halford, Katie, and Fatma Shapi. *A Lamu Cook Book.* Lamu, Kenya: Lamu Society, 1981.

Holtzman, Jon. *Uncertain Tastes: Memory, Ambivalence, and the Politics of Eating in Samburu, Northern Kenya.* Berkeley: University of California Press, 2009.

International Starch Institute. "Cassava." http://www.starch.dk/isi/starch/cassava.asp.

Kairi, Wambui. *Food and Festivals: Kenya.* Austin, TX: Raintree Steck-Vaughn, 2000.

Leonard, Robert. "Meaning in Nonlinguistic Systems." In *Advances in Functional Linguistics: Columbia School beyond Its Origins,* edited by Radmilla Jovanoić Gorup, Joseph Davis, and Nancy Stern, 309–34. Amsterdam, the Netherlands: John Benjamins, 2006.

Leonard, Robert. "Notes on *Uki,* East African Honey Wine." In *Oxford Symposium on Food and Cookery 1994,* edited by Harlan Walker. London: Prospect Books, 1995.

Leonard, Robert, and Wendy Saliba. "Food and Ethnic Identity: Theory." In *The Asian Pacific American Heritage: A Companion to Literature and Arts,* edited by George Leonard. New York: Routledge, 1999.

Leonard, Robert, and Wendy Saliba. "Food, Drink, and Swahili Public Space." In *Oxford Symposium on Food and Cookery 1991,* edited by Harlan Walker. London: Prospect Books, 1992.

Leonard, Robert, and Wendy Saliba. "Southeast Asian Food: The Durian and Beyond." In *The Asian Pacific American Heritage: A Companion to Literature and Arts,* edited by George Leonard. New York: Routledge, 1999.

Montgomery, Bertha Vining, and Constance Nabwire. *Cooking the African Way.* Minneapolis, MN: Lerner, 1988.

Mwangi, A. M., A. P. den Hartog, R.K.N. Mwadime, W. A. van Staveren, and D.W.J. Foeken. "Do Street Food Vendors Sell a Sufficient Variety of Foods for a Healthful Diet? The Case of Nairobi." *Food and Nutrition Bulletin* 23, No. 1 (2002): 48–56.

Nairobi Java House. http://www.nairobijavahouse.com/html/mamanginamenu2.html.

"Nutrition Country Profile, Republic of Kenya." ftp://ftp.fao.org/es/esn/nutrition/ncp/ken.pdf.

Oniang'o, Ruth K., and Asenath J. Sigot. *Complete Kenya Cookery.* London: Edward Arnold, 1987.

Osseo-Asare, Fran. *Food Culture in Sub-Saharan Africa.* Westport, CT: Greenwood Press, 2005.

Samuelsson, Marcus. *The Soul of a New Cuisine: A Discovery of the Foods and Flavors of Africa.* Hoboken, NJ: John Wiley & Sons, 2006.

Wandera, A.B.N. *Kenya Traditional Dishes.* Nairobi, Kenya: Nairobi Club-Soroptimist International, 1983.

Liberia

Overview

The Republic of Liberia lies in the heart of West Africa, bordered by Sierra Leone, Guinea, and Côte d'Ivoire. It and neighboring Sierra Leone are the only two countries created as a destination of resettlement for formerly enslaved Africans repatriated to the continent from the United States and the Caribbean. With a 360-mile coastline stretching along the Atlantic Ocean, the country has a population of about 3,500,000 people. The country is extremely hot and wet, with its capital Monrovia holding the title of wettest capital city in West Africa along with Freetown, the capital of Sierra Leone. Like the rest of West Africa, the dry winter season is signaled by the harmattan, the cool, dry, dusty wind that blows south from the Sahara desert and provides a bit of relief from West Africa's heat and humidity. In 2007, the citizens of Liberia elected the continent's first female president, Ellen Johnson-Sirleaf.

Liberia's recent history is one of an almost-continuous 20-year civil war among indigenous groups and descendants of freed formerly enslaved people of African descent from the United States, who refer to themselves as Americo-Liberians. In 1822, the American Colonization Society (ACS), a group of whites dedicated to returning black people (freedmen and escaped slaves) to Africa, sponsored the first group to establish a resettlement colony for free African Americans, and by 1847, the Republic of Liberia was born. Today, the descendants of this group still live in the country as a small but powerful minority among the 15 different ethnic groups in the country, which include the Grebo, Mende, Gola, Kru, Krahn, Mandingo, Bassa, Kpelle, Loma, and Vai. The country's history has led to difficult and tragic interactions among the Americo-Liberians and indigenous groups, most notably civil war that lasted throughout the 1990s. The official language is English, but a creolized form of English is the primary form of communication among people who speak more than 20 different indigenous languages throughout the country.

Liberia is Christian, but many people also practice various forms of indigenous religion. Islam accounts for the beliefs of the remainder of the population. Liberia was never colonized by European powers, but due to its unique history it has a close connection to the United States and has had positive diplomatic relations with the U.S. government for most of its history.

🍽 Food Culture Snapshot

Matina Kabba makes trips to Monrovia's Duala market almost daily for the provisions she needs to prepare meals for herself and her children. Matina is a seamstress and a single mother of two children; her husband was killed during the last of the civil conflicts, which ended in 2007. She is of mixed Americo-Liberian and Grebo heritage. Like most Liberians, Matina and her family usually eat only two full meals a day, but in the Americo-Liberian tradition, they sometimes eat a full breakfast of bacon and eggs with a cup of tea or coffee. More frequently, however, she and her family begin the day with a light meal of tea and bread or fresh fruits like pineapple, bananas, or mangoes that Matina purchases at the market.

An African woman beating cassava root in a mortar in Liberia, West Africa. (iStockPhoto)

Because most dishes contain palm oil or palm butter, which is prepared from palm fruit, Matina purchases both in bulk at the market and prepares various stews and sauces with them. A very simple lunch or dinner dish consists of red palm oil and rice, okra, chilies, and smoked fish. To prepare other dishes, Matina will purchase cassava and cassava flour, to prepare *dumboy* or *fufu,* respectively. Dumboy is a starchy dish of boiled fresh cassava root pounded until soft and pliable and eaten with various soups, while cassava fufu is generally made with cassava flour. Dumboy can also be made from plantains and breadfruit. Plantains can be eaten ripe or unripe; in either state, they are usually fried as snacks or accompaniments to a main meal. Unripe plantains have green skins, while ripe plantains are sweet and have skins that range from yellow to black; both are inedible raw.

Matina will stock up on the dried and smoked fish used to flavor the soups and stews that so frequently grace her table. Preserved ingredients are usually purchased in bulk while fresh ingredients such as meats, fruits, vegetables, and other perishables are purchased the day that they are used due to a lack of refrigeration.

Major Foodstuffs

The staples of the Liberian diet are palm oil, rice, cassava, and fish or meat; these ingredients are usually cooked together in various combinations. Almost 70 percent of the population is employed in the agricultural sector, in which cassava and rice are the major cash crops. Liberia also produces a number of other important food crops such as cacao, coffee, sugarcane, palm oil, and bananas.

Palm oil and palm butter are important foods that are both culturally and nutritionally significant in Liberia and throughout West Africa. Palm oil is a deep red-orange color with a high percentage of beta-carotene. It is one of the few vegetable oils with a high percentage of saturated fat—about 44 percent. Palm oil is used for frying, flavoring, and coloring foods and is also an important ingredient in Brazilian cooking, having traveled with captured Africans to the Americas during the transatlantic slave trade. The oil remains semisolid in more temperate climates because of its high level of saturated fat. Palm butter is prepared by soaking the pulp of palm nuts, then cooking the liquid extracted from them. It is used as the main ingredient in palm butter soup or is simply eaten with rice or cooked with leafy greens. Burnt or boiled palm oil loses its red-orange color and much of its nutritional value but is also an important cooking oil.

Liberians favor leafy greens in their cooking; they are generally referred to as "leaves." Sweet potato and cassava leaves are used most often in the preparation of soups and stews, better known as sauces. *Palava sauce* is made from a puree of slippery *plato* leaves, also known as bitterleaf; the leaves have a mucilaginous texture much like okra. Collard greens and spinach are also frequently eaten. All greens may be boiled, finely chopped or pureed and stewed with meat, or fried. Other vegetables such as bitter balls (eggplant); *pumkin,* which is similar in flavor and texture to butternut squash; cucumbers; mushrooms; and okra are prepared in various ways and provide great variety and essential nutrients in the Liberian diet.

Rice is an essential element of any Liberian meal and is often eaten for breakfast, lunch, and dinner. While rice paddies do exist within the country, indigenous rice is rarely eaten. Instead, cheap Asian rice is imported and consumed. *Jollof rice* is a beloved rice dish with many variations; it usually contains chicken and shrimp with vegetables like peas, carrots, and corn cooked in a spicy tomato sauce. It is a bit like West Africa's version of fried rice. Rice is also ground into flour and used to make *rice bread,* which is a heavy and cakelike bread that also includes mashed ripe bananas or plantains. Starchy foods are valued in Liberian cuisine because they are filling and nutritious and cut the richness of dishes that are oily from the prodigious use of palm oil mixed with herbs, spices, and other flavorings like chilies, onions, and dried or smoked fish or shrimp. Native to tropical South America, sweet potatoes (*Ipomoea batatas*) made their way to the African continent during the transatlantic slave trade and are eaten and cultivated throughout the region as an important food source for animals and humans. The tubers can range in color from white to pink, purple, yellow, and the familiar orange.

In other parts of West Africa, yams (*Dioscorea* spp.) are favored, but in Liberia the sweet potatoes are preferred and are eaten boiled, roasted, or fried and also make their way into dishes reflective of strong connections to the cooking of the American South, such as sweet potato pie and sweet potato pone made from grated sweet potatoes, ginger, and burnt palm oil. Sweet potato leaves are finely chopped and then cooked with ground shrimp, meat or fish, palm oil, and chilies in a dish called potato-leaf sauce; cassava leaves are prepared similarly. Cassava is a secondary staple in Liberia; it can be fried in palm oil, roasted, mashed, or processed into flour. Roasted cassava is grilled or roasted and then eaten with palm butter.

Liberians favor dishes with meat and fish cooked together and tend to consume all parts of an animal.

Pig's feet, cow skin, and other viscera, collectively known as offal, are prized for the flavors and textures they bring to a dish. Typical of this style of preparation is *okra sauce,* a sauce that calls for pig's feet, chicken, beef, and dried fish in addition to chili peppers and fresh okra. Unlike in many countries throughout the region, pork is used to flavor sauces and is consumed frequently. Goat, chicken, and beef make frequent appearances in dishes, with goat soup being a dish prepared for very special occasions. Meats are boiled together with chilies, onions, and tomatoes for flavor, then left to simmer slowly in the resulting broth to develop the rich, intense flavors so typical of the cuisine. While most dishes do contain meat, it is often not considered the centerpiece of a meal but rather an essential flavoring component that may not be omitted. The heavy use of pork in Liberian cooking also reflects the influence of Americo-Liberians whose cookery is so closely tied to that of the American South. Pork can be the primary ingredient of a dish or used as a flavoring when it is smoked or salted.

Smoked and salted fish are used to flavor sauces and even consumed as the primary protein in dishes such as yam or cassava porridge, which is boiled yams or cassava cooked with onions, tomatoes, chilies, and fish until soft. For such purposes, cod is preferred, but salt cod on its own is the basis for a dish in which the cod is soaked, seasoned, fried, and then simmered in a chili-spiked tomato sauce. The long Atlantic coastline makes fresh seafood abundant and important to the Liberian diet, and fish, shrimp, crayfish, and other shellfish are eaten regularly, fried, grilled, and stewed in the ubiquitous sauces.

Peanuts (*groundpeas*) and peanut butter are important sources of protein and used in dishes such as groundnut soup. Pigeon peas and cowpeas, of which black-eyed peas are a well-known variety, are also stewed and eaten regularly. Kidney beans, a legume native to South America, are often mashed and used as soup thickeners. The beans were brought to Liberia during the slave trade.

A penchant for savory and sweet baked goods and desserts reflects the influence of southern U.S. food culture on Liberian cuisine. Rice bread, a

A Liberian boy balances his catch of fish on his head. (http://www.travel-images.com)

much-loved specialty, is but one cakelike bread that holds a place in the Liberian culinary repertoire. Cakes and pies are filled with all manner of fruits (e.g., pineapple, mango, pawpaw—of the American *Asiminia* spp.—or papaya) and, of course, sweet potatoes. *Liberian cake,* heavy, sweet, and studded with raisins, is another favorite. Shredded cassava and sweet potatoes are also transformed into cakes spiced with cinnamon and nutmeg; other sweets include stewed fruits like mango, pineapple, and pawpaw. Savory baked goods include cornbread, once again reflecting the roots of the repatriated former slaves who resettled among local indigenous groups.

Cooking

The most common cooking techniques in the Liberian kitchen are stewing, boiling, and frying. Preparing meals is labor-intensive because most things are made from scratch. Dishes like dumboy, fufu, and palm butter all require much pre-preparation. In general, soaking, pounding, peeling, boiling, drying, and crushing of basic ingredients are often the first steps to be taken before any actual cooking can be done. Few processed foods are available for use by the home cook, and when they are, the preference is for homemade.

Mortars and pestles are used to crush spices and pound tubers like cassava and yams to the correct consistency for dishes like dumboy and fufu. Most cooking is done outside over a fire or in a building adjacent to the main living area. Wealthier families may have cooks, but it is primarily the women and girls of a family who prepare meals.

Typical Meals

Throughout English-speaking West Africa, including Liberia, food is referred to as *chop. Chop* refers to food in general and to entrées of main meals, while *small chop* refers to snacks and smaller meals. Civil war crippled agricultural production during the 1990s, which changed typical eating habits throughout the country and made access to adequate nutrition difficult. Liberia is slowly recovering. Typically Liberians might eat two meals a day, usually lunch and dinner; however, wealth determines the number of meals a family might eat. Liberians eat many dishes with their hands. It is customary to wash hands well before meals and use only the right hand when eating, since the left hand is used for personal hygiene. A sauce with a starchy staple will be the focus of the main meal of the day, and if a second meal is taken, it will usually consist of leftovers. Rice, the country's main staple, might be eaten in some form or another for all meals, since few Liberians would consider a meal complete without it.

Breakfast might be fresh fruit or baked goods like coconut bread with tea or coffee or perhaps a bowl of rice eaten with milk and sugar. Lunch and dinner will consist of stewed sweet potato leaves with a bit of meat and tomato sauce spiced with chilies and served with rice, fufu, or dumboy. The average main meal in Liberia will be a spicy tomato-based stew or puree of leafy greens with meat, poultry, or offal, eaten with a cooked starchy dish.

Palm Butter Soup

Palm butter is a thick cream extracted from boiled, crushed palm fruits. In Liberia, people usually make it from scratch, but it is also commercially available. Palm butter soup, or palm butter stew as it is sometimes called, is a very simple dish once the palm butter has been prepared. It is a rich dish with a complex flavor that is most commonly prepared with a mix of seafood, just chicken, chicken and seafood, or chicken and beef.

2 28-oz cans palm nut cream

1 lb chicken pieces, cut small

1 c shrimp

1 c crabmeat

1 Scotch bonnet or habanero chili, finely chopped

1 medium onion, finely chopped

Salt and pepper

Fish stock (optional)

Season the chicken and shrimp with salt and pepper and set aside for 30 to 60 minutes. When the chicken is ready, place palm nut cream in a pot to melt. When the cream has melted, it will be rather thin. Add the chicken, onions, and chili and simmer over low heat until the chicken is done and sauce begins to thicken, about 25 minutes. Add shrimp, crabmeat, and all other ingredients and simmer 2 to 3 more minutes. If using fish stock, add to pot with seafood.

Small chop can be anything from a small fried sweet or savory fritter to roasted corn or pieces of fried cassava, yam, or plantain. Fresh fruit is frequently eaten as a snack along with freshly roasted peanuts or groundnuts. Cakes and stewed fruit are also considered small chop.

In Liberia changes in economic status and particularly the growth of white-collar employment in urban areas can affect mealtimes as men and women shop, prepare, and consume meals based on a much different daily schedule than in more rural areas, where most people are farmers. The physical demands of a particular job also determine the nature of mealtimes and food preparation in modern Liberia.

Eating Out

While there are restaurants and food stands throughout the country, there is not a strong tradition of eating out in Liberia. Purchasing small chop in markets or on the streets of cities, towns, and villages is a common practice.

Special Occasions

Food is always a central element of celebrations in Liberia. Aspects of Christian, traditional, and Islamic religious traditions blend with cultural elements of the various indigenous and Americo-Liberian groups to form a vibrant amalgam of culture that is uniquely Liberian. Independence Day, celebrated on July 26, marks the day of full independence from the United States with celebrations around the country. Christian, Muslim, and traditional religious holidays are celebrated with feasts, as are life's milestones such as marriages, births, and deaths. Liberians celebrate Thanksgiving on the first Thursday of November each year, as well as Flag Day and Armed Forces Day.

Diet and Health

Liberians eat a variety of meats, fresh fruits, and vegetables; however, the starchy staples of rice and cassava that accompany nearly every meal make the cuisine a heavy one. With civil war and unrest, the diet and health of Liberian citizens have suffered immeasurably. The civil war left the country reeling, affecting all aspects of life, particularly food production and infrastructure, which has made it even more difficult for the Liberian government to feed its citizens. As such, malnutrition is a serious issue facing the country.

Rachel Finn

Further Reading

Celtnet Recipes. http://www.celtnet.org.uk/recipes/west-africa.php.

Ember, Melvin, and Carol R. Ember. "Liberia." In *Countries and Their Cultures,* 3:1281–89. New York: MacMillan Reference USA, 2001.

Gibbon, Ed. Congo Cookbook. http://www.congocookbook.com/.

Horace Hoffman, Selena. *African Recipes: Liberian Cook Book.* Petersburg, VA: Ebonics, 1989.

Jackson, Elizabeth. African Chop. http://www.africanchop.com/.

Olukoju, Ayodeji. *Culture and Customs of Liberia.* Westport, CT: Greenwood Press, 2006.

Osseo-Asare, Fran. Betumi. http://www.betumi.com/.

Osseo-Asare, Fran. *Food Culture in Sub-Saharan Africa.* Westport, CT: Greenwood Press, 2005.

Smith, Ifeyironwa Francisca. *The Case for Indigenous West African Food Culture.* BREDA Series, no. 9. Dakar, Senegal: United Nations Educational, Scientific and Cultural Organization-Regional Bureau for Education in Africa, 1995.

Wilson, Gibson Ellen. *A West African Cookbook.* New York: Avon Books, 1971.

Maasai

Overview

The Maasai are an indigenous African ethnic group, until recently seminomadic but now largely settled, located in Kenya and northern Tanzania. They speak Maa, a member of the Nilo-Saharan language family that is related to Dinka and Nuer. Maasailand today straddles the border of southern Kenya and northern Tanzania. Census figures for Kenya estimated 377,089 Maasai in 1989. Figures based on Maa speakers estimated 453,000 in Kenya (1994) and 430,000 in Tanzania (1993) for a total population estimate of close to 900,000 between the two countries.

According to their own oral history the Maasai originated in North Africa and migrated along the Nile River down to East Africa, arriving near Lake Turkana around the 15th century A.D. They subsequently spread southward, conquering other groups on the way, some of whom they displaced and some of whom they incorporated into their own group. By the end of the 19th century, the Maasai ranged an area of grassy plains 700 miles north to south, from Marsabit in northern Kenya to Kiteto on the south of the Maasai steppe in what is now Tanzania.

European contact from Germany and Britain did not occur until the 1840s. As a consequence of European contact at the end of the 19th century the Maasai suffered severe losses of people and livestock from diseases, such as smallpox and rinderpest, introduced by Europeans and exacerbated by severe famine.

Sections

Under British Colonial rule Maasai groups in northern areas such as Laikipia were forced to move out of the highlands, which were earmarked for white settlers. The Maasailand Reserves were divided into separate geographically based sections: Ilkisongo, Ilpurko, Iloitai, Imatapato, Iloodokilani, Ilkeekonyokie, Ilkaputies, Ildamat, Ilsiria, Ilwuasinkishu, Ildalalekutuk, and Ilaitaytok. The largest sectional group was the Ilkisongo, who occupied parts of southern Kenya and Tanzania. Each section occupied a specific territory with well-defined boundaries within which all members of the section were free to graze their cattle; to cross into another section with cattle, permission had to be sought from that section. Theoretically, the section was the largest political unit, but, in practice, it seldom functioned as such except in disputes with other sections or other groups.

Each section was divided into localities (*enkutoto*, pl. *inktot*): self-contained ecological units with contiguous areas of wet-season pastures to which camps dispersed during the rains. In each locality the ruling elders formed a local council (*engigwa enktoto*) that had regular meetings to discuss and act on the public affairs of the locality.

Clans

Maasai belong to any one of five clans whose members are dispersed throughout Maasailand, thus providing a wide network of potential support and obligation that supersedes section boundaries. Inheritance passes through the paternal line, and families usually acknowledge and remember a lineage of three generations, back to the father of the oldest living man. Clans have no formal clan leaders and are not organized as geographically cohesive local groups.

In addition, Maasai are organized according to age-grade and age-set systems, and each age-set has its own spokesman appointed from among the group. Men proceed through different age-grades as members of named cohorts or age-sets that are formed every 14 or 15 years. Age-grades determine the formal political structure, and the system is based on the primacy of elder males over younger males and men over women. Women do not have an independent age-set system but automatically join the age-set of their husbands when they marry.

🍽 Food Culture Snapshot

The ole Koringo family is a large extended family occupying several *engang* (bomas, a mud and cow dung–covered hut) in the vicinity of Loitokitok and Rombo in southern Kenya. Maasai are generally polygynous. Ole Koringo has two wives and many children and grandchildren. Each wife occupies her own house, to which her husband has access. Children live in their mother's house but often share in food from other households.

Little food is purchased except for grains to supplement the largely milk diet. Tea and sugar are highly prized and can be purchased or obtained in exchange for milk. Milk is also exchanged for some foods such as vegetables at the weekly markets. Honey is often acquired in exchange for milk or meat.

Major Foodstuffs

The traditional Maasai diet consisted of milk, meat, animal fats, and blood as well as wild plants, such as berries or wild greens. In recent times, these are being supplemented by tea sweetened with sugar; a variety of grains such as maize, rice, and wheat; and a limited range of cultivated vegetables. As in many pastoral groups, the symbiotic relationship between the Maasai and their livestock is reflected in specific behaviors that provide for the nutritional needs of herders' families while simultaneously ensuring the continued productivity of the herds. For example,

herders rarely cull large stock for meat except on special occasions, when meat is normally shared among a larger-than-family group. They rely on dairy products, supplemented by occasional culling of small stock, for their daily needs. In Maasai society, men control the allocation of meat, while women control dairy products.

Most of the Maasai's food comes directly from their animals, in the form of milk, meat, blood, and animal fats. Milk is often sold on market days, and the proceeds are used to purchase vegetables such as cabbages, beans, and onions or grains such as maize, rice, or wheat flour. Milk may be exchanged directly with horticulturalists for a variety of vegetables to be cooked with meat in stews or with maize or rice.

Although individual yields of milk from cows in arid and semiarid zones of eastern Africa are low, the milk is of high quality. The fat content is as high as 5.5 percent, compared with the average of 4.8 percent reported for yields from sedentary herds in more humid areas of Africa or the average in European herds of 3.5 percent fat. The main deficiencies of milk are the absence of iron and vitamin C. However, if milk is drunk fresh without further processing, 1 kilogram (a little over a quart) of milk can supply 20 milligrams of vitamin C. Milk also lacks vitamin D, but this is hardly a problem in the tropics since vitamin D can be produced in the human body when it is exposed to sunshine.

Maasai depend on milk for a high percentage of their dietary energy, anything from 94 percent in the wet season to 30 percent in the dry season. Milk is plentiful from just after the rains until just before the dry seasons begin. If a Maasai mother has a son who is a *moran* (warrior), she will allocate one to two calabashes of about three quarts each to him; if she has two moran sons they would be given two quarts or more each. Moran eat with their peers and move from one house to another, each moran leading the others to his mother's house. A child of about 8 to 12 years would take 1.2 quarts in the morning before going out herding and 1.2 quarts in the evening when he gets back. A younger child will take about half a quart but spread throughout the day.

In addition, the moran and elders take about three quarts of yogurt per week, boys and girls about

A proud Maasi herdsman with his cattle in Kenya. (iStockPhoto)

two quarts, and women and older men one to two quarts. This is when the season is relatively good and the number of lactating cows averages 5 to 10 per household. In a time of severe drought at Ol Girra in January 2006, the women were subsisting on one quart of milk a day with no other supplementation from meat or grains. Children would fare relatively better because, according to the women, the children are fed first in times of crisis and both women and men will go without to favor the children.

There are times when there is more than enough milk; allocations would be high, and even the dogs would be fed milk. Passersby would be called to drink since storage and handling become a problem and the family would like to get rid of the surplus before the next milking. Things have now changed because there is a ready market for milk in the towns.

Maasai, like many other pastoral groups, consume limited amounts of blood from living animals. Cattle blood contains 7.6 percent protein, 0.06 percent fat, and 0.05 percent glucose. It also contains some valuable minerals such as iron as well as small amounts of calcium and phosphorus. An arrow is shot into the animal's jugular vein, and the blood is collected in a gourd. Later it is mixed with milk to make a protein-rich drink, often given to senior elders when they are ill and to women after giving birth, but all ages drink blood and milk during times of scarcity. Although consumed as snacks, fruits constitute a major part of the food ingested by children and women looking after cattle as well as morans in the wilderness.

Cooking

Maasai men slaughter and butcher cattle at a kill site, which also is the site where the carcass is roasted and some choice parts are given to the cooks. Only men roast meat, and it is they who divide and allocate the cooked meat. Meals prepared at the homestead are organized by the women and can include meat from goats and/or sheep and various types of stews. All milk products are controlled and allocated by the women.

Typical Meals

Just before dawn the woman of the house rises and relights the fire, which has been left smoldering overnight. She then goes out to begin the milking. Calves are brought out one by one from the calf enclosure or house and led to their mothers. The calves are allowed to suckle from two teats while the milker milks the other two teats into a gourd. After enough milk is taken from any one cow, the calf can continue suckling its mother while the milker fetches the next calf. Milking can take an hour or hour and a half for each household. The woman of the house will then prepare breakfast, consisting of a thin porridge of milk and maize flour for the herdboys and other children; and milk, milky porridge, or tea for her husband and any of his guests. Warriors are given pure milk as specified by their status. Younger herders who may be away from the homestead until evening are given a calabash of milk or porridge to carry with them. Older herders may take breakfast and then go without eating until evening. After the herds have left the settlement, the women and girls clean their gourds with burning charcoal from special aromatic woods that give Maasai milk its characteristic flavor. When the herds return in the evening, the morning milking ritual is repeated.

Masai tribal people cooking meat over an open flame in Tanzania. (Randy Olson | National Geographic | Getty Images)

A study of the Maasai diet among the Laitokitok-Kisongo in 2007 included food diaries for adult male and female Maasai over a period of three weeks. The days were divided into five segments: daybreak, 10 A.M., lunch, 4 P.M., and dinner. All began the day with tea with milk prepared by the wives around daybreak. At 10 A.M. some but not all consumed tea with milk; yogurt; boiled fresh milk; or maize-meal porridge with yogurt. Lunch tended to be more varied, for example, boiled fresh milk, tea with milk, maize porridge with yogurt, *ugali* (maize) with bean stew, rice and meat, boiled banana and fresh milk, goat-meat stew with ugali, ugali with cabbage, ugali with beans, wheat chapati and tea, chapati with bean stew, or ugali with yogurt. Most took tea with milk at 4 P.M. At dinner, ingredients included chapati, rice, or ugali mixed with goat meat, beans, cabbage, potatoes, and/or fresh milk or yogurt. If milk was plentiful some took only fresh boiled milk for dinner.

Eating Out

Maasai seldom eat out unless they are in town at the market or doing other errands. If they can afford to, they may purchase roast meat with ugali and green vegetables, onions, and hot peppers at a café or bar. They are, however, invited to share food at any settlements they visit. They may be offered fresh milk, yogurt, sweet tea with milk, milk with maize meal or rice, soup with meat (with or without vegetables), or roast meat.

Special Occasions

Meat Feast

Meat is just one of a wide range of primary and secondary products supplied by Maasai cattle herds. Although cattle provide herders with meat, they are seldom slaughtered to supply food for the family alone; instead, they tend to be part of a ceremony or celebration, with the meat shared among a number of participants. For example, during the ceremony of Eonoto, which marks the passage of a moran to elderhood, three steers are donated for the feast, including the required pure black steer for the ritual

sacrifice. These are slaughtered and butchered by the moran. The meat is slowly broiled over smoldering fires of aromatic wood. The Eonoto ceremony occurs every 10 to 15 years, after the moran have spent the required amount of time together in a *manyatta* (warrior village). The ceremony itself lasts for over a week, with feasting and celebration. Lesser feasts include the initiation of boys or girls, weddings, burials, or hosting of important visitors.

Mature, fattened steers are chosen for most ceremonies. Slaughter of a malnourished animal is avoided unless the animal is near death and likely to die anyway. Every effort is made to keep animals alive, even through severe drought, so that they can be fattened later for more nutritive consumption. If an animal does die or is close to death due to disease or malnutrition, its meat will be consumed. A steer would be slaughtered for a number of occasions: the ritual feasting surrounding the initiation of morans or their subsequent passage to elderhood, the initiation of girls, dancing festivals, women's festivals, burial ceremonies, judgment of crimes, or a time of need. Traditionally, ceremonies for circumcisions and marriages were held during the "green" seasons, June/July and January, when everyone moved around to any home with an occasion to celebrate. Today, these ceremonies are held during the school holidays in August and December.

Men make all decisions on slaughter, cooking, and sharing of meat from cattle. Women can select small stock (sheep and goats) for family consumption and can give small stock as gifts to special recipients, such as new wives, daughters-in-law, or siblings. Under normal circumstances a family will slaughter about two goats and one sheep monthly and perhaps one steer every six months.

An ox is slaughtered and butchered in a prescribed fashion, and the meat is shared following a particular pattern of allocation. Even when the steer is slaughtered in a time of need and not for any ceremonial purpose, the pattern is followed. Most meat elements are paired, such as forelimb X being allocated to elders (or the moran cooks) and forelimb Y to wives. Some cuts can be allocated to elders or wives depending on the ceremony; however, out of 10 ceremonies listed, only 4, all involving women, would allow wives to receive the choicest cuts. In contrast, women are automatically entitled to inner thigh X, forelimb Y, the meat around the hips, and the midspinal strip X. Boys and girls tend to be allocated the paired element of an elder's or a wife's allocation; for example, ribs for boys or inner thigh for girls. It does, however, seem that women may be discriminated against in regard to taste since they are allocated the neck meat, thigh bones, liver, spleen, rumen lining, and reticulum, which are so despised by the elders that they will not cook them. On a taste rating of 1 to 8, the Matapato rated tongue and flank as a 1, the choice of the elders, while the liver, spleen, and reticulum, allocated to women, rate a 7. The rumen, allocated to women, and the brain, allocated to dogs, are equally rated as an 8. Despite these taste rankings the women are not necessarily nutritionally deprived. The liver of a steer, weighing on average six-and-a-half to eight-and-a-half pounds, supplies iron necessary for women during their childbearing years. During the ceremonial feasting, everyone partakes of the daily stews, which are heavily loaded with fat. Two meat cuts, lung and heart, that might be expected to be relegated only to women or to children, are given to the cooks in some ceremonies or presented to the moran as they pass from moranhood to elderhood.

Taste is not necessarily a measure of nutritional value. However, the relative value of the hindlimb (taste-rated 2), which is allocated only to elders, and the forelimb (also taste-rated 2), which is the highest-ranking element allocated to women, suggests that Maasai men do have access to considerably more meat and fat by weight and quality than women or children.

Exceptions to the meat-allocation pattern occur when an animal dies away from home, when all members of the group (elders, wives, children) are not present, or when moran retire to the bush to slaughter and consume meat during their time in the manyatta (the ritual warrior village). Several moran may get together, beg animals from their fathers, and seclude themselves for up to a month or more, eating meat daily. Digestion of such large quantities of meat is aided by special plant-derived digestives. During this time of feasting the moran do not drink milk.

Estimates of how much meat by weight elders, moran, women, and children might consume in a day of feasting suggest that elders could consume up to 8.5 pounds, women up to 4.5, children six to eight years of age about 1 pound, older children up to 2 pounds, and moran 13 to 17.5 pounds, the highest amount.

Fats

Fat is greatly valued in the pastoralist diet. When the carcass of a steer is cut up, the fat is separated from the meat and grouped into three categories: (1) The hard white lumps from the stomach region and rump (taste-rated 7 or 8) have no ritual uses and are regarded with distaste by the elders. These, along with other stomach parts, are relegated to the women. (2) Fat from the ribs and hump gets a taste-rating of 2 and goes to the elders to be used as a relish. (3) A rating of 1 is given to the brisket fat, which is allocated to the father of the elder hosting the feast. This is the most sought-after fat as it will keep indefinitely once the fat has been separated from the tissue. The scrotal fat is allocated to the mother of the host. Other sources of fat come from bone grease and bone marrow. The absolute yields of bone marrow vary with the size, species, age, sex, and nutritional status of the animal, hence the preference for mature, fattened steers. Sheep are slaughtered for their fat, especially in the dry season, when sheep retain fat longer than cattle or goats do. Fat also comes from milk and butter. Infants are encouraged to drink melted butter to build up their strength.

Blood

At the special rite-of-passage ceremonies such as entry into elderhood, blood is gathered in the dewlap of the slaughtered steer, mixed with milk. Each new elder is required to drink from it.

Diet and Health

High blood pressure, cardiac disease, and diabetes would be expected to be common among Maasai given their high-fat diet, but this is not the case as long as they continue to exercise, mostly walking long distances every day. Many Maasai succumb to disease when they give up the lifestyle of a pastoralist.

Soups are probably the most important medium for consumption of wild plant food by the Maasai. *Olkiloriti* (*Acacia nilotica*), a powerful digestive, is the most frequently used soup additive. The root or stem bark is boiled in water and the decoction drunk alone or added to soup. The Maasai are fond of taking this as a drug; it is known to make them energetic, aggressive, and fearless. Soups prepared during the time of a meat feast are laced with bitter bark and roots containing cholesterol-lowering saponins. Some that are added to the finishing stew on the last day of feasting have strong purgative or emetic effects.

Medicines derived from trees and shrubs are used in the treatment or prevention of a wide range of diseases and include remedies or prophylactics for malaria, sexually transmitted diseases, tuberculosis, diarrheal disorders, parasitic infestations, prostate problems, arthritis, and respiratory disorders. Particular attention is given to women's health during pregnancy and childbirth.

Kathleen Ryan

Further Reading

Amin, M., D. Willetts, and J. Eames. *The Last of the Maasai.* London: Bodley Head, 1987.

Grandin, B. "Wealth and Pastoral Dairy Production." *Journal of Human Ecology* 16 (1988): 1–21.

Homewood, K. M., P. Kristjanson, and P. Trench, eds. *Staying Maasai.* New York: Springer, 2008.

Homewood, K. M., and W. A. Rodgers. *Maasailand Ecology: Pastoralists Development and Wildlife Conservation in Ngorongoro, Tanzania.* Cambridge: Cambridge University Press, 1991.

Nestel, P. "A Society in Transition: Development and Seasonal Influences on the Nutrition of Masai Women and Children." *Food and Nutrition Bulletin* 8 (1986): 1–21.

Ryan, K. "Facilitating Milk Let-Down in Traditional Cattle Herding Systems: East Africa and Beyond." In *The Zooarchaeology of Fats, Oils, Milk and Dairying,* edited by J. Mulville and A. K. Outram, 60–66. Oxford: Oxbow Books, 2005.

Ryan, K. "Food Sharing and Nutrition: Differential Access to Food by Age and Gender in a Pastoral Society." Paper presented at Society of Africanist Archaeologists (SAFA), Calgary, 2007.

Saitoti, Tepilit Ole, and Carol Beckwith. *Maasai.* New York: H. N. Abrams, 1980.

Talle, A. "Ways of Milk and Meat among the Maasai." In *From Water to World Making: African Models and Arid Lands,* edited by Gísli Pálsson, 73–93. Uppsala, Sweden: Scandinavian Institute of African Studies, 1990.

Madagascar

Overview

The Republic of Madagascar is an island located in the Indian Ocean, about 250 miles off the southeastern coast of Africa. The nation sits just south of the equator and is separated from Africa by the Mozambique Channel. It is the fourth-largest island in the world, with an area of 227,000 square miles (587,000 square kilometers). The population in 2009 was estimated at 20.6 million, making it the 55th most populous country worldwide. Although three languages are officially recognized—Malagasy, French, and English—Malagasy, a derivative of Malayo-Polynesian languages, is the most commonly used.

Madagascar is divided into six provinces (*faritany*): Antananarivo in the central highlands, Antsiranana in the north, Fianarantsoa in the southeast, Mahajanga in the northwest, Toamasina in the northeast, and Toliara in the southwest. Antananarivo is the name of the capital city as well, which is located in the central highlands and the largest, most developed part of the country. The climate of the island is primarily tropical, especially along the coast. Inland areas tend to be more temperate, particularly the highlands surrounding the capital. To the south is an arid environment. Due to its relative isolation, Madagascar has an abundance of plant and animal species that are found only on the island, something that has attracted the attention of botanists, environmentalists, and tourists alike.

The people of Madagascar (the Malagasy) are of mixed ethnic descent including Indonesian, African, Arab, and European heritage. Evidence suggests that the first inhabitants of Madagascar were Malayo-Indonesian, arriving sometime around 500 A.D. Afro-Arabians are said to have appeared sometime thereafter, likely around 1000 A.D. Until it became a French colony in 1895, Madagascar had an independent kingdom, governed by indigenous ethnic groups, namely, the Merina and Sakalava tribes, who occupied the territory in the central highlands and along the western coast, respectively. Following independence from France in 1960, Madagascar became a democratic republic, but political instability ensued and government control fluctuated wildly, sparking widespread economic decline in the 1970s and 1980s. In 1992, a parliamentary democratic constitution was passed, yet political turmoil persists even to this day. In 2009, following the resignation of President Ravalomanana, a new leader, Andry Rajoelina, assumed control, backed by military support. Economic decline and political unrest have transformed Madagascar into one of the poorest nations in the world. Reports show that roughly 70 percent of the population lives on less than one dollar (U.S.) a day.

The history, people, and diverse terrain of the island have all played a role in shaping Malagasy culture and cuisine. Religion has also profoundly impacted the way people live, interact, and eat in Madagascar. Roughly 52 percent practice traditional beliefs (ancestor worship), 41 percent are Christians (both Protestant and Roman Catholic), 7 percent are Muslims, and a very small number are Hindus. The most common religiously based dietary restrictions imposed are food taboos (*fady*). Since many practicing Christians still observe ancestral rituals surrounding burials, and most of the remaining population strictly adheres to traditional beliefs, fady have become commonplace in society. Variation occurs from one ethnic group to another, and between women, men, children, and expectant mothers. One such fady, originating in the Sakalava tribe, prohibits the consumption of pork. Another, belonging to the Antandroy tribe, forbids the eating of sea turtles or cows without horns.

Food Culture Snapshot

The average household in Madagascar is made up of approximately six people, with a male and female head, children, and sometimes grandchildren. It is not uncommon to find an extended family living under one roof. Single females represent 12 percent of household heads; few of them are single men. Most of the time, meal preparation is the responsibility of women, although children are encouraged to help from a relatively young age. Young females begin to assist in cooking as early as five years of age.

Madagascar has an abundant market culture where the majority of foods are purchased. Supermarkets do exist on the island, but most of them are expensive and limited to urban areas. Daily markets run in cities and towns, and weekly rotating markets are held in rural areas. Men, women, and children participate in selling products, each with their own specified role according to gender and age. For example, men tend to sell meat whereas women sell dried fish and produce. Most of the goods sold at these markets are locally sourced, either harvested directly by the seller or bought from a nearby larger market. Teeming with activity, a Malagasy market represents an important part of social life.

The typical Malagasy family does nearly all its food shopping in local markets. Foreign residents, tourists, and affluent households may choose to patronize the supermarkets, but in rural areas markets may be the only substantial option for food. In some cases, small stores (epiceries) offer basic needs such as cooking oil, sugar, and matches. Everything else is found in the market.

A variety of meats may be purchased including beef (zebu), chicken (akoho), pork (henan kisoa), goat, and lamb. For everyday use, meat is bought in small quantities and served as an accompaniment to rice or used to make broths and stews. Larger portions are reserved for special occasions. Fish (hazan drano) and shellfish are plentiful on the island; thus it is common to find vendors selling lobster, prawns, squid, crayfish, octopus, eels, sea turtles, oysters, and sea cucumbers, as well as various kinds of fish. Much like meat, the average household uses seafood regularly albeit sparingly, with the exception of special occasions.

As a tropical island, fruits, vegetables, and spices grow in abundance on Madagascar, and markets are the best place to find them. Fruits such as mangoes, bananas, coconuts (the flesh and the milk are common in cooking), papayas, oranges, lemons, lychees, pineapple, and strawberries are everywhere. Among the many vegetables available, leafy greens (bredes) and tubers predominate. Cassava root and its leaves form an important part of the Malagasy diet, as do other types of leafy greens, sweet potatoes, corn, and taro. Additional vegetables may include tomatoes, beans, hot peppers, ginger, garlic, onions, and the like. Spices, nuts, and aromatics like vanilla, cloves, cinnamon, black pepper, peanuts, and cashews are used frequently, taking a prominent position in any market.

A typical Malagasy family cultivates their own rice, but since it is consumed in such enormous quantities, supplementing what is grown at home is necessary. Also, there are a few areas where rice is not grown, and markets may be the only place to find the staple. Additionally, (cow) milk may be sourced from within the household, provided the family has its own cattle. Otherwise, it can be found in markets or grocery stores.

Major Foodstuffs

Madagascar's rich biodiversity makes it a place where food crops grow in abundance, and, consequently, the economy is largely agriculturally driven. Approximately 26 percent of the nation's gross domestic product is made up of agricultural products, employing nearly 80 percent of the domestic labor force. Surprisingly, many crops are grown almost exclusively for export. They do serve as ingredients in everyday Malagasy cuisine, but the finest of the harvest is reserved for the international market. Madagascar produces more vanilla than any other country in the world, for example, yet its appearance in the local cuisine is not as prevalent as one might think. Some other examples are cacao, coffee, sugar, black pepper, cloves, and cinnamon. Cultivation typically occurs on large plantations introduced to the island in the 19th century.

The most abundant crop is rice, which alone accounts for around 13 percent of the gross domestic product. Unlike the cash crops, rice (*vary*) is grown mostly for domestic consumption and is the basis of the Malagasy diet. Many households cultivate their own rice fields. It represents nearly half of all calories consumed and about two-thirds of all available cropland. The average person eats more than 308 pounds of rice per year (2000 figures), an amount so high that Madagascar is now a net importer of rice to meet that demand. The Malagasy people perceive rice as a sacred gift and chief above all other foods, often appearing in religious rituals and festivals. The old saying "rice is a god" (*vary andriaminitra*) demonstrates the reverence with which it is regarded. The colloquial Malagasy word used for eating a meal (*mihinanabary*) literally translates as "to eat rice." The Malagasy believe they cannot in fact survive without it. Abundant yields of rice are seen as a sign of social status, a reflection of the blessing of God and the ancestors.

Rice is eaten at every meal—three times a day—and is considered the main dish. Any other food served is thought to be an accompaniment or relish (*laoka*). Several kinds are grown on the island, but those most commonly used are the partially refined "red rice" (*vary mena*) and the completely refined white variety. Rice is served at different consistencies depending on the time of day or the occasion. The dry method uses just enough water to cook the rice (*ampangaro*). When milk is used it is called *vary amindronono*. Alternatively, the wet or soft version is made using excess water, resulting in a soupy consistency (*sosoa*). Rice is sometimes ground into a coarse flour to be used in a variety of recipes. One such dish calls for the meal to be cooked in banana leaves, resulting in something akin to dumplings (*betrosa*). Roasting and crushing the grain (*lango*) is a traditional way of preparing rice, making it good food for traveling.

Rice even serves as the basis for a common beverage (*ranonapango*), where water is boiled in a pot of leftover browned rice. It is enjoyed either hot or cold.

In Malagasy cuisine, beef (zebu) is second only to rice in importance. It is a local breed of humpback cattle that forms a substantial part of social and economic activity. Though sources vary regarding the origin of the animal—some believe it came to the island from southern Asia, and others insist it is African—zebu's place in Malagasy culture is in any case significant. Since it, too, is considered sacred, cattle is often slaughtered as a sacrifice to the ancestors at funerals, reburials (*famadihana*), and other special occasions. Much like rice, zebu is perceived as an indication of wealth. Furthermore, no part of the animal goes unused: The finest meat is eaten on special occasions; the tough, cheaper cuts are used daily in soups or stews; the hide is used for leather; and the horns are used in traditional medicine or as an offering at burial sites. Most of the time, zebu is used sparingly, as a relish for the rice. There are various ways of preparing the beef including traditional recipes and those that have been brought by immigrants. One common Malagasy snack (*sambos*), fried dough stuffed with beef and/or other meat and vegetables, suggests an Indian influence, even in the name (in India they are called samosas). An example of a traditional preparation for zebu calls for the meat to be boiled in water with onions and then grilled until brown (*varenga*). Since the consistency of the meat is relatively dry, it is usually served with soft or wet rice (*sosoa*).

Varenga

Ingredients

2 lb beef, deboned and cut in 1-in. strips

1 tbsp salt

1 medium clove garlic, minced

1 small onion, sliced

Water to cover

Combine all the ingredients in a medium saucepan and bring to a boil. Cover the pan, and reduce the heat to low to maintain a simmer. Be sure to add water as necessary to keep the meat covered. Cook the beef for about 2 hours, or until it falls apart with a fork. Remove the meat from the pan, drain, and shred using a fork. Spread evenly on a baking sheet and roast at 400°F until the meat is golden brown, about 30 minutes. Alternatively, the stewed meat can be grilled until brown (about 10 minutes depending on the heat), using a heat-proof basket or aluminum foil to prevent it from falling into the fire.

In some areas of Madagascar rice is not cultivated; it is replaced by sweet potatoes, cassava, and corn. It is widely accepted that cassava found its way to Madagascar from the Americas via Africa, and corn from the Americas by way of the Portuguese. Meals might be accompanied by boiled cassava, sweet potatoes, or a cornmeal mush very much like grits. The leaves of the cassava plant (*bredes*) are used all over the island to flavor soups and other dishes. One of Madagascar's national dishes is a stew made with pork and ground cassava leaves (*ravitoto sy henakisoa*). Another very typical dish is a broth made with water and leafy greens (*romazava*), especially those from the cassava plant. Sometimes zebu is added to the soup as a flavoring agent.

The everyday mealtime rice drink (ranonapango) is unequivocally the most customary of Malagasy

Romazava, a typical dish of Madagascar, is made with water and leafy greens (romazava), especially those from the cassava plant. (Mark Waddle | Dreamstime.com)

beverages, but other interesting choices can be found all over the island. Along with the introduction of sugar plantations came the production of a potent local rum (*toaka gasy*), sometimes home-made and always present on special occasions. Other alcoholic beverages typical of the island are lychee liquor (Litchel), local Three Horses Beer (*THB*), fermented sugarcane juice (*betsabetsa*), fermented coconut milk (*trembo*), and local wine from the southeastern province of Fianarantsoa. Coffee is becoming popular in urban areas and is locally grown. If someone asks for it "white," it is served with sweetened condensed milk. Lemongrass tea (*citronelle*) serves as an alternative to ranonapango at breakfast or following a meal. Many roadside restaurants (*hotelys*) offer fresh fruit juices including orange, mango, pineapple, strawberry, and the like. Sodas (both local and international) and bottled water are gaining popularity in cities throughout Madagascar.

Cooking

Traditionally, the cooking area of most Malagasy homes was located in a kitchen outside the house to minimize the threat of fire. In some cases, this is still true today, but in urban areas houses will have kitchens. The dishes are prepared using various cooking methods including grilling, frying, or boiling in liquid (water, meat or vegetable broth, milk, and coconut milk). Milk is considered the most valuable of cooking liquids and is typically used to make a sort of rice pudding (vary amin-dronono) that is sometimes flavored with honey and vanilla. Foods may be grilled directly over the fire or on skewers (*tsatsika*), buried in the coals (root vegetables), wrapped in banana leaves and boiled, or cooked in a pot. Earthenware bowls were the preferred choice for cooking prior to the introduction of metal and cast iron pots. Most food is cooked on portable stoves made of metal or stone. The most typical fuel for home cooking is wood and charcoal. Historically, the chaff of rice grains made for excellent fuel in areas where wood was scarce.

Because rice is such an important part of the Malagasy diet, there is always a granary nearby where rice is milled and stored. Granaries are elevated above ground to prevent excess moisture and rot of the grains. Mortars and pestles (*leona*) made of earthenware are equally prevalent as they are used to grind rice into a coarse meal, as well as spices, nuts, and other starches.

Smoked and dried meat or fish (*kitoza*) are popular and characteristically served with a cornmeal porridge or soft (*sosoa*) rice for breakfast. The protein is cut into strips and hung to dry before being browned over a fire. The result is something reminiscent of beef jerky. Pickling is another common method of preserving foods in Malagasy cooking. A variety of fruits and vegetables are used to make these sides (*achards*) served alongside rice at lunch or dinner. The ingredients are first rubbed in salt and left to sit overnight, then heated in a mixture of vinegar and spices. They are left to macerate for a minimum of three days before serving. One of the most popular is made with green, unripe mangoes (*lasary manga*).

Typical Meals

In Madagascar, meals (*sakafo*) can vary from one household to another depending on ethnic identity, religion, social class, and locality, making it difficult to define a typical meal pattern. Nevertheless, some practices are common all over the island. Most Malagasy families, for example, eat three meals a day and two snacks. Broadly speaking, everyday dining tends to be light in fare, featuring a substantial amount of vegetables and broth flavored with meat. Heavier meals are enjoyed on special occasions and may include dishes with coconut milk and more expensive cuts of meat.

A traditional breakfast might consist of soft rice (*sosoa*) and dried meat (*kitoza*). When rice is not available, boiled cassava or soft cornmeal is eaten instead. Sometimes leftovers from lunch or dinner are enjoyed for breakfast the following day. Today, many Malagasy eat small fried rice cakes (*mokary*) or fried doughnut rounds (*mofo gasy*) with coffee. In cities, bread might be served with honey or jam and coffee, and in some cases eggs as well (in hotels), a reminder of the French influence. Typical beverages

Women work in the rice fields of Madagascar. Rice is the nation's largest food crop. (United Nations)

might include water, local citronelle tea (made from lemongrass), coffee, or a sort of browned-rice tea (*ranonapango*).

Lunch is most often the largest meal of the day, featuring the obligatory bowl of rice and at least three relishes (*laoka*). Hot chili paste (*sakay*) is always present, along with pickled vegetable and fruit relishes (*achards*). Sakay is made with spicy chilies (*pilypily*), ginger, garlic, and oil and is very spicy. Malagasy food is not particularly hot compared to that of Indonesia or other African countries, and thus sakay is not used for cooking but as a condiment, added based on the diner's preference. An additional meat or stew might be served, as in the national dish romazava, made with beef and an assortment of leafy greens (*bredes*). The term *ro* literally means "juice" and is used to classify any dish with a sauce, or a soup. Some of the greens used have a slightly spicy flavor (*anamalaho*), somewhat like mustard greens but more pungent, while others are mild in flavor (*mamy*). Seasonal fruit may be served for dessert, sometimes flavored with vanilla and/or coconut milk.

Romazava

Although this dish is traditionally made with beef, other meats may be substituted, including chicken or pork.

Ingredients

2 tbsp vegetable oil

½ large onion, diced

1 lb boneless beef, cut into 1-in. pieces

1 clove garlic, minced

2 tsp ginger, minced

1 chili pepper, diced

1 c canned tomatoes, diced

1 small bunch fresh spinach

1 bunch fresh watercress

1 small bunch mustard greens

Water, to cover

Salt and pepper to taste

In a large stockpot, sweat onions in oil over medium heat until translucent. Add beef and cook for approximately 10 minutes, stirring occasionally. Add garlic, ginger, and chili and cook for an additional 3 minutes. Add tomatoes and simmer for another 10 minutes. Add water and bring to a boil. Add greens and reduce heat to low. Simmer 1 hour or until meat is tender when pierced with a fork, stirring occasionally. Season with salt and pepper to taste.

Dinner follows a similar pattern to the lunchtime meal but is sometimes slightly lighter. In addition to rice, sakay, and achards, meats or vegetables might also be served. A typical vegetable dish (*vary amin anana*) calls for mixed leafy greens, tomatoes, and onions to be simmered in water together with a small amount of meat. Fresh salads (*lasary*) also accompany the meal. Dessert usually consists of seasonal fruit mixed together with sugar and vanilla. Rice tea (ranonapango) is the beverage of choice served with both lunch and dinner, but water or lemongrass tea may be substituted.

Snacks are very popular in Madagascar and can be found in markets, street stalls, or roadside restaurants (hotelys). They can include rice flour and fruit cakes cooked in banana leaves (koba ravina), skewered beef (*masikita*), Indian-style meat or vegetable fritters (sambos), fried locusts and other insects, small doughnuts (*mofo menakely*), sweet rice and peanut cakes baked in banana leaves (*koba*), sliced fresh coconut, fruits and their juices, yogurt, and grilled cassava. In cities it is not uncommon to find French bread and pastries like croissants, cakes, and baguettes available throughout the day.

As in any culture, the way a meal is eaten in Madagascar is significant and shaped by social norms. Traditionally, all meals were served on the ground using mats for the food and for seating. In some rural communities this is still a common practice, but Malagasy people living in cities prefer to sit at tables during a meal. Typically, there is no progression of courses, as in many Western meals, with the exception of fruit and rice tea (ranonapango), which follows the meal because it is made from the browned rice left at the bottom of the cooking pot. Before the introduction of modern dinnerware, earthenware pottery was used for cooking and serving food. Historically, gourds were used as bowls for storing food and for individual use at mealtime, but in contemporary Madagascar the use of modern plates and bowls is the norm. All components of the meal were eaten together on the same plate or even shared out of a communal pot in the past, but today individual plates are favored. Spoons are the eating utensils of choice, traditionally made from zebu horns or pottery but mostly from stainless steel today.

In traditional Malagasy culture, social hierarchy surrounded the meal, dictating the order in which food was served to each person. When families ate together, older men were always served first and received the best share of the meal. Likewise, the youngest children were served before their older siblings to ensure adequate nourishment. When food was passed from one person to another, it was considered polite to hold the wrist with the opposite arm. It was not unusual for male and female family members to eat separately, and the eldest always received first dibs. Roles of men and women are somewhat less stratified today, but many of the old customs prevail in spite of these changes.

Eating Out

Eating out is a relatively recent phenomenon in Malagasy culture, having been introduced by the French and other foreign inhabitants. The tourism industry has also played a key role in its growth. However, many Malagasy people still believe the best food is found in the home. Restaurants (*restos*) are virtually exclusive to cities and towns, with only a few in rural areas. While they are becoming popular among Malagasy urbanites, the overwhelming majority of them cater to tourists, featuring a variety of Western foods like French or Italian cuisine. *Steak frites* (French-style zebu with fries), locally produced foie gras (French-style duck liver), pizza, and pasta feature prominently on menus. Chinese restos are beginning to appear as a popular alternative to traditional cuisine. Here, bowls of fried noodles with vegetables and meat (*mi sao*) and noodle soup with fish, chicken, or vegetables (*soupe chinoise*) are typical menu offerings. Indian restaurants are appearing in various cities and towns as well. Regardless of the type, every restaurant has something in the way of traditional Malagasy cuisine available. Many restaurants offer an assortment of beverages including local tea, wine, beer, and liquors. Some of the more expensive French restaurants carry a selection of French wines.

Malagasy locals tend to patronize small roadside eating huts (hotelys), as they offer fast service, inexpensive traditional foods, and a more casual atmosphere. Some can be found in smaller towns and less populated areas. These small stands serve classic fare including rice (vary) with assorted accompaniments (*kabaka*) like beef, chicken, pork, fish, or vegetables. In coastal areas they might serve boiled and roasted crayfish and other seafood dishes. Apart from the market, hotelys are the best place to find snacks. Fruit juices, local yogurt, and Three Horses beer might be available as well.

In the largest cities, especially Antananarivo, tea cafés (*salons de the*) have become prevalent, thanks to the French cultural influence. Most offer a selection of French breads and pastries, and sometimes sandwiches or light meals. Locally grown tea and coffee are always available.

Malagasy chocolate is highly regarded in places like Europe or the United States but is surprisingly scarce in local cuisine. It can be found in Malagasy markets, but the majority of the harvest is sent overseas. There is one French bakery in Antananarivo called Chocolate Robert that offers high-quality pastries, candies, hot chocolate, and the like. It is said to rival any patisserie (pastry shop) found in Paris and is very popular with Malagasy natives, foreign residents, and tourists alike.

Special Occasions

Celebrations, festivals, and religious holidays are an important part of life in Madagascar. With such a large population of Christians, holidays like Easter and Christmas are celebrated as national holidays. Baptisms, circumcisions, and first communions are considered special as well. Traditional ancestral rituals have given rise to a number of other festivals and celebrations. And every special occasion in Madagascar is not complete without great feasts and plenty of singing and dancing.

One of the most celebrated events in Malagasy life is the Turning of the Bones festival (famadihana), in which the bodies of ancestors are exhumed from their burial sites, re-dressed, and then moved to the ancestral tomb, where they are buried a second time. In Malagasy culture, the worship of ancestors (*razana*) is based on the belief that they oversee the lives of the living, rewarding or punishing them accordingly. At least one zebu cow is slaughtered during the festival, as it is considered an offering to the ancestors. The horns are used to decorate the tombs of the dead, and the meat is eaten during the celebrations. The local homemade rum (toaka gasy) is seen as an offering and is consumed by participants in copious amounts. Drunkenness is not unusual. In fact, a glass of toaka gasy might even be served to the ancestor's remains after they are exhumed from the tomb, a custom that is meant to show honor to the dead. As with other celebrations, a feast is served including plenty of beef, rice, and accompaniments; it is followed by singing and dancing.

The Festival of Rice falls sometime in April or May every year and is intended as a celebration of the rice harvest. In the past, each family performed a ceremony in which prayers, various parts of the rice plant, and the toasted rice meal lango were given as offerings of thanks to the ancestral gods. For this reason, the rice harvest became a sign of wealth and prosperity. It was taboo (fady) for any rice to be consumed before the ceremony. Although the festival is not as strictly followed today, it remains a period of great celebration where extended family and friends gather together to eat, sing, dance, and enjoy one another's company. Dishes with fatty cuts of meat and coconut milk are enjoyed. One such recipe might be chicken stewed in coconut milk with tomatoes and onions (*akoho sy voanio*).

Akoho sy Voanio

Ingredients

2 tbsp vegetable oil

1 whole chicken, cut up

2 onions, diced

2 cloves garlic, minced

2 tsp ginger, minced

1 can diced tomatoes

1 can unsweetened coconut milk

Salt and pepper to taste

In a large stockpot, heat oil over medium heat. Season chicken with salt and pepper, then sauté for about 10 minutes, turning occasionally. Remove the chicken from the pot and set aside. Add onions to the pan and sauté until golden brown, about 10 minutes. Add garlic and ginger, and continue to sauté another 3–4 minutes, stirring frequently. Add the tomatoes to the mixture, and cook for 10 more minutes, stirring from time to time. Return the chicken to the pot and add the coconut milk. Bring mixture to a gentle boil and immediately reduce heat to low, being careful not to curdle the coconut milk. Simmer for at least 30 minutes and adjust the seasonings.

Diet and Health

Madagascar has a long history of traditional medical practices (*fanafody*) that are strongly linked with the worship of ancestors. Although modern, Western hospitals and clinics are beginning to appear, they are mostly located in cities and towns, making access difficult for those living in rural areas.

In addition, many Malagasy people view Western medicine, as a relatively new form of health care, with suspicion. Consequently, traditional health care is still commonplace, particularly in remote locations. Regional variations occur in methodology and treatment, but most adhere to the belief that illness is a punishment for behavior not pleasing to God—the traditionally accepted God (*Zanahary*) or the God of Christianity (*Andriamanitra*)—or the ancestors.

Traditional healers (*ombiasy*) are employed for both physical and spiritual healing, relying heavily on herbal remedies. An ombiasy is believed to have the powers of divination—connecting with the ancestors and the spirit world—to help individuals suffering from spirit possession and diagnose a variety of other illnesses. Indigenous plants and leaves are commonly used, often steeped in water as a tea or bundled and placed under the patient's bed. These herbs are believed to remedy a number of maladies including headaches, common colds, nausea, toothache, and many others. The greens (*bredes*) so prevalent in cooking today, for example, were first used as medicine, slowly earning a place in everyday life. Spices, roots, and animal bones are part of the ombiasy medical repertoire as well. Markets are the best place to find them; stalls overflowing with various herbal concoctions are everywhere, overseen by ombiasy eager to find patients to purchase their wares.

Rice, too, is believed to have healing properties; the soft version (*sosoa*) is typically served to the sick. The Malagasy believe that children are well only if they eat enough rice. Toasted, ground rice flour (*lango*) is considered the food of the ancestors and thought to be restorative to the health.

Perhaps the greatest threat to Malagasy health is malnourishment and the lack of potable water. As one of the poorest nations in the world, sanitation standards and access to electrical power, transportation, and running water are well below those of the West. And with 70 percent of the population living on less than one dollar a day, access to food is a serious problem. Thirty-eight percent of the population is undernourished, mostly from insufficient caloric consumption and protein deficiencies. Forty-five percent of children under the age of three have stunted growth, a result of their mothers' poor diet during pregnancy. The average life expectancy is only 55 years. Cities have the best living conditions and access to plenty of food by comparison to rural areas.

Jennifer Hostetter

Further Reading

"About Madagascar." http://www.air-mad.com/about_history.html.

"All about Madagascar." Tranofalafa 2.0, September 14, 2009. http://www.tranofalafa.com/culture/food.html.

Conservation International. "The Malagasy People." http://www.conservation.org/explore/africa_madagascar/madagascar/Pages/malagasy_food.aspx.

Donenfield, Jill. *Mankafy Sakofo: Delicious Meals from Madagascar.* Lincoln, NE: iUniverse, 2007.

"Flavors of Madagascar." The Worldwide Gourmet. http://www.theworldwidegourmet.com/countries/flavors-of-madagascar/.

Jacob, Jeanne, and Michael Ashkenazi. "Madagascar." In *The World Cookbook for Students.* Vol. 3, *Iraq to Myanmar,* 128–33. Westport, CT: Greenwood Press, 2007.

"Madagascar." http://www.africa.upenn.edu/Cookbook/Madagascar.html.

"Malagasy Recipes." http://www.youtube.com/lemurbaby.

Ramiaramana, Bakoly Domenichine. "Malagasy Cooking." In *The Anthropologists' Cookbook,* edited by Jessica Kuper, 104–8. London: Kegan Paul, 1997.

Mauritania

Overview

The Islamic Republic of Mauritania is a country in northwestern Africa. Its western border is the Atlantic Ocean; to the southwest is Senegal; Mali is on the east and southeast, Algeria to the northeast, and the Western Sahara to the northwest. Mauritania was named after the ancient Berber kingdom of Mauretania. It was part of French West Africa from 1860 until gaining its independence in 1960. It is sparsely populated, with about three-quarters of its land being made up of desert or semidesert. The majority of the population is of Berber, Arab, Tuareg, and Fulani descent and still lives a nomadic or seminomadic existence. However, many of these nomadic people have been driven into urban areas from long periods of drought. Almost all of the population is of the Islamic faith.

🍽 Food Culture Snapshot

Lina lives in Mauritania's capital city, Nouakchott. Lina and her daughter, Hawa, go to the market in the Ksar. Lina must go to the market every day to buy food because little to no refrigeration is available. In the hot season, it is necessary to go to the market to buy food for each meal because food can spoil after only a few hours. Many of Mauritania's people still rely on subsistence farming to live. Lina and Hawa live in an urban area, so most of what they consume is purchased in the market. Lina and Hawa are lucky to live in Nouakchott because they have a greater variety of items available to them than if they lived in a smaller town or village.

The market is organized in sections. Different boutiques and vendors specialize in specific products. There are separate sections where butchered meat, vegetables, fruits, bread, and housewares are available. Small grocery stores are rare but may be found in larger cities like Nouakchott. These are typically for Mauritanians who are better off or are Western expatriates. The grocery stores are unique in that their prices are fixed. In the market, people are expected to bargain for the price of the item they are buying.

Major Foodstuffs

Rice is a staple in the Mauritanian diet. It accompanies many dishes of fish, meat, and vegetables and is often mixed into stews. Mauritania's coastline is one of the world's richest fishing grounds, and there are many preparations of fish in the Mauritanian cuisine. Mauritanians in general prefer to eat dried fish, which is often served alongside rice. Lamb and camel meat are most often eaten. Dates are an integral part of Mauritanian cuisine because they provide both calories and minerals. They are typically eaten at the end of the meal or as a snack. Dates are available in abundance; Mauritanians consume all the dates that are grown there and do not export any.

The type of food Mauritanians eat largely depends on location and ethnic group. In the north, there is a more limited variety of foods, and the food itself is typically blander than in the south due to the influence of the nomadic Moors. The Moors relied mostly on food that traveled well and did not have to be cultivated, which limited the variety in their diet. In the north, Mauritanians eat mostly meat,

Women sit on the beach with their freshly cleaned fish in Nouakchott, Mauritania. (Attila Jandi | Dreamstime.com)

rice, and couscous. In the south, they have an abundance of fish, vegetables, and some fruits—mainly due to climate. The northern part of Mauritania is dry and arid, while in the south they have the Senegal River as a water resource and higher average rainfall. This environment is much more conducive to land cultivation, which accounts for the variety of fruits and vegetables in the diets of Mauritanians living in the south.

Cooking

How one cooks in Mauritania is largely determined by where and how one lives. Nouahdibou has a higher standard of living due to higher economic development from fishing industries. Many of the better-off people in this city cook in Western-style kitchens with electric appliances and running water. In smaller, more rural areas, the kitchen may be located outside or in a separate area of the home.

Oftentimes the kitchen is merely a covered structure. A small burner or burners, set on the ground and fueled by gas, is often the only means by which to cook. Nomads may use an open fire to cook their food, which usually involves a tripod that has a wok-like vessel hanging in the center over an open fire. Mauritanians use a lot of vegetable oil in their food preparation because it increases the calories in the meal. In addition, the high quantity of oil allows the food to be compressed so that it is easy to pick up and put in one's mouth.

Typical Meals

The variety of dishes in Mauritania is quite limited. Typically, a family will eat the same foods for breakfast every day, and even lunch and dinner may vary little. For breakfast, people eat a porridge made of millet and served with milk and sugar. French bread and butter is also a favorite breakfast food. It is usually served between 7 and 8 A.M.

The main meal of the day varies by culture. Black Africans prefer to make lunch the main meal, whereas Arab-Berbers have their main meal in the evening. In the south, the favorite lunch item is a Senegalese dish, *chub u gin* or *chubbagin,* which consists of rice and fish. It may be accompanied by vegetables such as eggplant, carrots, peppers, potatoes, and/or a green leaf called *bissap.* If fish is not available, goat or lamb may be substituted. *Yassa,* a simple dish of rice with onion sauce, is also popular. Lunch is usually served between 2 and 3 P.M.

Dinner is often couscous, which may be accompanied by goat or lamb. For special occasions, at dinnertime, people will have a plate of couscous with a goat's head on top. Dinner is usually served between 8 and 10 P.M. During Ramadan, dinner may be served as late as 11 P.M.

Camel meat is a Mauritanian specialty. The following is a traditional version of the national dish.

Chubbagin

I lb camel meat, cut into cubes (lamb may be substituted)

¾ c vegetable oil

2 tbsp tomato paste

I onion, coarsely chopped

I small eggplant, cut into chunks

2 carrots, cut into chunks

I small cabbage, cut into wedges

I large sweet potato, peeled and cut into chunks

I smoked and dried fish

I tbsp red pepper flakes, or to taste

I garlic clove

I small handful hibiscus leaves

2 lb rice

I bouillon cube

Salt and black pepper to taste

Fry the meat in the oil to brown on all sides. Add the tomato paste and a little water. Stir to coat the meat. Add the onion, and season. Cook until the onion softens, then add the other vegetables, including the garlic. Continue to cook, adding more water if necessary. Finally, flake the dried fish and add to the pot. Add the red pepper and hibiscus leaves. Cover and cook for 30 minutes. Carefully remove the meat and vegetables and place in a bowl. Pour the rice into the remaining liquid, add the bouillon cube, and cook until rice is tender. Remove the rice to a serving tray, and place the meat and vegetables on top to serve.

The ritual way of eating is important in Mauritania. There are no utensils—the meal is eaten with the right hand. The left hand is forbidden by Islam since it is seen as unclean. Food is usually served in a large bowl or plate that is placed on the floor, with everyone gathering around the dish. If there are a lot of people, there may be two or three dishes. Each person has an area of the dish that is considered his to eat. One must eat only the portion of food that is directly in front of one. If a desirable piece of food is lying outside this portion, one must ask if one may have it. Others will usually oblige and place it on one's portion of food. The meat is usually placed in the center of the dish, and the host will tear off the best pieces for visitors and guests.

The tea ceremony is very important in Mauritania. It is seen as a social event and a show of hospitality. It is believed to alleviate hunger, thirst, and fatigue. Tea is served at every meal. Green tea from China is typically consumed, or sometimes mint tea. The ritual of preparing and drinking tea can often take three hours. Three glasses of tea are usually drunk. There are three conditions in the ceremony of making tea: *ijmari*—placing the teapot on the charcoal embers; *jar*—slowly infusing tea leaves, serving, and drinking; and *jmaa*—assembling people. Each glass symbolizes a different aspect of life. The first glass is strong and bitter to represent death. For the second glass of tea, the pot is set back on the fire with mint and sugar in it. The flavor of the second glass is strong and sweet, symbolizing love. The last glass is a combination of the first two and is meant to symbolize life.

The actual act of serving the tea is also quite time-consuming and symbolic. The amount of foam in one's glass is indicative of how welcomed one is by the person who is preparing the tea. If there is a lot of foam—perhaps half the glass—one is welcomed, and the host greatly enjoys one's company. Very little or no foam means that the host is merely serving the tea to the guest as a hospitable, moral obligation. The foam is created by pouring the tea from one glass to another, often holding the glasses far apart and letting the tea cascade down into the glass. Foam in the tea is important because it takes time and care to produce it, showing that the host enjoys one's company.

Eating Out

In Mauritania, eating mostly takes place in the home. That being said, there are restaurants of many ethnicities such as Moroccan, Lebanese, Chinese, and French located in the larger cities like Nouakchott. Foreign cuisines generally dominate the restaurant scene in the larger cities. Local cuisine like lamb, goat, and rice is available at restaurants throughout the country. Restaurants have improved in recent years due to better distribution of food. A typical meal may cost US$7 to $10. Eating on the street is also popular. One can buy nuts, fritters or donuts, cooked meats, and tea.

Special Occasions

Festivals are celebrated all over Mauritania. Many of them are religious celebrations, such as the New Year, as well as more secular festivities like Independence Day. Often the feasts at these celebrations include a whole roasted goat or lamb. Sometimes, the head of the goat is roasted whole and served on top of couscous.

Animal sacrifice is a food custom that often takes place at ceremonial occasions. At the end of Ramadan, a married man is expected to offer a lamb. The meat of the lamb must be eaten within three days. It is also traditional to offer an animal on occasions like name-giving, initiation, marriage, and funeral ceremonies.

Diet and Health

Religion influences Mauritanian dietary practices in many ways. Almost all Mauritanians are Sunni Muslims. Sunni is the largest denomination of Islam and means the words, actions, or example of the Prophet Muhammad. Mauritanians consume only halal food, which Islamic law dictates is the only food that is permissible to eat. Halal meat must be slaughtered in the way set out by Islamic law. The animal must be killed quickly, with the knife slitting the throat while a prayer is said and the name of Allah is spoken. The Quran explicitly forbids the consumption of the following foods: pork; blood; carnivorous birds of prey; animals slaughtered to anyone other than the name of Allah; carrion; an animal that has been strangled, beaten (to death), killed by a fall, gored (to death), or savaged by a beast of prey; fish that have died out of water; food over which Allah's name is not pronounced; and alcohol.

In Mauritania, the cultural ideal of beauty encourages young women to eat foods high in fat so that they gain weight. A person who is overweight by Western standards is instead considered beautiful in Mauritania. This practice is slowly diminishing as the influence of Western culture through television shows and movies takes effect.

Annie Goldberg

Further Reading

Anderson, Sarah. *Anderson's Travel Companion.* London: Pallas Athene, 2004.

Stephens, Betsy, and Ron Parlato. *Mauritania Food for Peace: Title II Evaluation.* Washington, DC: International Science and Technology Institute, 1983.

Wiefels, Roland. "Mauritania: Fish Trade and Food Security in Mauritania." In *Report of the Expert Consultation on International Fish Trade and Food Security.* Rome, Italy: Food and Agriculture Organization of the United Nations, 2003.

Morocco

Overview

Morocco is in North Africa. It is bordered by the Atlantic Ocean on the west, the Mediterranean Sea on the north, and Algeria on the east and southeast. The southwestern border of the country is in dispute, because Morocco and Mauritania both claim the arid, sparsely populated Western Sahara territory. The country is dominated by mountains, primarily the Rif chain along the Mediterranean coast and the three much higher Atlas ranges (from northeast to southwest, the Middle Atlas, High Atlas, and Anti-Atlas), which roughly parallel the Atlantic coast some 100 to 150 miles inland. The population is largely concentrated around the Mediterranean coast in the northeast, in the plains running inland from the Atlantic north of Rabat, and in the central plateaus of the Atlas. The least populous part of the country is the southeastern slopes of the High Atlas and Anti-Atlas mountains, which lead down to the Sahara desert.

Before the coming of Islam in the seventh century, North Africans spoke languages of the Berber family. At present, the overwhelming majority of Berber speakers are concentrated in Morocco; scattered islands of Berber speech survive as far east as Egypt. Though three-quarters of Moroccans are of Berber ancestry, only perhaps 40 percent still speak the language, most of them in the highlands and the far south, with the rest of the country now speaking Arabic. Culturally, there is little difference between Arabs and Berbers. Many city dwellers also speak French.

Food Culture Snapshot

Lahsen and Fatma Ben Hammoud; their son, Merwan; and Fatma's mother, Meryem, live in a four-room house in Fez, the country's fourth-largest city. Lahsen works as a tourist guide in Fez's huge and mazelike medieval *souq* (market). Their diet is typical of the lower middle class. They shop for meat, dairy products, and vegetables in the souq, but they also raise herbs, a few vegetables, and four chickens in their small backyard.

Major Foodstuffs

The Moroccan diet is based on grains, primarily wheat and, to a smaller degree, barley, which provide about two-thirds of the daily calorie intake. Wheat is made into couscous, bread, and pastries, and both wheat and barley appear as porridges and soups. Morocco is no longer self-sufficient in grain and imports about one-third of the wheat it consumes.

The country raises 17 million sheep, 5 million goats, and nearly 3 million cattle. Beef and veal are eaten somewhat more often than in other Arab countries. Poultry, primarily chicken but also pigeon, is as important as red meat in the Moroccan diet. The advantage of pigeons is that, because they are free, once one has gone to the trouble of building a dovecote for the semiwild birds to live in, they don't need to be fed. Near the coasts, fish is a major food.

Milk is mostly consumed in the form of *rayeb* (a sweetened custardlike product made by curdling milk with wild artichoke) and *jebna* (cheese), made from sheep, cow, or goat milk curdled with sheep rennet.

Spices and herbs at Marrakesh bazaar. (Corel)

Cheese is usually eaten fresh, but it may be pressed to make a longer-keeping cheese called *ma'sura.* Yogurt is not traditional in Morocco.

The principal fats are olive oil, from Morocco's extensive olive groves, and butter, which is always clarified of its solids and whey into butterfat. This clarified butter (*smen*) can be flavored with spices and aged for months, even years, to achieve a highly prized rancid aroma, which in older examples suggests an aged cheese. The flavor of aged smen is essential to certain dishes such as the stews called *qedra.* In the south of the country, the nuts of the *argan* tree are pressed for their oil, which has a light, pleasant, hazelnut-like taste.

Pulses such as lentils, chickpeas, and fava beans are a significant source of protein. Chickpeas are added to many stews, and all the pulses are used in bean soups and *bisar,* a bean paste flavored with herbs and spices that is eaten with bread. Vegetables include tomatoes, peppers, zucchini, artichokes, cauliflower, fennel bulbs, and cardoons. Eggplant and leafy greens play a somewhat smaller role in Morocco than in Arab countries farther to the east. Cabbage, turnips, and pumpkins are also important. Morocco is the world's third-largest consumer of olives. In most countries south of the Mediterranean, olives are consumed only as snacks, but Moroccan cooks often throw them into cooked dishes.

A striking feature of Moroccan food is the very extensive use of herbs, above all cilantro, and especially of spices, often a dozen or more in a single dish. The famous spice mixture *ras el hanout,* for which there are countless recipes, may contain 30 spices along with other flavorings such as rose petals.

Because of its wide range of climates, Morocco produces fruits ranging from subtropical bananas to temperate-climate fruits like apples and plums. The important fruits include grapes, plums, peaches, apricots, quinces, pomegranates, lemons, and oranges. Grapes are eaten fresh or dried, and raisins are a very common ingredient in stews. Lemons that are not consumed fresh are pickled in brine, which gives them a sweet, plush, somewhat pinelike aroma. Pickled lemons (*lim mraqqed;* literally, "lemons put to sleep") are added to salads and stews.

Cooking

A Moroccan kitchen needs only a small range of pots and utensils: a brazier (*mijmar*) for frying, boiling, and grilling; the earthenware casseroles *tajine* and *qedra;* and a steamer called a *keskas* (in French, *couscoussier*), rounded out with a few knives, a mortar and pestle, and some sieves. Modern electrical appliances such as refrigerators and mixers are available in stores. Many people buy meat and produce in small quantities and cook it the same day. Any leftover food is covered and eaten at the next meal.

Couscous, the Moroccan staple food, is called *kesksu* in Arabic and *seksu* in many Berber dialects. In the center of the country it is often called *tt'am,* which is simply the Arabic word for "food." It is neither a whole grain nor a noodle but granules of flour, created by a special process that does not involve kneading. To make them, the cook sprinkles salted water into a bowl of flour and moves the fingers through it in circles so that granules form. From time to time, the flour is sieved to remove the granules and sort them into different sizes for drying. This is a time-consuming process, so factory-made couscous has been available for nearly a century. Many women of the older generations still make their own.

Whether packaged or homemade, the couscous is cooked by moistening it with cold water and then steaming it several times in the top of the couscoussier, alternating periods of steaming with more cold-water moistening and rubbing with butter or oil. The bottom of the couscoussier is filled with boiling water or, to conserve fuel, the stew that will be served with the couscous. Since the flour has never been kneaded, the gluten, the tough protein that creates the firm texture of noodles and bread, has not been activated, so the couscous granules are only loosely held together. This means that couscous must be steamed—if it were boiled, the granules would turn mushy. It also means that the granules can absorb far more water as they steam than noodles do in boiling, so couscous has a light and delicate texture. It can even be made from flours that totally lack gluten, such as barley flour, cornmeal, or, in a few places, acorn meal.

Rice is rarely served as a side dish. It more often appears as rice pudding or in the stuffings of roast birds and *bestilas* (large pies), for which it is steamed like couscous. A kind of pasta called *she'riya,* resembling short lengths of vermicelli, is likewise cooked by steaming, though it can also be boiled in soup.

Typical Meals

Simple pastries are often served at breakfast. One is a sort of pancake called *beghrir,* which is fried on only one side. Variously shaped pastries collectively known as *rghayef* are made from leavened dough rolled thin and folded to create a few layers. They are cooked by frying in olive oil until brown and puffed and are then dipped in honey. Other foods that might appear at breakfast are cheese, olives, bread, and the bean paste bisar.

The beverage will be green tea, usually flavored with mint and sometimes with orange blossoms, and nearly always served very sweet. Mint tea is drunk not only at breakfast but also throughout the day; Moroccans rank ninth in the world for tea consumption. For serving to guests, tea is prepared in a ceremonious way, and at the end the tea is poured with a flourish from a height of a foot or more above the teacup.

Lunch is a relatively large meal, typically consisting of a soup, several salads of raw or cooked vegetables, and a *tajine* (chicken, lamb, or fish stewed with vegetables), followed by fresh or dried fruit. It comes with round, dense-textured loaves of bread an inch or so thick that are flavored with anise. Many Moroccans knead the bread dough and shape it into loaves at home and then send it to a local bakery for baking.

Couscous is commonly served at lunch, and it is the traditional meal on Fridays after men return from morning prayer at the mosque. Moroccan meals are eaten sitting on the floor, with the diners taking food from a common dish, using only the right hand. The etiquette of eating couscous is to gather the granules into a ball with the fingertips and pop it neatly into the mouth. The stewed meat or vegetables that accompany it are transferred to the mouth separately. The leftover juices of any dish may be soaked up with a piece of bread. Soups are eaten with a spoon.

Dinner is ordinarily a less important meal than lunch. The characteristic foods are hearty soups, but salads, tajines, and couscous may be served. However, when guests have been invited, dinner may be a very grand meal.

Morocco is the only major Arab country that was never part of the Ottoman Empire. As a result, its cuisine shows little Turkish influence—there are no stuffed vegetables or baklavas—and it has its own traditional haute cuisine, which arose in the royal courts. Though everyday meals may be rather simple, for special occasions Moroccan cooks have a repertoire of grand dishes, some of which go back to medieval times, such as *mruziya* (a tajine of lamb with prunes and raisins) and *tfaya* (lamb stewed with almonds).

The grandest dish of all is the bestila, a large pie a foot or more in diameter, typically filled with stewed pigeon, toasted almonds, curdled eggs, and spices. Its name comes from the Spanish word *pastel* (pie), and the basic concept was probably brought to Morocco by Moorish Muslims who left Spain in the 16th century, or perhaps earlier, because there had been considerable traffic between Morocco and Spain since the Moors conquered the latter in the seventh century.

The bestila now bears little resemblance to anything in Spain, because its crust is made from *warqa* ("leaf"), a paper-thin pastry sheet somewhat like phyllo or strudel dough but stiffer and crisper. It is made by tapping a large lump of dough against a heated metal dish (*tebsi*) and removing the thin sheet that sticks once it's cooked. Sheets of warqa are also used for making pastries other than bestila. Most often they are wrapped around a filling (usually almond paste) to make small packets called *briwat* ("envelopes"), which are cooked by frying. A strudel-sized roll of warqa with an almond-paste filling—but baked rather than fried—is called *mhannsha* ("snake-shaped").

In the north of the country, the bestila is usually flavored with lemon, and in the south it is usually sweetened. The north and south also have different tastes in couscous. Throughout the country couscous is most often served with a tajine of lamb, raisins, and chickpeas, but couscous with lamb, caramelized onions, and honey is traditional in Rabat, and in Essaouira on the Atlantic coast, couscous may come with fish and turnips. Throughout the country, people make a dish known as *couscous au sept légumes,* which is served with a tajine of mixed vegetables and, if possible, some lamb. Despite the name, the tajine needn't include exactly seven vegetables. A typical mixture might be carrots, onions, turnips, tomatoes, sweet peppers, zucchini, and pumpkin.

In addition to couscous granules of the usual size, larger and smaller varieties are also made. Extra-large couscous, called *mhammsa* in Arabic and *berkukes* in Berber, is popular in the south. Northerners make an extra-small couscous called *seffa* or *mesfuf,* which they serve with butter, sugar, and cinnamon.

Whole spit-roasted lamb (*meshwi,* often spelled the French way as *méchoui*) is particularly characteristic of southern Morocco and rural Berber regions. City dwellers often make a stripped-down version of meshwi using smaller cuts of lamb and sending them to a bakery, rather than roasting the whole animal on a spit.

Soupe aux Carottes (Carrot Soup)

Serves 2

Fez was the capital of Morocco for four centuries and had a long connection with wealthy and sophisticated Moorish Spain. As a result, it is renowned for elegant cuisine. This dish—something between a cold soup and a sweet salad—shows the delicacy and refinement for which Fez is known. Fez is also a major citrus-growing area and, citrus fruits play an important role there.

4 carrots

Juice of 4 oranges

1 tsp orange blossom water

Sugar

Cinnamon

Peel and trim the carrots. Quarter them lengthwise and cut out the bitter, woody core. Having discarded the core, grate the carrots as finely as possible. Divide the grated carrots between two soup bowls.

In a mixing bowl, mix the orange juice and orange blossom water, and add sugar to taste. Pour it into the soup bowls. Pick up a pinch of cinnamon between the thumb and index finger and deposit a thin line across each bowl of soup, then repeat to make another line crossing it at right angles.

Serve cold.

Eating Out

Moroccans usually eat at home. There are grand restaurants in large cities that cater largely to foreign visitors who otherwise would have no place to sample the unique dishes of the country. Otherwise, when away from home, people eat street foods such as fried fish (*hut mqalli*) and the local variety of shish kebab, known as *qotban* in Arabic and *brochettes* in French.

Qotban (Brochettes)

Serves 8–10 as a snack or appetizer

Qotban (literally, "sticks") are typically made by marinating the meat with vinegar, onions, and pepper. This version from the Atlantic coast is more elaborately flavored, giving an idea of the variety of spices used in Morocco.

3 lb leg of lamb

2½ tsp cumin

2 tsp paprika

1½ tsp white pepper

1 tsp black pepper

1 tsp turmeric

1 tsp oregano

3 bay leaves, crumbled

½ onion, minced

3 cloves garlic, minced

¼ c olive oil

1 tbsp red wine vinegar

2 oz (½ stick) butter, melted

1 tbsp cumin

Cut the lamb into about 15 (¾-inch) cubes. In a mixing bowl, mix the cumin, paprika, white pepper, black pepper, turmeric, oregano, and bay leaves. Add the meat and rub with the spices. Toss with the onion, garlic, oil, and vinegar. Cover and refrigerate 24 hours.

Arrange the chunks of meat on skewers and grill until done to taste, about 7–8 minutes, basting with melted butter every 5 minutes. Dust with cumin and serve.

Qotban, a typical Moroccan dish. (iStockPhoto)

Special Occasions

Nearly all Moroccans are Sunni Muslims and observe the usual Muslim religious occasions: the Ramadan fast and the Feast of the Sacrifice. Since the Muslim calendar is strictly based on the phases of the moon, the Muslim year is shorter than the solar year and the months of the calendar fall about 10 days earlier every year. The foods served at Muslim feasts (*eids*) tend to be the usual special-occasion foods of the particular time of year.

During the month of Ramadan, Muslims are required to abstain from food and drink during the daylight hours but are permitted to eat and drink from dusk until dawn. Eid al-Fitr (the Feast of the Fast Breaking) is a three-day celebration that follows the last day of fasting. The most traditional way of breaking the fast—whether during Ramadan or at Eid el-Fitr—is to eat dates, but the dish particularly associated with breaking the fast is a hearty soup called *harira*. It is basically a meaty broth slightly thickened with a flour-and-water slurry (*tedouira*), enriched with chickpeas or lentils, tomato paste, and any choice of vegetables and flavored with spices, always including some red pepper. Moroccans consume harira at any time of year, but it is particularly welcome after a day of fasting—and above all when Ramadan falls in summer, because of its thirst-quenching qualities.

The Feast of the Sacrifice, Eid el-Kebir ("the great feast"), takes place on the 10th day of the month of Dhu 'l-Hijja, the day that the pilgrims to Mecca sacrifice a sheep (or arrange with a butcher to sacrifice a sheep). Muslims around the world are expected to do the same if they can afford to and to distribute part of the meat to those who can't. As a result, the foods of Eid el-Kebir tend to involve meat. One dish particularly associated with the occasion is couscous with a tajine of sheep's head, carrots, and fava beans.

Couscous is served at both Eids. In fact, couscous is the universal dish at special occasions, such as weddings and the celebrations of births and circumcisions. During the period of mourning after a death, friends and relatives send couscous to the home of the bereaved, who distribute it to the poor.

Diet and Health

Moroccans consume a Mediterranean diet featuring many fruits and vegetables. Fish is a major food in coastal regions, and garlic and olive oil figure in many dishes. The oil of the indigenous argan tree is high in unsaturated fats. However, it is laborious to produce and too expensive for most Moroccans.

On the whole, the Moroccan diet is rather high in carbohydrates, and in recent decades there has been a growing but not well-understood problem of obesity in urban areas, particularly among women, 18 percent of whom are now obese, as opposed to 5.7 percent of men. This is rate is more than triple what it was in 1980, when male and female obesity were roughly equal. The traditional dietary problem had been malnutrition, which still exists to some extent, particularly among children in rural areas.

A more serious problem in rural regions is availability of safe drinking water. In the countryside, only 58 percent of people have access to safe water, and many people suffer from gastrointestinal infections. In the cities, 100 percent of the water is considered safe.

Charles Perry

Further Reading

Heine, Peter. *Food Culture in the Middle East and North Africa.* Westport, CT: Greenwood Press, 2004.

Peterson, Joan. *Eat Smart in Morocco: How to Decipher the Menu, Know the Market Foods and Embark on a Tasting Adventure.* Berkeley, CA: Ginkgo Press, 2002.

Wolfert, Paula. *Couscous and Other Good Things from Morocco.* New York: Harper & Row, 1973.

Mozambique

Overview

The Republic of Mozambique is located on the southeastern coast of Africa and stretches for 1,535 miles along its eastern coast. The country is nearly twice the size of California, with about 309,475 square miles and a population estimated in 2009 to be about 21 million. It borders Tanzania, Zambia, and Malawi to the north; Zimbabwe to the west; South Africa and Swaziland to the south; and the Mozambique Channel of the Indian Ocean to the east. The terrain ranges from rain forests and swamps to mountains, grasslands, sand dunes, and beaches. However, the country is generally a low-lying plateau traversed by 25 rivers. The largest river, the Zambezi, an important resource, flows west to east and cuts the country into northern and southern regions. It supplies power through the Cahora Bassa Dam, one of Africa's largest hydroelectric projects. The capital, Maputo, formerly Lourenço Marques, is located on the coast in the southern part of the country. There are two main seasons: the wet season from November through March and the dry season from April through October.

The official language of Mozambique is Portuguese, a legacy of the country's colonizers, but various indigenous languages are also spoken, particularly in rural areas. After independence in 1975, there was an attempt to remove Portuguese as the official language, but no other language was spoken by a majority of the people. Mozambique's numerous African languages, all of which belong to the Bantu family, can be divided into three groups: Macua-Lomwe languages, spoken by more than 33 percent of the population, mostly in the north; Sena-Nyanja languages, in the center of the country; and Tsonga languages, in the south of Mozambique.

The population is divided among nine major ethnic groups. The largest group is the Macua, in the provinces of Nampula, Niassa, and Zambézia and the southern part of Cabo Delgado. In the northern part of Cabo Delgado and into Tanzania we find the Maconde peoples. The Tsonga are mostly in the provinces of Maputo, Gaza, and Inhambane. The Shona, Sena, and Ndau are mostly in Tete, Sofala, and Manica provinces. Roughly 3 percent of the population is European, Indian, Chinese, Pakistani, or mestizo (mixed race, mainly European and African). These people live mostly in the large coastal cities and are usually doctors, teachers, or shopkeepers or are employed in industry.

The earliest inhabitants, Bantu-speaking peoples from the Niger Delta in West Africa, moved slowly through the Congo basin about 3,000 years ago, in one of the greatest population migrations on the African continent. Over centuries they journeyed into eastern and southern Africa, reaching present-day Mozambique sometime around the first century A.D., where they made their living fishing, farming, and raising livestock. These groups also knew how to make iron. This enabled them to make tools and develop farming techniques that gradually led them to absorb the population of nomadic hunter-gatherers.

By the eighth century, sailors from Arabia arrived and began establishing trading posts along the coast. They intermarried with the indigenous Bantu speakers and created a hybrid culture and language called Swahili. These Arab traders and slave traders also brought with them the spicy cooking styles of the East. This culture still prevails and exerts a strong influence throughout Mozambique. The name *Mozambique* is thought to have come from the Swahili *Musa al Big,* or *Musa Mbiki,* the name and title of an ancient Arab sheikh via the phrase *Ilha de Moçambique* (Island of Mozambique). The most important of the Arab trading posts was at Sofala, near present-day Beira. Other important coastal ports and settlements were Ilha de Moçambique, Quelimane, and Ilha de Ibo. These ports were the main link between the old kingdoms and the inland gold fields.

In 1498 the Portuguese explorer Vasco da Gama was the first European to set foot on the territory that is today Mozambique. After rounding the Cape of Good Hope he landed on an island off the coast and claimed it for the Portuguese. By 1510 the Portuguese controlled all of the trading posts, from the town of Sofala in the south to what is now the country of Somalia; and by 1515 they had expanded their control east to Tanzania and Zimbabwe.

Over the next century the Portuguese subdued the inhabitants, whom they forced to work on their farms and in their gold mines. Their rule was finally recognized by the Mwene Matapa group in 1629. The Portuguese called the area *Terra da Boa Gente* (Land of the Good People). Slavery existed in the area before the Portuguese came, but they introduced the practice of exporting slaves, and by 1790 approximately 9,000 people were being shipped out each year. Even after slavery was outlawed by the Portuguese in 1878, it continued for many years.

During the Portuguese rule, the *prazeiros* (Portuguese landowners) formed the wealthiest and most powerful class. Below them were the mestizos, those of mixed African and Portuguese descent; and at the bottom were Africans, who constituted the vast majority of the population. Today, the way people dress reflects the confluence of different cultures as well as an individual's economic standing. In the cities, men wear Western-style suits to work. Women wear Western-style dresses and dresses made from fabric with brightly colored African patterns. Women in rural areas, however, generally have kept their traditional dress of *capulanas* (long pieces of traditional fabric that are wrapped around the lower body). These capulanas are also used to hold their small children around their bodies. They also have retained the traditional head scarf or turban made from traditional fabric.

Today, the country is still divided along both ethnic and linguistic lines. But despite ethnic and linguistic differences, there is little conflict among the various groups. The greatest disparities are those that divide the north of the country from the south. The groups north of the Zambezi River follow a system of matrilineal descent. Many of them are seminomadic, moving every few years to more fertile soil. Because they are far from the capital and most urban areas, these groups show less influence from the Portuguese. South of the Zambezi River, in the Zambezi Valley, the tribes follow a patrilineal descent. To an extent, however, they have adopted Portuguese dress, language, and Christianity, especially the Catholic faith.

Mozambique is divided into 10 provinces: Maputo, Gaza, Inhambane, Sofala, Manica, Tete, Zambézia, Nampula, Niassa, and Cabo Delgado. Maputo, formerly called Lorenço Marques, is the national capital. Its main products are citrus, sugar, and limestone. Gaza's capital is Xai-Xai. It is located between the Limpopo and Changane rivers and has a rich wildlife. Gaza Province is known as the granary of Mozambique due to the fertility of the Limpopo Valley, where there is extensive cereal and rice cultivation. Its main products are cashews, cotton, rice, and maize. Inhambane was established as a permanent settlement by the Portuguese in 1534. It is one of the oldest settlements in southern Africa. The province is characterized by its extensive coconut palms and cashew trees. The main products are cashews, coconuts, and tangerines. Sofala is one of the richest Mozambican provinces, producing primarily shrimp and sugar. The provincial capital, Beira, is built on a plain below sea level. It is also the location of Gorongosa National Park and Marromeu Buffalo Reserve. The province of Manica is essentially agriculturally based and an important producer of a wide range of vegetables and fruits. Its capital, Chimoio, is the center for the trade of agricultural products from the surrounding fertile areas.

Its main products are gold, tobacco, citrus, and vegetables. Tete Province is known as the location of the colossal Cahora Bassa Dam, which is the fifth largest in the world. The city of Tete is in one of the warmest areas of Mozambique and lies on a plateau 1,640 feet (500 meters) above sea level. This province also has the largest number of baobab trees, which are spread throughout the area. Fishing is one of its main products. Zambézia is an agricultural mountain region of extensive coconut and tea plantations. Quelimane, its capital, is an important river port located on the Rio de Bom Sinais ("river of good signs"). The area is famous for its traditional cooking, which is quite spicy. Zambezian chicken, grilled with palm oil, is known all over Mozambique. Products are coconut, tea, and shrimp. Nampula's capital, also called Nampula, is an inland town surrounded by flat plains. Mozambique Island, located off the coast, where buildings are constructed of

coral, was declared a World Heritage Site in 1992. Nampula is also known for the Makua tribe, where women paint their faces white with *muciro,* an extract from a root that is also used to paint houses. The area is also known for its cooking utensils made from black clay. Niassa province is the largest and most sparsely populated region of the 10 provinces. Its main products are cotton, maize, hardwoods, and precious stones. Cabo Delgado, the northernmost province of the country, is home to the famous Makonde people, who are known for their sculptures in hardwoods and ivory. The Makonde are also known as a fearless people and ardent followers of initiation rituals. Another cultural characteristic is the tattooing of the body and sharpening of the teeth, both for aesthetic purposes.

Music is a very important cultural tradition. Song serves several purposes, including religious expression, and the relating of current events. Most

Women in the Tete province of Mozambique fishing with nets. (Andrea Basile | Dreamstime.com)

musicians make their own instruments. Their drums have wooden bases covered with stretched animal skins. Wind instruments known as *lupembe* are used by the Makonde peoples and are made from animal horns, wood, and gourds. The gourds are dried and hollowed calabashes, which produce a sound similar to that of a trumpet. The *marimba,* a kind of xylophone that has been adopted in the West, originated in Mozambique, where it is popular in the south among the Chopi peoples. Chopi musicians also use the *mbira,* an instrument made from a hollow box with strips of metal attached to it and plucked with the fingers.

Dances are sometimes linked with religion, and the Chopi are known for their hunting dance, when they dress in animal skins, carry spears and swords, and act out battles. In the north, the Makua men dance around the village on tall stilts, wearing colorful masks and outfits. On Mozambique Island, women perform a dance that combines rope jumping with complex footwork. The *marrabenta,* a form of dance and a type of music, is very popular in the cities.

Food Culture Snapshot

João and Maria Mutemba are a typical middle-class couple in Maputo. They live in a middle-class neighborhood and have two children, a boy age 12 and a girl age 10, who attend private schools. João and Maria's lifestyle and eating habits are typical of the middle class. They enjoy both Mozambican and Portuguese-influenced dishes. Their day begins with a breakfast of coffee; Portuguese rolls; papaya, mango, or bananas; and preserves. Sometimes breakfast will include eggs, sausages, fried manioc root, and/or leftover meats. Their bread is purchased at the bakery, and the fruit, preserves, and eggs come from the local grocery store.

For lunch their meal might consist of any of the following: grilled chicken or fish with fried potatoes and a salad, *lumino* (fried fish and manioc stew), *matapa* (a stew made from pumpkin leaves, peanuts, shrimp, and coconut milk), *quiabos fritos com camarão* (fried okra with shrimp), or *feijoada de mariscos* (seafood stew). The lunch usually ends with coffee and a dessert such

as *doce de papaia* (papaya dessert, a fruit pudding). Snacks, usually eaten around 4 P.M., include *bolinhos de amendoim* (peanut balls), *chamuças* (spicy chicken or shrimp turnovers), *croquetes de mandioca* (manioc croquettes), *camarão grelhada* (grilled shrimp), and pastry with coffee.

The evening meal, usually served around 8 P.M., might consist of a soup made from pumpkin, corn, or manioc; *caril* (the Portuguese word for curry) with seafood, fish, or chicken; *camarão à laurentina* (shrimp in coconut milk); *frango à Moçambicana* (grilled chicken); or *churrasco Moçambicana* (grilled meats) with salads. Dessert follows, with *doce de batata doce* (sweet potato pudding), *bolo de ananás* (pineapple cake), or *doce de papaia,* served with coffee.

Major Foodstuffs

Most of the crops originally cultivated in the region have been supplanted by European imports. The exception is millet, a grain that is sometimes made into beer. The diet of rural residents is based on the cassava root, which is called *mandioca* in Portuguese. It is an edible tuber root and a main source of nutritional starch. When pounded, it is a useful sauce thickener. Its importance is testified to by its name, which translates as "the all-sufficient." This malleable food source can be baked, dried in the sun, or mashed with water to form porridge. To substitute for rice and/or potato, cassava can easily be cooked by cutting it into pieces and frying, similar to French fries. In its most common form, it is ground into coarse flour along with corn and then mixed with cassava leaves and water. The resulting dough is served in calabashes. Cassava leaves have a high nutritional value, and their use in many Mozambican dishes makes them a favored food. Corn is the other staple food; both corn and cassava were introduced from the Americas by the Portuguese. Cashews, pineapple, and peanuts, other important foods, found their way to Mozambique in the same manner.

Fish and seafood are some of the delicacies that Mozambique has to offer. Fishing along the coast accounts for one-third of the country's exports. The rivers also provide fish, and several fisheries produce mackerel and anchovies. Maputo is known for its excellent prawns, lobsters, and crayfish. Calamari (*lulas*) is also very popular and usually served grilled or fried. Crabs, cockles, clams, and various fish such as tuna, red snapper, rockfish, and swordfish (*peixe serra*) from the coastal waters are savored and prepared in a variety of ways, but the most common is grilled over coals. Fish is often just served with a simple sauce made by combining lemon juice, chili peppers, and salt and heating them for a few minutes. The oils used to cook these delicacies are peanut, olive, and sunflower.

Beans are a staple in Mozambique and are used in many traditional dishes. The most common are *nhemba* (a type of black-eyed bean), *feijão-manteiga* (butter bean), and *feijão soroco* (a green split pea). The Mozambican secret to perfect beans is not to stir them until they finish cooking.

Agriculture is by far the largest industry. Rice, also a major food product, is grown in the province of Gaza. The Limpopo River, which runs through the southern part of the province, creates a wide, fertile plain where rice is cultivated. Coconuts, tangerines, and sugarcane are also major crops. The spices that are most commonly used in Mozambican cooking are garlic, parsley, onions, mint, cinnamon, cloves, saffron, coriander, cumin, and red peppers.

Cooking

Cooking techniques vary throughout the country. In the rural areas most food is cooked over an open fire. Chicken is grilled over coals, and any leftovers are made into another dish and eaten with rice. Vegetables and stews are cooked over the coals in clay or metal pots. In the central and northern regions goats are raised by many farmers and are part of their diet. The goat meat is cooked over coal fires and eaten with vegetables and a white doughlike mixture made from ground maize flour. This dough is used instead of utensils to scoop up the meat and vegetables.

In the larger cities, middle-class families have their meals prepared by cooks. Those meals are mainly Portuguese influenced, although the Goan (Indian) influence is very evident. Most meals are prepared on gas stoves fueled by propane tanks. Charcoal grills are also popular for grilling meats and sea-

food. The utensils that are essential in a Mozambican kitchen include a *pilão* (mortar and pestle) to pound peanuts and corn, a straw strainer to sift out the small stones and husks from flour, a small mortar to crush garlic and chili peppers, an *mbenga* (clay pot) to soak corn, and a good wooden spoon. Also found are a large pot for soups and stews; a large frying pan; a meat grinder for meats, peanuts, and greens; and a grater for garlic and other spices. Nowadays, steel and aluminum pans are used, but in the countryside good pans are made from clay.

Piripiri, the hot chili pepper, is a major contribution to the art of cooking. It is particularly prevalent in the cooking of the provinces of Maputo and Beira. All Mozambican cooks have their own way of preparing the piripiri sauce. The most common way is to begin by squeezing lemons, passing the juice through a sieve to remove the pulp, and simmering the juice in a pan with the piripiri peppers. The peppers are then removed and pounded to a paste with salt in a mortar and pestle. The paste is then returned to the pan with the lemon juice and simmered until thickened. The sauce can be served brushed over steak, fowl, fish, or shellfish that has been cooked on the grill. It is also used to season many dishes.

Refogado, a sauce that is the basis of most soups and stews, is made with onions, tomatoes, garlic, and green peppers sautéed in olive oil. Rice is usually served at each meal and sometimes combined in a dish with fruit such as *arroz de papaia* (rice with papaya) and *arroz integral com manteiga de amendoim e bananas* (brown rice with peanut butter and bananas) and served with grilled meats. Rice is also mixed with vegetables as in *arroz verde* (green rice), which calls for the rice to be cooked with a refogado made from onions, bell peppers, cilantro, garlic, salt, and pepper with chicken broth. *Mucapata* (rice with split peas) is an enticing combination of rice, green split peas, and coconut milk from the Zambesia region in central Mozambique. It is prepared in a clay pot and is usually served with *frango à cafreal* (African-style grilled chicken). Peanuts are a main ingredient in many Goan and Mozambican recipes. They are usually ground to a powder and used to thicken the sauce. *Matapa saborosa* (collard greens with peanut sauce) calls for the collard greens to be cooked with shrimp, coconut milk, ground peanuts, and chili peppers. It is usually served with pork loin and white rice. Another very popular dish is *caril de amendoim e galinha* (chicken with peanut sauce): Chicken is served in a spicy curry sauce that calls for the piripiri pepper.

The Portuguese influence is very evident, mostly in the large cities, particularly in the use of wine in cooking, egg yolk desserts, and salads. Thousands of immigrants from the former Portuguese province of Goa, on the west coast of India, settled in Mozambique, adding a permanent Indian element to the culture. The Indian (Goan) influence is most evident in the southern part of the country. Caril (curry) is prepared using chicken, fish, or seafood. It is usually accompanied by mango chutney (*manga achar*), a hot chutney sometimes served with side dishes such as chopped peanuts, grated coconut, sliced cucumbers, and bananas. The chutney is also served with chamuças (samosas—triangular wedges of fried pastry filled with chicken, shrimp, meat, or vegetables). In the rural areas of the country and in restaurants and homes in the larger cities, we find African dishes such as African-style grilled chicken (frango à cafreal), cassava leaves cooked in a peanut sauce (matapa), chicken in lime-juice sauce (*galinha à Zambeziana*), and grilled meats, Mozambican style (churrasco Moçambicano). Along the coast the cuisine is more Portuguese influenced than in the interior, and in most restaurants excellent fish and seafood are available. In addition to grilled prawns, lobster, crayfish, and calamari (lulas), seafood dishes such as *macaza* (grilled shellfish kebabs), *bacalhau* (dried salted cod), and *chocos* (squid cooked in its own ink) are items on the menu. The food is seasoned with peppers, onions, and coconut.

Traditional drinks abound, and each region has its favorite. Some of the more common ones are made using cashew fruit, manioc, mango, and sugarcane. Normally, the fruits are gathered and washed and left to ripen completely. The fruits are then opened to loosen the seeds and rind, and everything is put into a large receptacle for a day or two. The mixture is then passed through a sieve, and the liquid is bottled and is ready for drinking. *Maheu,* a beverage commonly served at ceremonies or as a snack, is made with corn flour and water. After cooking it resembles a thick porridge. It is then refrigerated and sugar is added. Another popular drink served with food is *shema* (palm wine).

Chamuças (Chicken Turnovers)

Chamuças are one of Mozambique's most famous appetizers. They are of Indian origin and are common in much of southeastern Africa. But because of the Goan influence over centuries in Mozambique, this dish is now considered Mozambican. It can also be prepared with a shrimp filling.

Filling

2 lb bone-in chicken thighs

2 tbsp vegetable oil

2 large onions, minced

1 large tomato, chopped

1 tbsp curry powder

1 tbsp grated fresh ginger

1 tbsp red pepper flakes

1 tbsp garam masala

1 tsp salt

Pastry Dough

2 c all-purpose flour

¾ tsp salt

1½ tbsp oil or clarified butter

½–¾ c water

Vegetable oil for frying

For the Filling: Place the chicken thighs in a large pot, cover with water, and bring to a boil. Reduce the heat and simmer until the thighs are cooked through, about 30 minutes. Remove from the heat, and cool the thighs in the broth. When the chicken is cool, remove the skin and bones and shred the meat. Heat the oil in a large skillet. Add the shredded chicken and all the other filling ingredients to the skillet and simmer for 30 minutes, stirring frequently. Add a little of the broth if the mixture becomes too dry. Set aside.

For the Dough: Stir the flour and salt together. Make a well in the center of the mixture and pour in the oil and water. Stir briskly until combined, gradually adding more water if necessary. The dough should be slightly moist and stick together. On a lightly floured surface, knead the dough for about 10 minutes, until smooth and elastic. Cover with a damp cloth.

Preparation: Break off pieces of dough and shape them into balls the size of walnuts. Roll each ball into a circle about $\frac{1}{16}$ of an inch thick and 4 inches across. Cut the circle in half and place a heaping tablespoon of filling on one side of the half circle. Fold over the half circle to form a triangle. Brush a bit of water along the edges and pinch to seal. Continue in the same manner until all the dough and filling have been used.

Heat 2 inches of oil in a large skillet. The oil is ready when a piece of dough sizzles when dropped in. Fry 3 or 4 chamuças at a time until golden and crisp on each side. Drain them on paper towels. Serve at room temperature with mango chutney.

Variation: You can also use wonton wrappers in place of the pastry dough. In this case, place a tablespoon of the filling in the center of each wonton, brush the edges with egg wash, fold in half diagonally, and press the edges together to form a triangle. Fry in hot oil until golden on all sides.

Typical Meals

Mozambique with its 10 provinces has many regional flavors and ethnic food cultures. There are some differences in the type of food eaten in the interior and the major cities, but there are many meals that are typical and enjoyed throughout the country. Mozambican influence is evident in dishes such as peanut balls (*almondegas de amendoim*); collard greens with peanut sauce (matapa saborosa); rice with split peas (*mucapata*), which is prepared in a clay pot and served with grilled chicken or fish; African-style grilled chicken (frango à cafreal); fish and shrimp stew (*peixe à lumbo*), papaya pudding (doce de papaia); and sweet cassava (*doce de mandioca*). Goan influence is evident in dishes such as chicken curry (*caril de galinha*), chicken with peanut sauce (caril de amendoim e galinha), shrimp curry sauce (*molho de camarão com caril*), steamed rice bread (*sanna*), and chicken turnovers (chamuças).

Breakfast in rural areas is often different from what is eaten in urban areas (see Vignette). It might consist of *mealie,* corn ground into flour and prepared like porridge and mixed with goat milk. The cassava root is also eaten, either baked or mashed with water to form porridge. Other dishes include grilled meats, rice or potatoes, fruit, or leftovers from the previous evening meal. Occasionally omelets and scrambled eggs are served with a bit of meat and bread.

Lunch in rural areas might consist of stews, grilled meats, and manioc. All meat is cooked over an open fire. What is not eaten at lunch is often mixed with rice and served for another meal. Vegetables such as onions, potatoes, cabbage, and tomatoes, grown in home gardens, are cooked as side dishes or combined with leftover meats for stews. The evening meal might consist of leftovers from lunch, soup and bread, or grilled meats with cooked vegetables.

Maguinha and *upswa* are similar food staples that are widely consumed. Maguinha is made with cassava, and upswa is made with corn. Both are quite filling and are best eaten with a sauce, but when times are difficult and food is scarce, especially in the dry season, people will eat maguinha without a sauce.

In the rural areas, because of a frequent lack of electricity and gas for refrigeration, *meringues* are used to hold water. They are small containers made from clay and shaped like a balloon with a long neck and a lid. They are usually kept in the kitchen and will keep water fresh for at least three days.

Eating Out

Most restaurants and hotels in larger towns and provincial capitals offer Continental, Portuguese, and local fare. In villages and rural areas one might find only *barracas* (small food stalls). These small stalls are also found in the large cities and usually serve local fare such as maguinha or upswa and sauce, fried fish, grilled chicken, and local beverages. In hotels and restaurants in the larger cities the fare is varied.

A barracas, or street vendor, in Mozambique. (Amitai | Dreamstime.com)

There will usually be one or two local dishes on the menu along with dishes like *caldo verde* (a green vegetable soup) and other soups, grilled meats, chicken, seafood, fish, fruit salads, French fries, and sandwiches. There are also ethnic restaurants: Italian, Portuguese, Brazilian, Greek, and Indian. Most cities have cafés, *pastelarias* (bakeries), or *salão e cha* (tea parlors) where one can purchase tea, coffee, pastry, snacks, or light meals.

Special Occasions

Food is a part of many celebrations, and it is customary to serve a meal at parties, rituals, and other social gatherings. At private parties such as weddings and funerals, a variety of foods are found. Regional dishes as well as dishes with Portuguese, Chinese, and Indian influence are very popular at buffets. People celebrate festivals differently across the country, depending on the family's financial resources, regional foods, or religion. For instance, Tete Province, which is inland and separated from northeastern Mozambique by Malawi, has an estimated 1.8 million goats. Locals celebrate festivals by slaughtering a goat and preparing *caldeirada de cabrito* (goat stew made with potatoes, onions, tomatoes, carrots, peas, beer, curry powder, and lemon juice). In Zambézia Province, located southeast of Malawi, a celebration would not be complete without mucapata (rice with green split peas, coconut milk, and chili peppers, served with rice cooked in coconut milk).

In southern Mozambique, animals such as cows, goats, and pigs are slaughtered during Christmas or Family Day and New Year's Eve or Day. These two holidays bring families together more than any of the others, which are public and political events. Usually it is the religious holidays when special foods are eaten. For example, on Easter, meat is not eaten, and most who celebrate eat salt cod, other fish, and seafood. On Christmas Eve, because of Portuguese influence, bacalhau (salt cod) is the fish of choice for those who can afford it. Other dishes that are served for festivals are *caril de galinha à Moçambicana* (curried chicken, Mozambican style), *feijoada Moçambicana* (Mozambican bean stew), *lumino* (fried fish and manioc stew), matapa (collard or pumpkin greens in peanut sauce), frango à cafreal (African-style grilled chicken), and churrasco Moçambicano (Mozambican grilled meats).

Apart from national holidays—most of which are celebrated with parades, songs, and dance performances—Mozambique has few festivals. The public holidays and special events include New Year's Day (January 1), Mozambican Heroes' Day (February 3; commemorating the country's revolutionary heroes), Women's Day (April 7), International Workers' Day (May 1), Independence Day (June 25; commemorating Mozambique's independence from Portuguese rule in 1975), Victory Day (September 7; commemorating the signing in Lusaka of the treaty granting Mozambique its independence), Revolution Day (September 25; commemorating the initiation of Mozambique's independence struggle in Chai, Cabo Delgado Province), Day of Peace (October 4; commemorating the signing of the 1992 peace accords), and Christmas or Family Day (December 15). Each city or town also has its day commemorating its founding. Local businesses are closed on this day, and the city celebrates with parades and song and dance performances. Maputo Day is November 10.

Caril de Galinha à Moçambicana (Curried Chicken, Mozambican Style)

Curried chicken, Mozambican style, is very popular throughout the country and is served at many parties and formal ceremonies. This dish is one of a number of examples of the influence Indian food has had on Mozambican cuisine.

Chicken

½ c olive oil

1 large onion, chopped

2 cloves garlic, chopped

½ c chopped fresh parsley

1 whole chicken (3–4 lb), cut into 8 pieces, or 8 bone-in thighs

Curry Sauce

½ c olive oil

2 cloves garlic, minced

1 large onion, minced

2 medium tomatoes, peeled, seeded, and chopped

1 tbsp curry powder

1 tsp salt

1 tbsp flour

1 tsp red pepper flakes

2 c unsweetened coconut milk

For the Chicken: Heat the oil in a large skillet and sauté the onion, garlic, and parsley, stirring until the onion becomes transparent. Add the chicken pieces; cover with water, and cook over medium heat until the chicken is cooked through. Set aside (see note).

For the Sauce: In another large skillet, heat the olive oil over medium heat; add the garlic and onion. When the onion turns lightly golden, remove it from the skillet and puree in a food processor. Return the puree to the skillet, and add the tomatoes, curry powder, and salt. Stir well. Mix the flour with 2 tablespoons of water and add to the skillet along with the pepper flakes; mix well. Cook over low heat for 1 hour, adding ½ cup of coconut milk every 15 minutes. Add the chicken pieces, cover, and cook another 10 to 15 minutes, until the sauce thickens. Serve with white rice.

Note: After cooking the chicken you can remove the skin and bones and cut it into large pieces before adding it to the curry sauce.

Diet and Health

In 1975, when Mozambique gained its independence, the government created a free, nationalized health care system. Its goal was to improve the population's health through preventive medicine. They employed nurses to give vaccinations and to educate the population about sanitation and other basic health care issues. They established clinics throughout the country, many of which unfortunately were destroyed during the civil war. In 1992, when the civil war ended, the government began rebuilding those clinics. The government also abandoned a law prohibiting private practice in an effort to increase the number of doctors, whose numbers had dwindled due to the exodus at the beginning of the civil war. Today, the main health threats are malaria, AIDS, and sleeping sickness, which is transmitted by the tsetse fly.

Malnutrition is also a concern and is the most common health problem, mainly because there is a lack of a variety of foods in many residents' diets, and they do not consume an adequate amount of protein, vitamins, and other essential minerals. There is a movement for the population to introduce new crops and change their diet to a much healthier one. As a result, vegetable gardens are being encouraged, and beans, tomatoes, onions, potatoes, and cabbage are being planted. Many people would have to borrow money to buy the seeds to plant these crops because most Mozambicans do not have a bank account. Bananas and cashews grow well in most parts of the country and are part of the local diet. Goats are kept by many, and therefore goat milk is available. For those living along the coast and near rivers, fish and other seafood are an important part of their diet. Corn, which is often ground into flour, is eaten by people in the rural areas for most of their meals. Rice is not grown in the northern region, which means that villagers have to purchase it. Many cannot afford to do so.

Cherie Y. Hamilton

Further Reading

Hamilton, Cherie Y. *Cuisines of Portuguese Encounters.* New York: Hippocrene Books, 2008.

Rowan, Marielle. *Flavors of Mozambique.* Maputo, Mozambique: Edição do autor, 1998.

Namibia

Overview

Namibia is a country in southern Africa with a land area of 318,148 square miles. It is a little less than twice the size of the state of California. It has a population of just over two million, making it the second least densely populated country in the world, after Mongolia. Namibia shares borders with five countries: Angola, Zambia, Zimbabwe, Botswana, and South Africa. The country has over 900 miles of Atlantic Ocean coastline, much of it comprised of the western reaches of the Namib Desert, which encompasses over 31,000 square miles and is believed to be 55 million years old. The northern coastline of Namibia includes the notorious "Skeleton Coast," named for many shipwrecks and whale bones that washed to shore during the height of the whaling industry, due to dangerous ocean conditions created by cold water currents, surf, and thick fog.

Namibia gained its independence from South Africa in 1990, ending a long era of occupation that had begun with colonial Germany in 1884. While the Germans conceded claim to Namibia after World War I, their imprint of enforced segregation, relocation, and subjugation of indigenous tribes still echoes in contemporary Namibian society. German occupation was followed by South African control (initially as a British colony, then as a sovereign nation), which brought the system of apartheid to Namibia, further entrenching deep divisions between races by institutionalizing a system of disenfranchisement and discrimination. In 1966, the People's Liberation Army of Namibia formed a guerrilla military response to South African rule, demanding independence. The war was fought until 1988, when South Africa agreed to relinquish its administration of the country. Today, Namibia is a presidential representative democratic republic.

Whites and mixed-race Namibians (Coloured and Baster groups) together make up nearly 14 percent of the population, but the majority of Namibians are black Africans. The largest tribe is the Ovambo, which constitutes nearly half of the black African population of Namibia. The original inhabitants of Namibia are the Bushmen (San), who are hunter-gatherer nomads. English is the official language, though the multinational origins of Namibian society contribute to a country where German, Afrikaans, and Oshiwambo are widely spoken and often represent first languages for many citizens. Namibia is an interdenominational country but with Christians comprising 80 percent of the population.

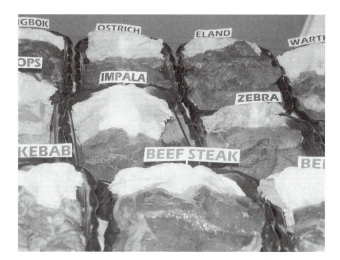

Various meats at a barbeque in Namibia, including zebra, impala, warthog, and ostrich. (Unique2109 | Dreamstime.com)

🍽 Food Culture Snapshot

Joyce Udjombala is married, with two children. She works as a librarian at a public branch in the Katatura Greenwell neighborhood of Windhoek, Namibia's capital city. Her husband, Thomas, is a middle manager at a power plant in the suburbs. Both Joyce and Thomas are ethnically Ovambo and grew up in northern Namibia but moved to Windhoek for postsecondary education. Joyce's oldest, a daughter named Maria, is an undergraduate at the University of Namibia, studying law. Her youngest, a daughter named Letha, is still in high school. Both daughters live at home with their parents.

Joyce grew up just outside Oshakati, the second-largest city in Namibia, located in the far north of the country. She grew up watching her mother and aunts prepare traditional dishes like *oshifima* (boiled millet) and *potije,* a vegetable and meat stew cooked in a three-legged metal pot. Now, living in Windhoek, Joyce prepares oshifima with cornmeal, more widely sold in the southern part of the country. She makes the thick cornmeal porridge with milk and often serves it with cooked meat. While Joyce and her family all eat their lunches at work or school, they gather most nights for a shared dinner. Provisions for the meal are purchased at the local supermarket on the way home from work and include a meat roast and gravy, canned or fresh vegetable sides, and bread. On special occasions, Joyce and her family will enjoy one of Windhoek's many restaurants, which specialize in everything from Cameroonian curry to *braai,* a grilled-meat tradition from South Africa that has spread through Namibia so widely that it is considered a national dish.

Major Foodstuffs

In Namibia, a main meal for all ethnic groups is not complete without meat. While cattle are raised and consumed widely in Namibia (the number of cows far exceeds the number of humans in the country), wild game such as springbok, zebra, and oryx is also very popular. Two preparations are most common, the first being the traditional grilled meat called *braai,* an Afrikaans word from South Africa, where the dish originated. This dish is so thoroughly woven into Namibian society that they have made it their own. The second preparation, called *biltong,*

involves air-drying small pieces of meat into strips of jerky. While braai makes a meal, biltong is seen in the cities as a snack, though in rural areas it is an important preparation to preserve meat for future consumption. Finally, German sausage varieties are widely available in Windhoek and other urban areas across the country.

With its long coastline, Namibia also boasts an array of seafood dishes. Fresh oysters are popular, along with fillets of hake and kingklip. Namibia exports horse mackerel and pilchard, a species of sardine. Recreational fishing is popular in Namibia, and licenses are available for enthusiasts. A seasonal Ovambo delicacy is the mopane caterpillar, or *omagungu,* which is fried with vegetables and often served with oshifima. The caterpillars can also be dried to eat as snack, much like biltong.

Grains and Starches

Grains are grown and prepared widely throughout Namibia. In the north, millet, or *mahangu,* is the staple crop. Millet is more drought resistant than other grains and can thrive in the unforgiving climate in much of the north of Namibia. Once harvested, millet is pounded and winnowed to release the chaff. It is typically prepared as oshifima, by boiling it with milk and water, and then served alongside a meat stew.

In southern Namibia, white maize is the common crop, so cornmeal often replaces millet when making oshifima. While the wheat industry exists in Namibia, it is a much smaller crop compared to white maize and millet. Wheat pasta dishes are popular in much of urban Namibia, but the pasta is often imported from South Africa, which has much more robust wheat production.

Oshifima

Serves 4–6

1¼ c white cornmeal or millet

1 c milk

1 c water

Heat a cup of water to boiling in a medium-sized saucepan. Meanwhile, in a bowl, gradually add ¾ cup of the cornmeal to the milk, stirring briskly to make a smooth paste. Add this mixture to the boiling water, stirring constantly. Cook for 4 or 5 minutes while adding the remaining cornmeal. When mixture begins to pull away from the sides of the pot and stick together, remove from heat. Transfer oshifima into a lightly greased bowl. With damp hands, shape it into a smooth ball, turning in the bowl to help smooth it. Serve immediately.

To eat in the traditional manner, tear off a piece of oshifima and make an indentation in it with your thumb. Use this hollow to scoop up stew or sauce from a communal bowl. Alternatively, the oshifima can also be shaped in the bowl as a vessel, and the meat stew can be poured in and over it and then served.

Many groceries and markets in urban Namibia offer a range of fruits (bananas, grapes, and oranges) and vegetables (tomatoes, onions, pumpkins, and potatoes), most of them imported from neighboring countries with longer growing seasons and more suitable climates. Much of Namibia is arid and particularly challenging for providing crops the irrigation that they require. However, there are indigenous fruits that thrive in pockets of Namibia, namely, the northeastern Caprivi Strip of fertile floodplain bordering Zambia and Zimbabwe. The *marula* tree bears a plum-sized fruit of the same name with a light yellow-green rind, which is rich in vitamin C. The dark orange *eembe* berry is also prized and is known by the term "bird plum." Both these fruits can be used for making jellies, jams, fruit juices, and even cakes.

While yellow maize and varieties of beans are grown in parts of Namibia, the yield is for feeding livestock, not humans. Nearly half of Namibians depend on subsistence farming for their livelihood, so small-scale gardens and crop cultivation in rural areas are the norm. Groundnuts (peanuts) are cultivated in Namibia but mainly for export to South Africa.

When the Germans arrived in the late 1800s, they brought their culture of beer brewing, which today manifests in the Namibian Breweries' popular brand Windhoek Lager, which, along with an assortment of other lagers and drafts, is sold throughout the country. In addition to imported drink traditions, Namibia has a number of indigenous alcoholic beverages. *Walende* is a distillate made from palm fruit, while *mataku* is a wine made from watermelon. Millet is used to prepare a fermented drink known as *oshikundu,* sold widely in northern Namibia in both alcoholic and nonalcoholic varieties. The German influence on cuisine is not limited to beer and bratwurst. German pastries and cakes are widely available in bakeries and restaurants in urban areas such as Windhoek and Swakopmund.

Cooking

The most common Namibian dishes are grilled over heat or fire, as opposed to baked. In the countryside, cooking is typically done over a fire, though efforts are underway to introduce solar stoves to take advantage of a plentiful natural resource. Cooking in some exclusive Windhoek neighborhoods largely takes place in kitchens that are outfitted with the full range of appliances one might expect in any industrialized nation: refrigerator, oven and stovetop, microwave, and dishwasher. Across town in more impoverished areas of the city, kitchens would more resemble their relatives in the countryside than their city counterparts. In the most arid climates of Namibia, which is much of the country, both meat and fruit are prepared for storage through a drying process that keeps the food preserved for months.

Outdoor cooking in a small village in Namibia. (iStockPhoto)

Typical Meals

For rural Namibians farmers, who make up roughly 70 percent of the population, meals revolve around an agricultural lifestyle. A porridge breakfast of oshifima might start their day at dawn before the heat of late morning and midday sends people into the shade of trees or indoors for lunch, which would likely involve a meat dish—fish for coastal dwellers, game or cattle in much of the north and south. Dinner would be taken after a second shift either herding or tending to crops. While both men and women work in the fields, it is expected that women will prepare the meals.

In Namibian cities, many families eat breakfast at home so as to arrive at work between 8 and 10 A.M., depending on the job. Toast, coffee, tea, eggs, and boxed porridge are common dishes. Families with European heritage likely add cold meat slices and cheese to the breakfast menu. Alternatively, some urbanites enjoy *kapana,* or a skewer of beef or other red meat, sold in roadside stands in many neighborhoods of metropolitan Windhoek. These inexpensive sticks of grilled meat are not limited to breakfast, as the vendors fire up their coals in the morning and then sell throughout the day into the evening. While some urbanites return home for lunch, many grab a quick take-out sandwich or salad in the neighborhood where they work at around noon. Dinner is served at home between 6 and 8 P.M. and is typically prepared by the matriarch of the household.

Eating Out

In rural Namibian villages there are no traditional restaurants, so eating out would involve an invitation by another household, most likely as part of a celebration of life (birth or marriage) or death (a funeral). In towns across Namibia, small eateries sell biltong, simple foodstuffs, and braai. In addition to small-scale restaurants, a range of street vendors offer everything from kapana to fresh fruit.

Windhoek, like any large capital city, has restaurants that run the gamut from fine dining to dives. Many of the most expensive ones line Independence Avenue and feature cuisines that have been introduced to Namibia, such as German, Cameroonian, Chinese, and U.S. Western barbecue. Independence Avenue is also home to malls that offer up dozens of coffee shops and fast-food eateries that sell pizza, sandwiches, and sweets. Joe's Beerhouse is a short drive from the city center and specializes in the array of meat dishes Namibia is famous for, from *sosatie,* the South African term for skewered meat in a spicy sauce, to classic braai. The restaurant Luigi and the Fish specializes in preparing the array of seafood found in Namibia.

Special Occasions

Namibian Independence Day, March 21, is marked with celebrations across the country. Families will mark the day with a braai, and parties are known for "sunrising," as the festivities continue through the night until the break of dawn. As a predominantly Christian country, a number of holidays are observed widely in Namibia and typically involve meals and traditional dishes. Christmas and Easter often involve meals following church services, where a centerpiece red meat dish would be joined by vegetable and pastry side dishes, followed by dessert. Turkey or goose, while popular in a few households in Namibia, is not common. Rural celebrants would most likely prepare a slaughtered goat. Specialty baked goods such as *veldt bread,* made with cinnamon, allspice, and cloves, grace many a table. In German Namibian households, Christmas would be celebrated on December 24, whereas in non-German Namibian households, the celebration would take place on the 25th.

Diet and Health

While urbanization has meant exposure to processed foods, supermarkets, and chain eateries for many Namibians, the majority of the country lives and eats in rural villages and towns where their diet has remained relatively unchanged for generations. Namibia has one of the widest gaps between rich and poor in the world, which affects diet and health indicators. While life expectancy in Namibia is an average of 51 years, if calculated along class and race lines, a more divergent set of ages would be revealed.

Anita Verna Crofts

Further Reading

Anandajayasekeram, Ponniah, Mandivamba Rukani, Suresh Babu, and Frikkie Liebenberg, eds. *Impact of Science on African Agriculture and Food Security.* Wallingford, UK: CABI, 2007.

Chavonnes Vrugt, Antoinette de. *My Hungry Heart: Notes from a Namibian Kitchen.* Birmingham, AL: Venture, 2009.

Nigeria

Overview

Nigeria is located on the western coast of Africa in the central region. Its name is taken from the Niger River, which is not only an important food source but also an important form of transportation. The country is quite large, approximately twice the size of California, and has a mostly humid, tropical climate. The majority of the topography is plains and plateaus; however, there are mountains to the eastern side of the country and the Sahara desert is to the north. These landscape differences introduce variation in the types of foods that may be grown. The rivers also enabled trading of foodstuffs and the migration of people. The slave trade was established in Nigeria by the Portuguese around 1400, with other European traders and eventually the British taking control and establishing Nigeria as a territorial entity in 1914. As a result, the food of the southern United States has been influenced by the traditional foods of Nigeria through the slave trade, while traders coming into the region introduced Asian spices such as cinnamon and nutmeg.

Nigeria has the largest population in Africa (148 million people) and accounts for just less than half of the total West African population. There are approximately 200 different ethnic groups, and around 500 different languages are spoken; most residents are multilingual. The largest ethnic groups are the Hausa-Fulani in the north, the Igbo in the southeast, and the Yoruba in the southwest. These ethnic groups also provide the lingua franca for each region, and their languages are designated as national languages. Government business is conducted and written in English. Despite this ethnic and linguistic diversity, the country is dominated by just two religions (90% of the total population). The northern region is largely Sunni Muslim although there are a number who belong to Sufi orders. Likewise, the Christians in the south may belong to a number of individual church sects, including Catholic, Methodist, Lutheran, Anglican, and Pentecostal.

Although one of the poorest countries in the world, the country is rich in natural resources, including oil and gas but also productive agricultural land able to produce a wide range of fruits and vegetables and support livestock. Nigeria has the second-largest African economy and accounts for 41 percent of the sub-Saharan gross domestic product. Over half of the country's population (54%) lives on less than one U.S. dollar a day. Life expectancy within the country is just 47 years. Families tend to be large, with an average fertility rate of 5.5 children per woman, and nearly 13 percent of teenage women have children. The infant mortality rate is high, at 19 percent (giving the country a ranking of 13 in the world). Literacy rates in Nigeria are better than for sub-Saharan Africa as a whole (69% compared to 59%), but boys are more likely to be enrolled in school (100%) than are girls (87%), and they attend school for a longer period (the average length of time in school for boys is nine years compared to seven years for girls). Economic data from 2007, however, suggest that inflation has fallen in recent years to around 5.5 percent (consumer prices) and that the current balance of payments is positive (exports exceeding imports). Most farming involves animal husbandry as well as crop production, and the majority of farmers operate small-scale farms

One of many street markets in Ibadan, Nigeria's second-largest city. Located about 100 miles from the Atlantic coast, Ibadan is an important commercial center that serves as the capital of Oyo state. (Corel)

of five acres or less that can be managed by hand. The Nigerian government argues that oil is now the primary foreign-exchange earner; however, there has been unrest in the region where oil is produced (the Niger Delta), which has reduced oil exports.

Despite the poverty, this is a country full of hope, creativity, and invention. In the recent past the country was ruled by the military; however, in 1999 the transition from military to democratic governance began, and in May 2007 the Umaru Musa Yar'Adua was sworn in as the third democratically elected president. This event is the first instance in Nigeria of a peaceful handover from one civilian government to another. Like the United States, the national governance structure is that of a federation, with a federal government presiding over 36 states.

🍽 Food Culture Snapshot

Adé and Ṣadé Òyélówò live in an affluent area of Lagos. Adé is a headmaster, and Ṣadé is a teacher. They have three children, a relatively small family by Nigerian standards. Abení, a daughter, is 14 years old. Tunde, their son, is 11 years old. The youngest child, Grace, is 8 years old. All of the children attend their father's school. The family is Christian and is Yoruba. Their house reflects their more affluent standing and has a kitchen with a gas range and a refrigerator. There is a veranda on the house that overlooks their garden, which has mango and orange trees and a small vegetable patch where Ṣadé grows yams, carrots, greens, peppers, and onions. The two girls help her with this.

Ṣadé prefers to go to the local market to purchase most of what she needs. She likes the markets because she can meet and talk with the market women and she feels that the food is better quality because it is fresh. For example, buying food in the market means she can also buy whole animals and then cut them up herself at home or live chickens that she can then kill when she is ready to use them. She can also get whole spices, such as nutmeg and pepper, that she then grinds in her mortar and pestle at home. Sometimes she will send the girls to the market after school to buy things for her. The market is not just a place to buy fresh food. She can also buy things like cooking oil for frying meat and plantains, sugar, and tea. She buys rice secretly from a woman who also has a stall at the market, because it is now illegal to import rice, so it must be smuggled into Nigeria.

Each day the family gets up at about 5 A.M. They have a small breakfast of thick toast or a porridge made of ground dry maize. The adults drink tea, while the children have hot chocolate. It is Abení's job to prepare this meal, but Ṣadé serves it to Adé on the terrace, where he will eat on his own until Tunde is 15 and will join him. The others eat together in the living area, where there is a table. Although school does not start until 8 A.M., Adé and Ṣadé leave earlier, as they must be at the school by 7 A.M. to prepare. The three children clean up the house and walk to school together later. The school day finishes at 2 P.M., when the three children walk home together unless they have a church or other function after school. The children have a snack on the way home that they purchase from one of the roadside vendors. This snack will often be *dodo* (fried plantains with chili), as this is a favorite, or *chinchin* (fried dough) if they want something sweeter. The snack is important because no lunch is served at the school. Ṣadé arrives home around 4 P.M. after stopping at the market. Ṣadé then starts preparing the evening meal, which consists of stew and either rice, if it is available, or a *gari* (ground cassava root) that is made into a thick porridge. The girls help with dinner preparations as it is part of their chores. Adé arrives home about 7 P.M. Once dinner is ready, at about 8 P.M., Ṣadé serves Adé his dinner on the terrace, bringing it to him on a tray. She and the three children then eat together at the dining table.

Major Foodstuffs

While a traditional Nigerian meal would consist of a thick stew and a starch, individual wealth, regional location, religion, and tribal affiliation play a key role in determining the specific character of these items. Meat and fish feature in Nigerian cooking; however, apart from those whose livelihood is through farming or fishing, these foods are affordable only to the very wealthy. As a result, a large proportion of Nigerians are vegetarian out of necessity. For those who have access to meat, this would include goat, cow, chicken, turkey, goose, guinea fowl, and pigeon. The country also has a good source of freshwater fish, such as carp available from the Niger and Sokoto rivers, and seafood, including shrimp and crabs. Various varieties of palms are widely available, and as a result palm oil, made from ground palm kernels, is used extensively. There is an abundance of fresh fruit in Nigeria; papayas, pineapple, coconuts, plantains, and mangoes are plentiful. The Muslims in the north do not drink alcohol as those who are caught drinking face strong penalties under sharia law. Non-Muslims sometime drink a fermented palm drink produced locally or wine, beer, or spirits that are imported. Throughout the country men are more likely to drink than women.

While Western foods are available in supermarkets, these are also frequented only by the very wealthy. Ordinary Nigerians tend to purchase traditional foodstuffs from local markets and roadside stalls. Because of this provisioning behavior, combined with the diversity of the physical geography of the country, foods take on a regional character. For example, people from the north, who are also mostly Muslim, have diets based on beans and sorghum; those in the eastern part of the country eat pumpkin, dumplings, and yams (not the same as the American sweet potato); the southern people, who are mainly Christian, eat groundnut (peanut)-based stews (see following recipe) and rice as well as pork; and those in the southwestern and central areas (Yoruba people) tend to eat cooked gari (cassava root powder) with okra stews, groundnuts, mushrooms (which are also a harbinger of the ripening of new yams), yams, and rice dishes such as *jollof rice.* Finally, those living on the coasts are more likely to have seafood stews instead of meat stews, while those near rivers will include freshwater fish stew in their diets. Foods made with milk and milk products are not common, except in the northern parts where the Fulani ethnic groups live. Women and girls from this region will hawk boiled cow milk (*mein-shanu*), which is then used in cooking. People also use milk in tea and on their breakfast porridge.

Groundnut Stew

Serves 6

1 stewing chicken or chicken parts (2–3 lb)

2–3 tsp oil for frying

1 tsp salt

A pinch of cayenne pepper

1 yellow onion, chopped finely

1–2 garlic cloves, chopped

4 c water

1½ c natural peanut butter (preferably with low sugar content)

Cooked rice for 6

Toppings: Chopped tomato, onions, pineapple, orange, papaya, banana, and grated coconut

In a large heavy-bottomed pan heat the oil and fry the onion and garlic until soft (5–10 minutes). Add the cayenne pepper. Once the onions and garlic start to caramelize, add the chicken and cover with water to form a broth. Simmer until tender. Once the chicken is cooked, remove the chicken from the broth and debone. Add the peanut butter to the cooking broth and stir until smooth. Return the deboned chicken to the broth and simmer for a half hour or more. If a thicker sauce is desired it can be thickened with cornstarch. Adjust seasoning to taste. Serve over cooked rice (as you would a curry) and sprinkle with fruit toppings.

Jollof Rice

Serves 6

½ tsp grated fresh ginger

½ tsp cinnamon

1 tsp thyme leaves

½ tsp salt

¼ tsp cayenne pepper

1¼ c chicken broth

16 oz chopped tomatoes (if using fresh tomatoes add 1 c water and 1 tsp tomato paste; otherwise, use the juice from the can)

2 tbsp peanut or cooking oil

2–3 lb chicken pieces

1 medium onion, chopped

1 clove garlic, chopped

1 bay leaf

1 c uncooked long-grain rice

Parsley, chopped

First, crush the ginger, cinnamon, thyme, salt, and cayenne pepper with a mortar and pestle. Combine the chicken broth, tomatoes, and either the juice from the can or, if using fresh tomatoes, the water and tomato paste. Add the crushed herbs and spices to this liquid. Set aside.

Next, in a large skillet heat the oil on high heat. Brown the chicken pieces on all sides (about 15 minutes). Once browned, remove the chicken from the skillet. Reduce heat to medium, and add the onion to the pan and cook in the same oil in which the chicken was browned. Soften the onion and add the garlic. Cook until tender but do not brown. Drain off the fat and return the chicken to the pan. Add the broth and tomato mixture to the chicken and the bay leaf. Do not stir. Bring to a boil, then reduce the heat and simmer for 30 minutes, covered. Skim off any fat. Add the rice, making sure the rice is covered in the liquid. Cover and simmer for an additional 30 minutes, until rice is cooked. Remove the bay leaf. Sprinkle with parsley and serve.

A vegetarian version of this dish can be made by omitting the chicken and substituting vegetables such as green pepper and okra and by using vegetable broth instead of chicken broth.

Food in Nigeria is often well seasoned with salt, pepper (*atalodo*), and chilies. Refined sugar, however, is not traditionally an important part of the Nigerian diet, as many snacks are savory rather than sweet and the norm is to drink water or fruit juice with meals. Examples of snack foods that may be made at home or purchased from street vendors include fried bean cakes, *kulikui* (deep-fried peanut butter), chinchin, and dodo. Where there is a dip, it is often made from chilies. Children buy and sell small, hard candies on the street. Globalization has meant the availability of sugary soft drinks, which are now increasingly consumed with meals instead of water or juice.

Cooking

Most Nigerian meals are made up of one course consisting of a starch and a soup or thick stew. Frying food in oil as part of the preparation of the stew is very common. Food is cooked on a small portable stove or hearth. The better off may have a gas or electric stove. In modern houses, the kitchen would be part of the house and have similar features to Western kitchens, with a stove, refrigerator, cupboards for storing things, and so forth. In rural areas, however, the kitchen may be separate from the main living area and include an area for the cooking fire with a support for a cooking pot. In these kitchens, where there may be no oven, baking is accomplished by wrapping the food in leaves and cooking it in the hot coals. Indeed, banana leaves serve many functions as a cooking utensil. The leaves are also used as lids for the cooking pot to keep steam in, as well as baking pans. All Nigerian kitchens will also have a mortar and pestle, which may be made of wood or stone, for crushing spices and mashing yams.

In Nigeria cooking is women's work. It is the wife's responsibility to teach young girls how to cook. This teaching is done through demonstration, as cookbooks are rare. Women tend to cook from memory, and a good mastery of timing and volumes is considered a valuable skill that relies on the ability to understand how dishes should taste, how much to prepare, and how long it should take. This practice of cooking by memory and intuition also means that each cook imposes her own tastes on the food. Because food is frequently shared, women aim to achieve a reputation as a good cook among family and friends. Indeed, a number of epigrams are directly related to acknowledging the importance of women's cooking, such as "the way to a man's heart is through good food."

Polygamy is common and legal for all men in Nigeria, though those who are Christian are less likely to adopt this practice. In a polygamous family, wives take turns feeding the husband, but each wife is primarily responsible for feeding and caring for her own children. Particularly in rural areas, however, families live in extended units, and the wives along with aunts, female cousins, sisters, and so forth will often help each other when needed. Because men and women tend to keep their money separate, in order to support their children, women take on jobs to enable their provisioning such as tending the family garden, processing palm oil, or selling vegetables in the local market. Young boys and female children help their mothers with these tasks after school.

Typical Meals

Breakfast, eaten at five or six in the morning, may be leftovers from the previous day, rice and mangos, dodo (fried plantains), stewed soybeans, or a porridge made from gari (ground cassava root). In wealthier urban households breakfast may be a cup of tea and toast with butter. Lunch may then be eaten around 11, and in many rural areas it is the main meal. In the evening a lighter meal may be taken. Throughout the day snacks are eaten, and for many children snacks are the only time when they are able to eat food without having to share it with their siblings.

While dining tables and cutlery are increasingly present in both rural and urban Nigerian households, this is a relatively recent phenomenon introduced by the wealthy. Traditionally Nigerians would eat with their right hand (use of the left hand is considered unhygienic) sitting around a mat placed in the central living area. This includes soups, which are eaten with a cupped hand. Because many Nigerians think that the eating experience is diminished

A group of men in Nigeria eating lunch. It is customary for the men to eat before the women and children. (FIFA | Getty Images)

by the use of utensils, traditional practices are still observed despite the availability of these items.

Nigerian households continue to be sharply divided along gender lines. This extends into eating practices, whereby the males would eat first and separately from the women and children. It is the wife's job to serve her husband his evening meal on a tray. In the poorer families, what is left on the plate is then eaten by the women and children. In wealthier families, where there is more food, women and children may eat at the same time as men, but they are still separate from the men. Very young children will share their mother's plate, but as they get older they will share a plate with other children of the same sex. When children reach adulthood, in wealthier households they are given their own plate. In households where men eat first, it is considered bad manners for

the male householder to eat all the food and leave nothing for the women and children. These gendered eating practices occur throughout Nigeria.

Eating Out

Because of poverty, most Nigerians tend to eat at home rather than eating out at a restaurant. Restaurants tend to be in the cities and are the domain of foreign visitors and the wealthy. There is the possibility of purchasing cooked food from market traders or small eateries (*bukas*) that serve local foods. Those eating this food are most likely to be men eating while at work during the day, rather than people eating out as a social or family event. Women who work prefer to bring food from home that they have prepared rather than purchase food out, as for many women it is considered disgraceful to have to buy cooked food.

While eating out in the commercial sense is limited, it is not uncommon for Nigerians to eat out at a friend's or relative's house. Indeed, there is an expectation that enough food should be made to feed visitors, who may arrive unannounced. Within Nigerian custom, all visitors are to be fed, and the more generous the meal, the greater the affection that is being shown by the host. Guests are not expected to eat all the food they are given; instead, this generosity should be reciprocated by the giving of gifts. If a person is invited to dinner at a Nigerian home, it is appropriate to bring fruit, nuts, or chocolates for the host and a gift for the children.

While it is often common to see Americans and British people eating "on the go," Nigerians, partly because of the nature of the food but also because of custom, tend to sit and relax while eating. Indeed, it is viewed as bad manners to eat while doing something else, including when eating food purchased from street vendors.

Special Occasions

As with most cultures, food is an important part of all Nigerian celebrations. While some celebrations are directly linked to the Muslim or Christian religions, others are linked to ethnic groups or particular regions, while still other celebrations are more national in their practice. The Christian holidays of Christmas, Good Friday, and Easter, as well as Muslim holidays of Eid al-Fitr, Tabaski, and Eid al Moulid, are all officially recognized. Eid al-Fitr celebrates the last day of Ramadan, which is the month-long observation of fasting (occurring in September). During daylight hours, those who are Muslim must not eat or drink. After dusk, families will buy food from street vendors to break the fast. For those who celebrate Christmas, this often involves traveling to be with relatives. Children will open presents in the afternoon. A typical Christmas feast will include *obe didin* (roasted goat), jollof rice, yams, liver, and other dishes.

Many of the regions have festivals to celebrate the various foodstuffs that are indigenous to that area. Examples include the Rgingu Fishing Festival, which takes place in Arugungo in Kebbi state. Arugungo is a village along the Sokoto River, and the festival marks a visit by a dignitary that occurred in 1934. While the original visit was in August, the festival is celebrated each year in February or March to mark the end of the growing season. Thousands of men enter the river with nets or in boats and for 45 minutes harvest perch and balloon fish. The largest fish that is caught is offered to the organizers of the event. What is caught is then grilled (barbequed) and eaten in a communal feast.

Perhaps more widespread are the New Yam Festivals, *Iri-ji,* celebrated in August, and the Second Yam Festivals, celebrated in November to January. These festivals are primarily celebrated by the Igbo communities. Each community will have its own day, much like European and North American communities that have harvest festivals or country fairs. The day symbolizes the conclusion of a work cycle and the beginning of a season. Only dishes made of newly harvested yam are served on this day. Prior to the festival, any old yams, which may have been stored whole or ground up, are disposed of. Before the celebration, new yams are offered to the god or yam spirit, Ifejioku, and ancestors first. Then the eldest and highest-ranking male member of the village will have the first taste of the new yam crop, as this position carries with it the privilege of being an intermediary between the gods and the community. Finally, the community and anyone who is visiting, not just those who grow and harvest the yams, will be invited to eat the new yam dishes, which are different from those that use old yams. The ritual of the new yam is meant to express thanks for the harvest to the gods. Yams are also considered a male crop signifying sustenance, strength, and endurance.

Similar to the New Yam Festival is the Benin Festival, which is held at the end of the rainy season after the harvests have been gathered. Unlike the other festivals, this festival is also intended to introduce marriageable (as defined in terms of wealth) girls to boys. While not all youth of marriageable age may participate in the festival matching, all of the villagers will participate in the feast. In some places the festival is held only every four years.

At the family level, most Nigerians will celebrate marriage, naming, and death with food. Kola nuts are used in wedding ceremonies to bless the marriage, and guests are invited to taste the symbolic foods used in the ceremony as well as to join in a meal afterward. Eight days after a child is born there is often a naming ceremony, when the child is given its names by its parents. After the ceremony there is a celebratory meal. Likewise, those who attend a funeral will also be invited to share a meal with the family afterward. Meat dishes will often be served at these events, even by poor families. In fact, celebrations may be the only times when less-well-off households eat meat. The purchase of a whole steer is not uncommon for such occasions, but unlike many westerners, Nigerians will use the whole animal, including the organs, feet, and head. What is not edible will be used in other ways.

Diet and Health

Given the relative productivity of the land and the possibility of growing a large variety of fruits and vegetables, the country offers the potential for providing access to a good, well-rounded diet. Indeed, recent estimates suggest that the average Nigerian's daily calorie supply is around 2,700. However, the extreme poverty of so many can be linked to health inequalities that are directly related to or are impacted on by diet. Of children under the age of five, about 39 percent are underweight, and over 39 percent are stunted (short for their age). Just over one-quarter of all children under five (27%) are estimated to be malnourished. Many in Nigeria also suffer from vitamin A deficiencies, which can result in blindness; these deficiencies result from inadequate access to greens, orange fruits and vegetables, and protein. As is the case with food supplies, access to clean drinking water is also divided by class. Just 51 percent of the population has access to safe drinking water, while the remainder are susceptible to waterborne diseases such as bacterial and protozoal diarrhea, hepatitis A and E, and typhoid fever.

Nigeria is also in a malarial zone. These diseases can also contribute to vitamin A deficiency.

Finally, while malnutrition and water-related illness certainly contribute to the short life expectancy, AIDS also takes its toll. Today, the estimated life expectancy of Nigerian men and women is 47 years. Nearly three million adults in Nigeria are living with AIDS or HIV. Antiretrovirals, which are used to treat AIDS, are costly and require doctor support; also, the person must take the drugs with food and must take them several times a day. Access to food and water plays an intrinsic role in the life chances of Nigerians today, because without access the cycle of poverty is further exacerbated.

Intergenerational transfer of illnesses such as AIDS and illnesses related to vitamin and mineral deficiencies such as goiter, night blindness, and rickets are also linked to poverty. The estimated infant mortality rate was over 7 percent, or about 74 infant deaths for every 1,000 live births. Importantly, newborns in Nigerian societies are regarded with pride. They represent a community's and a family's future and often are the main reason for many marriages (a large proportion of Nigerian households are characterized by polygamy). Throughout Nigeria, the bond between mother and child is very strong. During the first few years of a child's life, the mother is never far away, and Nigerian women place great importance on breast-feeding and the bond that it creates between mother and child. Children are often not weaned off their mother's milk until they are toddlers. If a mother is infected with AIDS or HIV or is vitamin deficient herself, then her milk will not be sufficient to adequately feed her child.

Both Western and traditional forms of medicine are available in Nigeria. The health care system is sponsored by the government; however, because corruption is high and there is a shortage of trained health care professionals, ordinary Nigerians' access to health care is limited. Traditional medicine, also known as *juju,* is commonly practiced and involves the use of a variety of plants and herbs in the cures. Most families also have their own secret remedies for minor health problems. Juju can also involve adhering to food taboos; for example, when suffering from breathing difficulties one should avoid hot food, kola nuts, and coconuts. Likewise, "slimy" food (e.g., okra soup) should be avoided when recovering from a wound because it is thought that the wound needs to dry out to heal and the texture of the foods will slow this process down. Some traditional remedies involve avoiding foods that, while not related to the characteristics of the malady, when eaten are thought to anger the gods. For example, smallpox is thought to worsen if chicken and grains are consumed because for some these foods are forbidden and the gods will not heal the patient if they are eaten. Finally, the character of the overall diet is also linked to understandings that combine taste with health benefits. Pepper, for instance, is not just used to improve the flavor of the dish but also because it is thought to act as a natural preservative and antibacterial agent and also to reduce the body temperature of the eater, which is important in a hot climate.

Megan K. Blake

Further Reading

Falola, Toyin. *Culture and Customs of Nigeria.* Westport, CT: Greenwood Press, 2000.

Gordon, April A. *Nigeria's Diverse Peoples: A Reference Sourcebook.* Santa Barbara, CA: ABC-Clio, 2003.

"Nigeria." Countries and Their Cultures. http://www.everyculture.com/Ma-Ni/Nigeria.html#ixzz0XOj8ktQf.

"Nigeria." Food in Every Country. http://www.foodbycountry.com/Kazakhstan-to-South-Africa/Nigeria.

Odebiyi, A. I. "Food Taboos in Maternal and Child Health: The Views of Traditional Healers in Ile-Ife, Nigeria." *Social Science and Medicine* 28, No. 9 (1989): 985–96.

Robson, E. "The 'Kitchen' as Women's Space in Rural Hausaland, Northern Nigeria." *Gender, Place and Culture* 13, No. 6 (2006): 669–76.

Senegal

Overview

The Republic of Senegal is located at the westernmost point of the African continent at the intersection of trade routes connecting Africa, Europe, the Americas, and the Arab world. It is bordered by the Atlantic Ocean on the west, Mauritania to the north, Mali to the east, and Guinea and Guinea-Bissau to the south. The country of Gambia lies almost entirely within Senegal's borders, separating the southern tropical region of Casamance from the dry Sahelian regions in the north and northeast of the country.

Due to high rates of urban migration since the 1970s, nearly half of Senegal's 11.9 million inhabitants live in major cities, including the capital Dakar, Touba Mbacké, Thies, Mbour, Kaolack, Ziguinchor, and St. Louis. The official language of Senegal is French, but national languages Wolof, Sérère, Diola, Pular, Malinké, and Soninké are commonly spoken.

Eating habits vary based on region and ethnicity, with the largest differences occurring between rural and urban areas and between northern Senegal and the Casamance region. Though many common dishes can be found throughout Senegal, each ethnic group has its own specialties and unique ways to prepare common dishes. Senegalese dishes generally consist of a cereal base accompanied by sauce. At lunch the base is almost always rice, especially in urban areas. In rural regions, millet continues to be frequently consumed, though, there too, consumption of imported rice is gaining popularity. In coastal regions, fresh fish is the main source of protein, but beef, chicken, dried fish, and beans are also commonly eaten, especially further inland. Pork, although obtainable, is rarely eaten, because the vast majority of Senegalese are Muslim and thus abstain from pork.

🍽 Food Culture Snapshot

Aissatou and Malik Sarr live with their two young daughters in Pikine, a suburb of Dakar. Although they have their own apartment, they eat meals and spend most of the day at Malik's parents' house a few streets away. The Sarrs' eating habits are typical of lower-middle-class urban citizens. They mainly eat Senegalese dishes and a few from other regions of West Africa. Western influence can be seen, especially at breakfast and dinner, though they always have a distinctly Senegalese feel.

Around 9 A.M., Aissatou brings her daughters to their grandparents' house for breakfast. By that time, Malik has already left for work, grabbing a coffee from a street vendor on the way. When she arrives, water is already hot for *café touba,* a spiced coffee, and *quinquiliba,* a tealike infusion. The family eats a French baguette with butter or a chocolate-peanut butter spread before Aissatou walks to the market.

Lunch is the largest and most important meal of the day in Senegal. Aissatou decides what to prepare based on the ingredients available at the market. She carefully chooses the fish or beef, carrots, onions, eggplant, okra, cabbage, potatoes, and cassava (a root vegetable common in tropical climates) that she'll need for lunch and dinner. She chooses spices among tiny bags of

A local market in the region of Casamance, Senegal. (Torsius | Dreamstime.com)

salt, pepper, vinegar, mustard, and dried hot peppers hanging above the tables of meticulously stacked vegetables. Once back home, she begins cooking, since preparation takes over three hours. She boils the meat and vegetables for hours, adding bouillon cubes, garlic, parsley, tomato paste, and peppers to flavor the meal. Aissatou prepares enough for her husband's immediate and extended families. She shares the responsibility of cooking with an aunt, each woman cooking for four days at a time. The Sarrs eat lunch around three in the afternoon. If family members are not present at lunchtime, a portion of the meal is set aside for them. Dinner is a lighter meal served around 8 or 9 P.M. Rice is generally avoided in the evening in favor of millet, the traditional grain staple in Senegal; Moroccan-style couscous; or European dishes such as pasta, omelets, or French fries.

Major Foodstuffs

Even though Senegal is mainly rural, environmental and infrastructural issues paired with politics that favor cheap international products have left the country dependent on imports for the majority of its food needs. Rice and wheat are most heavily imported, followed by products like powdered milk, bouillon cubes, and oil.

Rice is the main staple in Senegal, especially in urban areas. It has been cultivated in Casamance since the 11th or 12th century. However, most of Senegal is too arid for rice, better suited for growing coarse grains such as millet, sorghum, and *fonio* (an indigenous kind of millet). Today, despite significant political efforts to enhance the production of rice, cultivators are unable to keep up with the country's growing demand, linked to changing eating habits among groups who once favored millet and to growing urban populations. Senegalese generally eat broken rice, a by-product of rice processing that is less valued on the international market but preferred in Senegal.

Certain processed foods are gaining importance in the Senegalese diet. Bouillon cubes and mustard are used to flavor sauces. Breakfast is dominated by industrialized foods: bread, butter, cheese, instant coffee, and powdered milk. Although drinking beverages during the meal is uncommon, Senegalese often buy sodas (Western brands and local varieties) to serve while entertaining guests.

Senegal has a wide variety of fish, ranging in quality from the highly valued marlin to the bony and inexpensive sardinella, called *yaboy*. In coastal areas, fresh fish is the main source of protein, affordable for all social classes. Dried fish is also commonly consumed, especially farther inland. Beef consumption is widespread, and Senegalese regularly eat mutton, in part because sheep sacrifice is essential for Muslim celebrations. Chicken is mainly eaten among the middle and upper classes or for special occasions, due to its price and the fact that one is generally obligated to purchase an entire chicken. *Niébé*, a bean native to Africa, also provides a significant source of protein, especially among lower social classes.

Vegetables are a part of nearly every Senegalese dish. However, they are often regarded as an accompaniment to the sauce that adds color and flavor, rather than a principal part of the meal. Alongside vegetables native to Africa, like okra, bitter eggplant, and cassava, one finds vegetables introduced by Europeans, including onions, potatoes, cabbage, tomatoes, eggplant, and carrots.

Senegal has a wide variety of tropical fruits, including mangoes, papayas, oranges, grapefruit, bananas, and coconuts. One can also find native fruits like *madd* (*Saba senegalensis*), which could be mistaken for an orange from the outside but inside has seeds surrounded by a bitter, slimy fruit. Madd is sugared, or salted and spiced, before it is eaten.

Many fruit juices are produced in Senegal. The most common, *bissap,* is made from dried hibiscus flowers that give the juice a deep purple color similar to that of wine. Another common juice is made from the fruit of the baobab tree, called *bouye* or monkey bread. When dried, this fruit is chalky with a pinkish-cream color. It makes a sweet, viscous juice of the same shade. *Ditkah* (*Detarium senegalensis*) is a firm, round fruit the size of a small plum that makes a bright green juice. It has a brown shell that is easily peeled to expose a green, fibrous fruit. Juice is also commonly made from ginger, which can be extremely tart or sweet. Like the tea and coffee served in Senegal, fruit juices are often flavored with large amounts of sugar. Members of the Catholic minority also commonly drink wine and other alcoholic beverages, whereas Muslims generally avoid alcohol.

Milk products are most commonly consumed in the form of *lait caillé,* literally, "spoiled milk." This milk is slightly less viscous than yogurt and is sweetened. Most Senegalese primarily consume powdered milk, but the Peulhs, a traditionally nomadic ethnic group of herdsmen, keep dairy cows. Those with family in Peulh villages can often easily access liquid milk.

Cooking

In nearly every Senegalese household, two to three hours per day are devoted to the preparation of lunch. Senegalese tend to have large families and many generations live together, meaning there is nearly always a female family member at home who prepares the family meal. It is also common to hire a maid to help with housework and cooking, even among middle- and lower-middle-class families.

Little is done to minimize cooking time, because the care that a woman puts into the elaborate preparation helps to maintain her family's reputation. Attempting to save time when washing ingredients, mixing spices, or leaving the sauce to boil would be interpreted as cutting corners, which Senegalese presume could not produce a good meal and would furthermore not be considered respectable.

Girls begin to learn how to cook between ages 9 and 12, starting with simple tasks like grinding spices in the mortar. It is considered imperative among all social classes that women know how to cook, even in families where maids prepare the meal the majority of the time. The idea that a girl would marry without knowing how to cook all the basic Senegalese dishes is considered absurd and embarrassing. Girls take over cooking duties from their mothers in their teenage years, though only during vacation periods and on weekends if they go to school. Daughters-in-law who live with their husband's family are generally in charge of cooking. Though cooking is mainly a female task, as young men increasingly move out of the familial house before marriage, more Senegalese men are learning to prepare basic dishes.

Cooking often takes place in a courtyard outside the house. Meals are prepared in huge cooking pots

Members of various families eat a dish served during the mid day meal in the village of Merine Dakhar in Senegal, 2008. (AFP | Getty Images)

on burners atop gas cylinders. Wood charcoal is sometimes used because it is less expensive, though more time-consuming, than gas. Small woodstoves or grills are also frequently used. Many middle- and upper-class families have kitchens built into their houses, and some have Western-style cooking ranges, including an oven. Stainless steel pots, large metal spoons, and knives are the most-used items. Onions and other vegetables are skillfully sliced with one hand while they are held with the other. Even in the wealthiest households, spices are ground up by hand in a wooden pestle and mortar. Preparation often includes multiple methods of cooking. Fish is quickly fried before boiling, and meats are often both boiled and grilled for the same dish. Rice and couscous are steamed and are sometimes then added to the boiling sauce.

Typical Meals

In Senegal, people of different regions, religions, and socioeconomic classes share a surprising number of dishes. Meals are prepared in two forms: *ñari cin* and *been cin. Cin* refers to a marmite, a large cooking pot; *been* means "one," and *ñari,* "two." Ñari cin dishes consist of steamed white rice, cooked in one pot, accompanied by a sauce cooked in another. Been cin dishes do not include a separate sauce, because the rice is boiled in the sauce of the other ingredients. All Senegalese dishes blend a variety of bold flavors: garlic (often an entire head per meal), onions, black pepper, chili peppers, dried fish, and tamarind (the flesh of a sour pod native to Africa).

The national dish, *ceebu jën,* which originates from the colonial capital of St. Louis, is by far the most popular dish in Senegal. Eating and preparing this meal is perceived to symbolize a true Senegalese. Families often eat *ceebu jën* twice a week or more, switching off between the red and the white varieties (the former includes tomato paste). The preparation of other types of been cin dishes resembles that of *ceebu jën,* except that red meat is substituted for the fish in *ceebu yapp,* and *ceebu keccax* uses dried fish.

Ceebu jën

Serves 6

4 carrots

4 turnips

Large piece of cassava

1 small green cabbage

1 eggplant

5–6 okra

2 large onions, chopped

½ head garlic

Small bunch parsley

20 black peppercorns

1 bouillon cube

1 tamarind, pulp removed from pod, soaked in hot water and strained

1 small chili pepper or ¼ tsp cayenne pepper

2 or 3 lb whole fish (tilapia, or sea bass) or marlin steaks

1 lb dried, salted, or smoked fish such as cod or herring

½ c oil

6½ c white rice

1. Peel all the vegetables, then cut them into large pieces (halves or fourths). Clean fish, but leave whole (including the heads, which add flavor).

2. Grind the garlic, parsley, pepper, bouillon cube, tamarind pulp, and the chili or cayenne pepper (to taste) until it forms a paste, using a mortar and pestle or food processor. Cut 2–3 small slits in each fish and stuff them with the spice mixture.

3. Heat oil in a large pot. Fry the onions and the dried fish for a few minutes, then blanch the fish in the oil, frying on both sides for 1–2 minutes. Remove the fish and set aside.

4. Add the carrots, turnips, and cassava and enough water to cover them, and bring mixture to a boil. Add salt and pepper as needed. Reduce heat and let simmer for 30 minutes or more. Add the other vegetables and the fried fish. Simmer another 20 minutes until the vegetables are soft.

5. Remove the vegetables from the pot (you should be able to easily pinch off pieces with your fingers). Add the rice to the bouillon that's left (there should be twice as much liquid as rice). Bring water to a boil again. Cover, and let the rice cook for 15 to 20 minutes, lowering heat toward the end. Cook until the rice has completely absorbed the water.

6. Serve on a large platter with the vegetables and fish arranged in the middle, on top of the rice, which is spread out evenly.

After *ceebu jën* (called *ceeb* for short), the most common dishes are ñari cin. The sauces for these dishes vary greatly, and each originates from a specific ethnic group or region. The peanut butter–based *mafé* sauce is a Bambara dish. *Yassa,* based on onion, oil, and lemon juice, comes from Casamance. *Domoda* is a thick sauce made from peanut oil, tomato paste, onions, and flour. The *soupkànj* is an okra-based sauce that includes shrimp. When okra is ground up, it makes a thick, sticky paste to which red palm oil and vegetables are added. Besides these common Senegalese dishes, Senegalese often eat other West African specialties like *athiéké,* a dish from Côte d'Ivoire made from cassava.

Yassa

Serves 6

2 medium-sized chickens

2 c white vinegar

Salt

1 head garlic

1 bouillon cube

1 tsp Cayenne pepper or to taste

Pepper

8 tbsp lemon juice

6–10 large onions, chopped into rings or large slices

½ c peanut oil

2 bay leaves

2 tbsp Dijon mustard

1. Cut chicken into pieces. Remove the skin if you wish. Place chicken in a bowl with 1 cup vinegar and salt.

2. Grind the garlic, 1 bouillon cube, cayenne pepper, and 2 teaspoons of black pepper together with a mortar and pestle or food processor.

3. Remove the chicken from the vinegar. Cut slices (about 2–3 per piece) in the chicken, and stuff them with the spice mixture. Put the chicken back in the bowl with the vinegar and cover with the lemon juice. Add onions and another cup of vinegar to the mixture. Let marinate 10 to 20 minutes.

4. Heat grill or set oven to broil. Grill or bake the chicken until lightly browned but not done, making sure to cook all sides.

5. Heat oil in a large pot. Add onions, and cook for 10 to 15 minutes, until golden. Add the marinade the chicken was soaking in, bay leaves, mustard, and a cup of water to the pot. Cover and cook 20 minutes over medium heat. Add chicken and cook another 15 to 20 minutes.

6. Serve on a large platter over steamed rice, spreading the sauce evenly over the rice and arranging the chicken in the middle.

Senegalese generally eat around a large common bowl, seated on the ground or a low stool. This arrangement makes the meal easily divisible and is thus conducive to sharing. Guests, both expected and unannounced, are commonplace and (generally) welcome in Senegalese households. Food is eaten with the right hand, using either the fingers and palm to roll the rice into a ball or a spoon. The mother, or another member of the family (usually female), reaches into the middle and tears off little pieces of the fish or meat and vegetables, tossing them toward each family member. This way, everyone gets a fair portion, and guests receive the best bits.

Senegalese meals do not usually include a series of dishes but focus on one main dish. Dessert is relatively uncommon, although fruits are occasionally shared, and in some families French desserts are eaten from time to time. Certain families eat at Western-style tables, using plates and utensils. While this is more common among middle- and upper-class families, this practice is not generalized even among the upper classes.

The dinner meal varies from family to family more than breakfast or lunch, especially depending on economic level. In middle- and upper-class families, dinner has distinct foreign influences. Some common evening dishes include omelets eaten with baguette, pasta, Moroccan couscous served with Senegalese-style sauces, and steak with French fries. Millet-based meals are more common in the evening. While in some rural areas millet is eaten multiple times each day, in cities it is almost exclusively consumed at dinner. Residents of Dakar claim that eating millet at lunchtime seems so bizarre that it would throw off their perception of time. Millet can be eaten in a couscous or in porridge.

Evening meals often consist of a porridge-like substance made from boiled rice or millet flour that is served in either sweet or savory form. Among the savory dishes is *mbaxal,* a rice porridge prepared with fish or meat and vegetables that necessitates very little oil (unlike the dishes common at lunch, which oftentimes use half a quart of oil). *Daxin* is a thick dish prepared with peanut butter or niébé beans, cooked with peppers and onions. Other porridges are sugared and served with lait caillé (soured milk/yogurt). *Sombi* is a sweet porridge made from rice, and *fondé, caakry,* and *laax* are also porridges made from millet flour. Though these dishes are sweet, they constitute the evening meal and not a dessert. People of all socioeconomic classes eat these dishes, especially on Sundays or the day after a celebration, when Senegalese say they prefer something light. However, among many poor families, the evening meal is consistently a cup of fondé or laax, due to its inexpensiveness.

Eating Out

In villages, one's options for eating out are generally limited to a neighbor who sells snacks that she's prepared, while in urban areas the possibilities for dining outside the home are increasingly varied.

Vendors push moving stands through the streets, selling coffee and snacks. Others set up small tables in the road to sell peanuts, fruit and candies, or sandwiches and skewers of grilled meat. Plates of Senegalese dishes can be bought in restaurants, which sometimes consist of only a tent or a shack set up around a picnic table. There are many fast-food restaurants that sell hamburgers, hot dogs, pizza, and *chawarma* (a gyrolike pita sandwich of meat that has been cooked on a spit). But none of the franchised chains common throughout the world exist in Senegal. There are also a variety of sit-down restaurants that serve Senegalese dishes among European and sometimes Asian favorites.

Since the 1990s there has been increase in restaurants due in part to the introduction of the "continuous day," a bureaucratic change in the public school schedule that significantly decreased the length of the lunch break. This change also inspired transformations in employees' work schedules and thus led to an increase in consumption at university and company cafeterias, and at restaurants and sandwich shops near places of employment and schools.

The continuous day has made eating out a common activity for many urban residents, yet it continues to be viewed by many as a necessary evil. While people may enjoy restaurants, the underlying assumption is that eating at home would be preferable if it were possible. Some Senegalese favor home-cooked meals so much that they avoid taking a lunch break, preferring to eat leftovers from the family lunch when they return home at five or six in the evening.

The dislike of eating out is in part related to the strength of the value of community in Senegal. Social meals tend to be eaten with family inside of households, and eating out is often an individualized activity. There are also taboos against eating food prepared by strangers and fears that food outside the house is unhygienic. However, these beliefs are becoming increasingly uncommon, and exceptions are often made for certain types of restaurants or foods. Nonetheless, Senegalese mothers are often proud to announce that no one in their family eats in restaurants, even if certain members do sometimes eat out.

In general, restaurants are increasingly viewed as acceptable and even valued as a luxury. Certain families eat together in sit-down restaurants. This is especially common among those with relatives who live in Europe or the United States. Eating out with friends or siblings allows youth a sense of independence. Couples often go on dates to fast-food restaurants. Buying snacks from street vendors is widespread even among children, who receive a small allowance from their parents for this purpose. An afternoon snack could be prepackaged cookies, candy, Chinese-style egg rolls, *fatayas* (small fried pastries filled with spiced meat), or sandwiches filled with Nutella, tuna, or cream cheese.

Special Occasions

Religious holidays, baptisms, weddings, and funerals are all commemorated with a large gathering of family and friends accompanied by a feast. These festivals are very common, due in part to their extended guest lists. Some Senegalese attend two or three festivals per week. Children sometimes go from festival to festival, supplementing their diets with food provided at these feasts, especially in poorer neighborhoods. Thanks to Senegal's warm climate, celebrations take place outdoors under large tents set up in the street or a courtyard. Family members mill about, moving between the main house, the tent, the street, and the houses of close family members who live nearby and have opened their homes for this event.

Food is prepared in huge marmites (metal or earthen cooking pots with covers) by hired workers. Before, families tended to rely on *griots* both to provide the entertainment and to prepare food at festivals. Griots are the musicians and historians of West Africa. Traditionally, they would memorize songs that told of a particular village's history, genealogy, and great deeds. Today, those who prepare feasts are sometimes of the griot caste.

Meat at festivals is sometimes served with sauce and eaten with pieces of baguette, but other times it is cooked into a ceebu yapp. Food is served on a large platter, like at family meals. Guests gather around a nearby platter to eat under the tent or inside the house. Like at daily meals in Senegal, feasts generally focus around one main dish. Fruit juices and soda are served before and/or after eating, while guests mingle. Snacks, such as fataya, egg rolls, or meat on a skewer, are sometimes served while guests await the main dish.

The vast majority of Senegalese are Muslim. Islamic holidays like Tabaski (Eid al-Adha), Ramadan, Korité (Eid al-Fitr), and Tam Xarit (the Muslim New Year) are celebrated with a mixture of Islamic and Senegalese customs. Tabaski is the Muslim Feast of Sacrifice. It is essential that every family sacrifice at least one sheep on this day. The number of sheep sacrificed depends on the size of the family and their economic means. All parts of the sheep are consumed and are cooked in a variety of ways, including a tripe soup. The Muslim commitment to giving alms ensures that no one goes hungry on Tabaski; entire legs of mutton are given to neighbors or the poor.

During Ramadan, Muslims refrain from eating and drinking between dawn and dusk. Once the sun sets, the fast is broken with a small meal called *ndougu*. Senegalese drink hot tea or coffee and eat dates and foods commonly eaten at breakfast. A large meal is eaten later in the evening, which includes common Senegalese dishes. Senegalese often report that they spend more money on food during the month of Ramadan than at other times because they buy juices and more expensive ingredients than usual, indulging themselves slightly when they are allowed to eat.

The month of fasting is concluded with the festival of Korité. This day of feasting begins with the millet porridge laax. Sometimes Senegalese prepare variations of this dish with peanut butter and/or bouye. In early to midafternoon an elaborate lunch is prepared, which often includes chicken. Ingredients of particularly high quality and extra garnishes are used for both lunch and dinner on Korité.

Millet is considered the traditional grain of Senegal and is a critical part of many celebrations. In Senegal, the Muslim New Year is commemorated by eating millet couscous. Like on Korité, laax is served on the morning of baptisms, shared with those close to the family, who arrive early and spend the entire day at the celebration. In addition to laax, baptisms necessarily include two other symbolic foods: a sacrificial sheep and kola nuts. Sacrificing a sheep for a newborn is prescribed in the Quran. If parents cannot afford a sheep for their child's baptism, they borrow money or family members chip in to ensure that a sheep is purchased. If a sheep is not sacrificed, Senegalese believe that this will harm the growth and development of the child.

The kola nut is a small bitter red or white nut that contains stimulants and is the original flavoring of the soft drink cola. It is exchanged at many important events in Senegal. At baptisms, kola nuts are often distributed alongside candies made from rice and millet. Baptisms in Senegal take place eight days after a child is born and are also the day that a baby is named. Because guests cannot attend the naming ritual, the exchange of kola nuts is a symbolic way to connect the baby, the parents, and the guests at this celebration. Kola nuts are also distributed at weddings and funerals. At each event their exchange symbolizes social connections. At funerals the symbolic exchange of kola nuts and candies plays a central role.

Festivals in Senegal are generally elaborate and often expensive. Senegalese themselves often describe their celebrations as ostentatious but fail to see a way to change these rituals because they are part of a system of obligatory exchange. It would be considered disreputable to avoid or lessen the expenses associated with festivals. People often spend all their savings or borrow large sums to celebrate a baptism or wedding.

Diet and Health

Malnutrition has historically been and continues to be a serious concern in Senegal. In turn, calorie-dense foods like oil and meat are highly valued, because they are believed to give strength and to symbolize wealth. Until recently, in many parts of Senegal, it was said that when eating a good *ceebu jën*, one should have oil running down one's arm. The energy-filled carbohydrate bases of meals vary little, whereas the quantity of vegetables, fish, and meat lessens significantly in times of economic downturn.

Foods that are very sweet, salty, and oily are highly appreciated in Senegal, perhaps in part related to the constant threat of malnutrition. But diet-related noncommunicable diseases are increasingly widespread and are transforming ideas concerning health and nutrition. Diabetes and cardiac disease are extremely prevalent in Senegal and are a significant cause of death in the country. These degenerative diseases have been the subjects of many public awareness campaigns. Senegalese are thus increasingly familiar with problems related to obesity and consuming too much fat, cholesterol, and sugar.

However, awareness does not necessarily equate to transformations in eating habits. Senegalese often lament that their food is excessively oily, salty, or sweet but often feel that it is unalterable. This is, in part, due to the social role of eating in Senegalese society. Meals are a time of social exchange. Families eat together and welcome guests; meals link social networks. If one person or one family drastically changed their eating habits, this could isolate them and would seem individualistic and selfish.

The social difficulties of changing one's eating habits for health are obvious in the experiences of diabetics. Diabetics often explain that it is extremely difficult to avoid drinking sugary beverages because these play a critical role in welcoming a guest. To turn down food or drink one has been offered is considered discourteous. Familial celebrations pose a similar problem. To avoid appearing rude or ungrateful, diabetics often hide their illness and eat the foods offered, regardless of their nutritional content.

The price of ingredients and the cultural perception of ideal body size also play important roles in nutritional choices. It is cheaper to feed a large family a diet based on rice and oil than one based on vegetables. Many Senegalese simply don't have the economic means to consume the daily recommended amount of fruits and vegetables. In addition, heaviness is often associated with wealth, motherliness, and health. In turn, Senegalese women often prefer body sizes that are considered overweight by Western medical standards and make dietary choices based on these cultural perceptions rather than health considerations.

Despite the many cultural obstacles that inhibit proper nutrition, more and more Senegalese are attempting to make healthful changes in their diets. Many are trying to incorporate more fruits and vegetables into their diets and to avoid consuming excess rice, oil, salt, and sugar. These changes are mainly taking place in middle- and upper-class families, whose economic means allow them a certain nutritional flexibility that lower classes do not have.

Chelsie Yount

Further Reading

N'Dour, Youssou. *Sénégal: La cuisine de ma mère.* Geneva, Switzerland: Éditions Minerva, 2004.

Osseo-Asare, Fran. *Food Culture in Sub-Saharan Africa.* Westport, CT: Greenwood Press, 2005.

Sierra Leone

Overview

The Republic of Sierra Leone is a coastal West African country bordered on the south by Liberia and on the east and west by Guinea. The capital, Freetown, was established in 1787 by the British as a settlement for repatriated Africans and the descendants of those formerly enslaved during the transatlantic slave trade with the United States and the Caribbean. With an estimated population of six million, Sierra Leone is divided into four provinces comprising 12 districts that lie in environmental areas that range from mangrove swamps and the sandy beaches of the Atlantic coast to the savanna and mountainous highlands further inland. Locally, the country is known as Salone and its inhabitants as Saloneans.

There are about 18 different ethnolinguistic groups represented in the country with the predominant groups being the Mende, Limba, Temne, and Krio. Other smaller but no less significant groups include the Fula or Peuhl, Kuranko, Sherbro, and Mandingo. English is the official language of the republic, but Mende, Timba, Limba, and Krio are widely spoken. Sierra Leone and neighboring Liberia are the two African countries whose population boasts a significant number of descendants of formerly enslaved Africans. This group, known as the Krio, also speaks the Krio language, which is a creolized form of English mixed with elements of various West African languages. Inherent in Krio culture are strong elements of Western European culture due to the Krio history of enslavement in the Americas. These manifest themselves in food, cooking, dress, and speech, making the Krio quite different from the other indigenous ethnic groups. Large groups of Lebanese and Indians and their descendants add even more diversity to Sierra Leone's ethnic mix, and no one group claims majority status. Sierra Leone is predominantly Muslim, with about two-thirds of the population practicing Islam. Approximately one-quarter of the country is Christian, with the remainder adhering to traditional religions.

Sierra Leone is a rural country, and the majority of people are subsistence farmers. In urban areas, many grow vegetable gardens. Even so, food security is an issue due to the 11-year civil war (1991–2002) that stymied agricultural production from 1996 to 2007. The staple food of Sierra Leone is rice, predominantly varieties imported from Asia though indigenous rice production does occur in Sierra Leone.

🍽 Food Culture Snapshot

Manja and Edward Dauda are Mende and live in Kenema in southeastern Sierra Leone. They are a typical working-class Sierra Leonean couple with two small children. Edward runs a repair shop that also sells used auto parts. Manja's trip to the market yields purchases of rice, cassava, and plantains, all starches typical of the average Sierra Leonean diet. Fresh fruits like pineapple, pawpaw (papaya), citrus fruits, bananas, or soursop are purchased to eat or prepare as juices.

The family's day starts with breakfast, which may consist of fresh fruit like mango, pineapple, or pawpaw (papaya) with freshly squeezed lime juice or mashed butter pears (avocados) spread on bread or toast. A more elaborate way to start the day would be with a dish like rice pap, a cooked porridge made from rice flour, flavored with sugar and lime juice, and eaten with milk. Rice pap without milk is sometimes served to children as a snack. For lunch, Manja might buy rice at the market to be eaten with a groundnut (peanut butter) stew with chicken or beef and a side of *akara,* fried bean fritters made from indigenous ground cowpeas, of which black-eyed peas are a variety.

An evening meal might consist of a main dish like *jollof rice,* a one-pot dish of rice prepared throughout West Africa. It is cooked with a tomato-based sauce and any combination of mixed vegetables, often peas with chicken, meat, or fish. It is usually flavored with onions and plenty of hot chilies. *Plasas* is a stew of pureed leafy greens, usually cassava or sweet potato leaves, cooked with meat, smoked fish, chilies, tomatoes, and sometimes even pig's feet for flavor. It is known as *palaver* or *palava sauce* in other West African countries.

Manja, like most others, generally does her shopping at open-air markets where everything from cooking pots and cloth to shrimp or spices is sold. Because electricity can be unreliable or is nonexistent around the country for the majority of people, refrigeration is not always a viable option for most families, so food tends to be purchased on the same day it is eaten.

Major Foodstuffs

Many Sierra Leoneans raise chickens or have vegetable gardens and citrus or banana trees in their yards. They look to their local markets for meats, grains, and spices. The staple food is rice, and few consider a meal complete without it. There are permanent rice fields in the northwestern part of the country, where mangrove swamps dot the landscape. In other swampy areas of the country, rice production is also being developed, as imported rice accounts for nearly two-thirds of all rice consumed in Sierra Leone. Rice is even ground into flour for use in baked goods and other dishes.

Cash crops are produced by small farmers and include coffee, cassava (manioc), peanuts, cacao, millet, sweet potatoes, and palm kernels, which are used in the production of palm oil for cooking as well as beauty products that are important to the local and global marketplaces. Despite the presence of various waterways throughout the country and its location on the Atlantic coast, the commercial fishing industry is not developed, having been devastated by the civil war; the country is still struggling to rebuild it.

Besides rice, staples of the Sierra Leonean diet include cassava, palm oil, and groundnuts (peanuts). Cassava is often pounded into the ubiquitous West African dish *fufu,* a dish usually made from a starchy tuber that is boiled, then pounded in a mortar and pestle until it forms a sticky dough. Cassava root is also used as a base for spicy soups and stews. Cocoyam (taro) is a secondary staple and also an important cash crop, and it can also be used to make fufu. Sierra Leoneans also eat sweet potatoes (*Ipomoea batatas*) roasted and fried and have a preference for the leaves of the plant, which are cooked in thick sauces with palm oil. Yams (*Dioscorea* species) are also a significant food but much less important to the diet and culture than they tend to be in West African countries to the south, such as Ghana and Nigeria.

The fruits from which Africans produce their palm oil. (iStockPhoto)

Fresh fruits and vegetables are important to the Sierra Leonean diet, but vegetables in particular are very rarely eaten raw; they are most often part of a slow-cooked dish. Leafy greens such as leaves from the sweet potato and cassava are most common. Finely chopped, they are stewed with meat, chicken, or fish, flavored with chilies, and served with rice. Leafy greens are also valued for their mucilaginous qualities and added as thickeners to soups, much like okra. Okra, a vegetable indigenous to West Africa, is a much-beloved element in the Sierra Leonean diet and can be fried or stewed on its own or added to soups and stews for thickening and additional flavor. Corn, another important vegetable, is usually grilled and eaten as a snack. Fresh fruits like butter pears (avocados), bananas, papayas, pineapples, and citrus fruits are usually eaten raw, while fruits like soursop and passion fruit are most often used for refreshing juices. Plantains are a staple, eaten ripe or unripe. When ripe they are usually fried and served as a side; when unripe, they can be prepared similarly or boiled as part of a dish.

Plasas

This stew is the Sierra Leonean version of palaver sauce that tends to be found throughout West Africa. Meat and leafy greens are simmered in a tomato sauce. Any kind of greens can be used in the dish, although in Sierra Leone, cassava or sweet potato leaves might be preferred.

2 large bunches shredded collard greens

1 large onion, chopped*

1–2 Scotch bonnet chilies, chopped* (habaneros can be substituted)

⅔ c palm oil

1 lb beef stew meat

1 28-oz can crushed tomatoes

1-in. piece of ginger

2 c water

½ piece of smoked fish, cleaned and deboned

¼ c dried shrimp

¼ c natural unsweetened peanut butter

Salt to taste

*These two ingredients can be chopped together in a food processor.

Wash and shred collards by piling leaves atop one another and cutting thin strips; set aside. Chop onion and Scotch bonnet chilies. You may reduce the amount of chilies but use either habaneros or Scotch bonnets. Alternatively you may pulse the onions and chilies in a food processor; a very fine chop or puree will work well for this dish. Heat the palm oil in a large pot and fry the beef stew meat briefly. Add the tomatoes and the onion and chili mixture; grate the ginger, add to the pot, and cook for a few minutes more. Add 2 cups of water to the mixture and add salt. Reduce heat to medium low, and allow the mixture to simmer slowly for 20 minutes or until meat is fully cooked. When meat is done add shredded greens, smoked fish, and dried shrimp. Stir in the peanut butter and correct the seasonings. If liquid has reduced, add the rest of the water. Simmer 15 minutes more and serve.

The indigenous grain *fonio* (a kind of millet) is cultivated and eaten on a small scale. Corn and millet are commonly eaten. Corn is roasted or eaten fresh. It is also ground into meal for fritters or porridge. Rice is prepared in a similar manner.

Sierra Leoneans cook with coconut and peanut oil, but palm oil is the most important cooking oil. As in much of the rest of West Africa, the fruits of oil palms are harvested in Sierra Leone, and the intensely flavored, deep orange-red palm oil is extracted from those fruits. As much as the oil is valued for cooking, it is as highly valued for flavoring and coloring food. Palm butter is also extracted from the nuts and is a key ingredient in palm butter stew. The oil and butter are rich in beta-carotene, and it is one of the few vegetable oils high in saturated fat. It is, along with rice and cassava, one of the most important ingredients in Sierra Leonean kitchen.

Beans are important sources of protein. Indigenous cowpeas and pigeon peas are widely eaten, and white beans are also eaten on their own and used to thicken stews. Black-eyed peas form the base of highly seasoned bean fritters fried in palm oil and eaten as *small chop,* another name for snacks and appetizers.

Goat, chicken, and beef are popular meats, but pork makes an appearance in a fair number of dishes. Pork is often used to flavor soups and stews; pig's feet are the cut of choice. Afterward, the meat is usually chopped and then added to the finished dish; in the Sierra Leonean kitchen, nothing is wasted. The consumption of pork in Sierra Leone, a predominantly Muslim country, is most likely connected to the history of Freetown as a colony for formerly repatriated Africans from the United States and the Caribbean, where pork—smoked, salted, and fresh—was the primary meat made available for enslaved Africans to eat.

Smoked and salted fish flavor many dishes and are added to dishes as the focus of a dish or as a flavoring cooked along with other types of meat. Fresh fish, shrimp, and giant snails are also popular fried or cooked in spicy stews. Sierra Leoneans, like Africans across the continent, tend to use all parts of an animal, from nose to tail, including organs, known as offal. Trotters (cow's or pig's feet) are popular, as is cow skin, which is usually boiled in a soup.

Tomatoes, onions, and chilies are the base for many dishes; garlic is almost never used. Ginger and other herbs also flavor various dishes, but people like chilies above all. Generally, complex blends of flavors result from a mélange of spice, meats, and dried or smoked fish or shrimp slow-cooked together.

Cooking

Sierra Leonean cooking is labor-intensive, with most ingredients requiring a great deal of manual processing before cooking. Soaking, pounding, peeling, boiling, drying, and crushing of ingredients to be used in a dish are often the first steps to be taken before any actual cooking can be done. The most common cooking techniques are stewing, boiling, and frying. By and large, most things are made from scratch as Sierra Leonean cooks use convenience or processed foods infrequently, although some are widely available to the home cook: powdered plantain, yam, or cassava flours and canned meats.

Typical Meals

The average Sierra Leonean might awaken and drink tea or coffee and perhaps eat fruit or a piece of bread or cake to get the day rolling, but breakfast is not an important meal. Traditionally, people have tended to eat two meals a day—at midday and in the evening. These larger meals are referred to as *chop.*

A main meal might consist of a highly spiced soup or stew accompanied by rice or perhaps another starchy dish; food in Sierra Leone shares this general characteristic with food throughout much of the rest of the region. Dishes like plasas, pepper soup, or groundnut stew might be served, always with rice, cassava, cocoyam, or another starchy dish. The main meal of the day is generally served at midday and often eaten from a communal bowl, while leftovers from the midday meal are eaten in the evening for dinner. Like most West Africans, Sierra Leoneans snack frequently throughout the day on fresh fruit, roasted corn, plantains, and coconut. Small chop, as snacks are called, can also consist of baked or fried meat pies; savory and sweet fritters; or *suya,* kebabs of spicy grilled meat.

In Sierra Leone factors such as one's socioeconomic status and location, that is, whether one lives in an urban or rural area, affect the preparation and

A woman cooks rice over an open flame in Sierra Leone. (iStockPhoto)

consumption of meals. In cities, there is a shift toward more middle-class, white-collar jobs, and people may eat three meals a day in order to meet the demands of office hours. In rural areas the hard physical labor of agricultural work in fields may necessitate a heavier midday meal after the bulk of the day's work has been done. Because of poverty and food scarcity issues in Sierra Leone, two lingering effects of the 11-year civil war, many people eat only one meal a day—dinner. Because it is a very diverse country, many of the dishes are the same, but particular ingredients or slightly different cooking styles may be favored by a particular group.

Eating Out

There is little tradition of eating out in Sierra Leone, but cities and towns will have at least one cookery, which serves larger meals of the most traditional kind with rice, cassava, or plantain and grilled meat or fish. Restaurants generally serve only one or two dishes and plenty of different options for chop. One uniquely Sierra Leonean establishment is the *poyo house. Poyo* is fermented palm wine.

Special Occasions

Food plays an important role in celebrations throughout Sierra Leone. Everything from the unexpected visit of a stranger to special occasions like weddings, births, and funerals may be acknowledged with parties or celebratory dinners. As a country that has a Muslim majority and a significant Christian population, religious holidays such as the Eid al-Fitr, Ramadan, Christmas, and Easter are all celebrated, with feasting (or fasting) playing an important role in these celebrations. Sierra Leoneans celebrate Independence Day (April 27, 1961) with feasts, music, and dancing. *Awujoh* is a thanksgiving feast intended to acknowledge ancestors. It is also intended as a way for people to display gratitude and celebrate good fortune with family and friends.

Diet and Health

Sierra Leoneans have a varied diet that includes seafood, meat, many fresh fruits and vegetables, and very limited amounts of processed or sugary foods. Even with high amounts of rice and palm oil in their diets, most health problems do not stem from the typical diet itself. Rather, lack of food and subsequent malnutrition and inadequate sanitation are the primary causes of health problems in Sierra Leone. Civil war and governmental abuses have caused crushing poverty and a crumbling infrastructure. Basic food production and health care systems have been neglected, making it impossible to meet the needs of the growing population. While things are stabilizing slowly, hunger and malnutrition continue to be issues facing the people and government of Sierra Leone.

Rachel Finn

Further Reading

Celtnet Recipes. http://www.celtnet.org.uk/recipes/west-africa.php.

Ember, Melvin, and Carol R. Ember. "Sierra Leone." In *Countries and Their Cultures,* 1982–93. New York: MacMillan Reference USA, 2001.

Gibbon, Ed. The Congo Cookbook. http://www.congocookbook.com/.

Jackson, Elizabeth. African Chop. http://www.africanchop.com/.

Osseo-Asare, Fran. Betumi African Cuisine. http://www.betumi.com/.

Osseo-Asare, Fran. *Food Culture in Sub-Saharan Africa.* Westport, CT: Greenwood Press, 2005.

Smith, Ifeyironwa Francisca. *The Case for Indigenous West African Food Culture.* BREDA Series 9. Dakar, Senegal: United Nations Educational, Scientific and Cultural Organization-Regional Bureau for Education in Africa, 1995.

Wilson, Gibson Ellen. *A West African Cookbook.* New York: Avon Books, 1971.

Somalia

Overview

The Republic of Somalia is a country located in eastern Africa in an area known as the Horn of Africa. To Somalia's west and northwest is Ethiopia, to the southwest is Kenya, and to the north is Djibouti. The country's total land area is 246,090 square miles, about the same size as Texas.

Many of the people of Somalia live a nomadic or seminomadic lifestyle. They are organized by clans. The lifestyle of the nomad plays a major role in what foods they consume and how the food is cooked. Somalia has been a colony of England, France, and Italy. The influence of these countries can still be seen in their food and cooking. Religion plays a major role in the diet of Somalis, the vast majority of the population being of Islamic faith. They adhere to a halal diet, in which the consumption of pork and alcohol is forbidden and fasts are observed.

🍽️ Food Culture Snapshot

Ubah and her husband, Arale, live in Garas Balley, a small town northwest of Mogadishu. Some mornings, Ubah makes the journey to Mogadishu to go to the market. Mogadishu is about seven miles from her rural home, and it takes a little under two hours to walk there. Even so, she enjoys going to the market. Her two daughters, Amina and Nadifa, often make the journey with her. Not only is it a place where she can buy the food she needs to feed her family, but it is also an opportunity to socialize and enjoy the displays of handicrafts made from camel bone, wood, and fabric in the small shops located around the market.

The food at the market is fresh and local. A good variety of fruits and vegetables are available at a large market like the one in Mogadishu. She may also buy sorghum, rice, tea, sugar, dates, and pasta at the market. Ghee, which is butter that has been melted and its milky solids removed, is also purchased at the market. Ubah brings containers with her to the market so that she can buy milk. She will go from vendor to vendor, tasting the milk to find the one she likes best.

Major Foodstuffs

Vegetarianism is relatively rare in Somalia, so meals are mostly meat based. Nomadic groups raise livestock to sell to the rest of the population, and they also depend on the animals as a source of food. Mutton is favored, with goat meat also being quite popular. Beef is also eaten but rarely. The popularity of each kind of meat is largely dependent on its availability. A small amount of chicken is consumed, but Somalis don't generally eat any other fowl. Fish is consumed along the coast but is not a part of the diet of Somalis living further inland due to the lack of cold storage and transport. Camel meat is considered a delicacy and is reserved for special guests. The milk of the camel is prized for its health benefits and is usually given to children to promote health and growth.

Carbohydrates are a large part of Somalis' diet. Rice is one of the staples and usually accompanies the main meal. Corn, beans, sorghum, and pasta are also consumed. Spices are used throughout Somali cooking. For sweets, cinnamon, nutmeg, cardamom, cloves, and ginger are used. For savory cooking, black pepper, chilies, cumin, and parsley are commonly used. While most of these spices are not indigenous to Somalia, their common place in Somali cuisine illustrates the interaction Somalis have had with Asians and Middle Easterners. Somali farmers are able to produce a variety of fruits and vegetables including grapefruit, papaya, guava, pomegranate, mango, and citrus fruits. The selection of fruit available varies by region. Bananas are a very important fruit because they are one of Somalia's largest exports.

Cooking

Women do the cooking in the Somali household because it is perceived as a feminine role. Often, the women living in a village will gather together to prepare food and socialize. With very limited technolo-

gies at their disposal, cooking is a time-consuming and labor-intensive task. Grinding the grains to make traditional breads like *anjeero* and *muufo* is done by hand, with the women of villages or clans collectively sharing in the labor. The grinding is done with a Somali version of the mortar (*kal* or *tib*) and pestle (*mooye*), which is made of wood. It is done each day to make the bread. A small piece of the previous day's bread dough is saved for the next day as a source of leavening. Bread is baked in a covered, wood-burning clay oven or on a hearth.

The majority of the population lives in rural areas where kitchens often have no running water or electricity. In some areas, there are no kitchens, and food is prepared outdoors. In big cities and villages, the stove most commonly used is made from clay and stone and uses charcoal for fuel. In some villages, the stove is made of tin and uses charcoal and wood

A Somalian woman holds her baby as she prepares breakfast over an open fire. (AFP | Getty Images)

for fuel. The most common method of cooking in Somalia is frying, which is often done in ghee. Cooking meats that have been dried and then fried in ghee is a traditional method used by nomads. Meat may also be grilled over an open fire, broiled, or stewed.

Typical Meals

Somalis typically begin their day with *canjeero,* which is a pancakelike bread. They are usually eaten a few at a time with ghee and sugar. Canjeero is given to children—mixed with tea and sesame oil—to encourage growth. Liver and onions may also be eaten with the canjeero. *Boorash* or *mishaari*—a kind of porridge made of ground wheat and cornmeal—may be eaten for breakfast in the south. It is very similar to the polenta eaten in Italy. Somalis prefer to eat it with butter and sugar for flavor. Breakfast in the north might consist of shredded canjeero mixed with spices. Also popular is a spicy mixture of beef parts served with canjeero.

Canjeero

This bread is a staple in the Somali diet. It can be eaten with every meal. Traditionally, it is made with corn or sorghum flour.

2 c sorghum or corn flour

2⅔ c lukewarm water

Whisk together the flour and water until a smooth batter forms. Let the batter rest.

Grease a nonstick or cast iron pan with ghee and heat over medium low. Pour the batter into the center of the pan and rotate the pan so that the batter evenly coats the bottom. Cook until the batter has set and is no longer sticky. Do not flip the bread to cook on the other side. Simply remove it from the pan and serve it as an accompaniment to a meal or plain with sugar and ghee.

Qado, or lunch, is the largest meal of the day and can often be elaborate. It usually consists of a type of starch like rice or, in the south, *baasto,* or pasta, accompanied by a *maraq,* or stew of vegetables with meat served on the side. In the south, a mixture of rice and vegetables called *iskudhexkaris* is often eaten.

Dinner is often served as late as 9 P.M. and is a lighter meal than lunch. During Ramadan, dinner is eaten after the saying of the Tarawih prayers, which can be as late as 11 P.M. *Cambuulo* is a dish of slow-cooked adzuki beans mixed with butter and sugar. *Qamadi* is cooked in a similar way, with wheat replacing the beans. Muufo is another popular dish, similar to cornbread. It is baked in a clay oven and eaten by adding sugar and tea, then mashing it up. The evening meal may also be accompanied by a salad and is always served with canjeero. It is common to drink a glass of milk with cardamom before bed.

Throughout the day, many cups of sweetened tea or coffee are consumed by Somalis. They are drunk before or after a meal but never during it because many Muslims do not like to mix food and drink. Islam forbids the consumption of alcohol, so coffee, tea, water, and fruit drinks are the main beverages consumed.

Sambuusa, a popular Somali snack, are very similar to the Indian samosa. They are usually filled with ground meat and spiced with hot green pepper. *Bajiye* is also a popular snack. These deep-fried fritters are usually a mixture of maize, vegetables, meat, and spices and are usually eaten with hot sauce. Fresh fruits or homemade cakes may also serve as snacks throughout the day.

Gashaato or *qumbe* is a popular sweet consumed in Somalia. It is made of coconut, oil, sugar, and cardamom. In the south, *lows iyo sisin*—which is a bar made from peanuts, sesame seeds, and caramel—is a popular treat. *Jalaato,* which comes from the Italian word *gelato,* is a popsicle-like frozen fruit treat. Many varieties of cookies and cakes are also available, but these are usually reserved for holidays or special occasions. Table manners or rituals of eating are important to the Somali meal. First, before eating the meal, people wash their hands in a bowl of soapy water. Somalis often eat with their fingers or by using bread as a sort of utensil. Only the first three fingers are used. The left hand is never used for eating because Muslim tradition considers it the unclean hand.

Eating Out

The cities of Somalia have restaurants offering a wider variety of food. In the larger cities, such as Mogadishu, restaurants offering cuisines from other countries—such as Chinese, Italian, Middle Eastern, and American—can be found. Along the coast of Somalia, restaurants might offer freshly caught fish. Due to the influence of the Arabs over the seventh century, some restaurants offering traditional Arab food like kebabs might be found. By Western standards, Somali restaurants are quite inexpensive—a very nice meal costs about $10, and the cheapest meal costs only around $2 to $5.

Teahouses and coffeehouses are also popular places for people (mostly men) to gather and eat, drink, and socialize. Until recently, women seldom went to restaurants because women who were seen there were regarded as improper or as having a bad reputation. Many women still avoid restaurants in favor of socializing at friends' homes.

Special Occasions

Nearly all festivals and celebrations have religious significance in Somalia. Family, friends, clan members, and villages gather together to celebrate births, weddings, public events, and holidays. In Somalia, as in all other Islamic nations, the Muslim lunar calendar dictates the dates of religious festivals.

During the holy month of Ramadan, Muslim Somalis observe a month of fasting. Through fasting, they show a true devotion to Allah and Muhammad. During this month, from dawn until sunset, Somalis refrain from eating, drinking, smoking, and indulging in anything that is in excess. In the morning, they have to rise before dawn to eat *suhoor,* the meal used during fasting to replace the traditional breakfast, lunch, and dinner. It typically tends to be heavy and is highly regarded by Islamic traditions to avoid the typical side effects of fasting, such as fatigue and ill temperament. After the meal is eaten, prayers must be said, and fasting continues through the day until *iftar,* which is the evening meal. On the last day of Ramadan, the fast is broken. This festival is called Eid al-Fitr and lasts for three days. Somalis don their best clothes, which are often bought for the occasion, to attend communal prayer in the early morning. Prayer is followed by feasting and visiting relatives and friends. Food is usually plentiful at this time, with many dishes of meat, vegetables, homemade bread, and rice being served. Food is also donated to the poor.

Wedding festivities are also great times of feasting. Depending on what the families are able to afford, the festivities can last for three days. The first two days and nights of the festivities are attended by those of the younger generations. On the last day, everyone comes together for eating, drinking, and dancing. Circumcision ceremonies are also events where festivities take place. Male and female Somali children are circumcised. Parents invite friends, relatives, and neighbors for a feast that takes place after the ceremony.

Bur Katuunboow

Bur katuunboow are a type of fritter or donut. They are usually served during the month of Ramadan.

2 c all-purpose flour

½ c sugar

½ tsp active dry yeast

¼ tsp ground cardamom

Salt, to taste

1 c water

Vegetable oil to fry

Combine all dry ingredients. Add the water to the dry ingredients while stirring, being careful that lumps do not form. Cover directly with plastic so a skin does not form on the surface, and let rest overnight in the refrigerator. Heat the oil to 325°F. Using a small ice-cream scoop, form balls of dough and drop carefully into the oil. Let brown on one side, then turn gently. Remove the fritters from the oil and let them drain on a paper towel. Serve hot and fresh from the fryer.

Diet and Health

Religion influences Somali dietary practices in a number of ways. Nearly all Somalis are Sunni Muslims. Sunni is the largest denomination of Islam and means the words, actions, or example of the Prophet Muhammad. Muslim Somalis consume only halal food, which Islamic law dictates is the only food that is permissible to eat. Halal meat must be slaughtered in the way set out by Islamic law. The animal must be killed quickly, with the knife slitting the throat while a prayer is said and the name of Allah is spoken. The Quran explicitly forbids the consumption of the following foods: pork; blood; carnivorous birds of prey; animals slaughtered to anyone other than the name of Allah; carrion; an animal that has been strangled, beaten (to death), killed by a fall, gored (to death), or savaged by a beast of prey; fish that have died out of water; food over which Allah's name is not pronounced; and alcohol.

Annie Goldberg

Further Reading

Ali, Barlin. *Somali Cuisine.* Bloomington, IN: Author House, 2007.

Anderson, Sarah. *Sarah Anderson's Travel Companion: Africa and the Middle East.* London: Pallas Athene, 2004.

My Somali Food. http://www.mysomalifood.com.

South Africa

Overview

The Republic of South Africa occupies the southernmost part of the African continent and includes an area known as the "cradle of humankind," where three-million-year-old skeletons of the extinct hominid species *Australopithecus* have been found. Modern South Africa was not recognized as a unified territory until the early 20th century, after years of conflict chiefly between rival European colonists fighting to control the region's valuable resources, notably the Cape's strategic position as a layover for spice merchants traveling to and from the East, and the reserve of gold and diamonds discovered in the late 1800s, which led to the development of what is today a leading mining industry.

Following British defeat of the Boers, or Dutch settlers (also known as Voortrekkers), in the Second Boer War (1899–1902), the Union of South Africa began under British rule in 1910 and lasted until the country was granted independence in 1931. In 1948 the National Party took leadership of South Africa and legally instituted the system of racial segregation known as apartheid. South Africa was named a republic in 1961, and the National Party remained in power until 1994, when Nelson Mandela was inaugurated as the first president of the "new" South Africa after the country's first democratically held elections. Today, South Africa is a constitutional democracy, made up of a central government (parliament and the executive authorities of the president and his ministers), local governments representing each of South Africa's nine provinces, and traditional leaders (like King Goodwill Zwelithini, monarch of the Zulu people).

Its long history of political and social conflict has contributed to making cultural diversity one of the distinguishing features of the "rainbow nation" that is present-day South Africa. This is particularly evident in its many food cultures. Beyond European influences (mainly British and Dutch but also French from the Huguenots who arrived as Protestant refugees in the late 1600s, as well as some German and Portuguese influences), what is now considered traditional South African food includes richly spiced dishes based on those introduced by Malay slaves brought from Java and Indonesia to the Cape in the 17th century, and later by Indian laborers brought to work in sugarcane fields in the province now known as KwaZulu-Natal. Yet the most widespread food culture in South Africa belongs to the black majority who inhabited the country long before settlers from Europe and slaves from Asia arrived. Numbering almost 80 percent of a population of 49 million people, black South Africans are the main speakers of 9 of the country's 11 official languages, apart from English and Afrikaans. Though individual linguistic groupings have distinctive food cultures, black South African food traditionally consists of hearty portions of grains (maize, millet, barley, sorghum), vegetables (such as amaranth, known locally as *morogo*), beans (kidney, *jugo*, cowpeas), and meat when available.

The diversity of people and cultures represented by 11 official languages (which do not include the languages of the aboriginal Khoi and San people) gives some indication of the great variety of foods eaten in South Africa, although cultural groupings are not always accurate predictors of what individual

173

A student of the Rockefeller Foundation-funded African Center for Crop Improvement at the University of Kwa-Zulu-Natal, South Africa, inspects her maize project in July 2006. The Rockefeller Foundation and the Bill and Melinda Gates Foundation partnered to create the Alliance for a Green Revolution in Africa to increase the productivity of small farms and improve agricultural development in Africa. (Sharon Farmer | Bill and Melinda Gates Foundation)

South Africans eat. The combined effects of industrialization and internationalization, for example, have made more mass-produced convenience items (and fast food) available to a greater number of people, meaning that some traditional foodstuffs and preparation methods have been replaced. Also, while the boundaries between different traditional foods and those who eat them have never been static, social and political transformations in recent decades have made these lines even more permeable, particularly when it comes to eating in some of the many restaurants that now offer both traditional and/ or modernized versions of foods from all cultural groups. Most important, South Africa remains a country not just of cultural diversity but also of great economic inequality, meaning that those with financial means have a wide variety of food choices (particularly in cosmopolitan areas, where sushi is as standard as pizza and "Mexican" food), while approximately half of South Africans live under the poverty line and must eat whatever is cheap and available.

Food Culture Snapshot

Thabi and Lauren live in Cape Town with their two daughters, Naomi (age five) and Bianca (age three). They met at the university, where they both majored in English. Thabi went on to study communications and now works as a consultant for a new media firm. Lauren stayed at the university to complete her doctorate and now teaches in the English Department. Although they both have full-time jobs, their schedules are flexible, and they both do a fair amount of work from home. The university has a day-care facility that is open all day, though Lauren prefers to collect the children in midafternoon when she can.

They do most of their shopping for meat and dry goods like pasta, rice, and cereal on a weekly basis, but it often happens that they run out of something, so on most days Lauren stops at the local mall on her way home. When she does, the girls normally get a small treat like an *ice lolly* (popsicle), a piece of *biltong* (jerky), or a biscuit (cookie). The family subscribes to an organic vegetable box that gets delivered to their house every week, so they seldom buy vegetables from the supermarket. Their daily shopping generally consists of fruit, milk, and fresh bread.

When she has time, Lauren makes herself a fruit and yogurt smoothie for breakfast, while the girls have cereal or porridge (either oats or their favorite, Maltabella, a malted sorghum porridge that now comes in convenient portion packs that only take one minute to cook in the microwave). Thabi is only interested in coffee first thing in the morning, so he buys a muffin at around 10 A.M. from the coffee shop close to his office. The day-care center provides the children with a midmorning snack, but their parents need to send packed lunches, so Lauren makes sandwiches and cuts up fruit for their lunchboxes while everyone else eats breakfast.

Lauren gets her lunch from the food court on campus (usually a salad and sushi, or soup on cold days), and if Thabi is not at a business lunch, he picks up a chicken pie or a sandwich, which he eats at his desk. They employ Thelma three days a week to clean their house and do their laundry, so they also need to make sure there is enough bread on those days for her to fix herself lunch. If they have leftovers from dinner, Lauren usually gives them to Thelma to take home with her because she knows that Thelma has a big family to feed and struggles to make ends meet. For their evening meal Lauren and Thabi take turns cooking. Their standard weekday dinner is some combination of meat or fish, vegetables, and either rice, pasta, or noodles.

It is always fast and easy to prepare: They do a lot of stir-frying, and they use a range of sauces and condiments to turn otherwise-bland food into something more interesting. If the meal is very spicy, like when Thabi makes his favorite Thai green chicken curry, they simply cook a small portion of meat and vegetables separately for the children.

On Saturday mornings they enjoy going to the local organic market for breakfast and to buy interesting breads and meats for an afternoon *braai* (barbecue). They have a circle of friends who also have small children, and they regularly get together on Saturdays in one of their backyards where the adults can relax with a beer or a glass of wine while the children play. On Sundays they go to Lauren's parents' house for a traditional Sunday lunch with the whole family, including Thabi's parents when they are free. Lauren's mother always makes a roast of some sort, which she serves with rice, potatoes, gravy, at least two kinds of vegetables, and a salad, followed by one of her famous desserts, like trifle, lemon meringue pie, or a hot sticky pudding with custard. Lauren and Thabi are rarely hungry on Sunday evenings, so the children get something easy from the freezer, like fish fingers (fish sticks) or chicken nuggets.

Major Foodstuffs

Despite vulnerability to drought and an arable landmass of less than 15 percent, South Africa is self-sufficient in most of its major foodstuffs and also exports many agricultural goods to neighboring countries and overseas. Subsistence farming dominates in small rural communities, while commercial agriculture was deregulated in 1994, meaning that state-run cooperatives could be privatized and that, coincident with the withdrawal of international trade sanctions, South African commercial farmers could compete in the global market.

Maize (corn) is the country's main crop and also the national staple, followed by wheat, sugarcane, and sunflowers, used for cooking oil. *Mielie meal,* or ground maize, forms the basis of a number of starch-rich meals, including breakfast porridge, *pap* (thicker and drier than porridge, normally eaten with meat and/or vegetable stew), and *phutu* or *krummel pap* (cooked for longer and with less water until it reaches a crumblike consistency, also eaten with stew). Less finely ground than mielie meal, samp is made from boiling dried, chopped maize kernels and is often served with beans (*umngqusho,* or "samp and beans," is reputedly Nelson Mandela's favorite dish). Fresh maize cooked on an open fire is a popular roadside snack and also often an accompaniment to a braai, while fresh kernels mixed with flour and steamed in maize leaves produce *mielie bread.* Maize is also a main ingredient in *umqombothi,* a beer brewed with sorghum and yeast. Less traditional, but as popular, are the thousands of boxes of popcorn eaten in the country's cinemas on a daily basis. Beyond domestic consumption and mercantile exports, the maize industry is supported by government and private-sector subsidies that fund the distribution of food relief in South Africa and in surrounding countries.

Meat is consumed in great amounts in South Africa, whether simply braaied (barbecued) over coals (and no braai is complete without a ring or two of *boerewors,* "farmer's sausages," a combination of beef and pork flavored with coriander seed), oven-roasted, cooked into a number of stews or curries, or eaten as a snack in the form of biltong or *droëwors* (dried boerewors). Cattle, sheep, and poultry farming provide up to 85 percent of meat for domestic consumption with the remaining 15 percent being imported.

Fruits are also important, both as a major export item and for local consumption. Deciduous fruit like apples, pears, and grapes makes up 15 percent of agricultural earnings from export and are eaten locally either fresh, dried, baked into puddings, or preserved in the wide variety of jams (*konfyt*) and chutneys that South Africans eat regularly. Dried fruit also features in a number of savory dishes such as *bobotie* (curried meatloaf with raisins or sultanas and sometimes flaked almonds, topped with an egg custard before baking) and yellow rice with raisins. The country's most important fruit is the grape, first introduced by the Dutch settler Jan van Riebeeck in the 17th century and now indispensable to South Africa's position as one of the top 10 wine-producing

Lamb kabobs on a grill. The act of barbecuing, known as braai, is a popular social custom in South Africa. (Shutterstock)

countries in the world. With annual exports of over 300 million liters, the wine industry contributes significantly to the country's economy and to providing world-class wines for South African tables.

Beyond these key national industries, South Africa has several major regional foodstuffs, many of which are transported and consumed around the country but remain characteristic of particular areas. With approximately 1,750 miles of coastline, seafood is sourced from the Cape's western coast (where the cold Atlantic yields predatory fish like tuna, yellowtail, and *snoek*) all the way along the east coast to the northern border with Mozambique, where the warmer Indian Ocean provides sole, calamari, and pilchards. Crayfish (spiny rock lobster) are a South African delicacy, as is *perlemoen,* a local abalone. Oysters are naturally abundant (the West Coast town of Langebaan is famous for having one of the largest oyster graveyards in the world) but have also been commercially farmed since the mid-20th century. Other popular seafood includes mussels, hake (a favorite for fish and chips), linefish such as kingklip and *geelbek* (also known as Cape salmon), and small fish like *harders* (sold dried and salted as *bokkoms,* a snack food) and whitebait, typically deep-fried whole and served with lemon and tartar sauce.

The inland aridity of the northern Cape makes it a prime area for sheep and ostrich farming, where local delicacies include sheep's testicles, *pofadders* (puffadder is usually refers to a venomous snake, but these are sheep's intestines filled with offal, grilled over coals), *skilpadjies* ("tortoises," lamb or sheep's liver wrapped in caul), and *kaaings,* cracklings made from sheep fat. The area is also home to the Kalahari truffle (a species of *terfezia,* or desert truffle) and to much of South Africa's *rooibos* ("red bush") tea cultivation.

Bordering the landlocked Kingdom of Lesotho, the Free State has been known as South Africa's bread basket, thanks to extensive wheat cultivation. The area also produces potatoes, groundnuts, and asparagus, as well as hosting an annual cherry festival. Citrus, nut, and tropical fruit (mango, lychee, banana, avocado) farming are key to the province of Mpumalanga, while visitors to Limpopo can expect fried mopane worms, porridge made from the fruit of the baobab tree, and home-brewed *marula* beer.

Cooking

One result of industrialization in South Africa is that much traditional food preparation has been simplified and/or displaced. Making pap or porridge used to involve hand-grinding the dried maize kernels, whereas now a majority of people rely on factory-processed mielie meal (the practice of hand-grinding continues in rural areas, where subsistence farmers also grow and dry the kernels themselves). Where available, presliced factory bread (or "government loaf," so named because of legally instituted price controls and tax exemption) has largely taken over as a main staple, and for those with refrigeration facilities, frozen, chopped vegetables provide a convenient alternative to hand-chopping, particularly for food at large gatherings like funerals and weddings.

In rural areas, and in many traditional households across all racial groups, cooking remains the women's domain. This reflects both African custom and the class-based divides introduced by Dutch settlers, who hired Malay slaves as cooks in their homes in the 17th century. Dating from the colonial era and later throughout apartheid, it is still common for middle- and upper-class South African households

to employ domestic help to clean their homes, look after children, and, often, do the cooking. Known colloquially as *chars,* domestic workers are invariably women: Men have historically been employed to work in gardens, if not as migrant laborers in mines and other industries.

One notable exception to the norm of women cooking is the braai. Men are typically designated braai masters, and for many it is the only form of cooking they do. The task involves getting the coals ready, grilling meat, and declaring it ready—everything else is usually prepared by women. Cooking on a fire is an age-old practice in South Africa, beginning with the Khoi and San people (though now collectively referred to as the Khoisan, the two groups had distinctive ways of life: The Khoi were herders with domestic livestock, while the San were hunters), followed by the so-called Bantu tribes who migrated south from the Great Lakes region in central Africa to become "native" South Africans, and finally to the Voortrekkers, who introduced the three-legged cast iron pot known as a *potjie* ("little pot"). *Potjiekos* (*kos* is the Afrikaans word for food) continues today and refers to a stew (generally meat, vegetables, and potatoes) cooked slowly in a potjie set over coals. Potjies are also used to bake *potbrood,* or "pot bread," while *roosterkoek* ("grid cake") refers to bread buns cooked on the grid and *askoek* ("ash cake") to bread baked directly on the embers. Apart from steaks, chops, ribs, and boerewors, *sosaties* (kebabs, or marinated pieces of meat on a skewer, often interspersed with dried fruits and chunks of onion) are popular braai items, as is whole fish brushed with a jam-based glaze.

Frying is another common form of cooking in South Africa, from deep-fried foods like fish and chips to a number of savory snacks such as samosas, *slangetjies* ("small snakes," fried strands of a spiced pea-flour batter, sometimes mixed with nuts), *dhaltjies* (or chili bites, spicy puffs made from chickpea flour), and *vetkoek* ("fat cake," small pieces of fried bread dough, eaten either with sweet toppings like honey or savory fillings like curried mince). Deep-fried sweet foods include the Afrikaner *koeksisters* (twisted or plaited doughnuts dipped in ginger-and-lemon-flavored syrup) and the Malay variant, *koesisters,* small round doughnuts made from a spiced dough, dipped in a simple syrup, and rolled in dried coconut. Pumpkin fritters with cinnamon sugar are also enjoyed on their own or, following the practice of pairing sweet with savory, as an accompaniment to a meal. *Smoor* ("smother," or braise) refers to foods braised in a pan with onions. *Smoorsnoek* traditionally calls for dried, salted snoek, flaked and fried with onions, cabbage, potato, chili, and garlic, though smoked fish is more often used nowadays. Rice, cabbage, and other vegetables like eggplant are commonly smoored.

Typical Meals

A South African breakfast can be as simple as cereal, porridge, and/or *amasi* (curdled milk, prepared by natural fermentation in rural areas or available as a cultured dairy product from the supermarket). In traditional Afrikaner households, homemade baked goods are common, ranging from muffins and rusks (oven-dried biscuits typically dunked in coffee or tea; rusks provided useful sustenance for Voortrekkers and soldiers because they did not spoil) to breads. *Seed loaf,* referring to a whole-grain bread with a variety of seeds (sunflower, sesame, poppy, linseed), is widely eaten as toast with butter and preserves. A "full" South African breakfast, still eaten by some on a daily basis though more frequently reserved for weekend brunches in urban areas, mimics the traditional English breakfast with toast, eggs, bacon, fried tomatoes, mushrooms, sausage, and sometimes kippers, a piece of steak, or a lamb chop.

Apart from a Sunday roast, lunch is generally not the main meal of the day and often consists of a sandwich or other food item that can be eaten on the run, particularly for the large group of blue-collar workers. A typical lunch for many construction workers and other physical laborers is half a loaf of bread and some form of cooked or cold meat from a supermarket, if not something from one of the many corner cafés that sell hot foods like fish and chips, toasted sandwiches, savory pies, sausage rolls, and "Russians" (thick pork sausages). A favorite Cape fast food is the *gatsby,* a large hot dog bun filled

with cooked or processed meat, French fries, and sauce, or a *salomi,* curry wrapped in a roti flat bread. The *bunny chow*—half or quarter of a hollowed-out loaf of bread filled with curry and topped with the *virgin,* or the bread from the middle (the virgin is eaten first with the curry, followed by the gravy-soaked sides of the hollow loaf)—originated in KwaZulu-Natal as a convenient way of selling food without cutlery to indentured laborers, but it can now be found in most major South African cities.

In traditional Malay and Indian households, the evening meal typically consists of some form of curry served with rice and/or breads, and *sambals* (accompaniments like chutney; *atjar,* a spicy relish; and *raita,* a yogurt-based condiment). Malay curries are milder than Indian curries and often have a sweet element to them, like in bobotie, a recipe for which was selected to represent South Africa in a United Nations international cookbook published in 1951. Other Malay specialties include *denningvleis* (lamb stew flavored with cloves, allspice, and tamarind) and *bredie,* a lightly spiced tomato-based stew, the most unique version of which uses *waterblommetjies* (the flowers of water hawthorn, an aquatic plant that grows wild in the Cape). Lamb, mutton, and chicken are popular meats for curries, though the Malay community uses only halal meat (and therefore never pork).

The braai is the most typical South African meal because it is the one that most, if not all, South Africans are familiar with—so much so that the annual public holiday on September 24, previously known as Shaka Day (in commemoration of the Zulu king's assassination by his half brothers in 1828) and later renamed Heritage Day, has been dubbed National Braai Day (or Braai4Heritage Day), with Emeritus Archbishop Desmond Tutu as its patron. Both a noun ("let's have a braai") and a verb ("let's braai"), the occasion is most often a social one that can suit any demographic or income group. A braai can be a lavish affair with crayfish, fillet steak, and fine wine or a more casual gathering with virtually any form of meat (including chicken and venison), vegetables, boerewors, and plenty of beer. In addition to pap and grilled corn on the cob, a number of condiments are usually served with *braaivleis* (braaied meat), like chutney, pickles, and *chakalaka,* a spicy tomato-and-onion relish.

Eating Out

South Africa has a thriving restaurant industry that caters to most of its population and also to the tourist market, which has a wide choice of world-class restaurants to dine in. Le Quartier Français and La Colombe are notable as two restaurants (both in the Cape winelands) that have repeatedly been voted among *Restaurant* magazine's 50 "Best Restaurants in the World," though as their names suggest, the food they serve is inspired by French (or broadly international) trends. In the global market in which they participate, this class of restaurants offers extremely competitive value, but from a South African perspective only a minority can afford to spend more money on a single meal than many people earn in an entire month. Yet this relatively small market manages for the most part to sustain the high-end dining industry, and several South African chefs are recognized as celebrities in their local contexts. In 2009, Cape Town welcomed the country's first signature restaurants by foreign celebrities with the opening of Gordon Ramsay's maze and Nobuyuki Matsuhisa's Nobu.

Cosmopolitan areas do offer a wide variety of places to eat out that are affordable on a regular basis to the middle to upper classes. Wine and tapas bars, delis, and sushi restaurants have become popular in recent years, while less casual restaurants continue to be well populated for business lunches and dinners. Cities also abound in all kinds of middle-of-the-road eateries, from Italian to Chinese to burger restaurants, all of which are particularly successful in student neighborhoods (where street food also thrives, especially hot dogs made with boerewors). In suburban areas with a higher population of middle- to lower-income groups, franchised fast-food and family restaurants are very popular, including South African franchises like Spur Steak Ranches (burgers, steaks, and ribs), Nando's (Portuguese-style chicken), the Ocean Basket (seafood), a number of pizza chains, and global brands like McDonald's and KFC.

Eating out in rural areas generally falls into one of two categories that echo the historical divides set in place by apartheid. In traditional black communities, as well as in townships on the outskirts of most

A number of restaurants and store fronts along the coast of the Victoria and Albert Waterfront in South Africa. (Monkey Business Images | Dreamstime.com)

cities, restaurants often combine a butcher shop with braai facilities, so patrons first buy a piece of meat and then have it cooked for them on the fire, while pap, stews, and other accompaniments are available to order on the side. Mzoli's in the Cape township of Gugulethu has become a popular tourist destination for those looking for an "authentic" black experience, which here involves many people standing around their cars, playing loud music, and drinking copiously while enjoying Mzoli's meat and his famous secret sauce. In contrast, there are farm stalls along highways in sparsely populated agricultural areas. Originally small roadside stores selling fresh produce from (white-owned) neighboring farms, today farm stalls are sophisticated delis with an adjoining coffee shop or restaurant where travelers stop for refreshments and *padkos* ("road food") and also for hearty country meals.

Special Occasions

In traditional black communities, special occasions like weddings and funerals typically involve feasting, beer drinking, and often the ritual slaughter of a cow or goat. Cattle have long been a symbol of wealth, and the practice of using cattle for *lobola* (the bride price, with the main aim of establishing a relationship between two families) remains common in rural areas. Some wedding customs also include food taboos, such as the bride not being allowed to eat until a certain time. Similarly, where male initiation rites are still observed, boys undergo a period of fasting and isolation before the final feast, which also includes the slaughter of an animal.

Food, and its restriction, is also important to Muslim celebrations, and several lavish dishes are reserved for special occasions. During the fasting period of Ramadan it is customary for children in Muslim communities to take plates of sweets like koesisters to their neighbors to break the fast at sundown. *Boeber,* a spicy drink of milk and sago (a starch extracted from palm), is often served before the main evening meal and is typically drunk on the 15th day of Ramadan to mark the middle of the fast. The celebration of Eid to mark the end of the fasting period of Ramadan usually features expensive dishes like crayfish curry and a host of elaborate puddings and sweets. *Breyani* (adapted from the Indian *biryani*) is a typical wedding dish that is assembled in various stages, beginning with marinating mutton or chicken for a few hours in a mixture of yogurt, tomato, and spices (cardamom, cinnamon, chilies, turmeric, cloves, saffron). The final dish consists of meat, rice, lentils, fried potatoes, and onions, layered in a pot and cooked slowly. Etiquette requires the lid of the pot not to be lifted until the time of serving, when halved hard-boiled eggs are often added as a final garnish. *Doopmaal,* the naming ceremony for Muslim babies, is always followed by tea and cakes, and sometimes savory snacks or a more substantial meal.

With a Christian majority, South Africa observes the major Western holidays like Christmas and Easter. These are celebrated with the same commercial flourish as in many parts of the world, with supermarkets stocking Christmas cakes, hams, and turkeys from October, and Easter eggs from soon after Christmas. Beyond these ritualized festivities, special occasions like birthdays and anniversaries are celebrated in nonspecific ways across the country but generally with due attention to food and drink, be it at a fancy restaurant, at a Spur Steak Ranch (where the staff will sing "Happy Birthday" on request), or simply having a braai with friends.

Diet and Health

Echoing all other spheres of South African life, people with financial means can benefit from first-rate private health care, while the majority of South Africans currently have access only to the very rudimentary health care that the government provides free of charge. One result of this is an average life expectancy of 49 years, concentrated in the 80 percent majority who do not have access to adequate health services.

HIV is the biggest health challenge that South Africa faces, with a prevalence of close to 20 percent and over five million people living with the virus. It has also been the subject of the most notorious link between diet and health, when, in the period 2000–2005, then-president Thabo Mbeki denied the causal relationship between HIV and AIDS and publicly recommended eating a diet rich in fruit and vegetables to fight the disease, rather than prioritizing access to antiretroviral drugs. It is estimated that 350,000 people died unnecessarily during that time.

As cattle are a symbol of wealth, excess body weight is also traditionally regarded as a sign of prosperity. This continues in many black communities and is exacerbated by high rates of HIV and AIDS, now commonly considered a "slim disease" because of its associated weight loss. But the principle that being fat is healthy is also complicated by escalating rates of diabetes and related health complications resulting from overweight and obesity. While increasingly Western lifestyles in urban areas, involving higher consumption of fast food and convenience foods, have contributed to this development, it is also the result of traditional ways of life across most racial groups, as eating substantial portions of meat and starch, often coupled with large amounts of beer, is not confined to black communities (white men count among the most obese in the country).

In cities the opposite trend is widespread, with a visible increase in the number of gyms, many of which work in partnership with medical insurance companies to offer reduced membership rates. Also on the rise are healthy fast-food options, from chains like Kauai (which also operate in the ubiquitous Virgin Active gyms) and Osumo, both of which specialize in smoothies, salads, sandwiches, and wraps and offer nutritional information with their menus. Leading supermarkets also have health sections that offer a number of "lite" and "low-carb" snack and meal-replacement products under leading diet brands like Weigh-Less, as well as a full array of gluten- and sugar-free foods.

Signe Rousseau

Further Reading

Leipoldt, Louis. *Leipoldt's Food and Wine.* Cape Town, South Africa: Stonewall, 2004.

Mayat, Zuleikha. *Indian Delights.* Durban, South Africa: Women's Cultural Group, 1970.

Snyman, Lannice. *Rainbow Cuisine.* Cologne, Germany: Könemann, 2001.

South Africa. http://www.southafrica.info.

South Africa Online. http://www.southafrica.co.za.

Williams, Faldela. *The Cape Malay Cookbook.* Cape Town, South Africa: Struik, 1993.

Sudan

Overview

Sudan is a country in northeastern Africa with a land area of 2.3 million square miles, roughly the same size as the United States east of the Mississippi River. It has a population of 41 million. Sudan shares borders with nine countries and enjoys coastal access along the Red Sea. Two strands of the Nile, the White Nile and the Blue Nile, converge in the capital city of Khartoum and continue north to Egypt and eventually the Mediterranean Sea. Sudan's strategic location on the African continent has made it desirable to outside occupying forces, and both the United Kingdom and Egypt laid claim to parts of modern Sudan during the 19th and 20th centuries. The legacy of colonization is manifest in aspects of Sudanese culture today, from religion to food and language.

The contemporary history of Sudan is one of conflict. Two civil wars between Sudan's northern and southern states were fought for over 40 of the 50 years following independence from the United Kingdom in 1956. A peace accord was signed in 2005, but it was overshadowed by violence in the western Darfur region of Sudan, where it is estimated that hundreds of thousands have lost their lives since 2003. The combination of war and natural disasters has resulted in mass migration and displacement of the Sudanese subsistence-agriculture population. As such, Sudan has experienced rapid urbanization, with an estimated 40 percent of Sudanese living in cities today.

Given its land area and varied terrain, Sudan is home to a rich collection of indigenous tribes—over 100 of them—with an equal number of languages spoken. The official languages of Sudan are Arabic and English. Arabic is spoken widely in the north, while English is spoken in much of the south, a result of the British presence in the region during the 20th century. The majority of Sudanese are Sunni Muslims (70%), followed by indigenous and animistic faiths (25%) and a small minority of Christians (5%). Because of the strong Muslim influence in Sudan, alcoholic beverages are forbidden, as is the consumption of pork. The Sudanese economy has experienced tremendous growth because of its deposits of crude oil, which it began to export in 1999. While the standard of living has improved for some due to this new revenue stream, more than a third of Sudanese live on less than a dollar a day. In addition to disparities in household income, the population of Sudan is defined by the generation under the age of 14, who make up 40 percent of the population. In 2011, a southern Sudanese independence referendum is scheduled for a vote, which could potentially result in southern Sudan declaring itself a sovereign nation.

⦿ Food Culture Snapshot

Selma Hassan Mustafa is married with three children. She works as a director at the federal Ministry of Finance in Khartoum. Her husband, Mustafa Adelrahman, is a professor of economics at the University of Khartoum. While Selma's mother was one of multiple wives to her father, she and Mustafa do not practice polygamy, which is still common in parts of Sudan. Selma's oldest son, Mohamed, is a physician and is married and working in Saudi Arabia. Her middle child,

People try to earn some money by selling peanuts and sugar outside of their shelters in East Darfur, Sudan. (David Snyder | Dreamstime.com)

a daughter named Amel, is an elementary school teacher. Amel is unmarried and still lives at home with her parents. Selma's youngest son, Hisham, is still in college in Khartoum, studying urban planning.

Selma grew up outside of the capital in Blue Nile State, located eight hours south of Khartoum by car. She learned to cook from her mother and grandmother, who prepared traditional dishes like breaded and fried river fish and *waika,* a dish made with dried okra flour, which she still prepares for her family in Khartoum. While her children are no longer living under one roof, Selma continues to cook dinners for her husband, Amel, and Hisham, who look forward to suppertime and the dishes she prepares.

As a practicing Muslim, Selma looks forward to the religious festival marking the end of the month of Ramadan when devout Muslims fast from sunrise to sundown each day. To celebrate, her eldest son and his wife return from overseas, and the family is reunited for a feast that includes roast mutton or goat and *bellah,* or dates, for dessert.

Major Foodstuffs

Many standard Sudanese dishes have a grain as their main ingredient. In the west, millet is grown widely and is the base for *aseeda,* or boiled millet flour. This filling dish has the consistency of thickened polenta and is typically enjoyed with a *moullah,* or stew. Central Sudan produces sorghum, which is ground into flour called *fetareetah.* This flour is then used to form a batter that is fried into thin pancakes called *kisra* that are also served along with stews and cooked vegetables. In the north, wheat is produced and harvested for bread flour, used to make *gurassah,* flat unleavened bread fried in a pan. Cassava was introduced to southern Sudan in the 1830s by the British colonizers in an attempt to provide a crop that was more drought resistant and grew underground so that pests that fed on aboveground stalks would not damage the crop. This tuber is now a staple of southern Sudanese cooking.

In much of Sudan, meat makes the meal. The most common meats are lamb, mutton, and beef. Goat, camel, chicken, and fish are also consumed regionally. Meat can be prepared simply on skewers over a grill, or as a component of a stew or rice dish. Many meat varieties are ground and formed into kebabs, which are then served with bread and a spicy yogurt sauce called *shohta.*

Peanuts, or groundnuts, are a favorite ingredient and key export item for Sudan. Vendors serve roasted peanuts on streets across the country, and the nut is incorporated into fresh salads that accompany Sudanese barbecue, such as *salata dugwah.*

Salata Dugwah (Peanut-Paste Salad)

Serves 4 as a side dish

Ingredients

4–6 medium tomatoes

½ c finely diced purple onion

1 tsp salt

⅛ tsp ground cloves

⅛ tsp ground curry leaves

½ tsp ground coriander

1 tsp minced garlic

⅓ c ground fresh peanuts (unsweetened peanut butter can be substituted)

Dash of sugar

Wash and dice the tomatoes and place them in a mixing bowl. Add the diced onions and incorporate thoroughly. Stir in the salt, cloves, curry leaves, coriander, and garlic. Finally, add the peanut paste and a dash of sugar and mix well.

Fava beans, or *fuul,* are known for the classic dish of the same name that is widely eaten throughout Sudan and much of northern Africa and the Middle East. An excellent source of protein, fuul is often served as a morning or midday meal.

Date palm trees are cultivated along the banks of the Nile from the northern state of Sudan down south of Khartoum to Sinnar state. Sudanese dates, or bellah, are prized for their size and flavor and are found in snacks such as *bellah madeedah,* a smoothie made from wheat paste, clarified butter, milk, yogurt, sugar, dates, and honey. While not native to Sudan, mangoes were introduced 6,000 years ago and many varietals flourish today. The Sudanese town of Shendi is particularly famous for its mangoes. Banana trees are plentiful in parts of southern Sudan, and they are consumed in many parts of the country. Dates, mangoes, and bananas are all rich sources of essential vitamins. Sudanese recipes often call for onions, tomatoes, cucumbers, and green peppers. These ingredients are either incorporated into hot entrées or highlighted in salads or side dishes. Another popular leaf vegetable is arugula, served fresh as a side salad.

Among the popular drinks, *karkaday* is a magenta-colored juice or tea made from dried hibiscus flowers. The dried petals are prepared as either a cold or a hot drink rich in vitamin C. The *tibeldi* trees in southern Sudan produce fruit that is dried to a chalky, wrinkled consistency and creates a thick juice when mixed with water. The dried tibeldi fruit is sold widely in markets across Sudan.

Cooking

Most Sudanese dishes are cooked over heat as opposed to baked, regardless of whether one lives in the city or the countryside. Urban kitchens typically have a stovetop but might not include a proper oven. In cities, bakeries that produce cookies and popular breads are plentiful. In the rural areas, cooking is typically done over a fire. Finding fuel can mean seeking wood from a far distance, given the deforestation and desertification of much of Sudan. In southern Sudan, charcoal grills have replaced wood-fueled grills as the most popular cooking mechanism. In the most arid climates of Sudan, meat and fruit are preserved through a drying process that keeps the food edible for many months.

Typical Meals

Urban Sudanese often take only a cup of milk tea and a simple cookie (referred to by the British term *biscuit*) at home in the early morning before starting their workday at 8 or 9 A.M. Some might stop for a potent espresso-sized cup of *jebena,* or spiced coffee, on the way to work. Alternatively, a tray of such coffee might be fetched for an office from one of the many jebena vendors after the workday is underway. The coffee tradition in Sudan is strong, as it is neighbors with Ethiopia, the birthplace of the bean. The meal referred to as breakfast is eaten at around 10 or 11 A.M. and might consist of a simple sandwich made of a round individual-size loaf of white bread stuffed with *tamaaya* (falafel) or fuul. Lunch therefore comes much later in the day, usually sometime between 2 and 5 P.M. The meal is more robust than breakfast and could involve takeout from a growing number of fast-food establishments that sell kebabs, French fries, and, in Khartoum, even pizza. Workmates sometimes share a spread of gurassah (the flatbread) dipped in *sharmut moullah,* a meat stew. Given the later dining times for lunch, dinner is typically taken well into the evening, between 8:30 and 11 P.M. Women are expected to do the cooking, and while some might employ hired help, many still handle the task on their own. Bread is a component of the meal that would likely be purchased, while others, like *sheearia,* a sweet noodle dish, would be made at home. Simple salads of sliced tomatoes, purple onions, and cucumber are common.

Fuul Sudani (Sudanese Fava Bean Stew)

Serves 4

Ingredients

1 lb fava beans
Salt to taste

1 tbsp sesame oil

1 medium onion, diced

1 green pepper, diced

1 medium tomato, diced

1 tsp chili powder

1 tsp cumin

Juice of 1 small lemon

3 tbsp feta cheese

Soak the beans overnight (at least 3 hours), then boil them in water until they are tender. While the beans are cooking, heat a large skillet over medium-high heat, and add the sesame oil, then cook the green pepper and onion until they wilt, about 2–3 minutes. Then add the tomato and a dash of salt, cooking just until the tomato is warm but not cooked so much it loses its shape. Turn down the heat to simmer. Once the beans are soft, drain them, retaining 1½ to 2 cups of the cooking water, and place the beans in a mixing bowl. Then, with the back of a flat wooden spoon or curved spatula, mash the beans so that they break apart. Sprinkle with the remaining salt, chili powder, and cumin to taste. Add the beans and the reserved water to the skillet and combine thoroughly, incorporating the lemon juice and salt to taste. Turn the heat back up to medium high until it almost begins to bubble, and then take it off the heat and serve the fuul in bowls with the feta crumbled generously over the top.

For rural Sudanese farmers or herders, the rhythm of their day creates an alternative meal structure. In addition, different regions of Sudan produce distinct crops, which are reflected in the meals. Millet may be their staple, or it could be wheat. Dairy is emphasized in the west, where cattle are plentiful. Fish play a more central role in the fertile communities that line the White and Blue Nile rivers. Dates are grown in the north and feature prominently in their cuisine.

Eating Out

In rural villages, eating out involves being invited to another family's home for a meal, either as a gesture of friendship or because of a shared celebration. The Sudanese pride themselves on their hospitality, which is most often demonstrated by feeding guests. In towns and midsize cities, small eateries sell grilled meat, salads, and bread for eating in or takeout. In addition to restaurants, these locales have a collection of street vendors offering everything from roasted corn to *bakoumbah,* a sweet porridge made from boiled millet, yogurt, clarified butter, custard powder, sesame paste, and sugar.

Khartoum has a thriving restaurant scene, from fancy rooftop dining at the best hotels to corner restaurants in residential neighborhoods that serve a Sudanese favorite, *koftah,* or grilled meatballs. Lebanese, Egyptian, Chinese, Indian, Ethiopian, and Italian restaurants are popular with both locals and non-Sudanese residents of the city. The Kenyan restaurant chain Carnivore opened a branch on prime real estate facing the Nile and serves a wide range of meat that includes the traditional (beef and lamb) and the more adventurous (crocodile and camel). In addition to restaurants, Khartoum also has a vibrant street-food scene, where customers can enjoy kisra and moullah, or a grilled meat technique called *salat* that involves searing meat over hot river rocks and salt, to name just a few.

Special Occasions

For practicing Muslims in Sudan, there are two major holidays that involve food: Ramadan Bairam and Kurban Bairam. Ramadan Bairam is also known as Eid al Ramadan. Ramadan refers to the Muslim month of fasting, determined annually by the lunar calendar and lasting roughly 30 days. All Muslims are required to not eat or drink anything from sunrise until sunset. Pregnant women, the sick, children under the age of 13, and those in transit are exempt. The nights of Ramadan involve *fatour,* or the social breaking of the daily fast with a shared meal. Ramadan culminates with the Eid al Ramadan, which marks the end of the month of Ramadan. The celebration extends for three or four days and involves eating and visiting with family and friends.

Kurban Bairam, also known more widely as Eid al Kabier, is another Muslim lunar holiday that marks the 10th month called Zu al Hajj, the designated month of the year in which Muslims from around the world make a pilgrimage to Mecca. Eid al Kabier marks the day when those in Mecca will have journeyed to the neighboring city of Medina, where each pilgrim will perform an animal sacrifice. In Sudan, Eid al Kabier lasts for four to five days and is a celebratory time for shared meals and family visits. Every Muslim family with the means to do so will slaughter a ram to mark the occasion.

Diet and Health

While the introduction of fast food and large supermarkets in the urban areas has meant a shift in diet for some Sudanese, most Sudanese still live in small villages and towns, and their diet remains largely the same as that of their ancestors. As Sudan continues to urbanize, this trend will shift accordingly. The life expectancy in Sudan is an average of 51 years, not as a result of diet but instead because of a continuous cycle of food scarcity, war, diminished health facilities, and disease.

Anita Verna Crofts

Further Reading

Bacon, Josephine, and Jenni Fleetwood. *The Complete Illustrated Food and Cooking of Africa and the Middle East: Ingredients, Techniques, 170 Recipes, 650 Photographs.* London: Lorenz Books, 2009.

Grant, Rosamund, and Josephine Bacon. *The Taste of Africa: The Undiscovered Food and Cooking of an Extraordinary Continent.* London: Southwater, 2008.

"Menus and Recipes from the Sudan." http://www.sudan.net/society/recipe.html.

Swahili City-States

Overview

The Swahili (WaSwahili) are a Muslim people who live on the coast of East Africa. In some respects Swahilis differ significantly from other East Africans. They have always typically lived in city-state towns rather than in nomadic groups (like the Maasai or Samburu) or in dispersed farming settlements (like the Kamba or the Luyia). Among the Swahili, a prime differentiation is whether they are from a "stone town" or a "country town." The former exhibit more orthodox Islamic customs and claim more Persian and Arab ancestry.

Lamu is an ancient stone town, a Swahili city-state in the Indian Ocean off the north coast of Kenya. It is the main town of the traditional *Swahilini*—the original geographic crucible of Swahili culture. In December 2001, the United Nations Educational, Scientific and Cultural Organization granted World Heritage status to Lamu's Old Town, citing the fact that the old town had retained its traditional functions for over 1,000 years.

The Swahili language (called KiSwahili in the language itself) is the national and official language of Kenya and Tanzania and is probably the African language most widely studied outside of Africa. Swahili is spoken as a first language by the Swahili people on the Kenyan and Tanzanian coasts and the adjacent islands: Zanzibar, Pemba, Mombasa, Lamu, and more. This Swahili is a full and complex language (with 15 grammatical genders), but there is also a trade language based on simplified pidgin Swahili. The simplified version has led to a false reputation Swahili sometimes has as not being a real language. Swahili is spoken as a second (or third or fourth) language by tens of millions of people, mainly in Kenya, Tanzania, Uganda, and Congo (Democratic Republic of the Congo). There are also speakers in Mozambique, Rwanda, Burundi, Somalia, Zambia, Malawi, and the Comoros, and even in southern Arabian countries such as Yemen and Oman.

When the Europeans arrived in the 1600s, they found an urban, Muslim people who lived in stone houses, conducted trade with India and China, and had an active written literature. They viewed the Swahili as so different from other Africans that they assumed the culture to be a foreign transplant, for example, Arabic. But Swahili culture, while Islamic, is not Arabic: It is a unique, syncretic, African-based culture.

Swahili towns stretch along the eastern coast of Africa from Somalia to Mozambique. The East African coast has been important to Indian Ocean trade for the past 1,000 years, and small boats or dhows have sailed on the seasonal monsoon winds, which have blown ships from Arabia, Persia, and India toward the Swahili coast and then later in the year blown them back again toward home. Swahili food shows influences from Africa, India, Arabia, and Europe—not surprising, for the Swahilis have been the contact group, trading the goods of inland Africa and the rest of the world for many centuries. The group of greatest modern influence is undoubtedly the people of the Indian subcontinent. Swahilis' default seasoning is curry, and Indian spices are common; important snacks are samosas, *bhajia* (a kind of deep-fried onion fritter), and other Indian snacks; the default bread is a chapati; the most festive rice dish is *biryani,* a mixed pilaf (showing pan-Islamic origins as well).

A grove of coconut palm trees. Mnazi, the coconut palm, occupies a special place in Swahili culture. (Jonathange | Dreamstime.com)

In the modern day, Swahili meals center around *wali* (rice), chapati flatbreads made with white flour (*unga*) and whole-grain flour (*atta*), or cornmeal porridge (*sima, bodo,* or *ugali*), eaten with a *kitoweo*, an accompaniment of fish, meat, or vegetables. *Mchuzi* is the word for a sauce-based kitoweo; it is variously translated into English as gravy, soup, sauce, or curry. *Supu* (from English) is also used for soup.

🍽 Food Culture Snapshot

Sawiti bin Mohamed rises early, performs his *alfajiri* (morning) prayers, and arrives at the Lamu market just after dawn. He and other men (only men come to the market) congregate around the butcher, who is sectioning, cutting, and dispensing parts of the cow that was slaughtered just earlier. He orders a half pound of meat with bone. The butcher cuts what he thinks will

be about a kilo and puts it on a sheet of newspaper on one side of a balance scale, then puts a kilo weight on the opposite pan. In the vegetable area of the market Sawiti buys three onions, chilis, garlic, two European potatoes, a carrot, bananas, and coriander leaf (cilantro). He will cook a *mchuzi wa ng'ombe* to accompany the rice he plans to serve.

If he were cooking an extraspecial dish for this evening's meal—grilled meat—he might buy boneless *sarara* (filet), then find someone with a papaya tree that has a fruit, buy one, and marinate the meat, cut up, in the shredded papaya and a combination of spices. This will tenderize the meat to the point it can be chewed, as the cattle that have been coming to the market these days have been Somali cattle that have walked many miles on their way to slaughter. This meat makes good mchuzis, though, especially pieces with bone.

He exchanges lengthy greetings and news for a long while with the other men. They are dressed alike: a *kofia* (cylindrical hat), a *shati* (a collared shirt) or a *kanzu* (a full-length white shirt), and a *saruni* (a sarong), with rubber or leather *viatu* (sandals). He then leaves and stops at a *duka* (general store) to buy a small two-tablespoon tin of tomato paste and a packet of *bizari*, premade curry powder. Other days he will buy individual spices from bins and grind them himself on a grinding stone. He also buys two ripe coconuts and drops them off at his sister's house.

She cracks them in half, disposes of the water inside, then sits on an *mbuzi*, a seat of two crisscrossed boards with a sharp C-shaped saw blade—with the teeth on the outside of the C—stuck in the end of one board. She grinds the white part of the coconut with this blade, catching the result in a bowl underneath. She puts the ground coconut into a bag woven from fine palm fronds called a *kifumbu*, pours water into it, and squeezes out *tui* (coconut cream) into the bowl. She separates the first output from the second and third and will give them to Sawiti when he passes by again later.

Sawiti is a master professional *mpishi*, a cook. He is expert at Swahili, Indian, and European cuisines. Born in the area by the border with Somalia, he is a Bajuni Swahili and has lived up and down the Swahili coast. He has worked in restaurants and as the personal live-in chef for well-to-do Indians and Europeans. He can cook on a modern propane gas range using a baterie de cuisine and can make the same high-quality food when he needs to with only firewood and a battered *sufuria* pot if on safari (Swahili for "journey"), for example, on a sailing dhow trip to the northern islands of the Lamu Archipelago.

He is cooking with two friends and has no kitchen to speak of—not even a cutting board, only a knife, a kerosene cooker, one large spoon, and some sufuria pots. He peels the vegetables in a continuous single peel with the knife. One of the friends then holds the knife immobile, sharp side toward Sawiti, who grasps the meat and saws off pieces against the knife. Sawiti takes an empty tin can, puts peeled garlic and salt into it, and uses a stick to mash the garlic into paste. He mixes this with the meat and fries it with a piece of cooking fat from a small tin, adding the onion, bizari, and later the tomato paste. He adds water, the cut-up vegetables, and later the heavy tui and *dania* (coriander leaf). When the stew is done, he takes it off the

heat and covers it. There is no refrigerator, but this dish will be good to eat even the next morning if it is kept covered and no one eats from it with his hand.

It is nearly noon, time for the *adhuhuri* prayer, and Sawiti heads toward one of the many mosques in Lamu town. On the main street, Usita wa mui, a block behind the seafront, he passes and greets groups of men on benches talking, drinking from small cups, and smoking; children carrying and eating from trays of deep-fried foods their mothers have made for sale; and men eating meals at outdoor tables while meat is charcoal-grilled nearby. A group of women enter a restaurant to eat snacks and drink fruit juice while passersby purchase sweets from a shop to take home. There are no wheeled vehicles in Lamu; the streets—mostly so narrow that if one spreads one's arms out, one will touch the adjacent buildings—are left to pedestrians, donkeys, and handcarts.

Sawiti returns for a midday nap. Later, that evening, he cooks rice using the lighter second and third tuis. He turns the hot rice onto a *sinia*, a platter. The three men set out a mat on the floor and wash their hands with soap and water. They sit around the platter on the floor. Sawiti uses a large spoon to make a depression in the rice in front of each diner and ladles in some mchuzi. On top of the mound he places some peeled banana and whole chilies for those who want a bite now and again. The men say "bismillahi" and eat with their right hands, occasionally placing some choice piece of meat in front of their friend if they think they have gotten too many good pieces. From time to time Swahili replenishes the mchuzi from the pot.

After the meal they go across to a *hoteli,* a café or restaurant, to have a cup of chai (milk tea), or they stroll down the main street to a *tambuu* (betel-leaf) seller and sit on benches on the street side chewing tambuu while others smoke cigarettes and drink *kahawa tungu* (strong cardamom-scented coffee) and pass the news of the day.

Samaki wa Kupaka

A signature dish of the Swahili is *samaki wa kupaka* (also called *samaki paka*), fish coated with a paste of coconut cream and spices and usually cooked over charcoal. One could also bake or oven-broil it.

2–3 lb whole firm-fleshed fish like red snapper, scaled and cleaned, head on, tail and fins removed

Spice mix: ginger (a 2-in. piece), 1 head of garlic, and 2 hot chilies, all ground or mashed and chopped together (this is a common Swahili spice mixture—Swahili *sofrito*, so to speak—that one can make in quantity, storing the extra in a refrigerator)

About 2 c *tui mzito* (coconut cream; see note at end of recipe)

1 tbsp curry powder

½ c lemon juice or tamarind pulp or juice

1 tbsp turmeric

1 tsp chili powder, if desired

Slash one or two deep diagonal cuts in each side of the fish. Rub spice mix into the cuts and the inside cavity of the fish. Let sit for 30 minutes to an hour. Grill in a fish basket over a charcoal fire.

Meanwhile, combine tui mzito with curry powder, lemon juice or tamarind pulp or juice, turmeric, and chili powder, if using. Simmer together in a small saucepan until thick, about 10 minutes. When the fish is almost done, spoon coconut cream mixture onto the fish, letting it cook slowly into the flesh.

Serve with rice, chapati flatbreads, or sima (cornmeal porridge).

Tui mzito: If using canned coconut cream, do not shake the can; open and spoon off the creamy heavy part on top. If making your own, use only the first squeezings from each coconut. In either case you will need several cans or several coconuts.

Major Foodstuffs

Tui, coconut cream, is an important element in Swahili food culture. Largely because of the nature of its fats, it can transform what might otherwise be humdrum foods into dishes of depth, complexity, and richness. Tui deepens spices, blends flavors, and corrects asymmetries. Grated coconut is put inside a kifumbu, a woven bag, and water is added. The bag is wrung out over a bowl, which catches the fluid. One can use cheesecloth, or a potato ricer also produces excellent tui. Typically one does three squeezings. Classic meal preparation uses the first, most fat-rich squeezing in the mchuzi, and the second and third squeezings to make *wali wa nazi* (coconut rice). Others cook the mchuzi with the second squeezing and only put the first in to finish the dish.

Mnazi, the coconut palm, occupies a special place in Swahili culture. Conversations about the coconut caused the great poet and cultural historian Ahmed Sheikh Nabhany to present to this writer *Umbuji wa Mnazi* (The grace of the coconut palm), his book of first-rank Swahili *mashairi* poems extolling the coconut palm. Swahilis say that if people own a certain number of coconut trees they can retire happy, because the trees will furnish them with everything they need to live. The palm fronds are the roofing material of thatched *makuti* roofs. The husks are excellent firewood; the sap can be tapped and in a day or so becomes palm wine, which in a few days becomes *siki,* palm wine vinegar. And from the ripe coconut one can get tui. Tui is the richest substance in traditional Swahili culture, and there are proverbs and sayings with tui as their central theme.

Indeed, the coconut is king. (*Maji ya*) *Dafu,* "milk/juice (lit., fluid) of an unripe coconut," is a popular drink in the plantation fields and in towns is sold from pushcarts in the street. The husk and shell are whittled away from the top of the nut with repeated upward strokes of a knife (or just lopped off with a *panga,* or machete) until a small hole in the inner husk reveals the milk. Sometimes a straw is provided, though usually the customer drinks straight from the coconut. If the customer also wants to eat the meat of the nut (and many do not), the seller opens the hole wider and cuts a *kijiko* (spoon) from a piece of husk, which either he or the buyer uses to scrape the meat free. With the curved part facing the center of the nut, the spoon is used as a wedge between the meat and the husk. The meat drops into the bottom of the nut and the spoon is turned over, curved side down, and used to convey the meat to the mouth. It is acceptable to sit at the curb on a street to consume a dafu.

Swahili cuisine is a coastal one, and finfish is an important foodstuff, as are shrimp, squid, octopus, and cuttlefish. Swahilis do not typically eat crab or shellfish, nor lobster, though these are served to foreign guests (as opposed to, say, pork, which is never eaten, cooked, touched, or countenanced at all). The meat of cattle, chickens, and goats is widely used.

Fruits such as limes, pineapple, soursop, oranges, mangoes, tamarinds, and papayas are used widely, the papaya often for its meat-tenderizing properties. In Lamu for years the best *mishkaki*—meat on a skewer—was made by marinating the beef in a mixture of papaya and spices. The cattle were Somali animals that had been driven great distances, and yet the meat was tenderized by this mixture. Cabbage, onions, squash, and tomatoes are among the main vegetables.

Swahilis are Muslims, prohibited from drinking alcohol. Palms are tapped and the liquid is allowed to ferment, but it is proper to wait the few days until it turns to vinegar (*siki*) to use it, even in cooking. Other fermented foods include *maziwa lala* (yogurt) and *ng'onda* (salted, dried, slightly fermented fish). Popular drinks, apart from Western-style, fizzy bottled sodas, are tea, coffee, and a cinnamon beverage. Sweetened tamarind and lime juice are popular as well.

Eating Out

Swahilis normally eat meals at home. Restaurants are typically for those who are traveling, on pilgrimage, or working far from where they live. Tourists sometimes puzzle over why Swahili restaurants do not attempt to serve food in the fashion it would be served in a home. The reason is apparently that the intent of a restaurant is not to try to recreate the privacy and intimacy of home.

A Tanzanian woman carries a basket on her head while shopping at a street market on Lamu Island. (Christopher Pillitz | Getty Images)

As recently as 1985 there were essentially no restaurants other than in a tourist resort set away from the town. This was a period when Zanzibar was just about to open up to tourism and other outsiders, yet there was as yet no real impetus for restaurants. There were many snack vendors in the waterfront gardens in the evening, since a stroll (*matembezi*) and a snack are a common form of entertainment.

Lamu is a different story, for tourists and many government workers and others from non-Swahili areas now live there. Thus, there are cafés and restaurants (*hoteli* in Swahili) catering to them and to Swahilis looking for matembezi. There are complex rules concerning eating in restaurants. In Swahili culture, it is only fit for small children to eat while walking on the street. There is even a saying warning against such behavior, *Kula kitu kitamu kinjianjia mtu atasibiwa na shetani* (One who eats delicious food while walking will be possessed by a devil). One cannot eat in the street, but men may eat outdoors if seated. Such outdoor seating is normally separated from the street, if only symbolically, by a fence.

Women do not sit at outside tables. If women eat at a restaurant—a fairly uncommon occurrence—it is often in an all-female group in an inner, enclosed room away from the other patrons. One sometimes sees exceptions in restaurants that cater to travelers. Indeed, travelers are an exception to many rules. A Swahili proverb says *Msafiri kafiri*, "A traveler is (lowered to the level of) an unbeliever"; that is, one must do all sorts of things in the course of traveling that one would not do normally: Eat unclean foods and break other taboos.

Special Occasions

Food behavior comes under intense scrutiny during the month of Ramadan when all devout Muslims fast during daylight hours. They are forbidden to eat food, chew the stimulant *miraa*, smoke cigarettes, drink water, or even swallow their saliva. The signal that the fast is over each day is the evening call to prayer. Women break the fast at home. Many men, however, break the fast in the street. In preparation for breaking the fast, table upon table of food, sweets, and savories are set up right in the street in Lamu

and Mombasa. Kahawa and *maji tamu* (fruit juice; literally, "sweet liquid") are also set ready. Men buy their food and drink and in Lamu sit opposite it and wait for the call to prayer that will signal the end of the day. In Mombasa men sit or stand in groups on the street and pool the food they will break the fast with. After breaking the fast, the men then go quickly off to the mosque to pray, and then home to eat a full meal. Ramadan cooking is often special and festive, with many special dishes made during that time only. Eid al-Fitr ends Ramadan, and it is a public holiday in Kenya. Gifts are exchanged, new clothes are given as presents, and festive foods are abundant.

Diet and Health

Although many nutrition problems remain, Swahili have more access to protein than many other groups in the region given their routine eating of fish and other marine protein sources. This undoubtedly helps as well with ensuring enough iodine in the diet, a severe problem in some parts of East Africa.

Robert A. Leonard

Further Reading

Burckhardt, Ann L. *The People of Africa and Their Food.* Mankato, MN: Capstone Press, 1996.

DeWitt, Dave, Melissa T. Stock, and Mary Jane Wilan. *Flavors of Africa Cookbook: Spicy African Cooking—from Indigenous Recipes to Those Influenced by Asian and European Settlers.* Rocklin, CA: Prima, 1998.

Essuman, Kofi Manso. *Fermented Fish in Africa: A Study on Processing, Marketing and Consumption.* Rome, Italy: Food and Agriculture Organization, 1992.

Kairi, Wambui. *Food and Festivals: Kenya.* Austin, TX: Raintree Steck-Vaughn, 2000.

Leonard, Robert, and Wendy Saliba. "Food and Ethnic Identity: Theory." In *The Asian Pacific American Heritage: A Companion to Literature and Arts,* edited by George J. Leonard. New York: Garland, 1999, 171–180.

Leonard, Robert, and Wendy Saliba. "Food, Drink, and Swahili Public Space." In *Oxford*

Symposium on Food and Cookery 1991, edited by Harlan Walker. London: Prospect Books, 1992.

Montgomery, Bertha Vining, and Constance Nabwire. *Cooking the African Way.* Minneapolis, MN: Lerner, 1988.

Nurse, Derek, and Thomas Spear. *The Swahili: Reconstructing the History and Language of an African Society, 800–1500.* Philadelphia: University of Pennsylvania Press, 1985.

Oniang'o, Ruth K., and Asenath J. Sigot. *Complete Kenya Cookery.* London: Edward Arnold, 1987.

Osseo-Asare, Fran. *Food Culture in Sub-Saharan Africa.* Food Culture around the World. Westport, CT: Greenwood Press, 2005.

Samuelsson, Marcus. *The Soul of a New Cuisine: A Discovery of the Foods and Flavors of Africa.* Hoboken, NJ: John Wiley & Sons, 2006.

Wandera, A.B.N. *Kenya Traditional Dishes.* Nairobi, Kenya: Nairobi Club-Soroptimist International, 1983.

Swaziland

Overview

The Kingdom of Swaziland, one of Africa's last remaining monarchies, lies landlocked between South Africa and Mozambique. Swaziland is a small country, both in population and in geographic size. It is divided into four different regions: Highveld, Middleveld, Lowveld, and Lubombo. The landscape is mostly mountainous with hills in lower-lying areas. The climate is temperate with more tropical temperatures in lower-lying areas in the Lowveld. The majority of the population lives in the Middleveld where rainfall is less frequent than in the mountains. Its largest city and capital is Mbabane, located in the northwestern part of the country, in the Highveld. The food and diet of the Swazi traditionally were and still are affected greatly by seasonality.

Swaziland gained its independence from Great Britain in 1968 with its precolonial political system still relatively intact. The population of Swaziland is estimated around 1.2 million inhabitants. The population has, however, grown slowly due to the prevalence of HIV/AIDS, with 26 percent of its population being infected, the highest rate in the world. Its two official languages are SiSwati and English. Sixty-nine percent of the population is Christian, and the remainder practices traditional indigenous faiths. Religion has had an effect on food culture and eating. Swaziland's economy is made up mostly of subsistence farming and mining.

⦿ Food Culture Snapshot

Ndoro and Sikose live outside of Manzini on Swazi Nation Land. They have four children, all of whom attend a nearby school. With rising food prices, Ndoro is finding it hard to afford basic foods, especially since losing his job in the mining sector in South Africa last year. To help pay the children's school fees, Ndoro has planted some vegetables on his small plot of land. The rain of the previous summer helped them grow, whereas the previous year had been very dry and large amounts of the maize crops were lost. What vegetables he does not use to feed his family, he sells. In his garden he grows green leafy vegetables and pumpkins. Ndoro owns no livestock and therefore must buy his milk and meat from the grocery store. Every day, Sikose buys bread, and twice a week they buy milk because they don't have refrigeration. Meat is bought only for special occasions or when it can be afforded. Once a month and depending on the family's financial situation, Sikose will buy canned items, such as tinned tuna. The family doesn't eat much fruit, but last year Ndoro planted a banana tree for the family's consumption and also for income.

Major Foodstuffs

Traditionally, sorghum and maize were the main staples in the Swazi diet. Indigenous leafy greens and legumes accompanied the grains. While the base of the Swazi diet remains relatively the same, Western foods have been added due to availability and/or scarcity of indigenous plants and a shift from a hunting and gathering lifestyle to food purchasing. Western foods that have made their way into the Swazi diet as main staples are bread, rice, cabbage, tomatoes, and onions. Vegetables, such as carrots, spinach, beetroot, potatoes, peppers, chilies, okra,

An unidentified girl buys dried fish from a trader before a traditional Reed dance ceremony in Ludzidzini, Swaziland, 2009. About 80,000 virgins from all over the country attended this yearly event, which goes on for a week and which is the biggest in Swazi culture. (Getty Images)

pumpkins, and gourds, are also consumed. Fruit is limited due mainly to its price and availability. Some families may plant their own fruit trees, such as orange, guava, banana, and apple. Wild fruits indigenous to Swaziland have decreased in availability but can still be found. The most common are the monkey orange (*Strychnos cocculoides*), quinine berry (*Petalostigma pubescens*), and *marula* fruit (*Sclerocarya birrea*), a tart round fruit with a light yellow skin. The marula fruit (sometimes spelled merula) is fermented to make the traditional strong Swazi beer.

Meat, especially beef, is not eaten on a regular basis but generally reserved for special celebrations and ceremonies. Rural families keep their own livestock including cattle, goats, and chickens. Chicken is the most frequently consumed. Traditionally, game and birds would have been hunted; however, these

species have now decreased in numbers and are hunted less frequently. Insects, such as caterpillars, termites, and locusts, were traditional delicacies. Newer generations are aware of their edibility but do not have a taste for them. Fish has become a regular part of the Swazi diet, whereas traditionally it was not consumed due to an old belief that it was linked to snakes. Over the past 30 years, with the increasing availability of canned fish, it has become a popular food because it does not need refrigeration, an important consideration in rural areas.

Cow milk is consumed regularly. Fresh milk is available; however, sour milk called *emasi* is preferred. Emasi was traditionally ripened in a gourd. A hole at the bottom was plugged with a root. When the milk was ripe, the whey was drained from the hole in the base.

Cooking

Boiling, stewing, frying, and roasting are the most common cooking methods. Baking soda is used when boiling leafy greens to tenderize them, especially when the leaves are tough. The ash of aloe was traditionally used for the same effect. Legumes are boiled as well, with onions and tomatoes added as flavorings. Beans may be cooked with soup bones for added flavor. Meat is boiled, stewed, roasted, or fried. Fresh fish, caught in reservoirs near homes in rural areas, is generally fried, and tinned fish is cooked with fried onions and tomatoes.

The use of cooking fats, specifically oil, has aided in advancing cooking techniques among the Swazi people. This has allowed for more frying of foods, whereas before most items were stewed or boiled. Cooking equipment has also facilitated meal preparation. Prior to stoves and running water, firewood and water had to be brought to the kitchen, often from very long distances.

The traditional Swazi kitchen would have been inside a kitchen hut, called the *lidladla.* Cooking also took place outside over an open fire when the weather permitted. Inside the lidladla, a depression was created in the center of the hut floor, and a piece of iron was used to line the hearth. Iron rods were placed together to form a tripod to hold the pot over the flames. Today, food is prepared in a kitchen over either a coal stove or a portable camping-type stove. An open fire is also still used on occasion to prepare items like tea or porridge. To reduce the time spent preparing meals, as well as to save on fuel, the majority of meals are prepared once a day and then reheated as needed. Refrigeration is common in urban areas, but in rural areas not everyone has access to it. Cooking utensils were traditionally carved out of wood or gourds. Today, the use of aluminum, iron, and enamel pots and pans is common, as well as china or ceramic plates.

Typical Meals

Traditionally two meals were eaten during the day, one in the morning and one in the evening. The morning meal was informal and eaten midmorning.

Different age-groups and genders ate at different times. The evening meal was shared together at sunset and eaten in the *indlunkula,* the great hut.

Today, however, meals are eaten at unspecific times due to busy schedules. When possible, families eat together. Age and gender no longer specify mealtimes. Three meals are common today. Breakfast is usually eaten between eight and nine in the morning once the children have left for school. Lunch is eaten in the midafternoon around two once the children have returned from school, and supper is between six and seven. The main meal of the day is lunch, at which time food for the evening will be prepared. This helps save on food and water. Snacking between meals is not common. If something is consumed it is usually a soda or cordial. When the consumption of two meals was common, snacking was prevalent. *Jugo* beans (Bambara groundnut) would be boiled and carried to the fields as well as sugarcane, wild indigenous fruits, roasted groundnuts (peanuts), and *amahewu,* a fermented maizemeal beverage.

A typical breakfast consists of soft sour porridge with sugar, tea or coffee with creamer, and bread. Bread is spread with peanut butter or jam and sometimes margarine. Bread is replaced on occasion by scones or *vetkoek,* a traditional Afrikaner pastry that is deep-fried and filled with mincemeat or left plain and spread with honey or jam. Eggs are eaten when available but traditionally were restricted to women after the age of puberty, as it was believed that they would make them desire men.

Lunch is a stiff maize-meal porridge that is replaced at times by rice, mealie rice, or *phutus,* a maize meal cooked in such a way that it takes on the consistency of breadcrumbs. Phutus is served with fresh or sour milk (emasi) and sometimes relish. Relish in this sense refers to a side dish of leafy greens, meat, fish, eggs, or legumes. Maize is eaten daily. Dinner is leftovers from lunch. The maize-meal porridge is reheated and served with a different relish than what was served at lunch. A lighter supper without porridge would include a cup of tea with bread or scones. Tea is not part of the traditional Swazi diet. Its prevalence in today's diet is from British influence during the occupation.

The Sunday lunch is considered the culinary highlight of the week. Nontraditional foods, especially Western foods, are served to mark the special occasion. The Sunday lunch includes a fried, stewed, or roasted chicken served with rice and fresh and cooked salads, as well as pumpkin, mashed potatoes, or cabbage.

Meals are usually eaten with the right hand only, and utensils are used for softer or more liquid dishes that would be difficult to eat with the hands. The meal is an important way to express gratitude and hospitality as well as status. Meals are also used to perform rituals and mark certain celebrations. Children are taught from an early age to share their food with others. Food is often brought as a gift when visiting or given to guests upon their departure for the trip home. Food is always served to guests, and it is considered impolite to decline food when offered. It is also considered impolite not to serve food to a guest. Important guests are served meals similar to those served on Sunday. It is an important mark of status and shows respect for the distinguished guest. This meal includes rice, chicken, cooked and fresh salads, and a dessert that consists of jelly, canned fruit, and custard. Traditionally, men would be served in their own bowl, whereas the hostess and female guests would have to share the same dish.

The most prestigious foods in Swazi culture are beef and beer. Cattle are the main symbol of the accumulation of wealth. Green vegetables are regarded as women's food and suitable to serve to guests. Milk is regarded as a health food and used as a purifying medicine.

Eating Out

Eating out is reserved for the wealthy and tourists. More than half the population of Swaziland lives on less than $2.00 U.S. a day. However, a restaurant culture does still exist. Most restaurants are located in the town or on the outskirts of the towns. Mbabane, the capital city, Manzini, Lobamba, and Big Bend are among the places offering the widest selection of restaurants. While it is possible to eat local or traditional Swazi fare at some of these establishments, most restaurants boast French or Portuguese-inspired dishes.

Special Occasions

Food is also used to mark celebrations, for example, religious events, harvest, birthdays, and weddings. Foods associated with celebrations are often regarded highly. This is because these foods are often scarce, expensive, and time-consuming to prepare and are reserved for special occasions. Meat is an example of a food usually reserved for celebrations. An entire animal will be slaughtered and then consumed with all of the guests. For example, during *lobola,* the ceremony that marks the handing over of the bride's dowry, meat is consumed in large quantities along with strong beer. Cattle are associated with marriage and goats with birth. An exception to having to feed guests was traditionally during a funeral, when the family is considered to be too bereaved to have to cook and relatives and friends will bring food. Today, however, this is less widely practiced, and the family of the deceased will usually roast an entire animal and serve it with scones and bread.

The biggest and most important festivals are the *incwala* and the *umhlanga.* The incwala festival is a six-day celebration at the end of December or the beginning of January depending on the crops. It marks the beginning of the harvest. The consumption of the new crops is forbidden until the ceremony is performed. On the fourth day of the six-day festival the king, who has been in seclusion up until this point during the festival, must first taste the new crops before anyone else. On the final day a huge feast of cow meat and vegetables from the new harvest is eaten. The umhlanga, or the reed dance, is held in August and lasts five days. Unmarried girls gather to pay homage to the Queen Mother. These occasions are marked with the slaughter of a beast.

Impala (African Antelope)

Serves 12

1 impala leg (venison may be substituted)

4 cloves garlic, sliced thinly

1 c green olives, halved

Cooking oil

3 large potatoes, diced

3 large carrots, diced

4 onions, diced

1 c beef broth

10 dried prunes, pitted

Salt and pepper to taste

Directions

1. Rinse the meat and pat dry.

2. Remove the lower shank bone and set leg aside. Place the lower shank bone into a pot, and add water to cover. Set to simmer until reduced by half.

3. With a sharp paring knife cut slits throughout the leg. Into the slits place the garlic and olives. Season the leg with salt and pepper.

4. Place the leg into a roasting pan lightly coated with oil and cook at 325°F for 25 minutes per pound.

5. When done, remove the leg from the pan and set aside to rest.

6. Meanwhile, sauté the vegetables in cooking oil until they are soft and translucent but not browned. Add the prunes and cook until soft. Strain and set the vegetables aside.

7. Add the broth to the juices remaining in the pan and reduce by half. To serve, place the leg on a dish with the vegetables and prunes surrounding it, and drizzle the gravy over the top.

Diet and Health

Food restrictions in the Swazi diet are adhered to but not as commonly as before. Within the culture there is a strong awareness of the relationship between food, health, and body fat. Weight is a sign of prosperity. An underweight or thin person is a sign of poor diet. Milk is seen as an important beverage. It is drunk daily and seen as purifying during ritual occasions. While women are allowed to drink milk throughout most times in their lives, they are restricted from, or have limited contact with, the cows themselves. Depending on the woman's stage of life, contact between her and cattle is believed to affect the breeding and milk production of the cow.

Food restrictions were common. For example, adults who were still able to bear children were not to eat the meat of an aborted animal because it was believed that if they became pregnant they would have a miscarriage. Only the elderly were allowed to eat liver because, if younger people consumed it, it was thought that they would become forgetful. Men and older adults were not to eat soft porridge because it would cause them to become weak and lazy. Sugarcane and groundnuts were not to be consumed by pregnant women because of the belief that these would affect the baby once it was born. Sugarcane is said to cause a mucus-covered baby once it is born. Groundnuts are thought to cause the mother to give birth to a dirty baby. Some of the older generations still abide by these rules; however, the younger generations do not follow many food restrictions, as they cannot remember them.

Since the new millennium, food prices have been on the rise, making it difficult for the average Swazi family, especially when taking into account the prevalence of HIV/AIDS in the society. Many of those infected with the disease require well-balanced diets to facilitate the effectiveness of their antiretroviral treatments. With the increase in food prices it is difficult for these families to obtain the proper foodstuffs.

Kristina Lupp

Further Reading

Kgaphola, Mmantoa S., and Annemarie T. Viljoen. "Food Habits of Rural Swazi Households: 1939–1999, Part 1: Technological Influences on Swazi Food Habits." *Tydskrit vir Gesinsekologie en Verbruikerswetenskappe* 28 (2000): 68–74.

Kgaphola, Mmantoa S., and Annemarie T. Viljoen. "Food Habits of Rural Swazi Households: 1939–1999, Part 2: Social Structural and Ideological influences on Swazi Food Habits." *Journal of Family Ecology and Consumer Sciences* 32 (2004): 16–25.

Osseo-Asare, Fran. *Food Culture in Sub-Saharan Africa.* Westport, CT: Greenwood Press, 2005.

Welcome to Swaziland Web site. http://www.welcometoswaziland.com.

Uganda

Overview

Uganda is a country in equatorial East Africa measuring 241,000 square miles, a little smaller than the state of Oregon. Its population is about 32.3 million. Although Uganda is completely landlocked, a great proportion of the land lies adjacent to fresh water. There are many lakes such as Victoria, Kyoga, and Albert as well as the Nile River, and thus the land is extremely fertile in many places. This was one of the reasons the British designated the area a protectorate in the 19th century; their legacy is still apparent, in some food preferences if not in people of European descent, since white settlers were not permitted. Indians and others from throughout the British Empire were allowed to emigrate and have left a permanent culinary legacy. The population today on the whole remains relatively impoverished, and a large proportion of the wealth remains in the hands of a minority. Uganda is also a very young country, with a median age of 15 years (half the population is under 14 years old) and a life expectancy of 53 years. This is largely owing to widespread mortality associated with HIV.

The people of Uganda fall into dozens of separate ethnic groups, none of which constitutes a majority. The most powerful, centered around the largest city of Kampala, have historically been the Baganda. Their kingdom (officially recognized by the national government) is called Buganda, and an individual of this group is called a *muganda*. The Baganda comprise 17 percent of the total population. Other groups include the Banyakole with 9.5 percent, the Basoga with 8.4 percent, the Bakiga with 6.9 percent, and the Iteso with 6.4 percent, plus many others. As a legacy of colonial rule, English is an official language, though Bantu languages are widely spoken as well as Luo among the northern Nilotic peoples and Swahili as a kind of lingua franca in the north. Uganda has been an independent country since 1962 and has suffered great political vicissitudes, most notably under Idi Amin, who ruled for eight disastrous years in the 1970s. Its economy is growing rapidly today, however, despite the recent contraction of the economy globally. It is nonetheless still among the poorest nations on earth.

Roughly 80 percent of Ugandans work in agriculture, with coffee the largest and most important export. Tea, cotton, tobacco, and refined sugar are other important agricultural and industrial products. Many people still practice subsistence agriculture, though in larger cities and especially the cosmopolitan capital Kampala a large segment of the population works in public service and the service industries.

Most Ugandans are Christian, with 42 percent Catholics, 36 percent Protestants (mostly Anglican), 12 percent Muslims, and 10 percent other or none. Many indigenous practices have been melded with Christianity, though few still fully practice the traditional religions. There is also a tiny community of Jews, or Abayudaya (people of Judah), who live around Mbale.

🍽 Food Culture Snapshot

Madiina Nakazzi is the mother of six children and works at Makerere University in Kampala. The eldest

A family of coffee farmers in Uganda begin to husk their coffee beans. (Brian Longmore | Dreamstime.com)

of her children, Annette Nanziri Clark, is married to an American and lives in Atlanta. The two oldest boys, Roger Serunyigo and Douglas, live and work in Kampala but no longer with their mother. The three youngest children, Susan Nansamba, Enock Kakeeto, and Rose Nankya, still live at home. Rose is in her second year studying economics at Makerere University. The children have different fathers, and extended families are quite common, though monogamy is a growing trend.

Madiina is well known for her excellent cooking, of which her children are especially proud. They enjoy eating together when they can, though the pressures of work often mean the entire family gets together only on special occasions, especially birthdays. The older boys, who work in offices, often resort to street food or fast-food joints such as Zanzi, which specializes in pork and serves beer. But everyone appreciates the opportunity to eat traditional meals cooked at home by Madiina.

Major Foodstuffs

A great variety of starch staples are available in Uganda, though these differ according to ethnic group and also factors such as soil fertility, which determines which staple will grow well in a given area. People are largely identified by which staple they prefer, though several may be commonly served and most people enjoy a wide range of starchy foods.

Matooke is the starch staple of the Baganda. It is made from a green banana (considered overripe if yellow) not dissimilar to a green plantain. In the Luganda language the word *mmere* means simply "food," but it also refers universally to matooke. There is a strict procedure governing its preparation. The bananas are peeled and soaked. They are then tied into packages made of banana leaves, placed in a pot, and steamed until soft. The bundle is then squeezed and massaged until mashed and smooth. Matooke is often served with a sauce that is steamed in the same pot. This sauce may consist of ground peanuts or smoked catfish (*mukene*) or silverfish (*nkejje*). A mushroom sauce (*butikko*) is also popular. It is said that the flavor of matooke is best when cooked over a charcoal fire rather than on gas or electric burners, which don't lend a subtle smoky aroma to the finished dish. *Katogo* is another dish similar to matooke, but the bananas are left whole and unmashed.

Many of the now-popular staples were introduced to Africa from the Americas. One is called *posho*, which is made from white corn or maize flour. It is the dominant staple of the Samya tribe from the Mbale District in eastern Uganda, and it is usually eaten with fish, either fried, roasted, or steamed, and with groundnut sauce. It is similar to the *ugali* eaten in Kenya and throughout East Africa. It is essentially a thick corn-flour mush eaten by pinching off a round ball in the hand, creating a depression on one side to serve as a scoop, and then dipping it into sauces and stews. The whole seasoned ball is then placed in the mouth and eaten. In West Africa a similar dish is known as *foufou*.

Another import from the Americas is cassava. Similar to posho, the root is cooked and mashed into

A young African man is transporting a load of bananas on his bicycle on a dirt road. The meal called *matooke*, made of green cooking bananas, is the most important food for the rural people in Uganda, Rwanda, Burundi, and Congo. (iStockPhoto)

a thick porridge. This starch has largely displaced the native yam, a huge starchy white tuber not to be confused with the sweet potato, although the latter has also been brought from the Americas. Equally important is the potato, or Irish potato as it's called in Uganda, though it, too, originated in the Andes. It is eaten especially by the Bakiga people, though historically they depended more on local greens, gourds, and other vegetables.

The most important of native African grains historically are sorghum and millet. Sorghum looks like corn when growing, but instead of ears it has small round seeds at the top. Millet is a similar grain, familiar in the West as birdseed; it can be very tasty. These are eaten especially by the Banyankole ethnic group. *Kalo* is a thick mush made from millet flour

that is eaten much like posho, except that it is dark and heavy. Nonetheless, it is very nutritious and can keep a person energized all day. In the north the staples among the Alur and Lugbara are wheat flour and *simsim* flour, which is made from ground sesame seeds. In the north especially, simsim is cooked with spinach.

Groundnuts, or simply *g-nut,* are perhaps the most important flavoring in Ugandan sauces. The native African bambara groundnut has been largely replaced by the New World peanut, but they are similar and the name *groundnut* remains for both species. It is used in soups or in a sauce called *binyebwa,* which is served with matooke.

Ugandans eat a wide variety of meats and especially love beef, chicken, and goat, though there are many pork dishes as well. The following recipe is probably the most famous of Ugandan dishes; it can be made with any meat.

Luwombo

Serves 4

Ingredients

I chicken (can also be made with beef or goat)

2 c roasted peanuts

2 yellow onions

I tbsp grated ginger

4 tomatoes

Salt and pepper to taste

Banana leaves (available frozen)

Cut up a chicken (breast, thighs, and legs) into large bite-sized pieces without bones. Season with salt and pepper, and grill chicken until it begins to brown but is not cooked through. Next, crush the peanuts into a fine powder with a mortar and pestle. Chop the onion and sauté in oil until golden. Add the ginger. Dice the tomatoes and add to the onions. Cook until the liquid reduces, and then add the crushed peanuts and finish cooking the sauce. Add salt and pepper to taste. Place a few pieces of chicken, enough for a whole serving, with sauce in the center of a banana leaf. Draw in the edges, completely enclosing the ingredients, and tie at the top with a strand of banana leaf. Make four such packages. Place a few banana leaves at the bottom of a stockpot and arrange the bundles on top. Add a little water to the pot and steam for I hour or longer, checking to make sure the water hasn't evaporated. It is best cooked over a charcoal fire. When done, unwrap the bundles and serve one opened leaf package per plate. Serve with matooke—mashed steamed green banana. Plantains will work, but smaller green bananas from Southeast Asia are a better option. Men are advised to consider marrying only women who can properly prepare luwombo.

There are also a number of unique dishes, for example, cow's hooves, which are called *mulokoni* or *kigele,* often served with cassava. This is a popular meal late at night or at drinking parties. Probably the most unique food is green grasshoppers (katydids), which appear in the rainy season and are called *nsenene.* The name is probably onomatopoetic in origin based on the sound they make. They are caught in huge funnels, the legs and wings are removed, and they are fried in oil, salted, and served as a snack. In many rural places collecting nsenene dramatically enhances the household income.

Beans and peas are also a very important source of protein; the black-eyed pea and various relatives in the *Vigna* genus are native to Africa. Today, many varieties of beans and peas are grown and commonly included in stews and sauces. They can also be ground into a batter and fried. Fish are also very important to Ugandans who live near lakes and rivers, and smoked fish is eaten everywhere in cooked stews. Fresh fish, especially roast tilapia or other fish that is deep-fried or boiled with sauce, is a favorite at the beaches along Lake Victoria, such as at Entebbe.

A remarkably wide variety of greens provide essential vitamins in the Ugandan diet. There is *nakati,* a kind of spinach, either green or red, as well as *dodo* and dozens of other wild leafy greens. There is also a dish comparable to the Kenyan *sukuma wiki,* which is greens cooked down to a mushy and slightly gelatinous consistency that is highly appreciated. It is much like the consistency of well-cooked okra, another native African plant, which is also popular. The distant relatives of such dishes can still be found in the collard greens and gumbo of the U.S. south. There is also a small bitter eggplant called *ntula* as well as cucumbers, avocados (served in a salad reminiscent of guacamole), and many other native vegetables, which once formed the bulk of the diet. Among fruits Ugandans especially enjoy pineapple, which is grown extensively, as well as watermelons, pawpaws, mangoes, apples, jackfruit, and passion fruit. The juice of the latter is a popular accompaniment to meals.

The Banyankole also drink a lot of milk. Ironically, tea is the preferred local drink, a colonial legacy, despite the huge coffee production. Most

Ugandan coffee is exported and can even be bought in high-end coffee shops in the United States. Ugandans drink a lot of soda and also brew beer, most notably Nile Beer from Jinja, which is now owned by SABMiller. There is also a fiery liquor distilled from bananas called Uganda Waragi.

Typical Meals

Ugandans eat three meals a day: breakfast, lunch, and dinner. Many people eat a very small breakfast between 7:30 and 11 A.M. that consists of tea, with or without milk, and bread or fried cassava sticks or perhaps the Indian flatbread chapati—the legacy of a once-large Indian community who were exiled in the 1970s but have since been allowed to return. *Mandazi* is a kind of donut strip also eaten for breakfast. Some people, especially workers who may not have a long lunch break, eat a larger breakfast called *katogo,* which is matooke mixed with beef or beef chitterlings or offal. It is a heavy dish and thus can keep a person sated until dinnertime.

Lunch is a relatively late meal, eaten between 1 and 4 P.M., though in rural villages usually later in the afternoon since they will have spent much of the day tending gardens. City dwellers may go home for a lunch break, though increasingly they resort to fast-food and junk-food outlets that sell fried chicken, fries (called chips), and *chaps* (roasted ground meat in a kind of patty), or chapati and rice *pilawo* (another Indian dish, a kind of pilaf). Office employees without long breaks often resort to quick junk food.

Dinner is eaten very late, between 8 and 11 P.M., especially for those who work late and have no one at home who can cook. The cooking at home is almost always done by women, either the mother of the family or, if the family is affluent, a housemaid, and usually over a charcoal stove. Increasingly people do buy takeout from restaurants, which may sell rice, French fries or potatoes, chaps, beef, liver, kebabs, or sausages, which are all quickly cooked using gas stoves.

Eating Out

Chinese, Indian, and even Korean restaurants are popular for parties and special occasions. Often Ugandan families will prepare food at home and then transport it to weddings, birthday parties, and even sporting venues. There are also many restaurants specializing in pork products, like Zanzi, Outlook, Nicodemus, Yakobo's, and Rise and Shine, to name a few. Kebab stands were introduced by Parsis—Zoroastrians from India who came under British colonial rule.

There is also a flourishing street-food scene. One can purchase sausages, a chapati rolled around eggs and sometimes tomatoes called a *rolex,* or *kikomando,* a chapati with beans. There is also a version of the Indian samosa, or *sambusa,* which is a delicate triangular pastry filled with beans and spices. Roasted bananas called *gonja* are another popular street food as well as roasted chicken and the like. Street vendors usually come in from poorer suburbs into the center of town with their equipment and ingredients. Ironically, it is often the more affluent families and professionals who resort to street food and junk food, while traditional dishes are more common among the poorer classes, mostly because they are cheaper. There are also a number of Ugandan snack foods, such as nsenene, as well as fried sweet dough strips called mandazi and roasted corn, roasted peanuts, and olives.

Special Occasions

Among Christians special attention is given to holidays like Christmas and Easter, during which huge quantities of food are cooked for family gatherings, including matooke, beef, vegetables, chicken, beans, posho, and rice. Muslims celebrate their holidays with special foods such as a pilawo of fried rice and beef. They, of course, abstain from pork as do other Muslims. There are also secular celebrations such as the giving away of the bride, rites for the deceased, anniversaries, and birthdays. In the cities there are also office parties, which mostly include snack foods, fries and sausages, liver, and so forth.

Diet and Health

While many Ugandan adults over the age of 45 take health into consideration and have given up meat and fried foods, and instead resort to boiled food and low-sodium dishes, the young continue to eat both traditional foods and a wide array of Western junk foods high in fat, sodium, and refined sugar.

Ken Albala and Roger Serunyigo

Further Reading

Goode, P. S. *Edible Plants of Uganda.* Rome, Italy: Food and Agriculture Organization, 1989.

Henson, Erica. *The Food Holiday Uganda.* Atlanta: Echo Media, 2010.

Uganda: Growing Out of Poverty. Washington, DC: World Bank, 1993.

Zimbabwe

Overview

Despite having once been described as Africa's breadbasket, Zimbabwe, formerly known as Rhodesia, is now a country on the edge of starvation. While drought is part of the history of famine, the current situation is more the result of politics. Colonial exploitation by the British created an unequal farming system whereby the best and most productive lands were occupied by a minority of white farmers. These farmers, with the help of male, black farmworkers, were able to produce crops such as wheat, coffee, tea, and tobacco for export. The less productive land was largely subsistence farmed by women, which formed the backbone of Zimbabwean provisioning among the lower classes in both urban and rural areas, as rural women would trade their surplus in the cities. Recent land-reform efforts by President Mugabe, which reallocated plantations owned by white farmers to black Zimbabweans, did not redress the inequalities but instead had the effect of rendering much of this once-productive land unusable. This is largely because reallocation did not also come with training in large-scale agricultural practices. At the same time, efforts to "clean up" urban areas (operation Murambatsvina) resulted in the obliteration of the markets where women once sold their surpluses to poorer city dwellers and left millions, mainly women and children, homeless. Just less than 40 percent of the total population lives in the urban areas. Harare and Bulawayo are the largest cities.

Located in the southeastern part of Africa, Zimbabwe is a landlocked country whose borders are primarily formed by the Limpopo and Zambezi rivers. The climate is tropical, although this is moderated in much of the country by the altitude afforded to it by mountains that run the length of the country. From May to September the country's climate is cold and dry, which is usually offset by a rainy period between November and March. The most fertile areas are in the north of the country, leaving only about 8 percent of the whole area arable. In addition to the loss of productive agriculture in the country, the Zimbabwe Conservation Task Force estimates that 60 percent of Zimbabwe's wildlife has died since 2000. This is largely the result of poaching, as families are desperate for food after the collapse of farming caused by land reform.

Unlike many other African countries, Zimbabwe is relatively homogeneous in its ethnic and religious makeup. The largest ethnic group are Shona (77%), followed by the Ndebele, who comprise 18 percent of the population. Whites, mostly of British descent, are a very small minority at just under 1 percent of the total population. The vast majority of people (85%) consider themselves Christian, though like many who live in locations where Christianity was introduced by missionaries, Christianity is often practiced alongside or modified by more traditional forms of religion, which place particular emphasis on ancestor worship. Instead of religion or ethnicity, it is class that divides this country. The colonial expansion of the British South Africa Company introduced a class system that has profoundly influenced foodways. Those with greater incomes eat dishes that are more akin to what might be found in any British household. A considerably larger proportion of the remainder are lucky if they eat more than one meal of *sadza,* a ground-corn dish that has a texture similar to mashed potatoes, per day. Food insecurity is particularly high for those living in the southern parts of the country.

The recent past has been particularly difficult for the vast majority of Zimbabweans. Even those with professional employment struggled to feed themselves and their families as inflation reached unimaginable proportions. In 2008, the only legal currency was the Zimbabwean dollar, and at one point inflation was so severe that prices changed by the hour. Not only could people not afford to buy anything, but there was also very little to purchase. There were reports of people standing in line for hours to buy cooking oil or a loaf of bread. As a result people smuggled basic goods such as vegetable oil, cornmeal, and soap from South Africa. The Zimbabwean dollar is still very weak but has stabilized since changes in currency laws now provide for wages in U.S. dollars and it is no longer illegal to sell and buy goods in other currencies.

🍽 Food Culture Snapshot

Mapfumo is trained as a teacher. He used to live in Harare with his wife, Saki, and his three children. He now lives in Francistown, Botswana, just over the Zimbabwean border, working as a mechanic. Saki and his two youngest children, Fari (age 7) and Kati (age 12), still live in Harare. His other daughter, Rita (age 16), lives in the United Kingdom with her aunt, Saki's sister. Mapfumo makes the long journey back to the family home in Zimbabwe every weekend to be with his family. He moved to Botswana in 2005, when things in Zimbabwe started to become very bad, though not as bad as they would later become. He stopped teaching because the Zimbabwean government was not paying teachers regularly or enough to buy basic goods. One day he went to collect his pay packet hoping to be able to buy a hamburger for lunch. At that time the hamburger was $50,000 (Zim), or about $3 (U.S.). His total pay was only $25,000 (Zim) for a month's work teaching. He started going to Botswana to buy food and other goods, like soap, which he then brought back for Saki and the children. He and Saki also traded currency, but this became precarious when the government cracked down on market traders and the black market currency traders in 2005. He then decided to find work with some friends in Botswana, working as a garage assistant and tutoring privately. Until very recently he still brought back goods for his family from over the border, but now he can just bring money, as the shops are starting to sell goods again and it is legal to do business in currencies other than the Zimbabwean dollar.

Daily life for Saki is improving after the last hard years, though she has been forced to change the way she makes her livelihood. Now that it is possible to purchase goods in the stores again, and do so legally with the U.S. dollar, the Botswanan pula, and the South African rand, she is facing competition from legal businesses for the greens and vegetables she sells in the market. But at least she has a stall. Many lost their stalls when the government came through the suburbs in 2005 and removed what were identified as illegal buildings. This was not just stalls but also extensions

A child begins preparation for a meal in Zimbabwe, 2008. (GRANT NEUENBURG | Reuters | Corbis)

people had built onto their homes and garden sheds that were rented out to poorer families who could not afford their own home. Saki counts herself as lucky. She has a husband who is faithful and has not given her AIDS. He also gives her money. She is able to feed her family something more than bread each day. She can also send her two children to school. Her sister in the United Kingdom also sends her money regularly, though when it is transferred she spends the entire day waiting in line at the bank to get it out as no one trusts the banks. She misses Rita very much and knows she does not like living in the United Kingdom, but sending her to live with her aunt was the only way she could get formal schooling while the teachers were on strike for so long.

Saki starts the day at 5 A.M. She gets the children up and ready for school and gives them some sadza (ground corn mealies) left over from the previous evening. Sometimes there are leftover sweet potatoes. When she has milk, she boils some of this to pour over the sadza. It is best with a bit of sugar as well, but that is a luxury, as is the cup of tea that she likes in the morning. Mapfumo sometimes brings her red bush tea from Botswana, but she prefers the English-style black tea with milk and sugar that she used to have when she was younger. By six in the morning, she must be out of the house and waiting by the road for the farmer who brings her produce to sell in the market, so she is gone before the children start school. They leave together, and Kati drops Fari off at his school before heading on to her own. When the children finish school they will come to help Saki at the market. They tie bundles of amaranth leaves together to sell for the stew that goes with sadza. Sometimes they help grind peanuts into peanut butter. Kati stays with her mother now, although she used to sell roasted nuts at the bus station until a group of boys tried to take her away. A neighbor was also there and helped her get away from the boys. In the evening the family will have sadza with relish made from peanut butter and greens, which is better than a year ago, when all they would have was bread.

Saki is saving money to take a cooking class so she can work as a cook in a wealthy house. While she is a good Zimbabwean cook and her sadza has no lumps and is always the right consistency, wealthy people want cooks who can prepare English food. Saki doesn't understand why anyone would want to eat like that,

as traditional food, when there is enough, is healthy, fills one up, and is not difficult to make once you get the sadza right. She even read that a chef at one of the hotels won a competition for all of Africa with his traditionally inspired dish. This is not what the wealthy want, but working for one of them would mean more money. Saki dreams that, one day, her husband and all her children will be with her again in Zimbabwe. Mapfumo will be able to work as a teacher, and her children will have good jobs.

Major Foodstuffs

As in many other African countries, the traditional Zimbabwean meal consists of a starch and some form of stew or meat. The starch is usually sadza, which is made by mixing mealies (imported white corn) or mealie-meal with water to form a thick paste. Other grains such as millet are also used. The paste is cooked for a while, and then either more cornmeal is added to thicken it, or the water is squeezed out. What is left is a very thick, grayish porridge. When eaten, a chunk of sadza is taken and rolled into a ball. This ball is then dipped into the stew (referred to as relish). This relish might be some sort of leafy green, like spinach, amaranth, or collard greens, with squash and beans or nuts. Peanuts are very commonly made into a stew.

When Zimbabwe was more prosperous, meat (*nyama*) would be stewed with the vegetables and beans or grilled. Beef (*nyama ye mombe*) and goat (*nyama ye mbudzi*) were common, and to a lesser extent chicken (*nyama ye huku*), but also game animals such as springbok, kudu, impala (all types of venison), crocodile, and warthog. Freshwater fish, such as catfish, bass, and bream, are also available to those who can afford them or who live near a river or lake where they may be caught, something unavailable to most urban dwellers.

Dovi (Peanut Butter Stew)

Serves 6

Oil or butter for frying

2 medium onions, chopped finely

Garlic, crushed

1 tsp salt

½ tsp pepper

½ tsp cayenne pepper

2 green peppers, chopped

Chicken pieces (optional)

3–4 tomatoes

2 c water

6 tbsp peanut butter

1 large bag spinach or some other green leafy vegetable or okra

In a large heavy-bottomed pot, brown the onions over medium heat in the oil or butter. When the onions are just brown, add the garlic, salt, pepper, and cayenne, and cook for a further 3–4 minutes, stirring. Add the chopped peppers and chicken, if using. Cook for about 5 minutes or until the chicken is browned. Add the tomatoes and the water, and simmer for 10 minutes. Add the peanut butter, and continue to simmer for 5 minutes. Add the spinach or other greens, and cook briefly until the leaves are limp and tender. Serve immediately.

Because the seasons are distinctly divided, some foods are available only at certain times of the year, whereas others must be preserved. In rural areas in the summer mopane worms (flying termites) are caught and either eaten raw or fried (*modoro*) or made into a relish that includes baobab fruit (which looks like a coconut and has a sour pithy white interior), cassava, and nuts. Food is also preserved for the dry season in winter by drying it in the sun. *Biltong* (jerky made of seasoned meat that is hung to dry) and *kapanta* (dried fish) are two examples. Vegetables are also dried to be used in the winter dry season. *Nyemba* (a type of bean) leaves, pumpkin leaves, and tomatoes are all dried.

Cornmeal is sometimes made into a drink, called *whawha,* that is fermented and like beer. This and Chibuku beer, made from sorghum, are drunk by the poor, whereas those with more money may drink Lion or Castle brand beers. Lion beer is the stronger of the two. For those who do not drink alcohol, Rock Shandy (bitters, lemonade, and soda) or Malawi Shandy (ginger beer and bitters) are popular choices.

Cooking

The traditional way to cook is using a series of three cooking pots. The sadza pot is made of clay or cast iron and is balanced on a tripod of three stones set in an open fire, although those in urban places have gas or paraffin cookers in their homes instead of an open hearth. The other two pots, also cast iron or clay, are for cooking the stew. All children, including boys, are taught to cook sadza from the age of 10. People are judged on their ability to cook sadza. A good sadza is not lumpy and is neither too hard nor too soft. Cornmeal, along with other grains and nuts (especially peanuts), is often ground at home with a large rock and grinding stone. Larger pieces of meat will be barbecued using a spit or roasted slowly over a low fire. Recently, "hot box" cooking has been introduced into the country as an inexpensive and environmentally friendly way to cook with limited use of cooking fuel. The method involves cooking the food for 10 minutes in a lidded cooking pot. This hot pot is then placed in an insulated container, which may be as simple as a cardboard box stuffed with pillows or hay. The food in the pot will continue to steam and will be ready to eat in three or four hours. This method is particularly effective for cooking tough cuts of meat.

Typical Meals

While the norm for the majority of Zimbabweans is just one meal of sadza a day, the more traditional approach to mealtimes is to eat three meals a day. In the morning this may be sadza with jam, fruit, peanut butter, or sour milk and sugar, or a thinner porridge (*bota*) or bread (*pot brood*) with peanut butter. Tea or coffee are drunk with breakfast. Lunch and dinner are also likely to feature sadza dipped into a relish, which almost always includes some tomato. Sadza eaten at lunch is referred to as *sadza re masikati,* which means "sadza in the afternoon." Likewise, *sadza re manheru* means "sadza in the evening," or dinner. Many will also have a cup of tea at 10 A.M. and 4 P.M., a holdover from the British.

Before eating, a dish of water is provided for cleaning hands. The host or senior male member of the family will hold the bowl, and water is poured over the hands, which are then dried on a cloth. While utensils are available, typically people eat their food with their right hand. Serving of food varies and is culturally dictated. In some places food is served in a communal dish, usually wooden, on the floor, around which diners sit in a circle. Polite manners indicate that everyone eat at the same pace so that everyone has their share. More often, however, the order of eating is dictated by gender and age. Men eat first, starting with the husband, followed by older men, then younger men, then older women, then other women, and then children. The best parts of the meal are also given to the men; for a chicken this would mean the dark meat (thighs, wings, legs) is given to the men. Men will sit on benches if they are available, while women will sit on the floor.

The wealthiest are also the most likely to adopt the English diet. This typically consists of a meat and two vegetables. While ordinary Zimbabweans, including the middle classes, stick to one-course dishes of sadza and relish, the wealthy adopt multiple courses that include a starter, a main course, and a sweet course, but there may also be a soup and fish course prior to the main, much as the Edwardian colonizers would have done. Chicken roasted with bacon and served with apples, roasted potatoes, cheese, and grain mustard is an example of one dish that may be served as a main course. Victoria sponge cake may be served for dessert.

Eating Out

The woman is responsible for providing food for her children and paying for their schooling. As women are less likely to be formally employed, eating out would be reserved for the few and is most often not a family activity. There are restaurants in Harare, the capital of Zimbabwe, for tourists and elites. In Harare, one can find all types of cuisines, ranging from Italian to Chinese and Indian, as well as fusion cuisines that adapt local ingredients to foreign cuisines. Beer is available and the most widely consumed beverage, although in the hotels wine and other spirits may be purchased. When dining in a restaurant, table service is the norm. Licensing hours for bars are from 10:30 A.M. to 3 P.M. and then from 4:30 P.M. to 11 P.M. Street food is available, but it is technically illegal. Nonetheless, children and women will walk along the road or through the bus station with baskets of bread, fruit, boiled or roasted corn, peanuts, beans, and hard-boiled eggs, which they sell.

If invited to eat in a Zimbabwean home, one should expect to have one's hands washed first and to be served a separate portion of food rather than to help oneself from the communal dish. It is polite to leave a small portion of the food that is served, as this indicates that the host has provided sufficiently for his guests. The most likely occasion when one would be invited to a Zimbabwean home for a meal would be for an event like a wedding, christening, or funeral. Moreover, some guests will receive special food such as dried chicken because it is particularly expensive. In this case, the chicken is slowly roasted over an open fire and served with sadza and peanut butter.

Special Occasions

Zimbabwe is largely a Christian country and as such celebrates the major Christian holidays such as Christmas and Easter with food. Because of its location in the southern hemisphere, Christmas in Zimbabwe falls in summer and corresponds to the harvest. Fresh fruits and vegetables such as leafy greens and corn are eaten along with sadza. A roast is traditionally prepared using cow or goat, or perhaps game such as ostrich, kudu, or warthog. Additionally, the national day of Zimbabwe is celebrated in early April. In addition to sadza, the food that accompanies these celebrations may include squash soups or wild mushroom stews.

Weddings, christenings, and funerals are also marked with food. The size and scope of the wedding celebration largely depends on how much the family can afford to spend and may include a spit-roasted animal. A christening may be celebrated in a similar manner. Funerals, however, are not marked with special food. Instead, older family members and more distant relatives, such as a sister-in-law, will bring food to those who are mourning. It is expected that chief mourners, that is, the immediate family, will not be able to cook at this time because they are in mourning.

Diet and Health

The traditional rural diet is nutritionally sound in that it has few fats, uses natural rather than processed sugar, and incorporates many of the fruits that are able to grow in the country. Indeed, in the not-so-distant past, Zimbabwe was a net exporter of food. This diet has sometimes been impacted significantly by drought and crop failure, but the structural adjustment policies of the 1990s, and the more recent economic and agricultural mismanagement, have meant that this is a country plagued by an inadequate food supply. Lack of food contributes to a host of health problems that subsequently arise from starvation and malnutrition, such as blindness as a result of vitamin A deficiency and goiter due to lack of iodine in the diet. Children are stricken with kwashiorkor, a form of malnutrition linked to a lack of protein in the diet. Kwashiorkor usually affects children under five and exhibits symptoms such as a swollen belly or swollen ankles. Adults are more likely to exhibit pellagra, identified by dermatitis, diarrhea, and distemper, which is caused by niacin deficiency resulting from a diet solely of corn. Nearly two out of every five people are considered undernourished, and nearly one in every six children under age five is underweight, while one in five is stunted.

The life expectancy in Zimbabwe was identified as the lowest in the world in 2006. Men are expected to live to the age of 37 and women to the age of 34. This represents a drop in the life expectancy from 60 years in 1990. The infant mortality rate is also high, at 13.5 percent; about one in every eight children dies before reaching age five. Much of the decline in health is due to the prevalence of AIDS and HIV. Approximately one-fifth of those age 20–49 are currently infected with HIV. Additionally, the low life expectancy coupled with the economic disadvantages of women (employment is concentrated in the informal and illegal trading sector, and women are responsible for paying for their children's food) means that poverty is disproportionately borne by

children. Just over a third of the country's total population is composed of children under the age of 14, a large proportion of whom are orphans. Estimates in 2007 were 1.3 million orphans as a result of AIDS. They must fend for themselves or rely on an ever-shrinking pool of elderly relatives.

Unlike its neighbors, until recently Zimbabwe has had relatively safe drinking water. However, in 2008, large areas of the country were struck by cholera, which infected over 10,000 people. Typhoid fever, malaria, and schistosomiasis (a parasite-derived disease) are also present throughout the country, with those in rural areas more susceptible, as only 37 percent of those in rural areas have access to sanitation, compared with 63 percent of those in urban areas. Generally, access to water is increasingly under stress as a result of more frequent droughts brought on by global warming.

In Zimbabwe, the health system has largely failed. By the end of 2008, only one of the four major hospitals within the country was still open, and the medical school had closed. As a result, many turn to traditional healers for medical help. Traditional medicine is holistic and is concerned with healing the root cause of an illness rather than just the symptoms. The illness may be the result of having angered the ancestors by failing to follow socioreligious obligations and taboos such as those against elder abuse and promiscuity. Diet and herbs are important for curing these unnatural diseases. For example, among the Ndebele, eating food that shares one's name is prohibited. For instance, if a man's last name is "cow," then he should avoid all beef.

Megan K. Blake

Further Reading

Arnold, J. R., and R. W. Lener. *Robert Mugabe's Zimbabwe.* Minneapolis, MN: 21st Century Books, 2008.

Bonzo, Gertie, Norma Kitson, and Joan Wardrop. *Talking about Food: A Conversation about Zimbabwe, Cooking, Eating and Social Living.* 2000. http://motspluriels.arts.uwa.edu.au/MP1500jw.html.

Chataway, N. *The Bulawayo Cookery Book.* London: Jeppestown, 1909.

Middle East

Arabian Peninsula

Overview

The Arabian Peninsula, encompassing Bahrain, Kuwait, Qatar, Saudi Arabia, and the United Arab Emirates (UAE), is approximately one-third the size of the United States. Much of it is a desolate, waterless desert with meager stretches of pasture, mainly scrubby saltbush plants, occasionally enriched with other short-lived plants following the scanty rainstorms that occur only in the winter and spring. Mountain ranges, which have a pleasanter climate, run parallel to the southwestern and southeastern coasts. The Rub' al-Khali (Empty Quarter), one-fourth of Saudi Arabia, is so arid that even most nomads avoid traversing it, as it contains little grazing for their flocks. In some places, the exact boundaries between countries have not been determined because the land is so inhospitable.

The Kingdom of Saudi Arabia covers approximately three-fourths of the peninsula and is about one-fourth the size of the United States. The Kingdom of Bahrain, an archipelago of 33 islands off Saudi Arabia's coast in the Arabian Gulf (as Arabs call the Persian Gulf), is the smallest of the countries in this region, about one-fourth the size of Rhode Island.

The Kingdom of Saudi Arabia is a monarchy; the Kingdom of Bahrain and the Kingdom of Kuwait are constitutional monarchies; the state of Qatar is an emirate; and the UAE is a federation of seven absolute monarchies. King 'Abd al-'Aziz al-Saud brought together Saudi Arabia's four provinces in the first third of the 20th century, uniting several independent tribes with a combination of fighting

and democracy (although tribal affiliations remain strong in all countries of the peninsula). Bahrain, Kuwait, Qatar, and the UAE were once British protectorates; that is, they made a treaty with Great Britain that Britain would help them against their enemies, in return for which they would not do business with any other foreign rulers without getting permission from Britain. Kuwait became independent in 1961. The other three areas became independent in 1971 when Britain pulled out of the Gulf. Six of the seven emirates (Abu Dhabi, Ajman, Dubai, Fujairah, Sharjah, and Umm al-Quwain) then united to form the UAE; the seventh, Ras al-Khaimah, joined them in 1972. People who are unfamiliar with Qatar may have heard of its television station, Al Jazeera. Many Westerners first heard of Kuwait when Iraq invaded it in 1991, precipitating the first Gulf War. Kuwait has mostly recovered from the depredations of that invasion.

In an area this large, many different regional food habits exist; however, geography and climate, similar throughout most of the peninsula, played a major role in the original food habits in the area. Since the mid-20th century, the ready availability of imported foods of all kinds has greatly expanded food choices on the peninsula. Improved communication and mobility have contributed to homogenization of the diet. Most of the many foreign nationals working in the peninsula eat the traditional foods of their own countries.

Oil was discovered in Bahrain in 1932, in Saudi Arabia and Kuwait in 1938, in Qatar in 1939, and in Abu Dhabi in 1959. Before World War II, life on the

A traditional fishing dhow at dock in Waqrah, Qatar. (iStockPhoto)

peninsula was relatively primitive compared to the West, with the majority of the population being Bedouin. The discovery of oil led to increased contact with the West and a huge upsurge in the standard of living. Governments have moved many Bedouin into settled communities. Nomads still exist, but they often travel in sport-utility vehicles, and a camel is as likely to be riding with folded legs in the back of a pickup truck as walking in a caravan. Before World War II, if boys had any education, they attended religious schools that focused on memorizing the Quran; schools for girls didn't open until the 1960s. Now, all children attend modern schools, and many attend colleges and universities at home or in other Middle Eastern countries, Europe, or the United States.

The peninsula was not entirely isolated from the outside world before the oil companies arrived.

Ships sailing the spice routes from India to the Levant passed through both the Red Sea and the Gulf. Camels carried goods on the Incense Route from Yemen along the Red Sea coast. Experts disagree about whether early people living on the peninsula used the spices: Some assume they must have done so; others doubt they could have afforded them.

Beginning in the 620s A.D., after Muhammad founded Islam, Muslim armies fanned out through the peninsula, through North Africa into Spain and France, and along the north side of the Gulf and the Arabian Sea to the area that is now Afghanistan and Pakistan. They took Arabic foodways with them, and the foodways of the conquered countries filtered back to the peninsula. Once Muhammad instituted the pilgrimage (hajj) to Makkah (or Mecca, as it is usually spelled in the West), pilgrims came from far-flung countries of the Muslim empire. Some remained, making Makkah a cosmopolitan city. When the Muslim empire shrank, the Ottoman Empire moved in and occupied the Red Sea coast through modern Yemen, and the Arabian Gulf coast through present-day Qatar, bringing new food influences. 'Abd al-'Aziz al-Saud drove the Ottomans out shortly after World War I. Arabs who go to other countries for schooling, vacations, or jobs often enjoy foreign foods and add them to their diet. Add items from the Columbian Exchange, like tomatoes and peppers, and the peninsula's food demonstrates global influences.

The Arabian American Oil Company (Aramco, now Saudi Aramco) discovered oil in Saudi Arabia in 1938. World War II delayed development, but after the war, Saudi Arabia grew to dominate world oil production. The oil industry brought many foreigners whose food cultures have affected food habits in the area, as local merchants sell foods these people want. In its early days, to cut the expense of providing food to its employees, Aramco worked with local farmers, teaching them modern agricultural methods and introducing them to fruits and vegetables not formerly available in the area. Much of the peninsula receives five or less inches of rain per year, but the Saudis and other Arabs have developed sophisticated irrigation techniques, including using fossil groundwater and desalinated seawater. They now grow much of the food the country uses, and they export items like cucumbers, dates, grapes, tomatoes, watermelons, and wheat.

Bahrain raises some produce, goats, cattle, and sheep and eats local seafood, but it must import most of its food. Kuwait and Qatar grow few crops but raise livestock and catch fish off their coasts. The UAE produces foodstuffs such as cabbages, citrus fruits, cucumbers, dates, eggplant, mangoes, squash, and tomatoes; chickens and eggs; milk and dairy products; and local fish. However, it must import about three-fourths of the food it needs.

🍽 Food Culture Snapshot

Ali and Nura Abdulrahman live in Ali's family's compound in Riyadh, Saudi Arabia's capital. The compound's occupants include Ali's parents, his grandmother, his brothers and their wives and children, and his unmarried sisters. Ali and Nura eat breakfast at 6:30 A.M., as their workday starts early. Breakfast includes a grain porridge, fruit (often dates), and coffee. They both eat lunch at work: a light meal of meat (usually lamb or chicken), rice with pine nuts or raisins, and fruit. Most family members eat together in the evening. The meal consists of salad, rice, meat, vegetables, fruit, and occasionally a sweet dessert. The women of the household cooperate on the cooking; those who work outside the home usually come to the kitchen after work to help with final preparations and exchange news about their day and family developments.

Traditionally, meals were coordinated with some of the five daily prayers: breakfast after dawn prayers, lunch after midday prayers, and dinner after sunset prayers (sometimes much later). Mealtime schedules are now driven more by the needs of the modern business timetable, although Muslims still follow the traditional prayer schedule.

In some areas on the peninsula and in more traditional families, women are discouraged from shopping for food, with men or servants doing the shopping. People shop in both modern mega-supermarkets and local *suqs* (markets). Suqs often have a larger and fresher selection of fruits, vegetables, and fish, as well as live sheep and other animals. Suqs also sell whole, fresh spices, in contrast to the already-ground, bottled spices in stores.

Supermarkets offer the convenience of one-stop shopping, carrying both local and imported foods. Many products in the supermarkets are familiar to Westerners—but then there's fresh camel meat, packaged in the butcher section. Products from abroad cater to the tastes of foreigners. Supermarket owners must be careful in selecting items to import to be sure none of them contains any pork or alcohol. Imported meat must have been slaughtered according to Islamic requirements. Saudi consulates certify slaughterhouses in countries that wish to export meat to Saudi Arabia. Because large doses of nutmeg can be hallucinogenic or even cause death, Saudi Arabia classifies it as a drug, and stores there cannot import whole or ground nutmeg unless it is in a spice mix where nutmeg composes 20 percent or less of the mixture (presumably, this would allow for prepared mixtures of the popular spice mix *baharat,* which includes nutmeg). Poppy seeds are also banned.

Major Foodstuffs

Many people of the peninsula trace their ancestry to Bedouin who roamed the desert seeking pasture for their camels, goats, and sheep, and Arab food culture is rooted in that of the Bedouin. Their main foods were dates, bread, and the milk of their livestock, with occasional meat, usually for a celebration, to honor a special guest, or if they were lucky enough to catch some small wild animal (e.g., a hare or *gerboa*).

Ancient literature from the Gilgamesh Epic to the Bible to the Quran speaks reverently of dates and date palms. Scholars believe the date palm originated in the Arabian Peninsula. During the spread of the Muslim empire, armies and traders took along dates and, on purpose or by accident, planted date palms throughout the empire. Date trees are either male or female. Arabs hand-pollinate trees and tie paper

A man harvesting dates in Bahrain. Dates play an important role in the economies and cultures of the Arabian Peninsula. (StockPhotoPro)

bags around the flower clusters to protect growing dates from birds and insects. Birds nest in the trees, and many ground crops depend on their shade in hot oases.

Resourceful Arabs use every part of the palm. Arabs eat dates fresh and dried, and sometimes ground into meal that is mixed with water to make bread. Date seeds can be fed to livestock or be ground and made into flour. Syrup (*dibis*) pressed from dates can sweeten pastries or be poured over puddings. Dates are a good source of energy and contain several essential nutrients. With milk, they make a complete meal. Dried dates keep well for long periods of time because their high sugar content discourages spoiling and they are easy to transport.

Young date palm leaves, cooked, can be eaten as a vegetable. Hearts of palm are a delicacy, but Arabs rarely eat them, because the heart is the tree's growing tip, and cutting it out kills the tree. Woven fronds from the leaves become baskets or mats; the center ribs of the leaves make strong sticks (*jareed*) to build huts. The Arabs use palm wood for building. If anything is left, they use it for fuel. Arabs have many words to describe dates—not only names of different species, but also names for dates in different phases of growth.

Flatbreads are another staple food, and the Arabs have many varieties. Generically, bread is called *khubz,* but Arabs also refer to it as *'aysh,* meaning "life" (some also refer to rice as *'aysh*). Bedouin often cook bread by burying it under the embers of their fires. When it is done, they pull it out, brush the sand off, and eat it. Some Bedouin use a convex or flat piece of metal on top of the fire to cook bread. In villages, some women bring their bread to a communal oven. Some breads are cooked on stones on the oven floor; others are slapped onto the walls of the domed oven. If the oven isn't hot enough, the bread falls off into the fire. Some women stay by the oven and watch to be sure that their bread remains in what they consider the best place for it to cook. Some common breads in Arabia are *khubz 'arabi,* the simple pocket flatbread; *tamis,* a larger and crustier flatbread; *shurayak,* a soft, golden bread; *'aysh samuli,* a more loaflike bread; and *khubz ruqaq,* paperthin bread that includes date syrup.

Before the increase in contact with the West, Bedouin derived most of their protein from goat or camel milk. If they had more than they could use, they made it into *samna* (clarified butter; the Indian name ghee is more familiar to Westerners) or yogurt. It is usually made from goat milk because the composition of camel milk's fat makes it difficult to make butter from it. To make samna, one heats butter until it boils, the curds float to the surface, and the remaining liquid is transparent. The curds can be skimmed off or strained out and eaten; the remaining samna will keep for several months without refrigeration. Arab cooks often use samna for frying or add it to breads and desserts for richness. Bedouin allowed the liquid to drain from yogurt, leaving a hard substance that kept for a long time. When they were ready to use it, they pounded it into powder with a mortar and pestle and mixed it with water. If necessary, they ate the hard dried yogurt. They would also add salt and olive oil to yogurt, which made it keep for a longer time.

Coffee (*qahwah*) holds a place of honor in the Arab lifestyle as a major element of the hospitality ritual. Arabs prefer their coffee strong and bitter. They usually flavor it with cardamom but sometimes with cloves, rose water, saffron, or other spices. These spices impart some sweetness and help mask coffee's natural bitterness. Although most of the Arab world's cardamom used to come from India, much now comes from Guatemala. For everyday purposes, cardamom is added in a ratio of 1/50th to 1/25th the amount of coffee, but for an honored guest, a host may add much more. Because harvesters must pick each pod individually, cardamom ranks with saffron as one of the most expensive spices; thus, adding a large amount to coffee shows how much the host values his guest. Arabs also drink large amounts of tea throughout the day. They prefer sweet mint tea, sometimes with coriander seed added, which they drink from small glass mugs.

One must be a Muslim to be a citizen in all these countries, and Muslim practices, based on the Quran and subsequent Muslim teachings, govern food habits. Muslim eating traditions charge believers to exercise moderation in eating. Muslims are prohibited from eating blood and unclean animals, including pigs, mice, bats, monkeys, birds of prey, carnivorous animals such as dogs and cats, and land animals with no ears, such as frogs and snakes. Some schools of thought forbid eating any seafood that doesn't have fins and scales, but others allow Muslims to eat shrimp. Muslims may eat only animals that have specifically been killed for food (i.e., no carrion or animals that have died naturally), and the person killing the animal must say, "Bismillah, Allahu akbar" ("In the name of God, God is great"), when slaughtering it. Meat killed in the name of a pagan god is also forbidden. The slaughterer slits the animal's throat and allows all the blood to drain from it. Meat killed according to Islamic law and foods that are acceptable to eat are designated *halal*. Forbidden and unclean items are called *haram*. Although coffee is a symbol of hospitality strongly associated with the Muslim world, some schools of thought say it is not permitted because it is an intoxicant.

Alcohol is also forbidden to Muslims. It is not available at all in Kuwait and Saudi Arabia (although one can purchase malt beverages, i.e., nonalcoholic beer). Liquor is available on a limited basis to foreigners in Bahrain, Qatar, and the UAE, usually in the restaurants of large hotels. Foreigners living in these countries sometimes make alcoholic beverages. For the most part, governments ignore this activity as long as it is done circumspectly. The explosion of a still, public drunken behavior, especially drunk driving, or the discovery that a foreign national has given or sold liquor to a Muslim can result in jail and whipping or swift deportation. Visitors to these countries who are offered homemade alcoholic beverages should be cautious. Homemade liquor is often much stronger than commercial liquor, and it sometimes has impurities that make drinkers ill.

Cooking

Cooking is women's work. People traditionally live in extended matriarchal family groups, and all women in a family cooperate in food preparation, with the social aspect being as important as the nourishing aspect. At feasts or holidays, visiting women help in the kitchen. Until the mid-20th century, most women in the peninsula couldn't read or write. Girls started helping in the kitchen at a young age and learned to cook from their mothers. By the time they were old enough to marry, cooking was second nature—and besides, when they married, they moved into their husband's matriarchal family, where they joined other women who cooked together.

With growing industrialization, some families have left the traditional matriarchal mode and live in Western-style groupings of parents, children, and perhaps one or two other family members. Thus, some young women no longer have older women to help them with cooking. Toward the end of the 20th century, women began to publish cookbooks from various parts of the peninsula. Migration of families around the peninsula has encouraged the spread of regional recipes. Women who have spent time outside the peninsula have encountered the cooking of other countries and may try cooking foreign as well as Arab food. Television cooking shows, both from the region and from outside, have helped women learn recipes from all over. All these factors have increased the global influences on food in the peninsula.

Kitchens range from totally modern, Western-style kitchens in relatively new houses and apartment buildings to traditional kitchens or even a fire pit in a courtyard in older buildings. Pans and utensils may be Western style or may be traditional brass, copper, or wooden items. Bedouin still cook over a campfire, but that campfire may now be a camp stove.

Typical Meals

Traditionally, food is served on large communal platters set on a cloth laid on the floor or ground, usually on top of oriental rugs. People eat only with their right hands, preferably with only the thumb and the first two fingers. The left hand is considered unclean, as it is used for hygienic (toilet) purposes. Some families still eat this way; some use Western tables, dishes, and flatware; and some alternate between the two styles.

Men and women of a family eat together, although women may hold back until men have eaten. When there are guests, women, including female guests, eat separately from the men. Famously, on a 1979 visit, Queen Elizabeth of Great Britain was declared an honorary man so that she could eat with King Khalid of Saudi Arabia.

Arabs are famous for their elaborate rules of hospitality. This code developed from the Bedouin life, lived on the edge of starvation. Hospitality in the desert could mean the difference between life and death for the potential guest. Therefore, when a stranger came to a man's tent, even if he was an enemy, the man had to treat him with courtesy and extend protection to him for three days. The Arabic traditional greeting exchange that translates to "Peace be with you"—"And with you, peace" may now seem like a courteous formality, but at times, it had the power of a treaty. In exchange for hospitality, the guest would share news of weather conditions (especially rainfall), pastures, and other Bedouin he had encountered.

Since, in earlier days, a guest had probably made a long ride across the dusty desert, a host offered his guest a cool drink such as fruit juice. In modern times, even some shopkeepers continue this ritual, offering those who come in a soft drink or fruit juice. Customs regarding coffee figure strongly in the rituals of hospitality. A man shouldn't offer coffee to a guest too early in a visit, lest the guest think he was expecting him to leave. When the host did offer coffee (or food), the guest would refuse several times before allowing the host to persuade him to receive his generosity and partake. An Arab in the desert, having ground coffee with a brass mortar and pestle, uses the pestle to ring the mortar like a bell. The sound carries a great distance and might reach a weary traveler and guide him to a safe haven.

Before a meal, the host says the simple prayer, "Bismillah" ("In the name of God"), and when the meal is over, the host says, "al-Hamdu lillah" ("Thanks be to God"). Often, a host waits to eat until his guest has finished, serving the guest and scooping up choice morsels and balls of rice for him. Although hosts are supposed to provide for their guests according to their means, legends tell of hosts who essentially bankrupted themselves by killing their only goat/sheep/camel in order not to fail in hospitality.

Arabs do not separate out savory foods for the main course and sweet foods for dessert. Spices and fruit make many main-course dishes sweet (e.g., rice mixed with dates, cinnamon, and cloves), and some desserts contain items such as carrots. Although food in this part of the peninsula is often spicy, generally it is not hot. Flatbreads accompany all meals, since they serve as eating utensils.

Breakfast is usually a light meal—for example, bread with butter or samna; olives; eggs; fruit; and soft cheese or yogurt. In winter, it often includes a porridge such as *hunayua* (ground dates mixed with butter, semolina, and cardamom). *Balaleet,* a breakfast from Qatar, is a casserole of noodles or vermicelli cooked with sugar, cardamom, and saffron, topped with a flat omelet. Eaters use pieces of the omelet to scoop up the pasta. In the UAE, breakfast might be a pudding with saffron. Some people eat Western-style breakfasts.

The midday meal was once the main meal, but with the advent of Western-style work schedules, it is lighter, and the evening meal is becoming the main meal. Lunch is often a salad or vegetables; a mixture of meat or fish with rice; and fruit or pastries. Some people go to American fast-food restaurant chains for lunch. Dinner is similar to lunch but more elaborate. It begins with a salad (perhaps cucumbers and tomatoes), meze (a variety of foods served on small plates that are shared), or soup (lentil soup is popular). Arabs have imported the concept of meze from Lebanon, including hummus, baba ghanoush (a dip made of mashed eggplant, sesame paste, olive oil, lemon juice, and garlic), and tabbouleh. Soups tend to be thick rather than broth based.

The popularity of one-dish main courses in the peninsula stems from Bedouin cooking, where heat sources were limited, and also from the Arab tradition of hospitality. If extra guests show up, the cook can easily stretch the meal by adding more of some ingredient, or even just by adding water. So the main

Saudis gather around a traditional dinner. Saudi Arabia is home to a remarkably homogenous population; the peoples of Arabia are 90 percent Arab and 100 percent Muslim. (Corel)

course is often a stew, or meat served over rice. Other possibilities include lamb stuffed with rice, eggs, onions, and nuts; shish kebabs; or fried or grilled fish, especially in coastal areas. Popular seafood types include *hamur* (grouper), *shfri* (porgy), *kan'ad* (mackerel), *hamra* (red snapper), *zubaidi* (pomfret), crab, lobster, and shrimp.

Machbous

Machbous is the national dish of different countries on the peninsula.

2 tbsp samna (clarified butter) or butter

2 large onions, peeled and chopped

½ tsp turmeric

¼ tsp ground pepper

¼ tsp ground cardamom

¼ tsp chili powder

1 clove garlic, minced

2 lb lamb, on the bone

3 tomatoes, peeled and chopped

1 stick cinnamon

2 cardamom pods

2 tsp salt

1 bay leaf

1 clove

½ tsp dried lime (*loomi*), finely chopped, or 1 tbsp lime juice

2½ c water

2 c basmati rice

1. Fry chopped onions in samna until transparent. Stir in the first five spices, and cook for 2 more minutes.

2. Add the lamb; brown lightly.

3. Add tomatoes, remaining spices, and salt. Cover and simmer for 10 minutes.

4. Add water, cover, and simmer for 2 to 2½ hours until meat is tender.

5. Stir in rice. Cover and simmer 20 minutes.

6. Stir, remove from heat, and let stand covered for 5 minutes.

7. Remove the whole spices. Spoon rice onto each plate. Place pieces of meat on top of rice.

The most popular vegetables are those that thrive in warm weather, such as cucumbers, eggplant, olives, peppers, pumpkins, tomatoes, and zucchini and other squashes. Vegetable dishes are usually simple, emphasizing freshness. Often, larger vegetables (tomatoes, squash, peppers) are stuffed with a meat or rice filling. Lentils, chickpeas, fava beans, and black-eyed peas appear in many dishes. Fruits also tend to be tropical ones: bananas, citrus, dates, grapes, figs, mangoes, melons, and others. However, virtually all fruits and vegetables are available. If the Arabs can't grow it, they import it.

Desserts may be fresh fruit or a sweet pastry or custard. Some popular sweets are *halwa* (sweet sesame paste), *muhammar* (sweet rice served with dates or sugar), *Umm Ali* (a bread pudding), and *mehalabiya* (rice pudding with rose water).

Most dishes contain several spices. Traditional spice mixes, whose ingredients may vary somewhat, include *bahar* (cinnamon, cloves, nutmeg, and sometimes ginger or pepper); baharat (black pepper, cardamom, cassia, cloves, coriander, cumin, nutmeg, and paprika); *za'atar* (the Arabic word for thyme but also a popular spice mix of thyme, sumac, sesame seeds, and perhaps another spice or two). The sumac is deep red and not the same as America's poison sumac, though edible staghorn sumac is also native to North America. Cooks use large quantities of garlic and onions.

Arabs usually drink coffee and tea with meals; other favorite drinks are fruit juices and juice mixtures; goat, sheep, or camel milk; buttermilk; *laban*, a mixture of water and yogurt; mineral water; and soft drinks. Some favored snack items are baba ghanoush, falafel, *shawarma* (meat, usually lamb or chicken, spiced and roasted on a spit), kebabs, hummus, fruit, and *sambousas* (pastries with a sweet or savory filling).

Eating Out

Before the 1970s, almost no restaurants existed in the Arabian Peninsula except coffeehouses and those in the few hotels. Since then restaurants have proliferated, but natives of the countries rarely eat out. Restaurants range from formal eateries to fast-food outlets. High-end restaurants offer all types of cuisine, including Middle Eastern (more likely to be generic Levantine food than food specifically of the country), European, Indian and Pakistani, Indonesian, Chinese, Thai, Mexican, and many more.

Many American chains such as McDonald's, KFC, Pizza Hut, and so on have franchises in the Middle East. McDonald's even developed a special sandwich to appeal to Middle Eastern tastes: the McArabia, a sandwich of either grilled spiced chicken or spiced *kuftah* (ground meat) with lettuce, tomato, onions, and garlic mayonnaise, wrapped in flatbread. Shawarma shops offer a Middle Eastern fast food. The server cuts off thin slices of shawarma and folds them into flatbreads with vegetables such as cucumber, eggplant, onion, and tomato and dressings such as hummus or tahini. Traditional coffeehouses serve coffee, other drinks, and pastries and offer water pipes with flavored tobacco. Most restaurants in these countries have segregated eating areas: one for men only, one for families, and sometimes one for women only. Restaurants usually close during the day for Ramadan and on Muslim holidays.

Special Occasions

Dating back to Bedouin life, the traditional dish for Arab festive occasions, celebrations, and special guests is a sheep or camel roasted on a spit and served on a bed of rice. Roasting a sheep yields a delicacy that hosts bestow on the guest of honor: the eyeball.

Three major observances in Islam have strong associations with food, of which Ramadan is the best known. Ramadan, the ninth month of the Muslim year, in which the Quran was revealed to Muhammad, is set aside for fasting. This fast is one of the five pillars of Islam, the five duties enjoined on Muslims. Unlike fasting periods in many other religions, Muslims fast only from sunrise to sunset, whose exact times a religious official determines each day. Until recently, a cannon shot announced the beginning and end of fasting. Now, people are more likely to hear the news over the radio or television.

At sunset, Muslims break their fast, often with a few dates and water, a tradition initiated by the prophet Muhammad. In Makkah, the water is preferably from the well of Zamzam, traditionally the well that God showed to Hagar when she and Isma'il (Ishmael) almost died of thirst in the desert. In Bahrain, they may drink fresh lime juice. In other places, a drink made by dissolving apricot leather in water is popular. After prayer, Muslims eat a large dinner (*iftar*). Often, this starts with soup, to ease the empty stomach back into eating; an alternative is *harissa,* a porridge of pounded meat and grain. The cook soaks wheat overnight to soften it and pounds it until it is mushy. She debones the meat (poultry or red meat) and cleans it of fat. Then she boils the meat and grain together until they form a homogenized paste. Finally, she sprinkles cooked onions, dried lime powder, black pepper, cardamom, and other spices on top.

Iftars usually include more and richer dishes and desserts than meals at other times of the year. One popular dessert is dried fruits, sometimes soaked in rose or orange blossom water. Shops, especially pastry shops, remain open late, because some people party until late at night. Others spend part or all of the night meditating, praying, and reading holy books. Mosques schedule extra gatherings for prayer during Ramadan. A few hours before sunrise, people rise for another meal, *suhur.* This meal may be dates and barley porridge, or leftovers from the evening meal. In some areas, a town crier with a drum walks the streets a few hours before sunrise to wake people up for suhur.

While many Westerners understand Ramadan as a time of fasting alternated with feasting, the most visible aspect, the daytime fast, prohibits not only eating and drinking but also gum chewing, smoking, and sexual activity, the goal being to cleanse the soul. Some extremists go so far as to spit out, rather than swallow, their own saliva during the fast. Muslims say that fasting puts them in touch with the plight of the poor, who don't have enough food, and includes inviting people to one's home for iftar. These may be friends and relatives or strangers who pass by the house or whom the host meets in the street. Ramadan is also a time for discipline in other areas, including additional prayer and reflection. Muslims are exhorted to be more spiritual, to practice additional charity, to resolve outstanding arguments, and to reconcile with their enemies. While people are expected to work as usual during Ramadan, some people take time off, especially those who have prayed or partied through the night. Another Ramadan regulation concerns women who prepare food for the nightly feasting. Woman may taste food they are cooking during the daytime in Ramadan but may not swallow.

Certain people are exempted from fasting: girls younger than 12 and boys younger than 15; pregnant, nursing, and menstruating women; travelers; soldiers; the sick; and the elderly. Those who do not fast may make up for it by fasting at another time or by giving food or alms to the poor. While non-Muslims living in Arab countries are not required to fast, it is considered extremely impolite, and in some of the countries it is illegal, for a non-Muslim to eat, drink, chew gum, or smoke in public in the daytime during Ramadan.

Because Muslims use a lunar calendar, with a year of about 345 days, Ramadan comes slightly earlier each year when matched with the Gregorian calendar, in a roughly 33-year rotation. Thus, it can fall in winter (short days, long nights), summer (long days, short nights), or anywhere in between. Obviously, Ramadan is easier in winter. In summer, not only are the days long, but the temperature on the Arabian Peninsula can be well over 100 degrees Fahrenheit—even occasionally over 120 degrees—and going without food, and especially liquids, is an extreme hardship.

In most religions, a feast follows a ritual fast, and Islam is no exception. The three-day 'Id al-Fitr (or Eid al-Fitr, the Feast of Breaking the Fast) celebrates the end of Ramadan. Following a light breakfast, Muslims go to the mosque for prayers. Either immediately before the prayers or a few days earlier, they donate food or money, which are given to the needy so they can celebrate the 'Id. Dressed in their best clothes, they then visit friends and relatives. During the 'Id, people eat many sweet dishes, often flavored with rose water, giving the feast the nickname "the Sweet 'Id."

Religious leaders determine the start date of the 'Id al-Fitr based on sighting the new moon, and while it is narrowed down to one or two days, they must actually see the moon to determine that the 'Id will fall on the next day. This makes planning cooking for the 'Id difficult. Women must be prepared to start the feast on a particular day but also to hold the food over until the next day if the new moon doesn't appear. Since the feast often involves cooking a lamb or other large piece of meat that takes a long time to cook, women wait up to find out whether the new moon has been sighted and they should start cooking, or whether they must wait for the next night.

One of the rituals of the pilgrimage to Makkah, the hajj, is celebration of the three-day 'Id al-Adha (or Eid al-Adha, the Feast of the Sacrifice). This commemorates the willingness of Ibrahim (Abraham) to sacrifice his son Isma'il to God (the book of Genesis names Abraham's son Isaac as the one almost sacrificed, but the Muslim exegesis of this story says that the child, not named in the Quran's version of the story, was Isma'il). Muslims who are unable to make the pilgrimage also celebrate the feast in unity with those who are on the hajj. Each family sacrifices an animal, usually a sheep but possibly a goat, camel, or cow. The animal must be at least a year old and of good quality. The family gives part of the meat to the poor and keeps part for their own feast. Someone who, for whatever reason, doesn't wish to, or can't, sacrifice an animal can compensate by making a donation to charity. People on the hajj take their animal to a slaughterhouse in Miná. The meat from these animals is frozen and distributed to the poor in the Muslim world.

The hajj itself presents a major logistical challenge for Saudi Arabia: providing basic amenities, health care, and so on to over two million people, most of whom want to be in the same general area at the same time, to perform the prescribed hajj rituals. The government has an entire ministry devoted to it. Among other things, the ministry contracts with

A Saudi man carries his newly bought sheep prior to the Eid al-Adha, the four-day Muslim Festival of Sacrifice, December 29, 2006. The holiday, which marks the end of the the hajj pilgrimage, is celebrated by hundreds of millions of Muslims around the world by slaughtering goats, sheep, and cattle in commemoration of the prophet Abraham's readiness to sacrifice his son to show obedience to God. (AFP | Getty Images)

food vendors to provide food for the pilgrims. The employees of these vendors work long, hard days during the hajj.

Ma'mul, cookies made of a farina and samna dough stuffed with a mixture of sweetened dates, cinnamon, and sometimes chopped walnuts, and formed in a traditional wooden mold, are a time-honored part of both 'Ids.

Weddings involve a long period of festivities, mostly for the bride. Technically, the marriage happens when the groom and the bride's father sign the marriage contract. However, there is then a 40-day period when the bride stays at home. A week before the wedding, she and her friends have a henna party,

where they paint intricate henna designs on each other. Traditional foods for this party are sweets, harissa, breads, cheese, and olives. These are now ordinary foods but were once luxurious. Both the bride and the groom get new clothes to symbolize casting off their old life.

The actual wedding feast is quite different from Western weddings, because men and women have separate feasts, which start sometime after evening prayers and last into the early morning hours. Traditionally, these parties were held at home, but for those who can afford them, modern wedding parties take place in hotels or special wedding halls, although the groom's party may be in a tent, harking back to the Bedouin past. The bride's feast includes all female members of both her and her husband's family, plus female friends. The groom's feast, likewise, includes all male members of both his and his wife's family, plus male friends. The groom's feast is usually rice with sheep or camel meat, side dishes, and desserts. A more elaborate dish for wedding feasts is *khouzi*. This starts with a chicken stuffed with rice mixed with spices, nuts, and raisins and shelled hard-boiled eggs. The chicken and more rice are then stuffed into a lamb, which is then baked or roasted on a spit. Khouzi is one of several dishes that Middle Eastern food writers describe as a "national dish" of the Arabian Peninsula.

The bride's feast is more elaborate. It also includes rice and meat, but this is supplemented with meze, salads, vegetable dishes, and more. Desserts feature elaborately decorated cakes, imported chocolates, and other sweets. These feasts have grown more and more elaborate, to the point that a movement to scale them back has begun; some couples would rather spend less on the festivities and have money available to buy a home and furnishings. Currently, charitable organizations give money to help people afford weddings (especially the bride's dowry, given by her husband, which finances much of the feast), and some of the governments of these countries have started giving subsidies to men who want to marry, provided they marry a native of the country.

Around midnight, the men at the groom's feast escort him to the bride's feast. The women there put on their veils before the men come in. Once the men bring in the groom, they leave, and the bride and groom cut the wedding cake together.

Stuffed Camel

Serves approximately 100 people

Versions of this recipe have circulated among expatriates in the Middle East for years. Stuffed camel is also reputed to be the appropriate feast for a major Bedouin wedding.

1 medium camel

1 large sheep

20 medium chickens

1 gal samna

10 lb onions, chopped

5 lb almonds

5 lb pine nuts

2 lb pistachio nuts

2 lb raisins

2 c baharat spice mix

25 lb basmati rice, cooked

60 eggs, hard-boiled and shelled

Skin and clean the camel, sheep, and chickens. Brown the chopped onions in the samna. Mix in the nuts, raisins, and baharat, and add this mixture to the rice. Put an egg in each chicken, and add rice to fill it. Stuff the sheep with 5 chickens, and add rice and eggs to fill it. Put the sheep into the camel, and add rice and eggs to fill it. Roast the stuffed camel on a spit until done, and roast the remaining chickens. Put remaining rice on a large tray, and place the camel on top. Place the chickens and remaining hard-boiled eggs around it.

The Arab coffee ritual for guests rivals the Japanese tea ceremony. They roast the coffee beans on a specially designed flat pan, then cool them. They grind the beans into powder with a wooden or brass mortar and pestle. The host boils a pot of water over the fire, then adds the ground coffee. He allows it to boil again, pulls it off the fire, then heats it to another boil. He then places cardamom or other spices in a gracefully shaped brass coffeepot (*dallah*) and pours in the coffee. Palm fronds in the pot's spout filter out the coffee grounds and spices. He pours the coffee into small, delicate ceramic cups without handles (*finjans*), which are often white with colored or gilt decorations. Even the small cups are filled only about a third full. The host tastes the coffee to show that it isn't poisoned and then serves it to his guests and others who are present. Guests should drink at least three cups. After that, if they don't want more, they wiggle the cup from side to side, indicating that they are finished.

Diet and Health

The basic diet of the Arabian Peninsula is a healthy one, relatively like the modern Mediterranean food pyramid, featuring meat in moderation and an emphasis on fruit, vegetables, and grains. However, the area has developed an epidemic of obesity and related health problems. Causative factors include the social nature of eating, leading to long stays around the table; the relative abundance of food in the area since World War II; the extremely hot climate, which discourages outdoor exercise; and the prevalence of televisions and computers, encouraging a sedentary lifestyle.

Before the advent of the oil companies, for the most part, Arabs depended on traditional medicine, which made use of herbs, spices, and other natural ingredients. Some of these items were local plants; others are spices from India, China, and other remote parts of the world. Even petroleum, which was found in seeps in some areas, was used for medicinal purposes, both as a salve and taken by mouth. Even today, petroleum jelly is an ingredient in ointments and cosmetics.

Since the discovery of oil, the availability of modern medical care has increased greatly, with hospitals providing all the medical services found in the West, including organ transplants. In Saudi Arabia, the average life expectancy at birth in 1975 was 54 years, when good medical care was already available, and it has risen to the seventies. Other countries on the peninsula have similar numbers.

Christine Crawford-Oppenheimer

Further Reading

Al-Hamad, Sarah. *Cardamom and Lime: Recipes from the Arabian Gulf.* Northampton, MA: Interlink, 2008.

Bsisu, May S. *The Arab Table: Recipes and Culinary Traditions.* New York: HarperCollins, 2005.

Chapman, Pat. *Homestyle Middle Eastern Cooking.* Freedom, CA: Crossing Press, 1997.

Haroutunian, Arto de. *Middle Eastern Cookery.* London: Pan, 1982.

Heine, Peter. *Food Culture in the Near East, Middle East, and North Africa.* Westport, CT: Greenwood Press, 2004.

Jacob, Jeanne. *The World Cookbook for Students.* Westport, CT: Greenwood Press, 2007.

Khalife, Maria. *The Middle Eastern Cookbook.* Northampton, MA: Interlink, 2007.

Mallos, Tess. *The Complete Middle East Cookbook.* New York: McGraw Hill, 1979.

Mallos, Tess. *Middle Eastern Cooking.* North Clarendon, VT: Periplus, 2002.

Osborne, Christine. *Middle Eastern Cooking.* London: Prion, 1997.

Roden, Claudia. *A New Book of Middle Eastern Food.* New York: Viking, 1985.

Scott, David. *Traditional Arab Cookery.* London: Rider, 1983.

Suad, Joseph, ed. *Encyclopedia of Women and Islamic Cultures.* Vol. 3. Leiden: Brill, 2006.

Weiss-Armush, Anne Marie. *The Arabian Delights Cookbook: Mediterranean Cuisines from Mecca to Marrakesh.* Los Angeles: Lowell House, 1994.

Zubaida, Sami, and Richard Tapper, eds. *A Taste of Thyme: Culinary Cultures of the Middle East.* London: Tauris Parke, 2000.

Berbers and Tuaregs

Overview

The Berbers are the original indigenous people of North Africa and often refer to themselves as Imaghizen, which means "free" or "noble." Today, they live predominantly in Algeria, Morocco, Libya, and Tunisia. They have a long history stretching back to ancient times: They were mentioned by the Egyptians, flourished under Carthaginian rule when it was the most powerful seafaring state in the Mediterranean, and succumbed to Roman rule—in fact, there were many prominent Romans of Berber origin such as the poet Apuleius and St. Augustine of Hippo. The kingdoms of Numidia and Mauretania were Berber client states of Rome. In the seventh century the Berbers converted to Islam and made up a significant portion of those who eventually conquered and ruled Spain and northwestern Africa. The great medieval explorer Ibn Battuta was of Berber origin. In the early modern period North Africa fell under the sway of the Ottoman Empire, and in the 19th century Algeria was ruled by France.

In 1990, a department for the study of Berber culture and language was established at the University of Tizi Ouzou, and the following year another was opened at the University of Bejai; both schools are in the Kabyle. Liamine Zéroual, president of Algeria from 1994 to 1999 and a Berber from Batna, created the Haut Commissariat à l'Amazighité to help initiate policy and procedure for teaching Berber in schools and for its use in public spheres. In 1995, the Congrès Mondial Amazigh was established as an international Berber association based in Paris; in 1998 the Congrès adopted the Berber flag created by the Académie Berbère as the flag of the Berber people. In 2002, Tamazight, as it is called locally, was finally recognized as a national language in Algeria by constitutional amendment. Berber began being taught in schools the same year. Morocco, which has had similar issues with Berber language rights, also began formally teaching Berber in 2003.

The Tuaregs are also a Berber people. They live to the south in the Saharan desert, mostly as nomads and pastoralists, in Algeria, Niger, and Mali and to some extent in Burkina Faso. In the 11th century the Tuaregs founded Timbuktu, in present-day Mali, as a seasonal settlement. Timbuktu was an important city for the successive West African empires of Ghana, Mali, and Songhay. It flourished as a crossroads city between North and West Africa for trade and scholarship.

The largest concentrations of speakers of the Berber languages are found in Algeria and Morocco. Estimates vary, but they make up approximately 20 to 25 percent of the population in Algeria and 40 percent of the population in Morocco. Tunisia and Libya are predominantly Arab or Arabized, with small concentrated Berber populations on the island of Djerba in Tunisia and Jebel Nefousa in Libya. The largest population of Berbers outside of Africa lives in France; most are of Algerian or Moroccan heritage, and many are French born. Algerians from Setif and the Kabyle are often second-generation French citizens.

Food Culture Snapshot

Ahmed and Lilia Boudra live in Setif City in the second-largest province in Algeria. Although Setif is on the edge of the Kabyle, many residents refer to themselves as Chaoui, after the Shawiya Berbers of the Aures Mountains; however, everyone is a Staifi (Setifienne). The local dialect, or *derja,* is a Berber-Arab synthesis, not easily understood in other regions of Algeria.

Ahmed is the manager at a couscous and pasta factory. Lilia is a medical student at the University of Setif, where her classes are taught in French. At home, they speak their local derja; Khaled, their six-year-old son, is learning Modern Standard Arabic in elementary school. The Boudras begin their day at 6 A.M. with a breakfast of homemade *ghraif* (thick semolina pancakes) served with espresso. Khaled has a croissant purchased from a pastry shop and a glass of *lben* (buttermilk). Lilia packs lunches for the entire family. She and Khaled will have *kesra* (semolina bread) and a thick chickpea soup; Ahmed will eat a sandwich of grilled meat and salad rolled into flatbread. Ahmed and Lilia meet in town for afternoon tea or coffee at a café.

Dinner is around 7 P.M. and is the largest meal of the day. Lilia prepares pasta with a dough of barley flour and water, which she kneads and rolls into thin sheets, then cuts into little squares for steaming in a couscoussier. The pasta is served with a sauce of buttered turnips, peas, and carrots, a specialty of the Kabyle region that she learned from her mother. They have oranges for dessert.

The main meal on Fridays, often couscous, is eaten with members of their extended family after *salaat-ul-jumu'ah,* a congregational prayer held immediately after noon at the mosque. The local way of preparing couscous is called *berboucha;* it is made with lamb, chicken, and root vegetables. Lilia sometimes hand-rolls the couscous and sometimes uses an instant variety from the factory where Ahmed works; both are prepared by steaming. North Africans never cook couscous using the absorption method found on directions for packaged couscous in the West. Watermelon is the traditional dessert after couscous.

Setif City hasn't been affected as much by globalization as Mediterranean coastal cities. The Boudras shop for food at *souks* (outdoor markets) and *hanouts* (small shops); they purchase prepared foods from small vendors. Bakeries and pastry shops sell North African and European specialties. Most cooking is done from scratch. Small restaurants serve a limited range of regional dishes.

Major Foodstuffs

Political definitions of the Maghrib have shifted historically with changing seats of power and the birth of nations. It has been said that a culinary measure of the Maghrib, separating it from the Arab east, is found in an imaginary north–south line somewhere in Libya; rice is the staple food to the east, and couscous is the staple food to the west. Couscous is a Berber invention and the staff of life in the Maghrib countries of Tunisia, Algeria, and Morocco. Although there is theoretical unity through couscous, arguments about what constitutes a real couscous can range from lighthearted to fierce.

There is some evidence that the method for steaming couscous has a West African genesis. The prototypical couscous steamer was probably woven from grass; basket-type couscoussiers are still made in some rural areas of North Africa. In West Africa and Saharan North Africa, couscous is made with crushed millet or sorghum. The Maghribine (North African) Berber word for sorghum, *illan* or *ilni,* is

Chicken and couscous, or barboucha. (Typhoonski | Dreamstime.com)

related to the West African Songhay word for the same grain, *ille.* Couscous is also made with barley or cornmeal.

The most common and best-known couscous is actually a type of pasta made with durum or semolina flour. A mixture of coarse and fine semolina flour is lightly moistened with water while moving the flour in a circular motion with the right hand until tiny pasta "grains" are formed by aggregation. Adding more water and applying a heavier hand while rolling makes large pasta balls, called *berkoukes,* better known as Israeli couscous in North America or *Maghribiyya* ("make like the Maghrib") in the Middle East.

Couscous and derivative dishes were diffused widely during medieval Islamic times and the European age of exploration. One of the earliest written references to couscous is in an anonymous 13th-century Moorish cookbook. A 13th-century Syrian historian describes four recipes for couscous; one of them is called *Maghribian* (North African). The Moors of Spain and the Saracens of Sicily ate couscous.

During the Spanish Inquisition, couscous was banned as a symbol of Muslim behavior, but a derivative dish called *migas* (made of breadcrumbs) is still eaten in Spain. The Mexican dish *migas* or *migajas* differs from the North African and Spanish versions but is conceptually similar in that crumbs or tiny pieces of tortilla are used rather than bread as in Spanish versions. A Portuguese recipe for couscous from the 17th century calls for "flour of the earth," either maize or manioc, and looks very much like a modern Brazilian *cuzcuz,* a kind of steamed cake or pudding.

The North African and Arab influence in Sicily is still celebrated in what is called *cucina-arabic sicula* (Arab-Sicilian kitchen). The island hosts an annual event, Cous Cous Fest, that draws over 100,000 visitors. Sicilian *cuscusu* is usually prepared with fish. North African Jews introduced couscous to Israel. Today, semolina couscous is widely available as an instant food in Europe and North America.

The distinction between hard wheat (semolina or durum) and soft wheat (bread wheat) is important. Hard wheat has more gluten and less moisture than soft wheat, which makes it less prone to breakage during the drying process for pasta and gives it a longer shelf life than bread-wheat products. The capacity for extended storage and transportation would have been historically significant in eras of perennial famines and empire expansion. In some regions of North Africa, semolina flour and foods made from it, such as kesra (semolina bread), are strongly associated with Berber cultural identity.

In modern North Africa, pasta dishes tend to be concentrated in Tunisia and eastern Algeria. Berbers make rudimentary pastas with semolina flour, which are steamed or sometimes boiled. North African cookbooks often categorize pasta with either couscous or bread as related dishes or cooking techniques. Italian settlers introduced newer varieties of pasta during the colonial era. Pasta dishes that are categorized with couscous include *tlitli* and *dwiddat* (orzo). The method for making them is similar to the method for berkoukes, a rather tedious process of tearing off tiny pieces of dough and shaping each piece of pasta by hand.

Trid, or the diminutive *tridet* (derived from trid pastry sheets), are pasta squares. This shape of pasta is also called *m'kartfa* or *nawasar* (plural of *nasra,* square silver coins used during the Almohad dynastic period), and it is identical to Italian *quadratini. Tiftitine* are pasta strips made with semolina or bread flour. *Rechta* and *shariya,* vermicelli pastas, entered North Africa during the medieval Islamic period, and *fidwash* (fideos, a thin pasta still common in Spain) are Hispano-Moorish. *Maqaron* (macaroni) specifically refers to durum-wheat dried pastas.

Olives, olive oil, dates, figs, and semolina flour or a local grain are important regional staples. Chickpeas, lentils, or fava beans are added to many soups, stews, and *tagines* (stews simmered in a clay pot with a conical lid). Dairy products are primarily from cow, goat, or sheep milk. In sparse desert regions, camel milk is drunk as the primary source of protein. *Smen* is clarified or preserved butter. Clarified butter is used for cooking. Preserved smen tastes a bit like blue cheese and is used as a flavoring agent for couscous and tagines. Mint tea, herbal infusions, and lben are regional specialties.

Cooking

The word *couscoussier* is a French word derived from North African *kiskas,* which refers only to the steamer insert. The pot itself is called a *gdrah,* and the stew cooked in it, over which the couscous grains or pasta steam, is called *marga* or tagine. This ingenious method of cooking allows two dishes to be cooked over a single source of heat, a very important feature in a region that has historically dealt with shortages of wood for cooking. Some couscoussiers have two stacking steamer inserts. Couscous grains or pasta are usually steamed two or three times. Meat, poultry, seafood, and vegetables are also steamed in a couscoussier. Steaming foods is a very common North African cooking technique, used even for pasta.

The Arabic word *tajin* is derived from the Greek *teganon,* meaning "frying pan." Regional use of the word *tagine* varies in North Africa; in Algeria *tagine* refers to various pots and pans. The most common use for the word *tagine* is for meat and vegetable casseroles cooked in clay cooking vessels with conical lids. The cooking vessel and the finished dish are both called a tagine. The conical lid stays relatively cool during cooking and creates a kind of water cycle: Evaporated water from the meat and vegetables collects in the conical lid, then flows back down into the dish. The deliciously succulent results distinguish tagines from other casseroles.

Breads called *khobz tagine* are cooked on griddles also called tagines. Bread isn't as universally iconic as couscous, but it is more frequently eaten. And in some regions it is as significant as couscous. Meats and poultry are braised, stewed, roasted, or grilled. There is a preference for well-cooked meat; tagines and stews, in particular, are cooked until the tender meat is falling off the bone. Vegetables are grilled, roasted, or stewed, or added to soups, stews, and tagines.

Typical Meals

Berbers live throughout North Africa in vastly different economic, political, and geographic zones: in rugged mountainous regions, on islands, deep in the Sahara at desert oases, and in large cosmopolitan cities. Many have become assimilated into local or regional cultures.

There is no coherent Berber cuisine as such, since like the rest of North Africa, Berbers have been exposed to various influences. As for people everywhere, Berbers' meal choices are shaped by local availability of foods and personal finances more than anything else. Describing meals as "typically Berber" is impossible—at best, they are samples of what is eaten in different regions by Berber families. Berbers are predominantly Muslim and follow the same dietary laws and hygiene requirements as other Muslims. *Dadas* are female Berber cooks who work for wealthy families in North Africa. The tradition is especially strong in Morocco, where dadas have become important cultural icons as gatekeepers to traditional regional recipes.

Legend has it that the island of Djerba off the coast of Tunisia is the land of lotus eaters in Greek mythology. Today, the island's economy benefits from international tourism. The cooking style here is hot with *harissa* (chili paste) and fragrant with spices, like Tunisian cooking in general. Breakfast is *la bissara,* an egg poached in a spicy broth with fresh fava beans. Lunch is fish marinated in *chermoula,* a mixture of cilantro, onions, garlic, lemon juice, and olive oil, served with bread. Dinner is fish couscous with red peppers. The couscous is served in a large bowl, with the fish and peppers decoratively placed on top in a circular pattern and some of the fish broth poured on the top; the remainder of the broth is served in bowls. Harissa is stirred into the broth to taste. Dessert is *samsa* (fried pastry triangles) stuffed with dried fruit.

Kabylia is part of the Atlas Mountain range in northeastern Algeria. The region is known for olive trees, and many families make their own olive oil. Mint tea is rarely served in this region; proper coffee service is a matter of pride and considered an Ottoman influence. Herbal infusions made with fresh and dried herbs are very common. The Kabyle is a relatively poor region. The cooking is very simple, and expensive spices are rarely used; herbs and wild greens are plentiful. *Avrum* (flatbread) is made daily from semolina flour and is ubiquitous. Avrum is served for breakfast with olive oil for dipping and for lunch with *h'miss* (grilled pepper salad). Couscous is made several times a week; it is served for breakfast or lunch with lben (buttermilk), for dinner with a soup or stew, and even for dessert sprinkled with sugar and raisins. Dinner is *tikerbabin,* large semolina dumplings in a light soup of tomatoes, zucchini, and turnips. Watermelon is ubiquitous during the summer. Fresh and dried figs are also served for dessert.

Shawiya Berbers live in the Aures Mountains and parts of Setif. The style of cooking is very much like that in the Kabyle, as the landscape and resources are similar. The same or similar dishes have different names. Breakfast is kesra (a semolina bread like avrum) and a glass of lben. The meat of choice for Shawiya pastoralists is lamb. Lunch is *chorba* (soup) made with lamb and root vegetables. Dinner is lamb steamed in a couscoussier; the lamb is rubbed with olive oil and garlic and seasoned with salt. Bread is also served, with a salad and braised cardoons.

Tuaregs are perhaps the most romanticized of Berbers, not just by Europeans, but by other Berber groups as well. The "Blue Men of the Desert" are regarded for a fine sense of aesthetics that seems to permeate their lives; their elaborate style of dress, artistic craftsmanship, and poetry tend to be a focus of documentation. However, they are not known for their cooking. *Taguella,* bread made from millet flour, is traditionally cooked in hot ashes covered with sand. Millet is also made into porridge or couscous and served with a basic sauce of tomatoes and onions, or goat and camel milk. Meat is scarce due to the loss of huge numbers of cattle to drought.

Mint tea is called *eshahid* by the Tuaregs of Niger; it is an integral part of social life, and the finer points of tea making and service are of utmost importance. The preferred base for mint tea is strong Chinese green tea; the British introduced gunpowder tea into North Africa in the 18th and 19th centuries via two routes, Morocco and Algeria.

Twice a year, Tuareg salt caravans travel from Timbuktu, Mali, to the salt mines of Taudenni, Mali, and from Iferourane, Niger, to Salah, Algeria. Caravans are an important economic activity for Tuaregs; others depend on livestock for their livelihoods. However, erratic enforcement of national borders frequently severs trade routes; droughts and land degradation have left many Tuareg pastoralists even more impoverished. The Tuaregs of Niger live in what the United Nations calls the "ground zero of climate change."

Libyan Berbers, like Tuaregs, cook bread in hot ashes covered with sand. The dough is spiced with sesame seeds, fennel seeds, and aniseed, shaped into a round loaf with a hole in the center, and then baked. The bread is eaten with a thick green or black tea. Tea drinking is a social occasion involving several courses. A tea course might include roasted and ground peanuts or almonds mixed into the tea.

The Siwa Oasis, located in the Egyptian desert near the Libyan border, is famous for date palm agriculture and olives. For thousands of years, the main economic activity in the oasis has been exporting these products to the Nile Valley and beyond. The salinity of the soil and mineral content in the water are thought to produce exceptional dates. Until the early 1900s, caravans originating in West Africa or the North African Sahara used the oasis as the last stop in their northern routes. The Siwa Oasis is being developed for tourism. A typical meal is comprised of bread, olives, dates, and goat cheese.

Tetouan is located south of the Strait of Gibraltar. Fatima R'Houni wrote the first book of Tetounese recipes in the 1960s. Tetounese Moroccan cooking shares many similarities with Tlemcen, in western Algeria. The cooking is noted for the kind of elaborate medieval-influenced dishes that North Africa is perhaps most famous for. Both are very Andalusian cities that also had significant Jewish populations. Ottoman influences, which are considered very refined, entered the city via Algerian refugees during the French colonial period. *Tagine t'afia* is a chicken casserole perfumed with ginger and saffron, garnished with sliced hard-boiled eggs and toasted almonds. *Seffa* couscous is made with semolina couscous or broken vermicelli, doused with butter, sweetened with sugar and raisins, and

Tuaregs prepare a meal by a campfire in the Sahara desert, Algeria. (StockPhotoPro)

sprinkled with fried almonds. *Mhancha,* a sweet pastry made with phyllo dough and ground almonds, is an Algero-Ottoman influence.

Eating Out

Restaurants in Berber regions vary widely, and there is no Berber restaurant as such. Restaurants that market themselves as serving Berber specialties simply serve regional variations of general North African cuisine. On the island of Djerba, a Tunisian Berber chef with a culinary degree and international work experience serves a range of North African specialties at his restaurant. In the Aures and the Kabyle, a few regional dishes are served in mom-and-pop-type establishments. Moroccan dadas prepare elaborate regional specialties. Tea stops in the Sahara function as resting points and serve a limited number of refreshments.

Special Occasions

The vast majority of Berbers are Muslim to one degree or another. They celebrate the same holidays as larger North African society. There are, however, specialties that various groups or regions are known for, but that does not mean that that group invented the dish or that the dish is exclusive to a group.

Couscous is a celebratory dish for all North Africans, regardless of religion or region. Couscous with seven vegetables is a Berber dish; the number seven is considered to be lucky. Bedouin, who came to North Africa during the Hilalian invasion beginning in the 11th century, also make this dish. Various Bedouin groups are now considered Berber in North Africa.

Historically, North Africa had fluid borders between the Muslim, Christian, and Jewish worlds of the Mediterranean. The earliest evidence of Jewish presence in North Africa dates to late Roman times in Carthage and surrounding areas. Berber converts to Judaism have been documented even in relatively remote regions. The Shleuh of the Atlas Mountains in Morocco speak Judeo-Berber and claim to be descendants of Hebrew tribes who came to North Africa before the Christian era. The island of Djerba in Tunisia is predominantly Berber and still has a significant Jewish population, who trace their origins back 2,500 years. For Rosh Hashanah, they make a round challah baked with a piece of dough cut out in the shape of an open hand. *Adafina* (Arabic for "buried treasure") is a Jewish Sabbath stew of chickpeas, meat, potatoes, and whole eggs in the shell, made on Friday nights and left to cook slowly overnight. The dish is called *dafina* or *tafina* in Algeria and Tunisia, where it is still eaten.

North African Jews and Muslims have only nominal differences regarding religiously prescribed dietary rules. Both religions forbid pork. Wine is *haram* (forbidden) for Muslims but not for Jews. Shellfish and consumption of meat and milk together are *treif* (nonkosher) for Jews but *halal* (permitted) for Muslims. These differences are rarely encountered in North African cuisine: Pigs are scarce, wine is available in limited contexts, shellfish is only a minor component of coastal cooking, and yogurt marinades for meats are a nominal Ottoman influence.

Diet and Health

Berbers follow the same Islamic dietary principles as other North Africans. Regional folk beliefs tend be just that, and not particularly Berber in nature or even shared by all persons in a region. As in many regions of North Africa, folk remedies are being lost to globalization and urbanization. Many older people in rural areas know how to identify edible and medicinal wild greens, a skill that is disappearing with younger generations due to lifestyle shifts and changes to various ecosystems.

- Chamomile is collected in the spring and is used as an infusion for gastrointestinal problems. The leaves and stems are crushed and used to filter fresh butter to help preserve it.
- Musky bugle (*Ajuga iva* [L.] Schreb) is collected in the spring and summer in Morocco and sold as a dried herb. It is taken as a prophylactic against general illness and specifically as a detoxifying and purgative agent.
- In the sandy steppes of Tunisia, the perennial rose garlic is taken fresh to cure colds and used as a condiment for foods.
- Bishop's weed grows all over North Africa in wheat and barley fields. It is an invasive plant that is currently being cultivated by pharmaceutical companies. Bishop's weed is used as an antiseptic.

Currently, various academics and conservation organizations are cataloguing or trying to preserve local knowledge of medicinal plants. Conservationist-operated small farms exist in Algeria to support local economies by cultivating and selling medicinal plants.

In the Kabyle and in Setif, olive oil is highly valued as a locally abundant source of nutrition during times of scarcity. Infusions of herbs steeped in water are drunk regularly for general health and taste, as well as to cure specific ailments. An infusion of basil is believed to control flatulence and reduce stress. An infusion of thyme is drunk to detoxify the digestive system or inhaled to relieve sinus congestion.

Argan trees are native to the Souss Valley of southwestern Morocco and the Tindouf region of Algeria. Argan oil is valued as a flavoring in foods and as a beauty oil for protecting and softening skin. Cosmetic products containing argan oil are marketed in Europe.

In the Sahara, dates—often abundant and free—are prized for their nutritional value and caloric density. Dates from Biskra in the Mozabite region in particular are highly regarded for their flavor and texture.

Susan Ji-Young Park

Further Reading

Brett, Michael, and Elizabeth Fentress. *The Berbers.* Cambridge, MA: Blackwell, 1996.

Geller, Ernest, and Charles Micaud, eds. *Arabs and Berbers: From Tribe to Nation in North Africa.* London: Duckworth, 1973.

Gitlitz, David M., and Linda Kay Davidson. *A Drizzle of Honey: The Lives and Recipes of Spain's Secret Jews.* New York: St. Martin's Press, 1999.

Seligman, Thomas K., and Kristyne Loughran, eds. *The Art of Being Tuareg: Saharan Nomads in a Modern World.* Los Angeles: Iris and B. Gerald Cantor Center for Visual Arts at Stanford University and UCLA Fowler Museum of Cultural History, 2006.

Wright, Clifford. *A Mediterranean Feast: The Story of the Birth of the Celebrated Cuisines of the Mediterranean from the Merchants of Venice to the Barbary Corsairs.* New York: William Morrow, 1999.

Iran

Overview

Although widely considered part of the Middle East, Iran is a country in Near Asia with a landmass that is roughly one-third the size of the United States. Largely mountainous and hilly in the north, the country gradually gives way to arid lowlands, a large desert in its center, and finally more lush, tropical climes at its southern border in the Persian Gulf. In the north, the area around the inland Caspian Sea is verdant and cooler.

Iran shares borders with Turkey, Iraq, Afghanistan, Baluchistan, and the former Soviet bloc countries of Azerbaijan, Armenia, and Turkmenistan. At its largest, early Iran, or the Persian Empire, encompassed all of those nations within its environs. As a result, the cooking styles throughout the nation have been duly influenced by those who lived in the larger empire. Later, Greek conquest of Iran brought foodstuffs including stuffed items such as grape leaves, while skewered marinated meats like *souvlaki* are thought to represent Persian influence on the Greeks.

Throughout this period and earlier, the Silk Road brought spices and goods from India and China into Iran. Through both trade and conquest, Iran influenced the cuisine of northern India. At its height in the Mughal dynasty, which lasted from the mid-1500s to the early 1700s, northern India demonstrated an artistry of food in the Persian style including prodigious use of lamb, elaborately layered rice dishes, and savory preparations that featured fruits, the use of saffron, and warm aromatic spices such as cinnamon. Today, Iranian food can best be described as most similar to northern Indian cuisine minus the use of spicy peppers.

🍽 Food Culture Snapshot

Maryam Haghanifar, 27, is a typical 21st-century urbanite living in Tehran. She was raised in the northwestern city of Kermanshah, once a rural Kurdish stronghold but now a booming metropolis in its own right. Maryam's education brought her to Tehran, where she works as a sales analyst. Stylish clothes and jewelry are her passion, and like many young Iranian women who live in the city, she pushes the limits of Iran's Muslim sharia laws about *hejab,* or traditional dress for women.

Maryam and her husband, Farshad, 32, a musician, enjoy spending time in fashionable Western-style coffee shops or international-cuisine restaurants with friends, eating everything from sushi to pizza to Israeli falafel and fast food in the American style. At home the couple often eats take-out food for dinner, which is usually around seven or eight o'clock, because their hectic schedule doesn't allow for much cooking. Maryam, like so many Americans and Europeans, has adopted the habit of simply drinking coffee for breakfast while Farshad sticks to the more traditional tea and freshly baked bread with butter and jam. For both, lunch still follows traditional lines of being the larger meal of the workday and is usually a dish of rice with one of the many vegetable- and meat-based stews that are standard fare in Iranian cuisine.

When they do not purchase take-out food, the couple shops in Western-style supermarkets for their

An Iranian boy holds flatbread in a bakery in Tehran. (http://www.bigfoto.com)

staples. Tehran has a number of excellent bakeries, from the very traditional bread bakeries to patisseries in the French style, and like most people Maryam and Farshad get their breads and sweets in one of those two venues. The bazaar remains a traditional place to do all manner of shopping, particularly for spices and dried fruits.

For special occasions, such as weddings or feast days, Maryam enjoys specialties from both Kermanshah and Tehran. *Koreshte-khalal,* or a stew of lamb and sweet orange slices, is typical in Kermanshah and indicative of the Persian habit of using a variety of fruits in savory preparations, and *koreshte geymeh* is a beloved stew of lamb, split peas, and fried potatoes.

Maryam says she has noticed a change in the desire to cook and eat at home among Iran's younger generation. They prefer to eat out and are unaware of some of the nation's most traditional dishes. She notes that she is less interested in "old-style" dishes, and she mentions steak and pizza as high on her list of favorite foods.

Major Foodstuffs

Iran produces a wide variety of fruits and vegetables, thanks largely to a system of underground irrigation that brings water from mountainous areas through the drier areas of the country. Since ancient times, Iran has been noted for an abundance of fruits like pomegranates, mulberries, persimmons, quinces, and melons of various types. Peaches and plums originate in Iran, and in the tropical south,

oranges of many types are grown as well as a particularly succulent date that is prized throughout the Middle East. Up to 30 different varieties of grapes grow in Iran. In ancient times, these were used for prodigious wine production. As an Islamic republic, the consumption of alcohol is forbidden in Iran, so the grape harvest is eaten fresh, dried, and even pickled as an ingredient in various dishes. Even today, the classic Persian garden written about by both ancient historians and modern-era travelers still exists, and abundant and myriad fruit trees are a core part of its layout.

Iran grows a variety of vegetables including the slender Persian cucumber that is often served as a fruit, many different squashes, and eggplant, which is so ubiquitous in use that it is often called the potato of Persia. Pistachios are a major crop, and Iranian pistachios are widely exported to aficionados the world over. Almonds are grown and well used, as are English walnuts, which are Persian in origin. Saffron is also largely produced in Iran and considered to be the finest quality to be had on the market. Tea is also produced in Iran and is drunk in large amounts throughout the day. It is often spiced with cardamom.

Caviar is another major Iranian export and is largely considered to be the finest in the world. A traditional and beloved food in Iran, caviar fell under the strict eye of Muslim clerics soon after the 1979 revolution that changed the country from a monarchy to a theocracy. The clerics declared caviar *haram,* or forbidden, but both culture and economy made that an unpopular edict. Soon thereafter, a series of intricate studies as to the nature of caviar-bearing sturgeon, including a treatise on the scales of the fish, finally led them to declare this national food product permissible under sharia law.

Since wheat grows throughout much of the country, a wide variety of breads are made throughout Iran and often vary from region to region. Breads are cooked in a tandoor, a clay-lined oven, or in a brick oven. Flatbreads such as *lavash* or *taftun* will be familiar to those accustomed to eating wraps, tortillas, or flatbreads. More unique items, like *barbari,* a long, ovular flatbread that is slightly risen, and *sangak,* flatbread cooked over hot stones, are unique to Iran and best eaten hot. It is still common to see Iranians congregate at bakeries to obtain a daily supply of fresh hot bread.

The most important food to Iranians by far is rice; a long-grain basmati type is grown natively in the Caspian region. Called *domsiah* (black tail) for its black-tipped kernels, the rice is highly aromatic. Local production is supplemented by purchase of basmati rice from India. Rice is so ubiquitous in Iranian cuisine that it is eaten daily, sometimes at more than one meal. This varies according to income, and it is not uncommon for the poor, particularly in rural areas, to eat bread more often than rice.

Lamb and sheep are the major livestock in Iran because of their native adaptation to mountainous terrain, and Iranian sheep tend to be lean, carrying most of their fat stores in their tails. They are used not only for meat but also for milk, from which yogurt, a daily condiment in Iran, and cheese, akin to feta, are produced. Chicken is fairly popular as the number of chicken dishes demonstrates. Beef is eaten in small quantities, although it serves as the most common substitute for lamb for Iranians living and cooking outside of Iran. Pork is forbidden by Islamic dietary laws. In the north and south, a variety of fish—from the Caspian Sea and the Persian Gulf, respectively—is also consumed and throughout the rest of the country as procured from freshwater rivers and streams.

A close-up of traditional lamb biryani. (Monkey Business Images | Dreamstime.com)

Cooking

In Iran, cooking is as much a matter of artistry and etiquette as of culinary skill. Except in large cities like Tehran, where multinational takeout is rapidly becoming a norm, Iranians prefer home-cooked meals, and even "simple" everyday fare usually comprises four or five different dishes including rice or bread, stewed meat and vegetables, salad, yogurt, fresh greens, and pickled vegetables. Food is cooked abundantly, particularly for guests, so that the utmost hospitality is demonstrated.

The skill of a cook, particularly in more affluent families, is first gauged by his or her ability to master rice, the most precious part of any Iranian meal, followed by mastery of the preparation of complex items such as layered rice dishes or long-simmering stews. This extends to making one's own jams, pickles, and yogurts. It is not uncommon for an Iranian housewife to begin lunch or dinner preparation as soon as she has cleared the table for breakfast.

Rice is cooked one of two ways: The first is the more difficult *chelo*, in which rice is parboiled, then drained and mounded into a pot with oil or butter and a small amount of water, then covered and steamed. Chelo is fluffy with distinct grains, ideally featuring a crust of golden brown rice at the bottom, which is served separately. A second method, *kateh*, is made from boiling rice with oil or butter and salt until the water is absorbed, then allowing it to continue to cook over low heat. This is common for everyday meals. The kateh is overturned on a plate and sliced into like a cake. The crust is crunchy, but inside the rice is plump and fluffy, though not as separate as in chelo.

Chelo

Serves 4

1 c aged basmati rice (Koh I Noor and Lalquila are two good brands)

2 tsp salt

¼ c olive oil or clarified butter (melted)

1. Place the rice in a deep bowl and add enough cold water to cover by 1 or 2 inches. Swirl the rice

around with your hand until the water becomes cloudy, then gently pour off the water, being careful to not inadvertently discard any rice. Repeat this process four or five times or until the water runs clear.

2. After pouring off the last rinse water, fill the bowl with enough cold water to cover the rice by 2 inches. Add 1 teaspoon of the salt to the bowl as well. Set aside for at least two hours but preferably overnight.

3. When you are ready to cook the rice: Bring a saucepan (preferably nonstick) of water to a boil, and add the remaining salt. Pour off the soaking water from the rice. You can also pour the rice into a fine mesh strainer. Add the soaked rice to the boiling water.

4. Boil for 10–12 minutes on medium high, and remove from heat. Drain the rice into a fine mesh strainer.

5. Add 1 tablespoon of the oil or butter and 1 tablespoon water to the bottom of the same pan in which you boiled the rice. Swirl it around to coat the bottom of the pan.

6. Using a large spoon, carefully spoon the rice into the center of the pot to form a pyramid.

7. Mix 2 tablespoons water with the remaining oil or butter, and pour this mixture evenly over the rice pyramid.

8. Place a clean dishcloth over the pot and then place the pot lid over that, pressing down to secure it firmly and make a seal. Fold up the edges of the cloth over the top of the lid so they do not hang down and touch the burner. Alternatively, you may layer two pieces of paper towel and place them over the pot and then secure the pot lid on top of that.

9. Place the pot over low heat for 20 minutes. Remove lid and fluff rice. Once you spoon out the rice onto a platter, there should be a golden crust of rice on the bottom of the pan. This is called *tahdig*. Invert the pot onto a plate so the tahdig comes out in one golden crust. Serve alongside the rice. Serve with koreshte (see following recipe).

Koreshte Geymeh

½ tsp saffron, dissolved in ⅓ c boiling water

1 tbsp olive oil or clarified butter

1 medium onion, thinly sliced,

2 lb lamb, cut into 1-in. cubes

1 tsp turmeric

½ tsp cinnamon

1 tsp salt

Freshly ground black pepper to taste

1 tbsp tomato paste

2 *limou omani* (dried Persian limes) or ¼ c lemon juice

¼ c split peas

4 small Yukon Gold potatoes, peeled and sliced into matchsticks

Canola oil, as needed, for frying potatoes

1. Dissolve the saffron in the boiling water and set aside for at least half an hour but preferably overnight. The longer it steeps, the darker the hue.

2. Heat the olive oil or butter in a Dutch oven or heavy-bottomed saucepan on medium-high heat and add the onion. Sauté the onion until translucent, about 3–4 minutes.

3. Add the lamb pieces to the onion mixture, and stir well. Fry until the lamb is browned on all sides, about 8 to 10 minutes.

4. Reduce the heat to medium low, and add the turmeric, cinnamon, salt, and pepper and cook, stirring, for 30 seconds. Add the tomato paste and mix well. Cook, stirring, for 3 to 4 minutes.

5. Add enough water to cover the lamb pieces by 2 inches and reduce heat to a simmer. Add the limou omani, if using, and simmer uncovered for 40 minutes. If using fresh lemon juice, add in the last 10 minutes of cooking.

6. While the lamb mixture is simmering, place the split peas in a small saucepan with enough water to cover. Simmer on medium-low heat for 20 minutes or until tender. Drain and set aside.

7. Heat a large frying pan with 2 inches of canola oil. Test the oil by adding one small potato stick. If it bubbles and fries, it is ready. Add the remaining potato sticks and fry until golden brown on all sides. Remove from the pan with a slotted spoon and place on a tray lined with paper towels or on a rack set over a sheet tray to drain.

8. Mix the split peas into the lamb mixture in the last 10 minutes of cooking.

9. Serve koreshte in a deep bowl or serving dish and arrange fried potato sticks on top of the stew. Serve with chelo and tahdig, garnished with a tablespoon of the koreshte.

Most dishes start with some version of *piaz dogh,* or cooked onions. Stews follow the same method of preparation: Onions are fried, to which meat, most likely lamb, is added and browned. The mixture is then spiced, and a vegetable or fruit is then added to simmer for some time. This stew, or koreshte, is served with rice, and the form is commonly called *chelo koreshte* (steamed rice and stew). Iranian stews are named after the predominant vegetable since the meat tends most often to be lamb and is relatively little in relation to the vegetable or fruit. *Koreshte badamjun* (eggplant stew), for example, comprises meat and eggplant, but it is named after the eggplant. *Koreshte kadu* (squash stew) is named for the squash in the dish. *Ashe,* or soups, are incredibly popular and tend to be thick pottages that are mostly vegetarian in nature, thickened with yogurt or whey.

Layered rice dishes are very commonly cooked and are called *polloh.* They feature either a mixture of small pieces of meat and vegetables, in the nature of a *biryani* (a mixed rice pilaf), or nuts and dried fruits such as *zereshk* (barberries), a tart red berry that is used for culinary purposes mostly in Iran. As with koreshte these dishes are generally named according to the vegetable or fruit ingredient, including *albaloo* (cherry) *polloh,* *zereskh* (barberry) *polloh,* and so on. Pollohs are created using a method of steaming in which parboiled rice is layered alternately with cooked ingredients, then tightly covered and steamed over a low flame. Alternatively, sometimes pollohs are made by adding ingredients to steamed rice after both are cooked; "jeweled rice" is one example in which zereshk, dried fruits, and nuts are added after the rice is cooked.

Grilling, particularly of marinated meats, is a common cooking method and is most often used during picnics. It's not uncommon to see whole families picnicking on fine days with a portable hibachi-type grill, cooking kebabs. Baking of bread is most often left to the numerous bakeries throughout every city and village. Sweets, which include both traditional items made with nut and bean flours, rose water, and saffron and also Western-style cookies, cakes, and pastry, are most often purchased, though it is not uncommon for items like rice cookies and baklava, containing pistachios rather than walnuts, to be prepared at home, particularly around holidays.

Pickling vegetables is another skill that the Iranian cook must master. Collectively called *torshi,* or "sours," these pickled vegetables, ranging from pickled garlic or shallots to mixed vegetables and even herbs, are a condiment on the everyday table. Vinegar and a variety of spices are used, from angelica to nigella seeds and an allspice mixture called *advieh,* comprising ground rose petals, cinnamon, cardamom, pepper, turmeric, nutmeg, coriander, and cumin. This, too, can be made within the home by grinding whole spices or bought in the bazaar from a spice vendor.

Jams, compotes, and fruit syrups are other items cooked equally at home as well as purchased out, and they most often feature seasonal fruit, sugar, rose water, and spices, such as cinnamon or cardamom. Cold beverages called *sharbats* are made from various fruit purees, lightly spiced, or fruit syrups added to water. *Dugh,* a mixture of yogurt, mint, and flat or carbonated water, is also often made at home though bottled varieties are readily available.

Tea, the national beverage, is traditionally prepared using a samovar, a metal urn-shaped vessel with a heating chamber in the center that keeps the surrounding liquid hot. It steeps the tea leaves with a consistent gentle steam. Because a samovar is not practical for everyday use, Iranians use a system of two tea kettles: Hot water is added to tea leaves, often with cardamom, in a small kettle and placed on top of a larger kettle to gently steam. The resulting tea is strong and dark and is added to small glasses, in which additional hot water is added to thin it out. The tea is typically served with a bowl of fresh fruit, a mixture of dried fruit and nuts called *ajil,* and, perhaps, small cookies or pastries.

Typical Meals

An Iranian breakfast always features hot tea, though coffee is not uncommon. Breads such as lavash, taftun, or *barbari* are heated or preferably purchased fresh and warm and eaten with cheese or butter and jams. Eggs—cooked, fried, or in simple omelets—can be had as well.

As in most of the Middle East and part of Europe, lunch is the biggest meal of the Iranians' day, usually featuring chelo koreshte of some kind. The lunch hour, even for business, tends to be long to allow for some rest after the consumption of the heavy meal. Lunch (and dinner) is most often preceded and followed by the drinking of tea, which is consumed by placing a sugar cube in the mouth and taking small sips of the hot tea. Dinner features much of the same foods as lunch and is eaten fairly late in the evening, sometimes as late as eight o'clock.

Both lunch and dinner were traditionally served on a *sofreh,* or tablecloth, laid directly on the floor, around which diners would sit. A multiplicity of dishes are offered in addition to the main course, including *sabzi khordan,* or a plate of fresh herbs including mint, tarragon, parsley, basil, and scallion that are taken up with the fingers and eaten between bites of food. Radishes are also often included on the plate. Varieties of pickles, plain yogurt, and yogurt mixed with herbs or vegetables also dot the sofreh.

In modern times, most families eat at a dining table, though it is not uncommon for Iranians of all classes and level of urbanity to return to the sofreh during large gatherings or for special occasions. On a daily basis, dinner is increasingly more akin to the traditional lunch in its variety and length, as it is, like in the West, often the only time family members get to enjoy a relaxed meal together.

Snacks of dried fruit, nuts, fresh fruit, and small sweets are often eaten throughout the day, usually with tea. Savory snacks served in profusion are called *mezzeh,* similar to the Turkish, Arabic, and Greek styles. Desserts, while not typical daily fare, would be eaten with the postmeal tea and usually include small cookies, date-based confections, or even ice cream, commonly topped with compote or jam. *Paludeh,* or Iranian ice cream, has a unique taste as it is made with rose water and cardamom.

Eating Out

Until the 20th century, the most common manner of eating outside the home was in teahouses, at street-food stalls, and in *chelo kebabis,* or restaurants that exclusively served kebabs and rice with its accompaniments. The chelo kebabi remains popular today, as the method of preparation using the tandoor is often not present in the modern home, especially in major cities like Tehran, where most people live in some manner of apartment. While street stands or stalls are not common, smaller indoor eateries, usually without seating, prepare other items not normally prepared at home, usually because of the cooking method: the use of a direct flame, as with grilled lamb liver, or deep-frying, as for falafel.

Teahouses have always been popular in Iran and were at one time a male-only gathering place. Today, teahouses range from the most simple takeout to high-end establishments featuring decor in the classical style, including Persian rugs and throw pillows on which to sit. A variety of mixed fruit, nuts, and pastries accompany the tea.

Today, a large number of multinational cuisines are available in the larger Iranian cities, from fast-food joints in the American style to Indian, sushi, Chinese, other Middle Eastern cuisines, pizza, Italian, and much more. In urban areas, takeout is increasingly used to "solve" mealtimes, particularly dinner or for a quick midday meal during the workweek, although most Iranians prefer something more traditional like chelo koreshte for lunch, reserving takeout for the smaller dinner or as a treat. Increasingly, "foreign" eateries are taking on the tenor of traditional chelo kebabis or teahouses as places most valued for socialization. Sweets such as pastries and ice cream are common foods that are purchased and eaten out, particularly around festive occasions.

Perhaps the most prized form of eating out for Iranians is eating al fresco in the form of a picnic. Picnics usually feature grilled kebabs, which are traditionally cooked by men whereas women cook nongrilled foods. This is true both in the restaurant setting and within families, not dissimilar to the tradition of the backyard cookout in the United States. Breads, salads, fruits, pickles, and sharbats are typical. Picnics are common not only during good weather but also as an integral part of celebrations, particularly the 13th Day Festival of the Persian New Year.

Special Occasions

Foods for special occasions in Iran must follow the rule of extreme hospitality that is ingrained in the culture. A special occasion might range from the visit of a single guest to a wedding or celebration of a religious or national holiday. Regardless, the custom of *tarof* is key to meal preparation, serving, and consumption at those times.

The system of tarof is based on extreme selflessness and politeness on the part of both the preparer and the receiver of the food. A guest will enter an Iranian home and immediately be offered tea, fresh fruit, cookies, and bowls of dried nuts and fruit. The guest is expected to politely refuse the offer of refreshment, lest the host be put to any trouble. The entreaty to partake and refusal must pass back and forth at least three times until the host simply goes ahead and serves the items, to the guest's extreme thanks. When sitting down to eat the main meal, the host serves guests first, and guests, in turn, thank the host profusely for his or her generosity. As part of

entreating guests in the home, meals must be as expensive and generous as the host can afford. Guests should not be made to feel that they must curtail their eating, even if they want seconds or thirds, although it would be rude to eat that much.

The dishes prepared for special occasions must be elaborate enough to demonstrate the skill of the cook; layered rice dishes are popular. Also served are complex dishes that showcase the cook's ability to meld a variety of delicate spices and flavors, particularly, in many cases, showcasing the Iranian love for the sweet and sour.

Food is an important part of holidays in Iran. Not only are very specific dishes cooked but, in some cases, such as weddings and Noruz, the Persian New Year, ceremonial tables that use foodstuffs to highlight larger philosophical themes are the norm. At Noruz, an ancient Persian holiday that constitutes an ecumenical New Year on the first day of spring, a table is set with a *sofreh haft-sin,* or the "tablecloth of seven Ss." The Ss comprise items that begin with the letter S in Farsi and may include apples (*sib*), sumac powder (*sumogh*), garlic (*sir*), jujube fruit (*senjed*), vinegar (*serkeh*), and sweets (*shirini*), as well as coins (*sekkeh*), hyacinth (*sonbol*), or other items starting with an *s*. Each represents the possibilities for the year to come, including sweetness, abundance, wealth, spice, and even, at times, bitterness.

A table decorated with sofreh haft-sin or "tablecloth of seven Ss" in celebration of Noruz, an ancient Persian holiday that constitutes an ecumenical New Year on the first day of spring. (StockPhotoPro)

The Noruz dinner always features *ash reshteh,* a thick vegetarian noodle soup, as noodles represent long life, and whitefish served with herbed rice (*sabzi polloh va mahi*), as herbs represent the green and rebirth of spring. Noodle rice (*reshteh polloh*) and an herb omelet (*kookooyeh sabzi*) are served for the same reasons. Sweets abound at Noruz and are an integral part of the feast. Traditional cookies made from rice, chickpea, and almond flour abound, as do baklava and other treats, such as *gusht-e-fil,* or elephant ear cookies, and *zulubia,* a fritter of yeast dough dipped in sugar syrup perfumed with rosewater essence. It is very similar to the Indian *jalebi.* Thirteen days after Noruz is the celebration of *seizdah bidar,* or "the giving of 13," when families leave their homes for an elaborate picnic in a beautiful spot. Those who do not picnic try at least to eat their main meal outside the home.

Weddings are also an occasion for plentiful sweets similar to those served at Noruz. These include *noghle* (sugar-coated almonds) and *sohan assali* (honey almonds), which are placed on platters on a special sofreh that also features a plate of herbs, cheese, and bread to serve to the guests immediately after the ceremony to bring the couple good luck. Other items on the sofreh include a bowl of eggs to symbolize fertility, a bowl of honey for a sweet future, and other nonfood items—such as a needle and thread to "sew up the mother-in-law's mouth"—to represent a healthy and happy marriage. The wedding feast comprises the most intricate dishes that are within the families' means to provide. *Shirin polloh,* or "sweetened rice," is always served and is a layered rice dish featuring orange peel, carrots, pistachios, almonds, and zereshk. A whole roasted lamb is served as at most major feasts.

Ramadan, or Ramazan, as it is called here, is celebrated in Iran. In this Muslim fasting month, the daily fast is broken with a date and a traditional dinner. During this month housewives would have a large predawn breakfast prepared for their family, most often featuring foods more traditionally eaten at lunch or dinner, to fortify them for the day ahead. On the last day of the fast, the feast-day Iftar, a variety of both complex and humble dishes are placed on the table.

Diet and Health

The Iranian diet is particularly well balanced given that meat is eaten in relatively small proportion to vegetables and fruits, even when combined in the same dish. Sweets are eaten moderately, except during celebrations, and a variety of grains, in addition to rice and bread, including barley and whole-wheat germ, are consumed as well, providing additional sources of fiber.

According to the United Nations Food and Agriculture Organization, Iran's average proportions of dietary energy from protein (11%), fat (22%), and carbohydrates (67%) are desirable from a nutritional point of view. Food is considered a major part of health and well-being in Iran, not simply based on diet but based on its believed effect on personality and psychological well-being. A system of "hot" and "cold," called *garm* and *sard,* is similar to Ayurvedic and yin-yang principles of eating.

With a clear basis in seasonal availability the premise of garm and sard is an ancient one, believed to have originated thousands of years ago with Zoroaster, the founder of the Persian monotheistic religion of Zoroastrianism. The basis of the religion is the epic battle between good and evil, a battle that is thought to be waged within the human body and spirit as well. Foods must be used to balance the humors for best health, so, for example, if someone is "hot-natured," he or she must eat cold foods, and vice versa.

Garmi, or hotlike food, thickens weak blood and speeds up the metabolism, while *sardi,* or coldlike food, thins the blood and slows down the metabolism. It is important to note that those classifications have nothing to do with temperature or spiciness but rather a system that was developed millennia ago. Beef, for example, is "cold," while lamb is "hot." Duck is "hot," but turkey is "cold." Corn is "hot," but pumpkins are "cold," and so on. The classification applies to all manner of food, from meat to fish, fowl, grains, beans, vegetables, dairy, spices, herbs, and even beverages.

Ramin Ganeshram

Further Reading

Batmanglij, Najmieh. *New Food of Life: Ancient Iranian and Modern Persian Cooking and Ceremonies.* Waldorf, MD: Mage, 1992.

Mazda, Maida. *In a Persian Kitchen.* Rutland, VT: Tuttle, 1989.

Ramazani, Nesta. *Persian Cooking, A Table of Exotic Delights.* Charlottesville: University Press of Virginia, 1986.

Shaida, Margaret. *The Legendary Cuisine of Persia.* New York: Interlink, 2002.

Iraq

Overview

Iraq is a little more than twice the size of Idaho, with a population around 27 million, sharing borders with Iran, Turkey, Syria, Jordan, Saudi Arabia, and Kuwait. Its sole access to the Arabian Gulf is through the southern city of Basra. Topographically and ethnically, Iraq is diverse. The mountainous north is inhabited by Kurds, who make up 15–20 percent of the population. A bit farther south dwell the majority of the Turkomans and Assyrians, approximately 5 percent of the population. The central and southern zones make up a fertile alluvial plain inhabited mostly by Arabs, who constitute 75 percent of the population. There is also a small ethnic minority of Armenians, largely concentrated in Baghdad and Basra. The western and southwestern region is a desert sparsely populated by nomadic Bedouin. Iraqis are predominantly Muslims, about 97 percent, and the rest are Christians and other minorities such as Sabians and Yazidis.

🍽 Food Culture Snapshot

Ahmed is a 12-year-old boy who lives in Baghdad with his family of seven. Today is his turn to accompany his mother to the neighborhood marketplace, something to which he looks forward. He enjoys the sight and aromas of fresh vegetables and fruits, and he feels flattered that his mother needs him to carry home the grocery bags with her. These days she does grocery shopping more often than she used to because refrigeration is not dependable due to frequent power outages. She looks tired but never complains, and Ahmed is happy to help.

The first stop they make is at the butcher's. His mother purchases lamb chunks on the bone, which usually go into the stew pot. She also asks for chunks of beef to be ground for her, at which Ahmed gets excited. Ground meat is used to make delicious elaborate stuffed foods such as *dolma*, an assortment of vegetables stuffed with meat and rice, and *kubba*, disks of rice, potato, or bulgur stuffed with meat. Since they are expecting guests for dinner, they also stop at a fish place, where river fish varieties, such as *shabbout* and *bunni* of the carp family, are displayed. She also buys small inexpensive fishes called *zoori* at Ahmed's request. He loves them fried. The bigger fishes will either be cut into pieces and then fried or be baked whole in the clay oven (*tannour*) that Ahmed's father built outside the house in a corner of their small garden. Ahmed has already started fantasizing about the golden yellow rice with raisins and almonds that his mother usually cooks with fish.

Their next stop is the vegetable and fruit stalls, a place so much alive with the hustle and bustle of shoppers, the earthy aromas, and venders' loud chants and catchy phrases to attract customers. Ahmed's mother buys okra and fresh fava beans. "These are for the stews," she tells him. She further purchases eggplant, gourds (similar to zucchini), cucumbers, potatoes, tomatoes, peppers, green onions, white radishes with the leaves on, and small bundles of parsley, mint, basil, *kurrath* (similar to Korean leeks), and *rishshad* (garden cress). Most of the vegetables will be used for dolma, and Ahmed is hoping his mother will make his favorite, *poteta chap*, fried kubba made with potato. The herbs will be washed and served whole on a large platter with the main dishes. Were it wintertime, his mother would have bought spinach, Swiss chard, lettuce, and fresh green beans.

For fruit, they buy grapes, sweet pomegranates, a small cluster of fresh dates, and the locally grown small white apples. A large watermelon would have necessitated hiring a taxi to go home, but they already have one at home. In winter, fresh fruits of choice would have been oranges and mandarins, and perhaps imported apples and bananas if available and affordable.

Next, they make a short stop at the grocer's to buy tomato paste and dried white beans. For the fish dish, Ahmed's mother needs to buy some *noomi Basra* (dried lime). She further purchases a small bottle of pickled mango (*amba*), eaten as a relish with the meal. But Ahmed loves to have it stuffed in bread with slices of boiled eggs and tomatoes. The last stop is at the confectioner's, where they purchase a box of the syrupy pastries *baklawa* and *zlabya* (fried fritters), much to Ahmed's excitement.

Major Foodstuffs

To a large extent, Iraqi cooking is defined more by topography than by ethnicity, diverse as it is. The country is primarily agricultural. In the northern zone, it is cold in winter, and heavy snow sometimes falls on the mountains. Growing crops depends on rain, which falls in winter and spring. The central and southern parts are dry. There, the winter is mild and the summer is hot and completely rainless. The two major rivers, Tigris and Euphrates, are the main source for irrigating crops.

Grains, primarily wheat and barley, are the most important crops. They are planted in the fall and harvested in spring. Barley is more tolerant of salinity than wheat. Therefore, it is grown more in the middle and south than in the north, which is the land of wheat. In Iraq several varieties of rice are grown, the best of which by far is the aromatic *timman anbar*. It grows in paddies in the southern marshlands. In the course of the 20th century Iraq increasingly became more dependent on imported necessities to meet domestic demands, such as rice, wheat, vegetable oil, and sugar, among many other things, but they were all subsidized and hence affordable. That is why the economic sanctions after 1990 were devastating in their effects on the daily lives of ordinary people.

Meat comes from sheep, goats, and cattle. Iraqi sheep are distinguished by their fat tails (*liyya*), which have been a valuable source of fat, only recently shunned for health considerations. Mutton and lamb are preferred to other meat, particularly for dishes that require meat on the bone, such as *marag* (stew) and *thareed* (a stew with bread soaked in it). It is not cheap; therefore, quantities used depend on one's means. But since meat is a social gauge of some sort, when cooking for guests, more meat is thrown into the pot than usual. Goat meat is mostly eaten in the mountainous region, where goats abound. Beef is used for ground meat dishes, for kebab, both grilled and fried, and the endless stuffed dishes of kubba and dolma. Pork is hard to find since the majority of people are Muslims. Domestic poultry is not enough to meet the demand. Its meat is tough, and people always boil the chicken before doing anything else with it. Before the economic sanctions, substantial amounts of frozen chicken and eggs used to be imported.

Fish used to be plentiful in the Tigris and Euphrates and their tributaries. Fish dishes are more popular in the central and southern regions than in the north. Basra is the source for shrimp and *zubaidi* (pomfret), which, unlike river fish, has few bones. Southern marsh dwellers in Ahwar still salt and dry fish like their ancient ancestors used to do.

Traditional mutton briyani. (Paul Cowan | Dreamstime.com)

The richest yogurt, made from sheep and goat milk, is available in the northern region in springtime when the pastures are lush. Yogurt from the Kurdish city Arbeel is legendary. The best *geymer* (clotted cream) is made from buffalo milk. Fresh soft white cheese made from cow milk is called Arab cheese. Kurdish cheese made from sheep and goat milk is harder and saltier because it is aged.

The major fruit is the date. It grows in the central and southern regions. The north is too cold for it. Dates are eaten as fruit, both fresh and dried, and syrup, called *dibis,* is also extracted from them. In the northern region honey is more common. Fruits and vegetables are mostly locally grown and are all seasonal.

Basra has a long trade history with India, from where the best spices were imported. The basic *baharat* is a brownish spice mix of many ingredients including cardamom, cinnamon, ginger, cloves, and allspice. The yellow spice mix called *bahar asfar* is similar to curry powder. Iraqi cooks, mostly in central and southern Iraq, are fond of using the delicately tangy dried lime called noomi Basra (lemon of Basra), imported from Oman.

Cooking

Cooking with water was an advanced stage in the history of humans' attempts to make their food more palatable. This stage was already perfected in ancient Iraq millennia ago. One of three excavated cuneiform clay tablets written in 1700 B.C. in Babylon, south of present-day Baghdad, deals with 24 recipes for stew cooked with meat and vegetables, enhanced and seasoned with rendered fat from sheep's tail, leeks, onion, garlic, and spices and herbs like cassia, cumin, coriander, mint, and dill. Stew has remained a mainstay. Extant medieval Iraqi recipes and modern-day cooking attest to this. However, the introduction of tomatoes from the Americas around the 16th century revolutionized the way stew is cooked. They gradually replaced most of the thickening, souring, and coloring agents used in making the stews, such as nuts, sour fruit and vegetable juices, saffron, and pomegranate juice. Remnants of the medieval way of cooking tomatoless

stew can still be seen in the *summaqiyya* (soured and colored with sumac berries) of the northern city of Mosul and the *fasanjoun* (soured with pomegranate and thickened with walnut) of Najaf and Karbala, south of Baghdad. The preferred meat is lamb chunks on the bone, sometimes replaced with small, spicy meatballs called *ras il-'asfour* (sparrows' heads). Relatively recently, the saturated animal fat of rendered sheep's tail has been replaced with vegetable oil. Generally, the stews of the southern city of Basra are made spicier than the rest. The city is also known for its fish and shrimp stews and curries.

Related to stew is the traditional dish thareed, also called *tishreeb,* in which bread is soaked, because that was how stew was always served before rice became an affordable option through importation of American and Far Eastern varieties. Thareed prepared with chunks of lamb or chicken, *pacha* (a broth of sheep trotters, tripe, and head), and the meatless *tashreeb bagilla,* made with dried fava beans, are quite popular.

White plain rice is commonly served with stew, but it is also prepared in a variety of ways, depending on the occasion and affordability. It is garnished with almonds, raisins, and vermicelli noodles; made red with tomato juice; or colored yellow, most commonly with turmeric rather than the expensive saffron, and served with a whole browned chicken sitting in the middle. Rice is also offered as an independent dish, usually served with plain yogurt, as in *timman bagilla* (green rice with dill and fresh fava beans), *maqlouba* (upside-down eggplant dish), *timman tacheena* (with diced vegetables and meat), *mtabbag simach* (fried fish layered with rice), and *biryani,* which is a spicy mix of meat, vegetables, and rice reserved for festive occasions. Kurdish cooks in northern Iraq give biryani an elaborate touch by encasing the rice mix in thin sheets of dough and baking it in the oven. They call it *parda palaw.* Bulgur sometimes replaces rice, but this is more common in the northern region.

It is not customary to serve soup before the meal because it is a meal itself, eaten with some bread and salad vegetables. Unlike stew, soup does not have to contain meat. More commonly, it is prepared with grains and legumes. The most popular soups are *shorbat 'adas* (lentil) and *mash* (mung beans). For a treat, sometimes small meatballs of ras il-'asfour are added.

Bread consumed with the meals can be the flat variety baked in the commercial or household domed clay oven, the tannour. *Sammoun* bread is commercially baked in brick ovens. It is diamond-shaped, similar in texture and taste to the Italian ciabatta. In the north, *rqaq* is the bread to have with meals. It is made by flattening simple dough into a large thin sheet using a dowel, and baking it on a heated, large, domed metal plate called *saj*. In the southern marshlands where rice grows, *khubuz timman* is made by pouring a batter of ground rice onto a heated plate, resulting in thin sheets of rice bread.

Nawashif (literally, "dry") dishes are usually reserved for smaller meals, especially supper, or more conveniently offered, among many other things, at dinner parties. Most of them are fried, such as varieties of kubba, meat patties of *kufta* and kebab, and stuffed pastries like *boureg* and *sanbousa*.

The Iraqi cuisine is distinguished by the variety of stuffed dishes it offers. Kubba tops the list. The northern city of Mosul is especially renowned for its thin and huge flat disks of *kubbat Mosul*, usually boiled in wide pots. It is time-consuming and requires special skill; therefore, most cooks prefer to serve it as boiled small disks and balls. In northern Iraq, where it is more common to use yogurt in cooking, this sort of kubba is sometimes added to a delicate yogurt soup. *Kubbat hamudh shalgham* is rich soup made with chunks of lamb, cubed turnips, and chopped Swiss chard (which may be replaced with squash and mint in the summer) and thickened with crushed or ground rice. Then small balls of rice kubba are added to the pot. Iraqi Jews make it red by replacing the turnips with beets, and instead of rice flour, farina is sometimes used. They also add these kubba balls to okra stew.

Vegetables are stuffed in dishes like dolma and *sheikh mahshi*. For dolma, vegetables like cored eggplant and gourds, onion layers, and leaf vegetables like grape leaves and Swiss chard are stuffed with a mix of rice and ground meat and simmered in liquid until it all evaporates. For Lent, Iraqi Christians cook dolma without meat and use olive oil. For sheikh mahshi no rice is used, only meat, hence the name "master of all stuffed dishes." It is simmered in tomato sauce until it thickens nicely.

Most of the traditional desserts are simmered on top of the stove, since ovens in households did not become common until perhaps the middle of the 20th century. Light and thickened puddings are made with cornstarch, vermicelli noodles, dates, carrots, and other ingredients. Fried syrupy pastries like *luqmat il-qadhi* ("judge's morsel," deep-fried dough balls soaked in syrup) are also popular. Desserts are flavored with cardamom, rose water, or orange blossom water.

Typical Meals

All meals are served with warm bread, preferably purchased just before the food is served. To wash down the meal, several rounds of sweet hot tea are served in *istikan,* the small transparent glasses. A typical summer breakfast would be sandwiches stuffed with cheese along with watermelon or slices of peeled cucumber. In winter, it might be *bastirma* (Iraqi cured sausage) with eggs, or slabs of geymer (clotted cream) with date syrup or honey. Brunch on weekends can sometimes be elaborate, such as tashreeb bagilla. Dried fava beans are simmered to tenderness, and then broken pieces of flatbread are simmered for a while in the broth and then ladled onto a large platter. The fava beans are scattered all over it, and a generous amount of crushed dried *butnij* (river mint) is sprinkled over it. Then it is drizzled liberally with sizzling hot oil or clarified butter. Another typical brunch could be *kahi,* purchased from specialized bakeries. It is made of simple dough flattened into a large, thin disk, brushed liberally with oil, and then folded and baked. Kahi is eaten drenched in light syrup with a generous slab of geymer on top.

Lunch is the main meal for most families. Stew and rice (*timman w'marag*) are served almost daily, and the possibilities for variety within this category are endless. Okra stew is the most-liked summer stew, and for winter, white dried beans (*fasoulya yabsa*) and spinach (*spenagh*). Stew is customarily served in a big bowl. It is spooned out and mixed with some rice and eaten with condiments, such as pickles, amba (pickled mango), and plenty of herbs. A refreshing drink served with the meal in summertime is *shineena.* It is plain yogurt diluted with water, seasoned with a pinch of salt, whipped until frothy, and served chilled with ice cubes. On cold winter days, it is common to serve rich and hearty soups that stick to the ribs for lunch.

In the afternoon, the family gets together for a round of freshly brewed tea served with simple dunking cookies purchased from specialized bakeries, such as *ka'ak* and *bakhsam,* or *churek,* which is lightly sweetened yeast pastry. The afternoon is also fruit time.

Supper, usually served around seven or eight o'clock, is the time for nawashif (dry dishes), such as *kubbat halab* (rice dough stuffed and fried) or *'uroug,* which is fried patties of ground meat mixed with chopped onion and parsley. The family is often treated to simple puddings or the richer and thicker *halawa* (a fudgelike sweet made from nuts or sesame seeds).

Margat Bamya (Okra Stew)

Serves 4

To get rid of most of the slime inside okra, cut off both ends and wash it briefly. Fill three-quarters of a medium pot with water and bring it to a quick boil. Add okra and let it boil briefly (no more than 5 minutes). Then strain it and use or freeze for future use.

4–6 chunks of lamb on the bone (2–2½ lb)

2 tbsp oil

5–6 cloves garlic, whole

3 heaping tbsp tomato paste (one 6-oz can), diluted in 4 c hot water

1½ tsp salt

1 tbsp pomegranate syrup, or ½ tsp sugar and 2 tbsp lemon juice

1 lb fresh or frozen okra

2–3 small dried hot peppers (optional)

In a medium-heavy pot, sauté meat pieces in oil until browned, about 10 minutes. Add enough hot water to cover the meat. Bring to a quick boil, skimming as needed, and then let simmer gently, covered, on low heat until meat is tender and moisture evaporates, about 45 minutes. If meat is cooked and there is still some liquid in the pot, strain it and use it as part of the liquid required in the recipe. To the meat pot, add garlic cloves and stir for 30 seconds. Stir in the rest of the ingredients, and bring pot to a quick boil, skimming as needed, then reduce heat to medium low, and simmer gently, covered, until sauce is rich and somewhat thickened (35 to 40 minutes).

Serve the stew with a side dish of plain white rice or bulgur along with slices of onion and green pepper. Another popular way of serving okra stew is having it as *tashreeb:* Put bite-size pieces of flatbread in a deep dish and drench it with the stew sauce. Arrange meat pieces and garlic on top.

Eating Out

The first European-style restaurant opened in modern-day Baghdad in the 1920s. It boasted a menu, the first one in Baghdad, which offered Italian, Greek, and Lebanese dishes. However, Iraqis, even those who could afford it, were very slow to develop the habit of dining out for leisure, not doing so until the late 1960s.

For the majority of the population, the best option for dining out would be carry-out foods from stalls and small shops. A treat on an outing on a cool summer evening might be warm sandwiches of grilled meat, such as *mi'lag* (liver), *tikka* (cubed lamb), and kebab (skewered ground meat). Other options are *guss* (shawirma, similar to gyro) or grilled hamburger slathered with yellow mustard and *sos* (steak sauce similar to A1). At small specialized bakeries, succulent *lahm b'ajeen* might be another tempting option. It is flatbread topped with a thin layer of a spicy mix of fatty ground meat with chopped onion, tomatoes, and parsley. Cold sandwiches of sliced pot roast or boiled beef tongue are popular movie theater snacks.

An Iraqi family has a picnic at the Shrine of the Ezekiel. (StockPhotoPro)

A much more expensive summertime treat would be the famous Baghdadi *masgouf* fish barbecued and served in the open-air cafés scattered along the bank of the river Tigris. Customers are allowed to choose the fish themselves from small fish tanks. The fish is split open, washed, and sprinkled with coarse salt. Then it is impaled with other fishes on sticks arranged in a circle around a flaming wood fire. After an hour or so the fishes are placed flat on the smoldering fire so that their skins may crisp. Since river fish is riddled with numerous small, prickly bones, people usually eat it with their fingers.

The major bulk of the business of the small restaurants and food stalls that abound in the bustling city centers comes from the regular customers who work far from home for the day, or travelers. They usually serve the familiar staples of rice and stew or warm sandwiches of grilled kebab and guss. A hearty breakfast or a whimsical late-night meal might be the traditional dish pacha—a broth made with sheep's head, stomach, and feet. On cold winter days, passersby might find the aroma emitted from the steaming cauldron of *kubbat burghul* (stuffed disks made with bulgur wheat) at a street-corner stall too tempting to pass. The steaming pots of *lablabi* (boiled chickpeas) and *mayi' il-shalgham* (tender boiled turnips) might be equally hard to resist.

Special Occasions

During Ramadan, which begins and ends with the first appearance of the crescent moon, Muslims abstain from food and drink from sunrise to sunset. They usually break their fast first with a few dates and yogurt or water, in emulation of a tradition set by the Prophet many centuries ago. *Iftar,* which is the daily Ramadan meal, usually begins with soup, mostly lentil, followed by rice and stew, and platters of dolma, perhaps some kubba, or other nawashif dishes. A favorite drink with the meal is *sherbet qamar il-deen,* a refreshing, thirst-quenching beverage made from sheets of dried apricot. A few hours later, it is customary to enjoy some of Ramadan's favorite desserts, baklawa and zlabya. Before sunrise, a simple light meal called *suhour* is consumed.

The appearance of the new crescent moon announces the end of Ramadan and the beginning of one of the two major Muslim holidays, the Small Feast. It is a three-day celebration during which Muslims exchange visits and share meals. A variety of rice dishes with lamb or chicken and stews are prepared for guests, as well as dolma and kubba. Cookies called *kleicha* are offered to guests with sweet tea. The second major religious holiday is the Big Feast, which lasts for four days. It celebrates the end of the ceremonies of hajj (pilgrimage) to holy Mecca. Sheep are usually slaughtered to honor the occasion. Most of the meat is distributed to the needy, and with the rest some traditional dishes are prepared, such as pacha.

The dishes Iraqi Christians prepare for Christmas and Easter are not much different from the ones already mentioned. For Lent, a succulent meatless version of dolma is made with olive oil. Before the mid-20th century there was a thriving community of Jews in Iraq, who prepared special dishes for their own religious days and feasts. For the Sabbath, *tibyeet,* also called *tannouri,* was cooked. It is a rich chicken dish with rice simmered overnight in the clay oven (tannour). Both Christians and Jews share the Muslims' fondness for the festive kleicha cookies. The Christians bake them for Christmas and Easter, and the Jews for the joyous festival of Purim, which occurs in springtime. They call them *ba'ba' bil-tamur* (date-filled disks).

In Iraq, March 21 is a national holiday celebrating spring. The feast is called Norouz, and it is an essentially Kurdish festival, deeply rooted in the ancient Mesopotamian New Year spring celebrations. Typically, families would spend the day out in picnic areas enjoying huge pots of dolma.

The Muslim New Year, which occurs at the beginning of the lunar month of Muharram, is not

Date-filled cookies called Kleichat Tamur. Christians bake them for Christmas and Easter, and Jews bake them for the joyous festival of Purim, which occurs in springtime. (iStockPhoto)

celebrated by Iraqi Muslims the way Christians do the first day of January. Specifically, for Shiite Muslims, it begins a period of religious ceremonies that mourn the martyrdom of the Prophet's grandson al-Hussein, who was killed in battle on *'ashoura,* the 10th day of this month. For this occasion, wheat porridge called *hareesa* is cooked in huge cauldrons on wood fires set in the street. Pearled wheat is simmered with fatty lamb all night long, and neighbors take turns stirring and mashing it almost constantly until it looks like smooth, thin paste. Early in the morning it is distributed to the neighbors and offered to passersby, drizzled with sizzling hot clarified butter and liberally sprinkled with sugar and cinnamon.

Offering meals for the spirits of the deceased is customary. The family of the deceased Muslim offers evening banquets the first three days after the burial rites are concluded. The beverage offered on such occasions is sugarless Arabic coffee served in small cups. On happy occasions like weddings, guests are greeted with a sweet drink called *sherbet.* It is made by diluting syrupy condensed fruit juice (similar to cordial) with chilled water. As for the wedding feast itself, the centerpiece will typically be *qouzi,* a whole lamb stuffed with rice and roasted and served with different kinds of stew. Other elaborate dishes are also offered, mostly of the nawashif (dry) type, such as varieties of kubba, stuffed pastries (boureg and sanbousa), grilled meats, and so on.

When social gatherings were still strictly gender segregated, perhaps in the 1980s and earlier, women used to hold afternoon parties called *qaboul.* They would discard their *abayas* (black cloaks covering the body from head to feet) and have a good time, singing, belly dancing, cracking toasted watermelon and pumpkin seeds, and enjoying the dunking cookies ka'ak and bakhsam, along with kleicha and *khubz 'uroug* (traditional flat tannour bread with meat and vegetables).

Men sometimes get together to share alcoholic beverages, such as the indigenous *'arag* (distilled date wine) and beer. They are usually consumed with the familiar little *mezza* dishes of *tabboula* and hummus, or simmered dried fava beans (*bagilla*) and chickpeas (lablabi), along with some nawashif dishes like grilled meat. In springtime, a favorite mezza dish in northern Iraq outside the city of Mosul would be grilled sparrows (*'asafeer*). They were particularly popular in medieval drinking sessions, as they were believed to be an aphrodisiac.

Kleichat Tamur (Date-Filled Cookies)

Makes about 25 pieces

3 c all-purpose flour

1 tbsp sugar

½ tsp each of baking powder, cardamom, and ground aniseed

¼ tsp each of cinnamon, crushed nigella seeds, and salt

¾ c oil or melted butter

⅔ c water, room temperature

1 egg, slightly beaten, for glaze

Preheat oven to 400°F. In a big bowl, combine dry ingredients. Add the oil or butter, and rub mix between the fingers until it resembles breadcrumbs. Add water, and knead for about 5 minutes to form a pliable dough of medium consistency.

Take a piece of dough, the size of a walnut, and flatten it with fingers into a disk. Put a heaping teaspoon of date filling (recipe follows) in the middle, and gather the edges and seal well to prevent the date from showing. Put the stuffed piece into a wooden mold (available in Middle Eastern stores), press it in well, and tap it out. Repeat with the rest of dough. Arrange the cookies on a baking sheet, brush them with beaten egg, and bake them in a preheated oven until golden brown, 15 to 20 minutes.

Date Filling

2 c pitted dates

About ¼ c water

2 tbsp butter

½ tsp each cinnamon, cardamom, and coriander seed, all ground

¼ c toasted sesame seeds

1 tsp rose water or orange blossom water

Put dates, water, and butter in a heavy skillet. Cook over low heat, mashing with the back of a spoon, until the dates soften. Add the rest of the ingredients, and mix well. Allow to cool and use as directed.

Diet and Health

It is difficult to generalize about the diet and health of the Iraqi people today as the country has been going through trying times for at least 20 years. Years of economic embargo and military attacks have left most of the population, especially children, malnourished. These adverse circumstances are also believed to be the cause for an increase in diseases, especially cancer, and environmental pollution.

Under normal circumstances, however, the Iraqi diet is reasonably healthy and balanced, with more emphasis on vegetables than meat, which is indeed mostly dictated by economic constraints rather than health concerns. The majority of cooks have embraced vegetable oil and abandoned saturated animal fats, such as *dihin hurr* (clarified butter) and liyya (sheep's tail fat). Still, most of the traditional foods, collectively called nawashif, are fried, a vice Iraqis share with other Middle Eastern cooks.

Dessert is not served after a meal on a daily basis. People are more accustomed to having dates and melon, for instance, than rich pastries. The favorite beverage to drink after meals is black tea, which indeed has been acknowledged to possess healthy properties. But people usually prefer to have it very sweet. While this might offset the tea's benefits, it does, nonetheless, satisfy the sweet tooth of many.

During medieval times, the predominant dietary theory in the region was influenced by the classical doctrine of the four elements, that is, that the world, including food and the human body, is basically composed of fire, air, water, and earth, each of which possesses innate qualities. For instance, fire is hot and dry, while water is cold and moist. To maintain good health, the elements need to be kept in harmonious balance. Although this theory is now obsolete, remnants of its practices can still be recognized in the way Iraqis look at food. For instance, gourds are considered an ideal summer vegetable because they are cold. People with short tempers should not consume eggplant in excess because it is hot. Iraqis eat a lot of dates, and to balance their hot properties, they are usually served with cucumber or yogurt, both of which are cold.

Nawal Nasrallah

Further Reading

Bottéro, Jean. *The Oldest Cuisine in the World: Cooking in Mesopotamia*. Chicago: Chicago University Press, 2004.

Goldman, Rivka. *Mama Nazima's Jewish Iraqi Cuisine*. New York: Hippocrene Books, 2006.

Karim, Kay. Iraqi Family Cookbook. http://www.iraqifamilycookbook.com.

Karim, Kay. *Iraqi Family Cookbook: From Mosul to America*. Fall Church, VA: Spi, 2006.

Nasrallah, Nawal. *Annals of the Caliphs' Kitchens: Ibn Sayyar al-Warraq's Tenth-Century Baghdadi Cookbook*. Leiden: Brill, 2007.

Nasrallah, Nawal. *Delights from the Garden of Eden: A Cookbook and a History of the Iraqi Cuisine*. 2nd ed. London: Equinox Books, 2010.

Nasrallah, Nawal. Iraqi Cookbook. http://www.iraqicookbook.com.

Nasrallah, Nawal. "The Iraqi Cookie, *Kleicha*, and the Search for Identity." *Repast* 24, No. 4 (2008): 4–7.

Salloum, Habeeb. "Foods of Iraq: Enshrined with a Long History." 2006. http://www.thingsasian.com/stories-photos/3592.

Waines, David. *In a Caliph's Kitchen*. London: Riyad el-Rayyes Books, 1989.

Israel

Overview

The State of Israel, founded in 1948, is a Middle Eastern country located on the Mediterranean Sea. Lebanon and Syria form its northern border; Jordan is to the east and Egypt to the south. Israel is a democracy with slightly over seven million citizens. The vast majority are Jewish while approximately 20 percent are Arabs. Two languages are primarily spoken in Israel, Hebrew and Arabic, but a large portion of the population is fluent in English and/or Russian. Throughout the history of modern Israel, waves of Jewish immigrants have arrived from all over the world. From the 1990s on, close to a million Jews from the former Soviet Union have arrived in Israel. In smaller numbers, Jews from Ethiopia, Argentina, and France have also moved to Israel. Thus, Israel has become culturally and gastronomically a heterogeneous society as each group of immigrants have brought with them unique culinary traditions.

Israel is identified as the Jewish State, and therefore all its public institutions are required to follow the traditional Jewish dietary laws of *kashrus*. Kashrus, or "keeping kosher," involves compulsory rules for the slaughter of animals and food restrictions including avoiding pork products and shellfish and refraining from mixing dairy and meat products. Fifty-three percent of Israeli Jews identify themselves as keeping the ritual dietary laws. On certain holidays such as Passover, Jews abstain from eating leavened bread. Although the majority of Israelis are secular Jews, many still abide by some or all of the rules of kashrus. For example, it is not unusual for a family to keep a kosher kitchen but eat nonkosher meals outside the home. Nonkosher food is available throughout Israel in certain food chains, open-air markets, small delicatessens, and restaurants. However, all kosher restaurants are required to be closed on the Sabbath.

In general, the Israeli diet is rich in fresh fruits and vegetables, along with a variety of grains, bread, poultry, and milk products. These foods are readily available at reasonable prices. Certain items are under price control by the Ministry of Commerce and Trade in order to assure that everyone in Israel can afford to purchase white bread, flour, sugar, margarine, oil, eggs, and milk. Israelis have a wide variety of dietary practices based on income, ethnicity, education, and level of religious observance. Therefore, it is difficult to talk about the typical Israeli diet.

🍽 Food Culture Snapshot

Naomi and Dan Cohen can be found on late Thursday afternoon at the local supermarket doing their weekly shopping in a Tel Aviv suburb. Naomi is buying the favorite foods of her family (husband, two children, and a dog). Their typical cart is filled with two or three kinds of bread or rolls and a box of sweetened breakfast cereal along with milk and milk products such as flavored yogurt, yellow cheese, and a large variety of white cheeses. Vegetables and fruits take up considerable space in the cart. Most are fresh, although frozen and canned are available. It should be noted that consumption of fruits and vegetables is on the decline in Israel, as these are being replaced by convenience foods and snacks. At the meat counter, Dan chooses fresh chicken and turkey breast. A carton of eggs and packages of frozen fish fillets and chicken cutlets are also added to the cart. Other foods like pizza and hot dogs along with rice, noodles, and potatoes are part of the weekly shopping. Middle Eastern foods such as hummus spread and tahini sauce are eaten by the family regularly. If the family is planning a weekend picnic at a local park, the Cohens will buy prepared eggplant and cabbage salads along with kebabs, steaks, and pita bread. Snack foods are quite popular. The adults prefer roasted sunflower seeds, nuts, energy bars, and dried fruit, while the children choose potato chips, cookies, candies, and locally produced peanut doodles (bamba). Every week a case of mineral water and a case of soft drinks are also purchased. Next to the supermarket is a small store specializing in organic foods. Some of the Cohens' friends prefer this store or frequent local farmer's markets. However, the prices for organic foods tend to be high and choice is limited.

The Hatib family, Ibrahim and Suhad, live in an Arab town near the city of Hadera, a medium-sized city in central Israel. Although some of their shopping is done in a large supermarket, they tend to purchase much of their food from smaller shops in their town. Meat (chicken, turkey, and beef) is purchased from the family butcher, who is considered a trustworthy merchant. Spices and legumes are also bought in stores that cater to this sector of the population. Bread is bought fresh daily at a local bakery. Often, one of their children will go to a nearby restaurant to purchase hummus. Suhad is often busy preparing dishes at home and devotes significantly more of her time to cooking than her Jewish counterparts do. She often pickles olives, eggplants, cucumbers, and turnips for her family and purchases most of the family foods as basic ingredients rather than in prepared forms.

Major Foodstuffs

Israel is a modern developed country and produces almost 70 percent of its food requirements. Due to the global nature of the world food market, food is exported to Europe and America, and products from around the globe can be found in most Israeli supermarkets. Fruits and vegetables are locally grown and are available in season. In the winter,

common fruits are citrus, kiwi, apples, persimmons, quince, and bananas, and, in the summer, strawberries, peaches, apricots, mangoes, cherries, cantaloupe, watermelon, plums, figs, dates, and grapes are available. Vegetables are grown in greenhouses and are often available year-round. The tomato is probably the most popular vegetable, with cucumbers and peppers coming in close behind. Carrots, fennel, turnips, parsnips, eggplant, cabbage, zucchini, beets, yellow squash, onions, spinach, potatoes, broccoli, cauliflower, mushrooms, lettuce, radishes, artichokes, okra, and string beans are all found in the produce section. A new trend is purchasing fresh herbs, which are sold prewashed and packaged.

Although Israel is a small country, there is a large diversity of climates, soils, and weather. Consequently, agronomists have worked hard to develop methods to produce high yields of crops in desert soil and have used innovative technologies to grow grapes in saline water and melons and citrus in sandy soil. Israel is a leader in agricultural development, and on its markets' shelves new products can be found, such as peppers in virtually every color, red curled parsley, and pagoda cauliflower.

The dairy industry in Israel is well known for its production of a rich variety of yogurt and cheeses. Unlike in Europe, most of the cheeses are white cheeses similar to a curdless cottage cheese that can be spread on bread or crackers or put in salad. These cheeses range in fat content from 0 to 30 percent, with the most popular being 5 percent fat. Some of the cheeses are made with spices and vegetables for additional flavor. Yogurt is sold plain or with added fruits, candies, or granola, and new varieties and flavors are continually appearing on market shelves. Israelis also enjoy milk-based flavored puddings and creams.

Meat or poultry dishes are eaten daily, with chicken and turkey being the most popular. Surveys show that Israel consumes the highest amount of turkey per capita in the world. Unlike the typical 10-pound American turkey, Israeli turkeys are significantly larger and not sold whole. Turkey legs, breasts, necks, and wings are sold separately and used in foods ranging from cold cuts to shawarma (shaved turkey cooked on a skewer). Beef, lamb, and pork are all eaten but in smaller quantities. Commonly, beef is imported frozen from South America, while poultry, pork, and lamb are raised locally. Fish is also part of the Israeli diet and sold fresh, pickled, or frozen as fillets. Some fish are imported, and others are raised locally in both fresh- and saltwater ponds. Eggs are an important part of the Israeli diet. On average, Israelis consume one egg per day. Sources of fat include soy, canola, and olive oil along with margarine and butter. Common grains eaten in Israel are rice, corn, and wheat (bulgur, semolina, and pasta). Legumes are part of many traditional foods, but their popularity is decreasing. Chickpeas (hummus) and lentils (*majadara*— rice with lentils and onions) remain popular in both Jewish and Arab homes. Beans are consumed more in winter months and are eaten as part of the overnight cooked Sabbath stew (*cholent*). Israel has a well-developed soy-food industry, and imitation meat and milk products are very popular.

The most distinctive feature of the Israeli diet is diversity. It is impossible to characterize Israeli cuisine as a genuine entity as one might describe French food or Italian food. Within the Israeli diet, there are North African dishes, Asian dishes, South American foods, and Eastern European delicacies. There is also a strong Middle Eastern and American influence on locally eaten foods. The majority of Israelis are first- or second-generation immigrants, many of whom arrived as refuges; therefore, little attention has been given to the development of a hedonistic ethos of dining. Cooking and eating have served a functional role until more recently, when Israel has become more exposed to global culinary trends and fast foods. The younger generation of Israelis is well traveled and attempts to produce at home the exotic dishes consumed abroad. In addition, Israeli television broadcasts a multitude of cooking shows from around the world, and Internet access is widespread.

Israel has a hot climate, and it is important to consume sufficient amounts of liquids. Many Israelis drink large amounts of tap water, while others opt to purchase mineral water. This is available in small bottles or home coolers. Expensive filter systems are

Pizza being made at a Jewish restaurant in Israel. (iStockPhoto)

sold for personal and office use that dispense both hot and cold water. Common beverages include soft drinks, coffee, and tea. Coffee preferences range from a quick cup of instant to gourmet varieties of cappuccino and espresso. Beer, wine, *arak* (a clear spirit flavored with anise), vodka, mixed drinks, and cocktails are all consumed in Israel.

Cooking

Preparation of traditional foods is time-consuming and labor-intensive. As in most cultures, it was customary for women to prepare food for their families. Israel was founded on an egalitarian ethos and socialism. The early pioneers living on kibbutzim, socialist collective communities, strived for equality between men and women. Both genders were equally responsible for food preparation in collective dining halls. However, in more religious homes and in the Arab community, women retained the role of domestic cooks. Today, a large portion of the workforce is female, and less time is available for food preparation in the home. Consequently, microwaving is popular, and slow cooking is most often done, if at all, on the weekend, for the Sabbath meal and for religious holidays. Baking is rare, and ready-to-eat cakes and cookies are sold in bakeries and supermarkets. In some homes, a revival of home-baked bread can be found, often with the aid of bread machines.

Modern Israeli homes are outfitted with the latest cooking equipment, from microwave ovens to food processors and espresso machines. Expensive cookware from around the world is available in local stores. A wide variety of cooking methods are used in homes, including boiling, roasting, broiling, sautéing, stir-frying, and deep-frying. Israelis enjoy outdoor grilling, and on national holidays and weekends it is common to see families enjoying a cookout. As in the case of barbequing, men are most often the chefs on these occasions.

In the Arab community, home cooking is much more common. Regardless of their level of education and employment status, most women cook on a daily basis. Modern cooking devices are employed to save time and labor, but traditional foods are still eaten regularly. Local bakeries produce pita bread, which is bought fresh. Grilling and broiling are not commonly performed for cultural reasons. It is thought that serving a guest broiled meat is an insult, as it takes little effort to prepare and thus suggests that the guest was not worthy of being served foods that were specially prepared.

Typical Meals

Israel is ethnically and socially heterogeneous, yet there are some typical eating patterns and meals that have arisen over time. During the week most Israelis eat breakfast on the run. Readily available foods such as yogurt, breakfast cereals with milk, toast and white cheese, a slice of cake with coffee, or fruit often make up the first meal of the day.

Many have a 10 A.M. snack, in particular school-age children. This snack most frequently consists of a sandwich, fruits, yogurt, cookies, or pretzels. It also may be a fresh roll and chocolate milk sold in small plastic bags. In the Arab community, the traditional breakfast is no longer common, and many families eat breakfast cereals, flavored yogurts, or white bread with chocolate spread.

Lunch is the major meal of the day and usually contains a serving of protein-rich food. Most popular are chicken or fried breaded chicken cutlets (schnitzel), meatballs (chicken, turkey, or beef), fish (breaded and fried, baked, formed into fish cakes, or grilled), or soy meat (hot dogs, hamburgers, tofu). This is accompanied by two side dishes, one a carbohydrate and the other a cooked vegetable or salad. The carbohydrate is rice, potatoes, or pasta alongside a wide variety of seasonal vegetables. A dessert of fresh fruit or cake is also common. Schools in Israel do not have cafeterias, and most children return home for a midday hot meal. Others are served a hot meal by catering companies at afterschool programs. Adults also eat the main meal of the day during work hours, either in a company cafeteria or in small restaurants.

In Arab families, a hot meal is served at home upon return from work or school. Fewer women work outside the home in this community, and even if they are employed, they are still expected to prepare a home-cooked meal every day. Legume and rice dishes are more common, and traditional Middle Eastern foods are often served. However, more and more families are imitating the Jewish food practices and incorporating dishes such as fried breaded chicken cutlets (schnitzel), pizza, pasta dishes, casseroles, and vegetable soups into their meals. Commercial soup powder and ketchup are now used in most homes.

During the workweek, dinner is a lighter meal consisting of salads, sandwiches, eggs, hummus, pizza, grilled cheese, and milk products. This fits in well with the hot climate. On Friday night, the Jewish Sabbath, a special dinner is prepared (see the following).

Traditionally, Jewish families ate all meals together. This was an important aspect of daily life and helped to build strong connections among family members. In modern-day Israel, where much of the workforce is female and working hours are longer than in the past, there is less time for the luxury of family meals. Today, it is common to see latchkey children who return from school and are responsible for heating their own lunch. Although families do make an effort to eat dinner together, work schedules and afterschool activities often interfere. In Arab families the men traditionally ate separately from the women and children. Even today, in some homes, women eat with their children and serve their spouses a meal when they return from work.

Eating Out

Israelis eat out for many reasons. A growing portion of the workforce chooses to eat lunch either at work cafeterias, which are often subsidized, or at small restaurants that serve inexpensive, home-style meals. Eating out has also become a form of leisure activity, and many families dine out on a weekly basis. Special occasions are often celebrated in restaurants. Every variety of cuisine in all price ranges can be found: Chinese, Eastern European, Italian, Indian, American, Mexican, Argentinean, Romanian, Russian, Ethiopian, Thai, French, Japanese, Spanish, Brazilian, Turkish, Middle Eastern, and more. These restaurants are designed to capture the atmosphere of similar ethnic restaurants in other countries. Many of the dishes served have been modified to meet the local tastes, while others claim to provide authentic versions.

Fast food is also available on most street corners, and falafel stands compete with the large American chains. Pizza, hamburgers, tortillas, ice cream, fried chicken, frozen yogurt, pasta, crepes, and noodle dishes are all easy to find in most Israeli cities. In the last 15 years, there have been dramatic changes in the culinary scene. This has been fueled by an ever-increasing number of tourists and a growing number of middle-class Israelis who have been exposed to foods and restaurant culture around the world. A small number of gourmet restaurants with internationally trained chefs serve food that can compete with some of the best restaurants in the world.

Cafés are an institution in Israel. Israelis spend much of their time sitting in outdoor cafés, leisurely drinking coffee and eating light meals. The clientele includes professionals with their wireless computers, students, pensioners, businessmen, and, of course, the traditional coffee klatch. In the evenings one may find young couples on a date or groups of friends spending the evening together. On the weekend it is not uncommon to find families dining with their children. The café tends to be less expensive and more relaxed than other eateries. Cafés in Israel fulfill a similar function to the European pub.

Israeli breakfasts, served in hotels and many cafés, have a reputation for being unique. The most modest of these breakfasts consists of two eggs prepared to order, an Israeli salad, two or three varieties of cheese, tuna salad, freshly baked hot bread with butter, jam and honey, fruit juice, and coffee. This is often expanded to include a large buffet with several types of bread and rolls, numerous types of vegetable salads, fruits, smoked and pickled fish, breakfast cereals, and yogurts, alongside cakes and puddings. On Friday mornings (the Israeli weekend is Friday to Saturday) the cafés are filled with people enjoying a late Israeli breakfast. The meal is substantial enough to tide one over until the traditional Sabbath meal.

Israeli Salad

Ingredients

3 large tomatoes

3 cucumbers, unpeeled

3 scallions or 1 small red onion

1 green or red pepper

Parsley and *nana* (mint leaves), to your liking

Olive oil

Freshly squeezed lemon juice

Salt and pepper

Chop the vegetables. Before serving, add the herbs, olive oil, lemon juice, and spices to your liking. Serve with an omelet, fresh bread, olives, and cheese.

Shakshuka (Eggs with Tomatoes)

There are many variations on this recipe, but this is the basic dish.

Ingredients

1 large onion (not a red onion)

Olive oil

3–4 large ripe tomatoes or 5–6 plum tomatoes

1 red, green, or hot pepper, or a bit of each

A spoonful of fresh herbs to your liking (optional)

Salt, pepper, hot paprika (chili pepper is optional but go easy on it), and turmeric (optional)

2 eggs

Chop the onion, and fry it in olive oil until it turns translucent. Chop the tomatoes (you may want to peel them first), and add to the pan. Add herbs and spices. Cover, reduce the heat, and let cook until tomatoes are cooked but not as cooked as you would cook them when preparing a tomato sauce (15–20 minutes). Make two holes in the mix, crack eggs, and pour an egg into each hole. Cover and let cook until the eggs are firm (around 5 minutes).

Serve with fresh bread, pickles, and an Israeli salad.

Special Occasions

In the Jewish tradition, most holidays and celebrations are centered on food. Life-cycle events, births, bar or bat mitzvahs, and weddings are all accompanied by lavish amounts of food. Even in mourning, it is traditional to serve refreshments. There are no set menus for these events, and the food served reflects both the socioeconomic status and ethnic background of the family.

In most homes, a special Sabbath meal is prepared each week, and often the extended family and close friends gather to eat together. There are many ethnic and class-related variations on what is served; however, it is always different from what is served during the week. In many households this is the one day that is devoted to home-cooked meals. In religious or traditional families the meal will begin with the ritual blessings over the Sabbath bread (challah) and sweet red wine. This is followed by a serving of fish, either gefilte fish (ground carp in jelly) or *hriime* (a North African dish of fish in a spicy red sauce). Chicken or vegetable soup is served with soup almonds (*shkedei marak,* a kind of crouton made of flour and palm oil, sometimes called *mandlach* in the United States). The rest of the meal is usually a meat dish (often chicken) with side dishes and salads. Summer desserts are often fresh fruits, but compote (stewed fruits) and cake may also be served. Variations of the traditional Friday night dinner are common. Some families use this opportunity to prepare new recipes and entertain friends. In families where children return home for the weekend (soldiers, students, etc.), many mothers make an effort to prepare their favorite dishes.

There are long lists of Jewish holidays, each of which has its own traditional foods. For the most part, these foods are part of large festive meals with many servings. On the Jewish New Year it is traditional to eat apples, honey, and honey cake to symbolize the wish for a sweet and good year to come. Hanukkah is known for its fried potato pancakes and doughnuts, and on Passover unleavened bread (matzo) is served. New traditions have also emerged, and the Israeli state likes to mark its annual Independence Day with outdoor barbeques with kebab, skewered meats, hamburgers, and steak.

Latkes are one of the traditional foods of Hanukkah, the Jewish eight-day festival also known as the Festival of Lights. (iStockPhoto.com)

Diet and Health

Overall, Israelis enjoy good health, and over 50 percent defined their health state as "very good" in a national survey. The life expectancy for women and men is 82 and 78.5 years, respectively. This is among the highest in the world. These statistics are commonly attributed to the national health care program, in which every citizen is insured and has access to primary care doctors, inexpensive medications, and hospitals. However, many health care professionals feel that Israelis, on the whole, do not practice healthy lifestyles and that the next generation of Israelis will suffer from considerably more chronic diseases than their parents. The once-healthy Israeli diet is rapidly deteriorating and is mimicking other developed countries that consume high quantities of processed foods, simple sugars, and saturated fats. Women in the workforce have less time to prepare home-cooked meals, and the availability of prepared products and fast food plays a large part in these dietary changes. Obesity is on the rise, and a disproportionate number of older Arab women are overweight. Along with dietary changes, Israelis are less active than ever before. Most families have cars, and the use of computers and television viewing are common nationwide. Fewer and fewer individuals work in jobs that require manual labor, and despite two to three years of army service for most young adults, the lifestyle is quite sedentary. There is a trend to increase physical activity for all ages, and health clubs are popular. However, only a small percentage (~20%) of the population actually exercises regularly.

Overnutrition does not guarantee adequate nutrients. Iron-deficiency anemia is not uncommon in small children, teens, and female adults. Surprisingly, in sunny Israel, vitamin D deficiency has also been documented. This is most evident in sectors of the population that dress modestly, including religious populations, both Muslim and Jewish, and Ethiopian women with dark skin and modest dress. Despite the availability of a wide variety of dairy products, calcium intake in every sector of the population has been shown to be significantly lower than recommended daily intakes.

There is great interest in the connection between diet and health, and most newspapers and magazines have columns reporting the most recent findings in nutritional research. Alternative eating practices such as vegetarianism, vegan diets, and fruitarianism are popular. Diet books written by local authors, but also translations of fads from around the world (Atkins, Blood Type, South Beach, and Weight Watchers), can be found in bookstores or purchased on the Internet. In addition, yoga lessons, Pilates, and Feldenkrais lessons are offered in studios and community centers. However, there is a large gap between the population's knowledge and their practices. There are definite attempts to improve nutritional consumption at both individual and national levels. Organic foods are available, and a wide selection of new products has been marketed by the food industry: eggs with omega-3 fatty acids; low-fat cheeses and mayonnaise; reduced-calorie cookies, crackers, and cereals; soy hotdogs, hamburgers, and tofu; whole-grain breads; and dietetic ice cream. This reflects the population's awareness of the connection between diet and health, but purchase of these products is not sufficiently widespread. If supermarket shelf space reflects the consumption patterns of a community, soft drinks, candies, cookies, cakes, and salty snacks still fill a large proportion of market shelves. There are attempts by the Ministry of Health and the Ministry of Education to improve knowledge and attitudes regarding a healthy diet, but major changes still need to be made to improve the overall diet quality of the Israeli population.

Aliza Stark and Liora Gvion

Further Reading

Ansky, Sherry, and Nelly Sheffer. *The Food of Israel: Authentic Recipes from the Land of Milk and Honey.* Boston, MA: Periplus, 2000.

Gurr, Janna. *The Book of New Israeli Food: A Culinary Journey.* Tel Aviv, Israel: Al Hashulchan Gastronomic Media, 2007.

Gvion, Liora. *Culinary Bridges versus Culinary Barriers: Social and Political Aspects of Palestinian Cookery in Israel.* Jerusalem: Carmel, 2006.

Heine, Peter. *Food Culture in the Near East, Middle East, and North Africa.* Westport, CT: Greenwood Press, 2004.

Israeli Ministry of Health and Israel Center for Disease Control. *MABAT—First Israeli National Health and Nutrition Survey, 1999–2001.* Israel Center for Disease Control, publication 225. Tel Hashomer, Israel, 2004.

Kleinberg, Aviad, ed. *A Full Belly: Rethinking Food and Society in Israel.* [In Hebrew.] Tel Aviv, Israel: Keter, 2005.

Sirkis, Ruth. *Popular from Israel.* Tel-Aviv, Israel: Sirkis, 2004.

Jordan

Overview

The Hashemite Kingdom of Jordan is a young country that occupies a region with a tremendous amount of ancient history. Situated in the Middle East and bordered by Israel, Saudi Arabia, and Syria, Jordan was the location of several Bronze Age settlements, numerous Old Testament events, a number of Roman cities, and the remarkable "lost city" of Petra, once part of the huge Nabataean spice-trading network.

Most of the country was abandoned after the fall of the Roman Empire, left to small bands of wandering Bedouin herders. There was some habitation in the slightly more arable north, and a Crusader castle shows that more than just Ottoman Turks fought over the area. However, there was no urban center or area of greater population around which to build a state. Much of the interior, including Jordan's capital, Amman, was not inhabited from the time of the ancient Romans until the late 1870s, when Circassians—a Muslim group from the Caucasus Mountains—settled here after fleeing persecution in Russia. The Circassians introduced both wheeled carts and settled agriculture on previously uncultivated pastureland. They also engaged in commerce. Their success began to draw others to Jordan. This was the seed that would lead to the growth of the new country. Today, there are approximately 40,000 Circassians in the Amman area, but they are now a minority in a country whose population has grown explosively to more than six million.

The emergence of Jordan as a political entity began after World War I and the Arab Revolt against Turkish occupation. After the war, the Hashemite princes, believed by Muslims to be descendants of the prophet Muhammad, were given positions of authority in the newly liberated region, though under the protection of the British. King Faisal, who hoped to unite all Arab states into one, was declared king of Syria by the Syrians and was given authority over Iraq by the British. Abdullah, brother of King Faisal, was declared ruler of the region of Transjordan (so called because it was beyond the Jordan River). Abdullah made Amman his capital. By 1928, Transjordan had gained its independence, and after the Arab-Israeli War of 1948, having seized the West Bank, Abdullah declared himself king and renamed the country the Hashemite Kingdom of Jordan. Palestinians were outraged that Jordan kept control of the Palestinian land it had captured during the war, and in 1951, one angry Palestinian assassinated Abdullah. The throne, and the responsibility for establishing Jordan and its place in the world, passed to Abdullah's popular 17-year-old grandson, Hussein. King Hussein, supported by Britain and the United States, ruled Jordan until his death in 1999. He helped to stabilize the region and build a country that was the safest and most peaceful in the volatile Middle East.

At 34,277 square miles, Jordan is slightly smaller than Indiana. Its population is 98 percent Arab, with almost half of that number made up of recent Palestinian and Iraqi refugees. The population is approximately 92 percent Sunni Muslim, 6 percent Christian, and 2 percent "other." About 75 percent of the population is urban. Bedouin who retain their traditionally nomadic lifestyle make up close to 10 percent of the population. However, many Bedouin have been made to live in cities, and urban residents who trace their roots to the Bedouin make up more than one-third of Jordanians. The rest of the population lives in rural areas, where small villages perch on the edges of fields and orchards.

Most of Jordan is rocky desert, with a rainy season only in the west. Water is a rare and precious commodity. There is only a 16-mile shoreline, at Aqaba, where the country's hem brushes the Red Sea. Only 3.32 percent of the land is arable, and just under 3 percent of the population works in agriculture. The primary agricultural products are citrus, tomatoes, cucumbers, olives, sheep, poultry, stone fruits, strawberries, and dairy.

While there are Roman ruins at the center of the city, Amman is a clean, bright, modern city, in sharp contrast to the ancient capitals of surrounding countries. The dominant influences on both the culture and cuisine of Jordan are Syria, Lebanon, Palestine, and the traditional Bedouin who have so long wandered across this region. While those familiar with Middle Eastern food will recognize many of the dishes on offer in Jordan, there are still specialties that are particularly identified with the country.

Food Culture Snapshot

Maryam and Asef Bani Sakhr live in one of the older parts of Amman. The parents of both live in the same neighborhood, but their grandparents had not been city dwellers. On a typical day, Maryam was in the kitchen, watching her daughter, Nour, working with the yogurt. Nour was putting it to drain, to make *labneh*, the yogurt cheese that was a favorite breakfast item. Nour was now old enough to make it without Maryam's guidance, but Maryam still loved working alongside her daughter. Maryam poured bulgur into a

Grove of date palms in the Jordan River Valley. (Photo courtesy of Zev Radovan, Land of the Bible Picture Archive)

bowl and added water, to allow it to soak, and checked the chickens roasting in the oven. Her boys, Salah and Sameer, should be home with the groceries soon, and preparations for lunch would begin in earnest.

Maryam knew that an increasing number of Jordanian women actually left the home to do their own shopping, at least in the city. Women were even beginning to have jobs outside the home, but that was still not terribly common, especially among married women. For most families, the women did not go out unaccompanied. Maryam imagined that the world into which Nour was growing would be different. Nour even went to school. Most of the girls in the neighborhood did these days. However, the family remained traditional about Maryam going out alone, and that included for shopping.

In wealthy families, the women just sent the servants to the supermarket, Safeway. The prices were high there, but many foreign items were available. For most families, however, the husband and sons shopped locally or in the *souk*, or market, downtown. Almost everything Maryam needed could be purchased nearby. Every neighborhood had almost as many shops as residences. There was a bread baker pulling fresh bread out of his brick oven, a butcher with lamb and mutton hanging in the window, a chicken seller with cages of live chickens piled high, herb and spice shops, fruit vendors, nut and sesame seed sellers, tahini shops, milk and yogurt vendors, and more, plus there were little markets on almost every corner.

Maryam knew the boys might stop and talk to their friends, perhaps buying falafel at one of the many street vendors, especially as there were so many shops to visit. However, they could be relied on to remember everything. Asef had brought home lemons, zucchini, eggplant, okra, and fresh chickpeas last night from the souk, as well as chickens from the shop down the street. She had roasted the eggplant already, and the chickpeas had been cooked and pounded with tahini for the hummus they would enjoy this evening. She had coffee and cardamom, tea, and most of the spices she needed—cumin, coriander, garlic—plus rice, sesame seeds, yogurt, eggs, sugar, flour, clarified butter, and olive oil. However, the parsley, tomatoes, cucumber, sumac, parsley, mint, apricots, and maybe a watermelon would arrive with Salah and Sameer. Then they would not need to shop again for another week, except possibly for bread and some fresh produce.

Major Foodstuffs

Jordanian food is essentially an Arab cuisine, and it has much in common with other Middle Eastern countries, as well as Arab-dominated North Africa. Dishes such as baba ghannouj, falafel, hummus, and *bourek* (cheese-filled pastries) appear here as well as in most surrounding countries. Olives and olive oil are consumed at every meal. Eggplant, bulgur (also often called *burghul*), tomatoes, yogurt, mint tea, garlic, and unleavened bread are staples throughout the region. However, the influence of the nomadic Bedouin has contributed to the cuisine of Jordan, and among the country's Arab neighbors, Lebanon, Syria, and Palestine have had the strongest influence. Because of the Ottoman Empire, foods one often associates with Turkey and Greece have also spread throughout the region, including baklava and gyros-style meats (called *shawarma* in Jordan, where it is made as often with chicken as with lamb).

Because Jordan is a Muslim country, there is no pork. Most main-course dishes include chicken or lamb. Fish is available as well, though it is more common in the south, nearer the port of Aqaba, and goat is eaten on occasion, though most goats are kept for milk. Eggs, milk, yogurt, cheese, fava beans, and chickpeas are other important protein sources.

The bread one sees most often in Jordan, as throughout the Arab world, is the round, unleavened, pitalike loaves called *khoubiz* (also spelled *khobz*). One is served khoubiz in homes and in restaurants; it is found at neighborhood street-food vendors and fine hotels; and bakers everywhere can be seen piling it high in displays or on carts or trays. It is a little thicker than pita but is similar, including having the pocketlike quality that makes it ideal for making sandwiches with falafel or shawarma (or *shwarma*). The second kind of bread, seen somewhat less often, is Bedouin sheet bread, called *shrak* (also spelled *shirak*), which is about 13 inches in diameter and $1/4$-inch thick, and as soft and flexible as a child's blanket.

Tahini, a paste made from sesame seeds, appears at almost every meal, including breakfast, alone or incorporated into one of the many dishes for which it is a key ingredient, including the nearly ubiquitous pureed chickpea dip, hummus, and the smoky eggplant dip, baba ghannouj. Yogurt is another staple. It can be bought at the local market, but in more traditional homes, it is homemade, with mothers handing down recipes to their daughters. Yogurt is used plain and in sauces, or it is drained to create the creamy yogurt cheese called labneh.

Rice can be a bed for roasted meats, a pilaf, or part of the stuffing for cabbage rolls. Bulgur, or cracked wheat, is featured in many recipes, including the popular bulgur-and-parsley salad called tabbouleh. It is also a key ingredient in *kibbeh,* a tremendously popular dish that combines the bulgur with finely ground lamb, which, depending on the version of kibbeh being prepared, may be served raw (like steak tartare), baked, fried, stuffed, or in soup.

Coriander, cumin, cinnamon, and black pepper are common spices, but the most distinctive regional spice is sumac (also spelled *sumaq*). This is not the poison sumac of North America, though it is a distant relative. The spice is ground from the berry of a shrubby tree that grows wild in the Middle East. It has a deep rusty-red color and a tart, astringent taste that adds a pleasant sourness to dishes. In addition to being added to recipes or used to add a splash of color to an appetizer, sumac is a key ingredient in the spice mix *za'atar*. Za'atar is a flavorful blend of sumac, toasted sesame seeds, salt, thyme, oregano, and marjoram. Amounts of each ingredient may vary, and blends may appear red or green, depending on the proportion of sumac to herbs. Also, basil and/or savory may be included in the blend, as this can be very personalized. While it can be purchased commercially, za'atar is often blended at home. Two of the most popular applications are sprinkling za'atar on bread that has been spread with olive oil and sprinkling it on labneh. Even breakfast buffets in hotels will include a large bowl of za'atar for diners. The word *za'atar* can also refer simply to the herb thyme, but it far more often refers to the spice blend—and thyme is always a featured ingredient in any za'atar.

Flatleaf parsley is used so heavily that it actually constitutes a vegetable or salad green rather than a mere herb. It does sometimes appear as a garnish, but it is a major ingredient in such salads as *fatush* (a bread salad) and often dominates the bulgur in tabbouleh. Mint appears almost as commonly, in salads and other recipes, and is also almost always used in tea.

Fuul is the garlicky, lemon-scented, stewed fava bean dish that is Egypt's national breakfast, but it is most often found as an appetizer on lunch or dinner menus in Jordan. Lentils appear in soups, and chickpeas most commonly appear in hummus or in falafel, the fried veggie balls that are among the Middle East's most common snack foods.

Lebanese influence is most responsible for Jordan's splendid pastries. Delicate, layered, honey-drenched sweets and rich cookies laden with pistachios, walnuts, and/or sesame seeds line the shelves of pastry shops. Pastry is usually both baked and exhibited on a large, round baking tray called a *sanieh.*

Cooking

Modern homes are beginning to get modern conveniences, such as food processors, but few in Jordan are wealthy enough to have such appliances, and many simply do not believe they are as effective as traditional tools. The cornerstone of most traditional kitchens is a range of mortars and pestles: a large, heavy one, usually made of stone, for making kibbeh; and smaller ones of stone or brass for making hummus, baba ghannouj, and other purees and pastes. Generally, anything that will be put in the oven is cooked on a sanieh. Heavy pots and pans are used for thick soups and dishes containing yogurt.

Bedouin sheet bread is cooked on a *sorj,* which is a large metal dome that looks something like a shield or an inverted wok. It is put over a fire and the dough is stretched out over its surface. The bread cooks in only a few minutes. Skewers (for shish kebab, among other dishes) and grills are common everywhere, as are spits for roasting ranks of chickens or whole lambs.

In urban homes, cooking gas is used for cooking, but it is not piped in; individual tanks are delivered to homes. Gas company trucks cruise the neighborhoods each day, playing cheerful tunes to announce their presence, much as an ice cream truck would do. Water must be delivered as well. Jordan is among the most water-scarce nations on earth, so water is strictly rationed and must be conserved, because one must make the water last until the next delivery. Amman's recent rapid growth has further strained resources, and the government is looking for ways to ensure a regular water supply for all, regardless of economic status.

Typical Meals

Breakfast for most Jordanians comes after the dawn prayers that start the day throughout the Muslim world. Lunch is usually eaten around 2 P.M. and is frequently the biggest meal of the day. Dinner is generally eaten late, around 9 P.M. However, this schedule alters during the month of Ramadan, when Muslims are required to fast from sunrise to sunset; lunch is skipped, and dinner becomes the big meal of the day.

All meals include rounds of unleavened Arabic bread. Breakfast usually includes eggs (as omelets, hard-cooked, or baked with yogurt and garlic) and labneh, a soft, tangy yogurt cheese that is spread on the bread and often sprinkled with za'atar. The main meal will almost inevitably include hummus, soup, bread, yogurt, olives, salad, vegetables (cauliflower, eggplant, potatoes, okra, tomatoes, or cucumbers, or some mixture of these, often stuffed or with a sauce), a main course with rice and lamb or chicken, and fruit (apricots, apples, bananas, melons, and oranges are most common). However, depending on the occasion and whether there is company, lunch can expand to a lavish affair that spans hours. The hummus may be joined by a whole range of other *mezze,* or appetizers, including kibbeh, tabbouleh, bourek, spiced olives, beef sausage, fuul (cooked fava beans), stuffed grape leaves, baba ghannouj, and more. The mezze offerings are often so elaborate that this course seems like a feast on its own.

Generally, for meals, a covering is placed on the floor, and a large tray with the main course is placed in the center, surrounded by platters of bread and bowls of yogurt, salad, and whatever other dishes are being served. Often, the bread is the primary utensil for eating the food, torn in pieces, folded, and used as a scoop. Often, even at home, the genders do not mingle at meals. Men and older boys sit in a circle around one array of food, women and older girls sit in another circle, and, if the family is large, the youngest children, boys and girls, might be in yet another circle. This will usually occur even when there are guests. While seasonal fruit is the most common dessert, the presence of guests will usually find the meal ending with decadent pastries, either homemade or from one of the local pastry shops.

Nothing is wasted. Recipes abound for brain omelets, lamb-tongue salads, and stuffed tripe. Even day-old bread finds a second life in the flavorful, refreshing salad known as fatush. Fatush, a bread and vegetable salad, is identified most commonly as Jordanian/Palestinian or Lebanese/Jordanian. These countries are so close, and their populations are so intermingled, that many dishes don't change names or recipes as they cross borders. Because of differences in the types of unleavened bread available, especially for Jordanians living overseas, some recipes simply call for "local bread." Others will specify Arabic bread or pita. Any good unleavened flatbread will work.

Fatush (Flatbread Salad)

Serves 6

1 pita

1 heart of romaine lettuce, shredded

2–3 tomatoes, roughly chopped

1 cucumber, peeled and cut into ¼-in. chunks

3–4 scallions, white and light green parts, thinly sliced

1 sweet pepper, red or green, chopped

¼ c chopped parsley

¼ c chopped mint leaves

1 clove garlic

1 tsp salt

1 tbsp sumac

½ c lemon juice

½ c extra virgin olive oil

Freshly ground black pepper

Preheat oven to 400°F.

Cut the pita into approximately ¾-inch squares. Place on a baking sheet and toast in the oven until golden brown, about 8–10 minutes.

Put the lettuce, tomatoes, cucumber, scallions, sweet pepper, parsley, and mint in a bowl, and toss to combine.

Crush the garlic clove in a bowl with the salt and mix into a paste. Add the sumac and lemon juice, then whisk in the olive oil. Just before serving, add the toasted bread to the vegetables, pour the dressing over everything, and toss to combine. Chopped radishes or purslane are also common additions to this salad. Grind black pepper over to taste.

Za'atar and other typical breakfast items from Jordan. (iStockPhoto)

Eating Out

Wonderful, savory street food is found on almost every block of Jordan's cities. Most common among the offerings of the small food shops are falafel (balls of mashed chickpeas mixed with herbs and spices and deep-fried) and shawarma (slowly rotating pillars of spiced lamb or chicken, where the outside is shaved off as it roasts). Both of these are usually stuffed into pockets of khoubiz, that round, unleavened flatbread of the Arab countries. Shops selling roasted chickens are also close to ubiquitous.

Restaurants are increasing in number in rapidly modernizing Amman. However, even here, Islamic law generally keeps the sexes apart. Coffee shops and bars usually have all-male clienteles, though some foreign-run establishments (usually with obvious names like Irish Pub) welcome women. Still, women from traditional families would be unlikely to ever go to a bar. While an increasing number of restaurants in big cities, such as Amman, allow gender mingling, especially if the diners are foreigners, many eateries are for men only. Often, these restaurants will have a family room set aside for women and children.

There are a few American-style restaurants, mostly popular with homesick tourists, some excellent Mediterranean places, and a few good Asian restaurants, and most of the nicer hotels have restaurants that offer a range of "Continental" cuisine. Pizza, wraps, and smoothies are available for upscale Jordanians who are more familiar with Western culture, either through association or travel. However, even when dining out, most Jordanians are looking for traditional foods, though perhaps on a grander scale than is possible at home. The mezze spread can be fairly astonishing, and the national dish of Jordan, *mansaf* (lamb cooked in a dried yogurt sauce served on a big platter over flatbread and rice, and garnished with almonds and pine nuts), is eaten for all special occasions. It is the specialty of many restaurants offering traditional fare. One can even dine in a traditional "hair house," as the Bedouin call their camel-hair tents, in the courtyards of some popular restaurants. For a special occasion, this recalling of one's roots is a popular option. One does not sit on the ground in restaurants, as one does in homes, but low chairs surround low tables. As at home, myriad small dishes and platters are passed, and everyone dines from the huge trays in the center of the table.

Dining out, other than street food, even at relatively modest places, is generally the domain of the middle class or wealthy. Most Jordanians do not go to restaurants, or go rarely. However, as the middle and upper classes grow, this is changing. Some hip, high-end places not only allow women but also don't even require head coverings. At these places, the food may be European or fusion but is just as likely to be the same food found at more traditional spots. However, while some younger, better-educated Jordanian professionals are pursuing greater freedoms, Jordan is still a country where most women stay home until they're married and still often accept arranged marriages. So it seems likely that the restaurant scene will not change dramatically in the foreseeable future.

Special Occasions

Jordanians follow the Islamic calendar. Religious holidays include Ramadan, Eid al-Fitr (the end of Ramadan), Eid al-Adha (the Feast of the Sacrifice), Ras as-Sana (the Islamic New Year), the birthday of Muhammad, and Leilat al-Meiraj (the Ascension of Muhammad). National holidays include Arbor Day (January 15), Arab League Day (March 22), and Independence Day (May 25). Celebrations also surround engagements, weddings, and births.

Mansaf, the national dish of Jordan, is served for all important holidays and special occasions, as well as to honor the visit of a relative or guests. Of course, the usual mezze are served first, though more abundantly for a celebration, and strong, cardamom-scented coffee—the wine of the Arab world—will flow more generously. In some homes, real wine, or possibly *arak,* the strong anise-flavored spirit of the region—will be served, despite the fact that Islam forbids the drinking of alcohol.

Mansaf is a lavish feast dish that appears at special occasions everywhere, from Bedouin tents to high-end restaurants in Amman. This feast is taken seriously, with hours going into its preparation—and heated discussions often erupting over differences of opinion as to precisely how it should be made.

Mansaf

Many of the traditional ingredients in mansaf are not widely available outside of the Middle East. One key ingredient is *jameed,* a defatted sheep- or goat-milk yogurt that is formed into a ball, salted, and dried in the sun until rock hard. Then, when needed, it is soaked in water and heated, to reconstitute it. Mansaf is cooked in this reconstituted yogurt, which gives mansaf its distinctive, slightly gamy taste. Plain cow-milk yogurt cannot simply be substituted, as it curdles with long cooking. However, goat-milk yogurt is available at many ethnic grocery stores, and it will work in the recipe without curdling, or one can stabilize the cow-milk yogurt—directions follow the recipe. Also, liquid jameed can be found at some Middle Eastern stores.

Other essential ingredients, besides the jameed, include a spice mixture known as *baharāt* and the cooking fat called *samneh.* Bahārāt always includes black pepper, cinnamon, and allspice but may also include cardamom, nutmeg, coriander, or cumin. In the United States, it can be found premixed in many Middle Eastern markets, but in this recipe, the individual spices are used. Samneh is clarified goat- or sheep-milk butter, but any clarified butter, including Indian ghee, can be used.

Normally, an entire sheep is cooked, and the boiled head is prominently displayed in the middle of the mound of food. The recipe has been revised for a more reasonable, and headless, amount of lamb. For the presentation, Bedouin sheet bread is mounded on a large tray, rice is piled on top, the lamb is piled on the rice, the yogurt sauce is poured over everything, and then the dish is sprinkled with pine nuts. Almonds may also be sprinkled on the dish.

Mansaf is traditionally eaten in the Bedouin style, from a large, communal platter, with people sitting or standing around the mansaf, with the left hand behind the back, using the right hand instead of utensils. A piece of lamb is pulled off the bone (it is cooked until it is falling apart, so this is easy), and then a bit of rice, bread, and some of the yogurt sauce are gathered around it. This is rolled into a ball and popped into the mouth, without having the fingers touch the mouth. This is traditional good manners but also a good health tip when everyone is eating from the same platter. In restaurants serving mansaf, chairs are more usual, rather than sitting on the ground, and forks are available, as well as individual plates, for diners (usually foreign guests) not accustomed to Bedouin dining.

Mansaf

Serves 6

3 lb lamb shoulder on the bone, cut into 6 similarly sized pieces

Water

1 tsp salt

¼ c clarified butter

¼ c pine nuts

1 large onion, coarsely chopped

1½ tsp ground turmeric

½ tsp freshly ground black pepper

½ tsp ground allspice

½ tsp ground cinnamon

1 batch stabilized yogurt (see following)

3 c cooked, buttered rice

2 sheets Bedouin bread or 3 pitas, split

Additional salt and pepper, as needed

Place the lamb in a large pot and cover with cold water. Bring slowly to a boil, skimming as needed. When no more scum is forming and the water is boiling, add 1 teaspoon salt, or to taste. Cover, reduce heat, and let simmer for 30 minutes.

In a frying pan, heat the clarified butter. Add the pine nuts and fry, stirring frequently, until golden brown. Remove the nuts with a slotted spoon, leaving the butter in the pan. Set nuts aside. In the remaining butter, fry the onion until it is transparent. Stir in the turmeric, pepper, allspice, and cinnamon, and cook for an additional 2 minutes.

Add the onion and spice mixture to the lamb in the pot, and let the lamb continue to simmer, covered, for another hour. Then remove the lid and let the liquid reduce until it half-covers the lamb.

When the liquid has reduced sufficiently, add the stabilized yogurt (or goat yogurt, if you've found it), shaking the pan to blend the yogurt evenly into the liquid. Let the lamb simmer gently on low heat until the lamb is tender and the sauce thickens, about another 30 minutes. If the sauce does need to be stirred, do so gently and in one direction, to avoid breaking up the lamb. Add salt and pepper to taste.

To serve, line a large platter with the bread, mound the rice on top of the bread, and put the lamb on top of the rice. Pour the sauce over the lamb and rice, and sprinkle the fried pine nuts over the whole dish.

To stabilize cow-milk yogurt: Put 2 cups plain, full-fat yogurt in a heavy saucepan. Beat with a fork until smooth. Beat an egg white until frothy, then beat it, along with 2 teaspoons cornstarch and ½ teaspoon salt, into the yogurt. Put the saucepan over high heat. Stir with a wooden spoon as it heats, stirring in only one direction. Stir constantly until it starts to bubble. Reduce the heat to medium, and let it boil for about 3–5 minutes, or until thick. It is then ready to use in the mansaf.

Diet and Health

Before Jordan was a country, many people in the region were poorly nourished, unless they had herds or farms, but this was due to poverty and the scarcity of food, rather than flaws in the food traditions.

As the country grew and food was more widely distributed, whether through aid, as at the beginning, or later, as the economy improved, the traditional diet was essentially wholesome, with a good balance of meat, dairy, vegetables, legumes, nuts, and fruit. Also, like other Mediterranean countries, Jordan relies heavily on olive oil in its cuisine. With increased urbanization, sugar consumption increased, which had its biggest impact on dental health. A bigger concern for most health organizations was the long-standing cultural encouragement of smoking. Even today, approximately 62 percent of males smoke, though fewer than 10 percent of females smoke.

As with many countries, nutrition has declined with increased education, urbanization, and modernization, especially among the young. While fast food and soft drinks are not often consumed by adults or those in rural areas, they have been adopted by students in cities. In the past, the consumption of sweets was at least partially offset by a high consumption of dairy products, but with soft drinks increasingly replacing milk, health is suffering. Students who focus on fast food, modern snacks, and soft drinks are rarely getting enough vegetables and meat. Health organizations are making an effort to get nutrition programs into schools to help stop the deterioration of health.

Cynthia Clampitt

Further Reading

Abu-Jaber, Diana. *The Language of Baklava: A Memoir.* New York: Pantheon Books, 2005.

Bsisu, May S. *The Arab Table: Recipes and Culinary Traditions.* New York: William Morrow, 2005.

Heine, Peter. *Food Culture in the Near East, Middle East, and North Africa.* Westport, CT: Greenwood Press, 2004.

Jaimoukha, Amjad. "Circassians in Jordan." Circassian World. http://www.circassianworld.com/Circassians_in_Jordan.html.

Mallos, Tess. *The Complete Middle East Cookbook.* Boston: Charles E. Tuttle, 1995.

"Meeting the People of Jordan: General Rules and Etiquette." Jordan Jubilee. http://www.jordanjubilee.com/meetfolk/behavior.htm.

Robins, Philip. *A History of Jordan.* Cambridge: Cambridge University Press, 2004

Lebanon

Overview

Lebanon is bordered by Israel on the south, Syria on the north and east, and the Mediterranean Sea on the west. It consists of a relatively narrow coastal plain, the Lebanon mountain chain just inland, and the Bekaa Valley between the Lebanon and the Anti-Lebanon mountains, which form the Syrian border. It has a Mediterranean climate of mild summers, with rain concentrated in the winter months. Because of its mountains, Lebanon receives sufficient rainfall that three-quarters of its cropland needs no irrigation. The largest river is the Litani, which flows through the Bekaa Valley and enters the Mediterranean between the southern cities of Tyre and Sidon. A quarter of the country's land is agricultural, and the only foodstuffs Lebanon imports in any quantity are meat and dairy products from Syria. Despite its agricultural productivity, the population of 3.8 million is 87 percent urban.

The mountains have also influenced the country's religious makeup. After Sunnite Islam became the majority religion of the Middle East in the 11th century, Christians and other religious dissidents retreated to mountainous areas. The Lebanon Mountains are home to the largest Christian population in the Arab world (mostly Maronite Catholics but also Orthodox and other eastern Christian denominations) and to many Druze, members of an offshoot of Shiite Islam. The base population of the Bekaa is Shiites, locally called *mitwalli,* while Beirut is dominated by Sunnites. This uncomfortable diversity of faiths has contributed to a number of conflicts in Lebanon's history, notably the disastrous civil war of 1975–1990.

Food Culture Snapshot

Maroun and Afifa Nader and their daughter, Brigitte, live in a new apartment house in Kesrouan, a busy and prosperous area east of Beirut that has exploded into suburbs since the 1970s. Maroun works at a design firm; Afifa supplements the family income with a small Internet business trading in traditional craft jewelry. They are representative of the professional class. As Maronites, the most Europeanized segment of the population, they have a cosmopolitan lifestyle, but they often visit Maroun's relatives in the mountains and bring home village specialties such as the paper-thin bread *marqouq* and various gathered foods, including hawthorn (*za'rur*) and wood sorrel (*khubbaizi*). Afifa does not visit her family's ancestral village, which they left because of bitter fighting during the civil war.

The war devastated Beirut's market quarter. As a result, Beirut is the only sizable Arab city without a traditional *souk,* or marketplace, and Beirutis now shop in American-style supermarkets. The Naders live conveniently close to one of the largest, which uses as its symbol a giant shopping cart 40 feet high. It stocks the usual Mediterranean produce—tomatoes, eggplant, zucchini, potatoes, spinach, chard, olives, citrus fruits, grapes, apples—and a few items more typical of the Arab world: grape leaves for stuffing, fresh chickpeas in season, and a grain delicacy known as *friki,* which is unripe wheat grains scorched to give them a smoky flavor.

This market also has a fish department, a butcher shop (mostly lamb and chicken, with some beef and goat meat), a dairy section, and a wide selection of imported goods such as wines and cheeses. It also stocks Lebanese wines from the Bekaa. It sells frozen foods and an extensive selection of ready-to-eat dishes. When she's in a hurry, Afifa can pick up a carton of chard and lentil soup and another of lamb and okra stew, leaving nothing to make for her family's dinner but rice and salad.

Outside Beirut, people still shop in traditional souks, where the choices are more limited but prices are commensurately lower. Rural people eat less meat, getting a higher proportion of their protein from dairy products and pulses, consumed as bean soups and porridges.

Major Foodstuffs

The favorite meats are lamb and chicken. Beef is available to a limited degree, and so are pork products in Christian districts. Wheat and rice are the chief grains. Pita bread (called simply *khubz,* "bread") is eaten at most meals, even when rice is served. Wheat is also consumed as *burghul* (bulgur): Wheat grains are boiled until the starch gelatinizes and are then dried and crushed, making a product that can be made ready to eat simply by boiling or even soaking in water. Bulgur soaked in yogurt and then sun-dried makes *kishk,* a sort of instant soup mix with a tart, slightly musty flavor. Wheat is also used in sweet and savory pastries.

The leading cooking fats are olive oil, vegetable oil, and butter. Lamb fat, from fat-tailed sheep (which have been bred to deposit their body fat in their tails), plays a minor role; bits of tail fat are often threaded between the chunks of meat in shish kebab, and a little tail fat is traditionally added to the butter in baklava to give a subtle gamy tang.

Milk is rarely consumed fresh (except as ice cream). Mostly it's soured into yogurt (*laban*) or processed further by straining the yogurt to make the even more noticeably tart *labni,* which has the consistency of a soft cheese. Both keep quite well in the warm climate. Fresh milk is also curdled to make cheese, mostly consumed fresh as *jibneh baida* (white cheese) or preserved in brine, but a cheese called *musanara* is made from a boiled curd, like mozzarella or string cheese. Some cheeses are flavored with spices such as *mahleb* (ground cherry pits).

Butter is nearly always clarified of its solids and whey to make pure butterfat (*samni*), mostly used in making sweets. A product called *qaymaq* is made by simmering whole milk so that a skin of rich cream forms on the surface, being removed as it forms to make a very rich product comparable to English clotted cream—it can be eaten by itself or used as a filling for pastries. Other dairy products include *shanklish,* which is dried balls of yogurt cultured to produce an aged-cheese flavor, and *ayran,* a tart drink made by diluting yogurt with water.

While the civil war was destroying the old souk and paving the way for supermarkets and convenience foods, it had the ironic side effect of reviving some traditional homemade foods, because people often had to rely on themselves during the war. Today, Lebanese food lovers patronize shops that specialize in once-endangered foods such as *qawirma* (fried lamb preserved in jars under a layer of lamb fat) and homemade pickles, preserves, and cheeses.

The eastern Mediterranean is not particularly rich in fish, but Lebanon does have a fishing industry and a repertoire of fish dishes. Fish is most often fried in olive oil and eaten with rice and a squeeze of lemon, accompanied by rice and a salad, or as *sayyadiyyi,* the dish of fish, fried onions, and rice prepared throughout the Arab Mediterranean, but there are also fish kebabs, stews, and casseroles, even fish *kibbi* (fish pounded to a paste with bulgur wheat).

Grape leaves stuffed with rice, a common Lebanese dish. (Shutterstock)

Samak bi-Tahini (Fish in Tahini Sauce)

Serves 4

This is a rich special-occasion dish using the sesame paste tahini, which also flavors dips such as *hummus bi-tahini* and baba ghannouj, the smoky eggplant dip. Traditionally it's made with a whole fish, but these days some cooks use fish fillets instead to avoid having to pick through a lot of fish bones. It's served at room temperature.

Note: For frying, Lebanese cooks don't cut onions crosswise into rings. They make cuts from the top of the onion nearly to the bottom to produce narrow wedges about ¼ inch at the widest. These separate into lengths known as "wings" (*ajniha*).

1 fish (about 2–2½ lb)

Salt

4 tbsp olive oil

2 onions

1 clove garlic, crushed

1½ c tahini

¾ c lemon juice

Water

½ tsp cumin

Clean the fish and rub inside and out with about 1 tablespoon salt. Refrigerate for at least 2 hours to firm up the flesh.

Rinse the fish and pat dry with paper towels. Spread 2 tablespoons olive oil in a baking dish, place the fish in it, and bake at 350°F until the flesh flakes when poked with a fork, about 20 minutes. Remove the baking dish from the oven.

Meanwhile, cut the onion lengthwise into "wings" and fry in 2 tablespoons oil until just starting to turn golden. Remove and set on paper towels to absorb oil.

Place the garlic and the tahini in a bowl, and add the lemon juice and ¼ cup water. Stir, adding more water as needed, until it has the consistency of thick cream. Stir in the cumin, ½ teaspoon salt, and the

fried onions. Pour this sauce over the fish and return to the oven until the sauce is thickened and bubbling, 20–25 minutes.

Remove from the oven and allow to cool to room temperature.

Cooking

City people use gas or electric ranges, though villagers may still cook on a wood-fired range made of brick or stone. The cooking utensils of a Lebanese kitchen are much the same as in Europe, with one notable exception: the *siniyya*. This is a round baking pan about 16 inches in diameter with sides about an inch high. It's used for baking baklava-type pastries, a sort of flat meatloaf called *kibbi bi-siniyya,* and certain stews, such as *masbahet al-darwish* ("the beggar's rosary"), made with summer vegetables and tomatoes.

The siniyya owes its existence to the fact that traditional kitchens did not have ovens, so dishes to be baked were sent to the village bakery to cook after the day's bread baking was over. Its flat shape made it possible to fit a number of these pans into a brick oven at the same time. In villages it's common to see children balancing siniyyas on their heads on the way to the local bakery; it was not uncommon even 30 or 40 years ago in Beirut. These days city people more often use the siniyya in the oven of a home range. By its nature, cooking in a siniyya exposes a large amount of the food's surface to heated air, so stews baked in one develop a special flavor because of evaporation and browning.

Traditional kitchens have a large marble mortar (*jorn*) and a pestle (*mdaqqa*) about the size of a baseball bat, which are used for making kibbi, a versatile paste of meat, bulgur, and onions. In the Bekaa Valley, the mortar is replaced by a flat grinding stone (*rahaya*). Making kibbi with either utensil is a laborious process requiring an hour or more. Many people own a food processor, which reduces the process to a matter of minutes.

One notable feature of Lebanese food is the heavy use of lemon juice and olive oil. Fish and even eggs are fried in olive oil; the most usual salad dressing is lemon juice and olive oil (often with the addition of mint). Since medieval times, olive oil has been a particular feature of Christian fast-day dishes, such as vegetables slowly stewed in oil. Grape leaves (*waraq 'inab mahshi*) may be stuffed with meat, but the vegetarian version, stuffed with rice and tomatoes, is served cold with olive oil.

Mjaddara (Pockmarked Rice and Lentils)

Serve 4–6 as a main dish with salad or 10–15 as a dip
This filling vegetarian dish is often eaten by Christians on fast days, but it belongs to the general repertoire of Arab cooking. In fact, it is recorded in several 13th-century cookbooks. The name means "pockmarked," because of the grains of rice among the lentils. The addition of onions well browned in flavorful olive oil makes the dull-sounding combination of rice and lentils very attractive.

1 c lentils

7¼ c water plus more for washing the lentils

2 onions

¾ c olive oil

½ c rice

½ tsp allspice

½ tsp cinnamon

Salt

Wash the lentils by putting them in a bowl and covering them with water. Remove any floating debris and any stones or other extraneous matter. Drain. Put 6 cups of water in a 2-quart saucepan, bring to a boil, add the lentils, and cook until soft, about 35 minutes.

Meanwhile, peel the onions and slice into "wings." Put the olive oil into a pan and fry the onions over medium heat, stirring often, until distinctly brown (but do not let them burn). Drain onions on paper towels.

When the lentils are done, drain them and set aside. Put 1¼ cup water in the saucepan, bring to a boil, throw in the rice, allspice, and cinnamon, reduce the heat, and cook over low heat, covered, for 10 minutes. Stir in the lentils and add salt to taste. Stir in the fried onions and oil, and cook uncovered over medium-low heat for another 10 minutes.

Typical Meals

A usual breakfast for city people would be flatbread (plain or perhaps topped with *zaatar,* a mixture of wild thyme, sesame seeds, and tart ground sumac berries) and white cheese along with a handful of olives. Croissants, an imported soft cheese, and the rather syrupy local fruit preserves (*mrabba*) are typical. Turkish coffee is usually served with breakfast. Farmers often start the day with a hearty soup of kishk and qawirma fried with a good deal of garlic.

Lunch for city people is often a hasty kebab or falafel sandwich, but on more leisurely occasions a lamb and vegetable stew or kibbi baked in the siniyya might be served, or just a spread of the appetizer dishes known as *mezzeh,* such as hummus, falafel, tabbouleh, stuffed grape leaves, lebni (a kind of yogurt cheese), and pickled turnip spears. Mezzeh also appear at picnics and feature at afternoon parties.

A typical dinner might be lentil soup, followed by lamb stewed with a vegetable, accompanied by plain pilaf (*rizz mfalfal*) or pilaf garnished with toasted vermicelli (*rizz bi-sha'riyyi*). Tomato and cucumber salad is likely to appear on the side. Rural people eat the same sort of dinner so far as their budgets allow. Urbanites sometimes cook international recipes (mostly French, Italian, Iranian, and Indian) from their favorite cooking magazines. The traditional beverages are water, ayran, or (among Christians) '*araq,* an anise-flavored liqueur, but some people prefer wine. Coffee and fresh fruit end the meal. The famous Middle Eastern pastries are not usually served with a meal but consumed as snacks during the day.

Two features of Lebanese food survive from medieval cookery, though in an altered form. In the Middle Ages, most Arab stews contained a sour fruit juice, such as lemon, pomegranate, or even rhubarb juice, and all were flavored with complex spice mixtures. Both practices are still known, but all fruit juices except lemon have been replaced by tomato juice, and allspice, or a mixture of allspice and cinnamon, usually substitutes for the old spice mixtures. Other spices such as cumin, coriander, and saffron, when used, usually appear alone rather than mixed with other spices. On the table, salt and allspice appear instead of salt and pepper.

Kibbi is one of the most versatile Lebanese foods. The meat, bulgur, and onion paste can be rolled into meatballs and grilled on a skewer, baked in a siniyya with a filling of fried onions and lamb fat, made into tangerine-sized, torpedo-shaped meatballs with the same filling and then deep-fried, or made into meat-stuffed flying-saucer disks and grilled or fried. It can even be served raw, and often is at important dinners, because raw kibbi can be made only from the best-quality lamb.

Lebanon is a small country, but it does have regional specialties. The Sunnite grandees of Beirut were known for their fine food (a nearby village, Dfoun, traditionally provided their cooks), and the best hummus, falafel, and tabbouleh are still considered to come from Beirut. A specialty of the mountains is *fattoush,* a salad of tomatoes, cucumbers, purslane, and crisp croutons made by toasting pita

Fattoush, a traditional Lebanese salad made with tomatoes, cucumbers, purslane, and crisp croutons made by toasting pita bread. (Edward Karaa | Dreamstime.com)

bread. The mountain village of Ehden has a specialty of raw kibbi made with goat meat. Fish kibbi is a dish of the northern coastal region, and the northern city of Trablus is known for making elegant, miniaturized versions of baklava and other pastries.

Eating Out

The end of the civil war led to an explosion of restaurants in Lebanon, and today it has restaurants serving a wide variety of Asian and European cuisines. Still, most public eateries serve traditional roast meat dishes such as shish kebab (*lahm mishwi*) and *shawerma* (thin-sliced meat arranged on a vertical spit; browned portions are sliced off for serving as they are done). The meat may come with rizz bi-sha'riyyi, turnip pickles, and a tomato-cucumber salad, or it may be sold in pita bread with garlicky tahini sauce. These places also offer dips such as hummus bi-tahini and baba ghannouj and various salads. One new development after the civil war was a sort of restaurant/dance club called *taksh-wa-faksh,* where people eat the usual mezzeh snacks and then dance to disco music, on the tabletops if there's no dance floor.

Lebanon has a famous restaurant village, Zahle, located in a shady gorge at the western edge of the Bekaa Valley. Open-air restaurants extend out along a little creek for about a quarter of a mile up the gorge. They specialize in mezzeh and above all in roast chicken, which is served with a strong garlic sauce.

As everywhere in the Arab world, coffeehouses are a male preserve. They serve much the same function that bars do in Europe or America: as a place for male socializing. They serve Turkish coffee and a variety of pastries. More westernized men of the more affluent classes, however, are likely to patronize modern (and sexually integrated) espresso shops instead.

Special Occasions

The chief religious celebrations of the Muslim majority are Eid al-Adha (the Feast of the Sacrifice), which falls on the last day of the pilgrimage to Mecca, and Eid al-Fitr (the Feast of the Fast Breaking) at the end of the month of Ramadan. Eid al-Adha is the day when Muslims around the world, as well as those on the pilgrimage, sacrifice sheep (or other animals) in remembrance of Abraham's faithful willingness to sacrifice his son at the command of God, who allowed him to sacrifice a sheep in his place. It is a festive time of year when people dine and make sociable visits to family and friends.

Some Muslims do slaughter their own sheep for the occasion, but most arrange with a butcher shop for meat. Those who can afford to buy meat are expected to distribute some of it to families who can't. Naturally, Eid al-Adha spotlights meat dishes. Because the Islamic calendar is based entirely on the phases of the moon, Eid al-Adha can fall at any time of year, so on the whole the dishes served are the usual dishes of the season, rather than dishes unique to the Eid.

One of the principal religious obligations of Islam is abstaining from food and drink during the daylight hours of the month of Ramadan. From sunset to sunrise, in contrast, the faithful are permitted to eat and drink whatever they wish. They tend to avoid salty foods, which would make them thirstier during the following day. At the end of Ramadan, Eid al-Fitr is a day of feasting and socializing. In distinction from Eid al-Adha, it emphasizes pastries and other sweets, rather than meat dishes.

The Shiites observe Ashura, the 10th day of the month of Muharram, with bitter mourning for the seventh-century martyrdom of the imam Husain ibn Ali. *Ashura* is also the name of a dish associated with this day; it consists of boiled whole wheat enriched with raisins and nuts. Grains and other seeds symbolize rebirth and/or the afterlife, and a similar dish is prepared by Christians at Easter and the feast of St. Barbara. Christians abstain from meat on Fridays, during Lent, and on other days of abstinence. They have a repertoire of meatless dishes such as fish or lentil kibbi.

Happy occasions such as weddings and births are celebrated with sweet foods—puddings and pastries. By the same token, sweet foods are considered inappropriate at sad occasions. After a funeral, guests are always poured bitter coffee.

Diet and Health

The Lebanese diet is rich in fresh fruits and vegetables, so vitamin deficiency is not a serious problem. In particular, it uses lemon juice more abundantly than most cuisines. It also provides other healthful ingredients such as fish, nuts (which figure in the fillings of both pastries and stuffed vegetables), yogurt, and garlic.

Because of the availability of fish and olive oil, the Lebanese diet is lower in saturated fats and higher in omega-3 oils than that of some of its neighbors. However, although the Lebanese diet is the classic Mediterranean diet in many ways, sedentary city people tend to consume large amounts of sugar, butter, and refined wheat. Men who socialize in coffeehouses are at particular risk, because nothing but pastries is regularly served there, posing the danger of diabetes and cardiovascular problems. Many Lebanese are aware of these problems and explore health-food options.

Traditional medicinal concepts were derived from ancient Greek and Persian medicine and analyzed most complaints as due to an imbalance of the bodily humors. Medical treatments aimed to correct this supposed imbalance. All foods were held to have medicinal qualities, so medieval doctors often prescribed particular dishes—they even gave recipes, which cookbook writers eagerly plagiarized. These theories no longer exert much influence on diet, if any. Lebanon was the first Arab country to have modern medical schools, and it uses up-to-date pharmaceuticals and techniques. Folk remedies survive, however. Tea and yogurt are often recommended to those suffering from diarrhea, and mothers brew bitter medicinal teas for sick children.

Charles Perry

Further Reading

Batal, Malek. "Wild Edible Plants: Promoting Dietary Diversity in Poor Communities in Lebanon." http://www.wildedibleplants.org/

Heine, Peter. *Food Culture in the Near East, Middle East, and North Africa*. Westport, CT: Greenwood Press, 2004.

Helou, Anissa. *Lebanese Cuisine*. New York: St. Martin's Griffin, 1998.

Khayat, Marie, and Margaret Keatinge. *Lebanon, Land of the Cedars*. Beirut, Lebanon: Khayats, 1960.

Malouf, Greg, Lucy Malouf, Anthony Bourdain, and Matt Harvey. *Saha: Chefs Journey through Lebanon*. Berkeley, CA: Periplus, 2007.

Palestinian Territories

Overview

Palestine occupies the area between the eastern shore of the Mediterranean and the Jordan River and includes the Palestinian territories of the West Bank, the Gaza Strip, and East Jerusalem—though East Jerusalem is under full Israeli jurisdiction. The West Bank is inhabited by some 2.46 million Palestinians, the Gaza Strip by approximately 1.55 million. Palestine occupies, in total, only 4,163 square miles (6,700 square kilometers) of territory. Palestine has several distinctive languages, ethnicities, cultures, and cuisines.

Palestinians follow many religious traditions, but the main demographic, 98 percent, is Sunni Muslim. A significant minority is Christian—2.6 percent—with even smaller groups such as Druze and Samaritans. Cultural displacement means that many of the original Bedouin population of Palestine have transmigrated to Israel, Egypt, and Jordan. The current number of Bedouin accounts for 0.5 percent of the population, an Armenian community makes up 0.1 percent, and a Jerusalem-based Indo-Aryan Dom community (Gypsies) less than 0.1 percent. Palestinians represent a highly homogenized community who share one cultural and ethnic identity: South Levantine Arabic.

The output of the Palestinian economy is almost exclusively agricultural; there is some minor expansion in small-scale industry, but unemployment is widespread. Fifty-seven percent of the population lives below the poverty line.

The upsurge in the consumption of processed food as a result of westernization and altered work patterns has meant a move beyond the home and the basis of fresh fruits and vegetables that underlay the Palestinian diet. As yet, none of the organizations working in this area has conducted comprehensive surveys of the impact of the geographic, socioeconomic, or political situation on the Palestinian diet. According to a 2007 "Food Security and Vulnerability Assessment" study by the World Food Program, 34 percent of Palestinians could not afford a balanced meal. In 2009 the United Nations World Food Program began a food voucher system to help 30,000 people in urban areas of the West Bank. This was a response to the nearly 70 percent increase in the price of basic food commodities such as oil and milk. A similar smaller-scale project is planned for the Gaza Strip. Such voucher schemes are the result of a 2008 study by the World Food Program, which found that residents of Gaza and the West Bank were particularly vulnerable, due to their dependence on imports, to the repercussions of global food prices on domestic markets.

Palestinian food culture can be aligned to eastern Mediterranean Levantine food culture, a culture that also exists in Syrian, Jordanian, and Lebanese cuisine. Historically, Palestinian food originates in the many diverse civilizations that colonized or resided in Palestine, with particular lines of inheritance drawn from the Arab Umayyad conquest and its establishment of a caliphate. This can be traced back to the food cultures of Mecca and then Damascus. Further influence comes from Abbasid Caliphate, with its Turkish, Syrian, and Iranian food strands, and Turkish food culture via the Ottoman Empire.

Food Culture Snapshot

Yasir and Reem Abbas live in an affluent area of the West Bank city Nablus. Yasir, originally from Ramallah, is a civil servant; his wife, Reem, indigenous to Nablus, is a teacher. Their food choices typify middle-class urbanites whose diet is very Western as well as Palestinian. Yasir and Reem start their day at 6:30 with breakfast. This is a light meal of omelets, called *iljeh*, and Jenin fig jam, with both eggs and jam bought from the local minimarket. The *khoubz* bread they eat is bought by Yasir from a modernized bakery. The Abbases will meet again for lunch, the largest meal of the day, eating rice with a *yakhneh* stew of a small amount of lamb with squash and *mahasi* (stuffed vegetables). For the mahasi they will have bought eggplant. They bought the lamb and squash in a supermarket, although the spices that Reem used for the dish were from a reliable *'atar* in the local *souk* (spice market). If guests drop by, they may drink coffee, bought ready-ground in the souk. After work, at 8 P.M., Reem prepares a dinner of *shakshuka*, prepared using eggs and tomatoes bought from the minimart. Later, after dinner, comes *'hilew*, which is a light snack of *kanafeh* (a confection made of a shredded wheat–like pastry, cheese, and syrup) with mint tea, the mint coming from the souk. The pastry will have been bought from a local specialized Nablusi pastry shop in the Old City. Nowadays, there is more processed and fast food available to the Abbas family than in the past. They eat out more now than before, with wider choices, but often as part of their wider family unit. Westernization is more clearly evident in cities: Hamburgers replace *kiftah* (the traditional ground lamb dish), pizza replaces *sfeeha* (a flatbread topped with peppers, tomatoes, and lamb).

Major Foodstuffs

From the humid coastal strip of Gaza, to the land-locked hilly lands of Bethlehem and snow-capped Beit Jala, to the West Bank, with its high rainfall and mountainous highlands, to the desert landscapes of Jericho: All of these landscapes shape Palestinian food culture. Predominantly, though, more than 90 percent of Palestinian dishes are made of vegetables, but vegetarianism, as a discrete cultural choice, is rare. Meat consumption spikes at seasonal, religious, and cultural events. The differences between the interior and the coast alter food culture: The proximity of the north to Lebanon means that many dishes are yogurt based (using the dried yogurts of *jameed* and *kishk*); tomato-based sauces appear in the south and center of the country. Gaza's coastal reaches mean that fish and vegetables predominate, but the Egyptian culinary influences mean that dried hot red peppers and fresh green peppers are featured. Lamb is the main protein in the interior: Their complex meat dishes distinguish Nazarenes. Rural and urban differences can be seen.

Urban food is open to global food influences: The northern West Bank city of Nablus is home to wealthier, more cosmopolitan Palestinians, and so the food culture of Nablus tends to be aligned to that of cities such as Lebanon's Damascus. The settlement of Europeans from the mid-19th century through to the further demographic changes of the last 50 years has affected urban food culture. Furthermore, the closed borders of the Palestinian Occupied Territories can result in food shortages and

Shakshuka, a traditional dish made with eggs and tomatos and often served for dinner. (iStockPhoto)

imbalances: Staples such as flour and pulses have been estimated by the United Nations to meet only about half of the population's immediate needs. Food insecurity has a dramatic impact on Palestinian access to food, affecting the majority of people. For example, nearly 40 percent of Palestine's inhabitants live in Gaza, on only 6 percent of the total land area, making access to adequate food precarious.

Agriculture is a central sector of the Palestinian economy, a buffer in times of economic difficulty. However, agriculture also needs access to land, water, and markets, none of which are givens. Agricultural production in Gaza and the West Bank has declined steadily. Only 6 percent of the land cultivated by Palestinians in the West Bank is under irrigation. Rain-fed cultivation accounts for around 95 percent of cultivated land but is dependent on climatic conditions and is found in its highest concentration in the northern West Bank Jenin area.

Vegetables, including onions, cucumbers, tomatoes, cauliflower, squash, and okra, provide minerals, vitamins, and trace elements. In excess of 30 different vegetable crops are grown in Palestine, the number accounted for by plant diversity and varied planting times. A number of green leafy plants, bought in the market or often acquired gratis—even picked by the roadside—are popular but preponderate in the area of Jericho: Strong-tasting *jarjeer* (arugula) appears in abundance in winter, while in spring the grasslike *hindbeh* (wild chicory), *hwerneh* (mustard greens), and *khubbeizeh* (wild mallow) appear. Jarjeer and hwerneh are eaten raw in salads, while hindbeh and khubbeizeh are fried. Tomatoes flourish in the cooler, more northern climes in Palestine. Areas to the north of the West Bank, with their fertile soils and high rainfall, like Jenin, Tulkarm, and even Ramallah, lying in the middle of the West Bank, enjoy varied crops. In contrast, in the Gaza Strip, the capacity of agricultural production has been outstripped by consumer demand, and the last of the sand dunes has been leveled for intensive horticulture. The fertile West Bank lands of Jenin, far north of Nablus, are home to palm and fig trees, and also produce watermelon, a useful source of thirst-quenching water in a dry climate. The culinary tra-

dition of mahasi, the stuffing of vegetables such as pumpkin and eggplant, continues. Vegetables are cored and stuffed with rice and meat. Cabbage leaves and chard may be stuffed, or vine leaves to make *waraq al-'ainib*. Vegetable soups are also popular, based on such combinations as potatoes, Swiss chard, dried beans, and cauliflower. Zucchini can be used all year round, as these can be preserved dried.

Only small numbers of *fallahat,* women farmers, continue to sell domestically produced, rainwater-irrigated vegetables, purportedly low on pesticides, known as *baladi* vegetables, grown by *fellahin* (peasant farmers) on small plots in villages beyond the city. Vegetables include prized Rihâwi eggplant, fresh bush tomatoes, garlic, and onions. Despite displacement and urbanization, the persistence of vestigial fellahin culture means there is still an emphasis on the private cultivation of vegetables, even in urban areas. Seasonal vegetables and the fellahin who supply them still alter the food available: The spring brings apricots, the summer cucumbers, the autumn apples and olives, the winter bitter oranges and lemons. Many fellahin offering baladi-grown food must enter cities by circuitous back routes in order to avoid checkpoints, as the Israelis prefer to supply Israeli-grown vegetables to the Palestinian Occupied Territories. Za'atar is also one of the Palestinian foodstuffs that have become politicized. In 1977, ecologists ruled that overharvesting had left wild za'atar endangered: The Israelis declared it a protected species and banned its collection from the wild. Offenders would be heavily fined. The Israeli authorities have placed a similar ban on gathering za'atar in the West Bank. Palestinians, objecting to this, claimed an ancestral knowledge of how to preserve the yield of wild za'atar. Since 2006, Israel Defense Force checkpoints confiscate za'atar plants.

Dietary products derived from animal milk are a key source of protein. *Laban,* meaning "milk" or "white," is a fermented-milk yogurtlike product, often processed to allow year-round storage. Historically, the Bedouin have supplied the Palestinian market with goat and sheep meat and dairy products. After the rain of winter, fresh green pasture opens up in spring, and with it comes the production of white goat- or ewe-milk cheese, like *jibneh baida,* and cow milk–based, increasingly popular *ackawi*. Unfortunately, Bedouin food culture has suffered from the impact of droughts and lack of mobility: Restricted access to traditional grazing land in the West Bank has compelled the Bedouin to buy fodder for their livestock. This, then, has escalated in cost, forcing some Bedouin to give up their traditional livelihood or sell portions of their livestock. Cheeses derived from ewe and she-goat milk are made using gum Arabic or mastic (gum acacia, a pistachio-tree resin) and can be flavored with the aromatic spice *mahlep*, made from ground cherry kernels. The cheese is preserved in salted water. The production of *laban jameed* is staged: Once the milk has been churned to extract the butter, the buttermilk is left to drip through a cheesecloth for several days; the resulting sour paste is kneaded and mixed with such spices as turmeric, cumin, mahlep, nutmeg, and cinnamon (the Bedouin in the area of Bethlehem use fenugreek instead of cumin), then shaped into small balls. After being dried, the cheese is stored in cloth bags. The individual balls are rehydrated for cooking. Laban jameed is a staple in many Palestinian dishes, used in *mahashi* (stuffed cabbage), *fatteh* (stock and dates on leftover flatbread), *mansaf* (stewed lamb) for sauces, and in many stews. *Labaneh*, another yogurt derivative, is a ubiquitous side dish on the Palestinian table and, as *labaneh wa za'atar*, is served with olive oil and *za'atar* (a herb compound of dried thyme, hyssop, sumac, sesame, and sometimes oregano).

Butter is also derived from ewe milk, and clarified butter, *samneh baladieh*, is strained after being boiled with *burghul* (bulgur) wheat, the musky spice turmeric (giving samneh its distinctive taste and iridescent yellow color), and nutmeg. Where samneh would have been used for the deep, rich flavors it affords, because of heightened awareness of the dangers of saturated fats, its use is limited. Urbanized young people may prefer instead to use olive oil or vegetable oil in cooking.

Staple foods such as rice, bread, and wheat are grouped together under the term *aish*, from the Arabic verb "to live," and *arruz* (rice) is derived from *araza*, "to be miserly or tight-fisted"—the starch in rice, when cooked, huddles together in balls, like the fists of the miser. Rice is not cultivated in Palestine, a fact that bears testimony to Palestine's position as a point of intersection for trade routes. Rice appears during ceremonial eating and in dishes such as the Gaza-based dish *sumaggiye* (a stew of beef, chickpeas, and chard flavored with sumac and tahini paste) and the upside-down meat and rice dish *makloubet* or the stuffing for mahasi.

Wheat-derived products are the oldest aish foods in Palestine, served cracked in the form of burghul wheat, derived from durum wheat, in dishes like tabbouleh and *kubeh* (ground lamb dish). *Freekeh*, roasted young green wheat, can supplant rice in makloubet and mahasi, while semolina, the kernel of the durum wheat, is used to make the sweet Palestinian *harisseh*. Many wheat-based products are steamed, like *maftool*, popular in Gaza, where it is served like a couscous with a sauce flavored with dried sour plums, but maftool may also be shaped into tiny peppercorn-sized balls and steamed over a savory stew or broth. Pulses incorporated into soups are often used as a staple food among poorer eating communities. *Adas majroosh* is a popular seasonal winter soup, using crushed lentils (*majroosh*), chopped fried onion, and cumin. Freekeh is a second cereal type: Harvested yellow wheat, with soft inner seeds, is placed into piles and set on fire. This process leaves only the seeds, which are then thrashed or rubbed (from which the word *freekeh* is derived).

The next key staple, bread, may be homemade but is most often store-bought from modern bakeries. Commonly consumed, *kmaj* is a double-layered flatbread with a pocket of air inside, and this double-layering technique becomes multiple layering when *mtabbak* (meaning "folded") is made. Bread such as *mabsoos* is kneaded with olive oil and za'atar. Taking its name from the *tabun* oven, *tabun* bread is a combination of whole-meal and white flours. *Tanoor*, a thinner version of tabun made solely of white flour, is baked on the outside of the tabun. The hot, dry back of a type of local wok is used for pitalike *saj* bread. At most street corners in Jerusalem, circular breads called *ka'ek* are sold, sprinkled with sesame seeds.

Key herbs and spices recur. Za'atar is the generic name for a number of herbs and for Palestine's distinctive spice compound. Za'atar and other spices used include cumin, allspice, cardamom, and cinnamon. Fresh spices are readily available from a spice vendor, or 'atar; herbs such as mint, dill, thyme, coriander, parsley, and rosemary can be grown in the garden, although thyme and rosemary grow wild. Ideally, the herbs and spices used in Palestinian food should meet the required level of sourness, or *hmudah.* Spices and spice compounds such as dark red bitter sumac, unsweetened tamarind, or pomegranate molasses give this taste, as in the Gazan dish *rummaniyya* (made with eggplant, tahini, peppers, and lentils). Immature fruit can contribute to hmudah, such as the green fruit of the almond tree, *el-khader,* sold in the markets in early April. Several spice-based pastes and oils like za'atar, samneh (spiced, clarified butter), or *baharat* (a Levantine mix of allspice berries, cinnamon, black peppercorns, and nutmeg) inform the deeper tones of Palestinian food.

The culture of the olive tree is central to Palestinian food, although land confiscation has impacted olive cultivation. Home-pickled olives go with every meal. Olive oil is a base for stews and frying; integral to the construction of appetizers and salads, it also moistens *hummos* (hummus) and adds sharpness to *m'tabbal,* a pungent eggplant dip. Early morning workers in Palestine might douse their tabun bread in olive oil and a little sumac to ease the "dizziness" of an early morning start, while a small cup of olive oil can aid digestion. The highest density of olive orchards under irrigation is in the Tulkarm district in the northern West Bank region, which produces greenish oil, as opposed to the lighter, yellowish olive oil of Ramallah. Olive harvesting in October and November remains a key social, communal, and familial event in Palestine. Sesame oil, *sirej,* used in frying, is an element in the ubiquitous *tahineh* (sesame paste), and a tablespoon is added to dishes such as mahasi. Sirej, when combined with pistachios and sugar, makes the sweet *halaweh.*

Lamb, mutton, chicken, and beef dominate meat consumption in Palestine, although such meats are pricey and hard to come by in certain restricted areas, such as the Gaza Strip—lamb smuggling occurs in the occupied territories, but cattle smuggling less so. Lamb, its slaughter, and its presentation intersect with the fabrics of ritual, celebration, and daily

Harvesting olives in Palestine. The olive tree is not only a source of livelihood and a symbol of the people's connection to the land, but it has also been employed as a symbol of cooperation between peoples. (iStockPhoto)

life, fitting as it does with the concept of sacrifice in the twin traditions of Christianity and Islam, and the key theistic celebrations of Easter and Eid al-Adha.

Fish is a main element in the staple diet of specific regions of Palestine, namely, in coastal regions such as Gaza. Freshwater fish include carp, grey and golden mullet, tilapia, salmon, and freshwater prawns. Fish farming is a developing industry, as pollution, particularly in the Red Sea and the Jordan River, is increasingly problematic, as are falling water levels in the Sea of Galilee. Sardines and sole, *arous* (similar to sea bream), tuna, sea bass, turbot, slipper lobster, and a wide array of shellfish including squid, shrimp, and crab are representative of saltwater fish. Gaza was the traditional supplier of saltwater fish, but this is now under serious threat. According to the United Nations Office for the Coordination of Humanitarian Affairs, from 2000, the number of nautical miles from the coast in which fishing was permitted was limited to six. By 2008 fishing accounted for merely 1.5 percent of Gaza's economy (agriculture accounts for a further 8.5%). Most recently, a three-kilometer (about 2-mile) restriction has been enforced, limiting fishing to the overfished spawning grounds of shallow coastal waters. Gaza's fishing authority is trying to establish fish farms. Lack of fuel has also had a detrimental effect on the fishing industry. Popular fish dishes are the fish broth of *sayyadiy* and *zibdiyit gambari,* shrimp stewed with fresh dill, peppers, olive oil, tomatoes, chili, and garlic. Grilled fish, rubbed with or marinated in lemon juice, coriander, cumin, and chili, is popular.

Water is often used with meals; Arabic or Turkish coffee is popular at informally established times: in the morning, during the private time of siesta after afternoon prayer at around 3:30 P.M., or when visitors call. Coffee may be spiced with cardamom and sweetened or unsweetened. Mint tea is most often consumed in the evening, made with fresh green mint (*na'ana*) leaves infused in hot water; fresh sage (*maramiyyeh*) may also be infused. Coca-Cola is encroaching on mint tea consumption: Soft drinks can be found in most Palestinian homes. Hebron, Nablus, and Gaza have distribution centers for Coca-Cola (though Gaza's was shut down in 2007), and Ramallah has a Coca-Cola bottling plant.

While alcohol is not widely consumed, less conservative Muslims and Palestinian Christians drink light beer (the West Bank town of Taybeh has the only beer brewery, producing Tayibeh but also alcohol-free beer for conservative Muslims). Scotch whisky or the clear aniseed digestive *arak* may be consumed. Arak is diluted and made milky with water and is consumed with meze (small dish appetizers) and at high points in the cultural calendar. Christian monasteries may produce wine.

In winter, *sahlab,* warm milk thickened with *salep* starch, which is derived from the orchid bulb, and sweetened with orange blossom or rose water, appears. *Sharabat* is a category of soft drink made by adding ice and cold water to fruit syrups, such as the lemony orange citrus syrup *khushhash* and *toot*

made from mulberries. At key celebratory points such as Ramadan—or in periods of hot weather—people make drinks from the following: tamarind (*tamar hindi,* meaning "Indian dates," an Arabic appellation for tamarind), a licorice drink called *sous,* carob, and *mishmash* (apricot) juice. The pulp from carob is also used as a sweet substitute among children of poorer communities.

Cooking

Women are chiefly responsible for home food preparation, with a higher concentration of women rurally. However, social forces have impacted on this as women have joined the public workforce, and more food is processed. Traditionally, the centerpiece of cooking in the Palestinian household was the tabun, a cone-shaped oven of yellow clay and straw, fueled by wood or, more traditionally, by dried sheep or camel dung, situated in the open backyard of the home. The tabun featured in both public and private spaces in rural Palestinian villages, with families taking turns to use the tabun for bread making, as communal property. The use of the tabun has decreased substantially, almost disappearing, with a few exceptions in rural communities. Ironically, there has been some resurgence in its use, as supplies of more modern cooking fuels have become subject to restrictions. Predominantly, though, as shown by a survey by the Palestinian Bureau of Statistics in 2006, 96.1 percent of households use petroleum gas as the main fuel for cooking, while 9.4 percent depend on electricity as a secondary fuel and 8.5 percent on wood as a secondary fuel. Many Palestinians buy ready-made bread at local markets. Modern bakeries fueled by gas have replaced the tabun, and these can now be found on every corner. In this context, tabun use can be accounted for more by restaurants and bakeries aiming to attract customers who are nostalgic for old-fashioned tabun bread. However, many of the new so-called tabun are often operated by gas and bear no resemblance to the old-fashioned tabun. Fuel for cooking has been a compromised commodity: The illegal piping of cooking gas has been attempted, particularly beneath the southern Gaza Strip and Egypt. It was estimated that in the border town of Rafah, as many as 400 illegal pipes were laid. Fuel disputes led to some unexpected developments: Cooking oil has been used to fuel cars, which led to unexpected profits for restaurant owners. Much of this came about because Israel, once the sole supplier of cooking gas and fuel to Gaza, imposed sanctions following a spate of violence that disrupted a six-month ceasefire in November 2008.

Cooking utensils in modern Palestine are very similar to Western utensils, replacing the earthenware dishes such as the *zibdieh* or tagine-like *fukhar.* Various traditional implements were used in the past for grinding, but the most commonly used device is a mortar and pestle—although electric blenders and grinders are popular. Most Palestinians buy their spices from the souk or shops. A core set of spices like turmeric and nutmeg arrive in Palestinian dishes through other elements of the dish like samneh or laban jameed. Others are newcomers: Traditionally, coriander seed, with its delicately fruity undertones, has been used, only to be upstaged in recent years by an increased use of fresh green leafy cilantro. Coriander seed is used for such dishes as *mulukhia* (bitter leafy green), *bamiah* (okra), and *yakhni fasuliah* (beans).

Pickling, a means of extending the shelf life of seasonal foodstuffs, is common, with chilies, olives, turnips, and cucumbers being pickled in a multitude of different styles. Green olives not sent for oil production are lightly cut by the farmer, and then water with salt, sugar, or vinegar is poured over them and they are stored. Common also are techniques for drying and preserving; for instance, the many jams popular in regions such as Gaza are all ways of extending the shelf life of fruits: These can be fig, orange (*khushkhash*), or sour plum (*arasiya*). With only a short two-week season in July, the cherry-sized plums are sold in local markets and jammed or dried, in their dried form enriching the flavor of dishes like beef and pumpkin stew, *ari' bi tahina.* Jam making is, again, prevalent in West Bank cities such as Hebron, where grapes are a primary crop in spring and summer. Grapes are dried to make raisins, a molasses *dibs,* and jams.

Typical Meals

There is a central daily ritual of eating that Palestinians will adhere to, given the economic means to do so. There are four meals a day: breakfast (*iftur*), lunch (*gheda*), a predinner snack (*'hilew*), and dinner (*'asha*). The largest meal of the day is lunch, which may be anytime between 12 and 2, and, as eating is so integral to family life, meals may well take one or two hours.

Meals are sites of family connection and cultural identity for Palestinians. Traditionally, the family group, seated on the floor, would eat around the *tabliyeh,* a round table. In a more contemporary setting, food will always be placed on a surface above ground level. Nuts and olives, sometimes mixed with fresh rue, and cheese will already be on the table. The traditional notion of Palestinians eating with their right hands, seated in a circle around a dish (as is still practiced at weddings), is outmoded; many modern Palestinians will sit at a table to eat, using a knife and fork, with the fork in the right hand. The etiquette of right-handed eating is firmly and immovably established across Arab Christian and Arab Muslim food cultures. Traditionally, though, if guests and family are to eat using their hands, the right hand is used to scoop up food (always solely from the section of the communal plate directly in front of the diner), which is then shaped with the right hand into a golf ball–sized piece.

Bread is also ubiquitous: The bread is torn, shaped into a scoop with the fingers, and used instead of utensils to scoop up dips, salads, meats, and sauces. Bread dough also reappears in *manaqeesh* (flatbread covered with cheese or herbs); *sfiha,* with its crust of minced lamb; or *fatayer* (stuffed dough pastries). Pizzalike bases spread with pastes are popular, for instance, *manaqeesh jibneh,* when goat cheese is combined with oil and garlic; or *manaqeesh bi za'atar,* flatbread covered with the spice mixture za'atar; or *manaqeesh beid,* when eggs replace the za'atar.

Various salads and vegetables will be served: *salatat bandura* (tomato salad), *fattoush* (bread salad), *dagga* (tomato and chili pepper salad), and tabbouleh. Mahasi would also be served. A key element in typical meals is beans, such as broad beans, fava (*ful*) beans, and chickpeas in falafel. The chickpea-paste hummos, of which the most popular is *hummos bi tahineh,* comes in many varieties for both lunch and dinner. Chickpeas can also be combined with ful to make the brownish *mukhluta.* Other dips such as the eggplant baba ghanoush are popular, as is the spicier version of this, m'tabbal. Depending on where one is in Palestine, it is customary to serve a sweet such as baklava, made by layering honeyed walnuts and pistachios with sheets of unleavened dough, or a West Bank favorite from Nablus, kanafeh, with honeyed Nablusi cheese beneath the finely shredded noodlelike pastry, dyed orange and sprinkled with crushed pistachios. A sweet milk pudding such as *heytalliyeh* or *muhalabiyeh* might be served after meals.

Breakfast (iftur) may be eaten on the move from street vendors selling manaqeesh bi za'atar and jibneh baida; in its more sedentary form, breakfast is a quick, light meal of eggs (boiled, fried. or in iljeh), hummos, *foul mudammas* (stewed fava beans), cucumbers, tomatoes, olives, labaneh, and khoubz bread and quince, carob molasses, or *safarjil* (sweet lime) jam. In Jerusalem, breakfast may be the local specialty of a boiled egg and sachet of za'atar with the ring-shaped, sesame-seed bread *ka'ek bi simsim.* Hot tea infused with mint leaves accompanies breakfast. At its most basic, breakfast can be hot tabun bread, drenched in olive oil.

Lunch (gheda) lies later in the afternoon. Characteristically, lunch would be rice with a *yakhneh* stew, based on a single vegetable and sometimes lamb; mahasi or waraq al-'ainib, rice wrapped in vegetable leaves, is also popular—but the labor-intensive nature of waraq means its appearance can be limited to festivity. Kubeh, such as the pounded lamb and burghul wheat *kubeh bi-saniyeh,* are served warm. Lunch comes with an array of small dishes of pickles, salads, olives, and dips. Increased affluence and times of economic boom have meant that urban Palestinians are attracted to Western eating styles. However, Palestine's vigorous and indigenous street fast-food culture thrives, with inexpensive *shawarma* in khoubz bread and fatayer. For shawarma, lamb is grilled on a vertical spit, shaved, and then rolled up, with pickled turnip, onions, cucumber, tomato, and tahineh, in a long roll of khoubz bread. However,

most offices will shut down over lunch, to allow workers to have lunch at home with their families. It is often the case that all courses are served together.

A brief eating interlude called 'hilew acts as a satellite snack to dinner, coming before or after. 'Hilew consists of pastry shop–bought baklava or homemade muhalabiyeh. Dinner, 'asha, can be eaten after 8 P.M. and includes small, light dishes, such as little omelets or shakshuka, eggs cooked in tomatoes, peppers, and spices; soups; and unleavened dough cakes, sweetened with syrup and stuffed with nuts, called *fteereh.*

The following are examples of typical meals in middle-class families in three regions of Palestine: the Triangle (incorporating Galilee), Gaza, and the West Bank.

The Triangle

Cities such as Nazareth, Haifa, and Akka are counted as part of northern Israel. The Triangle, as this is referred to, is a contested area of land. The food culture of Galilee, or the Triangle, places an emphasis on kubeh, the combination of burghul wheat and meat, revealing its close affinity to Lebanese cuisine. The practice of serving burghul wheat raw reveals a direct affinity. A main dish would be *kubeh bi-siniyee,* which uses burghul wheat as a crust encasing minced lamb or beef, baked in the oven. Kubeh is associated with mood, particularly happiness, and its inclusion in a meal can signify the end to a time of mourning. Manaqeesh appears as a popular breakfast food, as does *lahm bi ajeen,* spiced ground lamb on a thin dough base, accompanied by tea or a yogurt drink, labaneh, and olives. Meze also predominate, accompanied by skewered meat. Roast lamb would be the focal dish for special occasions. Ackawi cheese, originating in the city of Acre, now part of Israel, on the coast of Galilee, is popular.

Gaza

Eighty percent of Gaza's occupants are refugees, bringing food traditions from throughout Palestine. Nonetheless, there is a distinct Gazan food culture: reliance on fish, on cheap foods such chickpeas, or on free seasonal wild foods such as mustard greens (hwerneh). Variations in the ingredients used in Palestinian staples also appear: Okra or fresh chopped basil may be added, and a side dish of green chilies is ubiquitous in Gaza. The distinctive tastes brought to Gazan food through chilies, dill, and cumin, as well as the sour fruit taste of tamarind, pomegranates, and plums, distinguish it in dishes such as the summer and autumn vegetarian dish rummaniyya, named after the pomegranate. Late autumn sees the harvest of root vegetables and squash, and the bright red dish *mahashi jazar ahmar,* plump, short, stuffed carrots in a tamarind stock.

Ironically, the artificially isolated nature of life in the monitored and check-pointed Gaza Strip means that it maintains a very distinctive food culture: This, the sea, and culinary connections to Egypt influence Gazan eating. For instance, dagga, a salad with distinctively hot peppers, dill, crushed tomatoes, olive oil, lemon juice, and raw garlic, is distinctively Gazan, as is the seasonal chard and lentil stew *fukharit adas.* Economic deprivation has determined the preponderance meatless dishes such as *bisara* (made of dried beans) or *saliq was adas* (chard and lentils). The price of fish is making it unaffordable for most inhabitants of Gaza, but calamari (*habbar*) remains plentiful. An emphasis on chilies and garlic in fish cookery exposes the Egyptian connection, as does the use of *shatta,* a hot pepper paste. A dish often associated with Gaza is the meat-based sumaggiye. The dish derives its name from its main ingredient, sumac seeds or powder. Sumac, soaked in water, is mixed with tahini. This is then combined with chard (another sign of Egyptian influence and a chief ingredient in much Gazan food), pieces of beef, chickpeas, garlic, dill, and chili. It is eaten with khoubz or kmaj bread. Popular during the Muslim Eid al-Fitr holiday, each family will distribute its own sumaggiye to friends and neighbors, who will, then, fill the bowl with their own bespoke version of sumaggiye—or some cinnamon, nutmeg, and date cakes, ka'ek bi ajwah.

The West Bank

With a population in excess of 33,000, including the refugee camp, Jericho has a moderate climate and a high degree of agricultural production, its most noted products being citrus, bananas, and dates. A heavier diet is consumed on the West Bank, with more meat protein and rice. In the northern cities of Tulkarm and Jenin the layered chicken, onion, sumac, and tabun dish *musakhan* originated. *Ma'lube* typifies the region and is an upside-down braised lamb, tomato, eggplant, and rice casserole. When turned, the casserole has a scarlet red top from the tomatoes (which are placed in a solid layer at the base of the casserole). As it is customary never to eat food dry—*nashef*—ma'lube is dressed with lemon juice or yogurt. In the West Bank region, grapes are the second-largest fruit crop, with Hebron being the greatest producer and, hence, supplier of grape leaves for waraq al-'ainib. Beit Jala, in close proximity to Bethlehem, and the village of Jifna are renowned regionally for their apricot harvest and jam, while Tulkarm is famous for olives. Seasonally, Artas, south of Bethlehem, is famous for its lettuce crop, and the seasonal dish to accompany this is lettuce leaves stuffed with tabbouleh.

Eating Out

Although much eating is domestic, eating out has become more popular. Restaurants still widely focus on Palestinian food, and, instead of single people or couples, whole families will eat out. Pickles and meze will often function as the starter courses, followed by kebabs and grilled meat and fish as a main. There is a vibrant food subculture that often involves the use of the grill, as opposed to the stove-based stews of home cooking: Kebabs, falafel, and shawarma are available. Western cuisine is popular, and most hotels, restaurants, and cooking schools explore a weak array of Palestinian food while offering French, Italian, and European dishes. Jacir Palace Intercontinental in Bethlehem has tortellini and gorgonzola or chicken breast dijonnaise. Foccacia bars and pizzerias are very popular. Hamburgers are widely popular, and Jerusalem has seen a huge expansion of restaurants serving French fries and European sandwiches. Ramallah sandwich shops such as the Ziryab Café have westernized fillings inside processed white bread rolls. Meze remain popular, with their staples of hummos and grilled or fried eggplant. Coffee shops still remain the province of

Two traditional food stalls selling beigele breads and Palestinian pastries in Old Town Jerusalem. (StockPhotoPro)

A centerpiece at many celebrations, and particularly weddings, is *mansaf,* a leg of lamb or sections of lamb, served on tabun bread with yellow rice. Although the use of Western tableware is widespread, mansaf is traditionally served on a *sidr,* a large communal dish. *Mansaf* means "to finish off food," and its inclusion on the table signifies respect for a guest. Another key thread in Palestinian food culture emerges, too: This food culture's fidelity to traditional food practices can be a determined act of cultural expression within the more hegemonic culture of Israel.

During Lent, Christian communities will eat specific dishes, although the more Orthodox a Palestinian Christian is, the more likely it is that they will eat a nondairy and vegetarian diet. Ramadan comes with a clearly discernable food culture. Fasting is central to religious obeisance, a central tenet of the five pillars of wisdom of Islam, and the ceremony of breaking the fast at sunset is deliberate and controlled. Daily iftars, the breaking of the fast, are marked with a drink of water or a mixture of strained tamarind and rose water, fatteh, a combination of clear stock and bread, and dates. After fasting, traditional drinks are based on bitter almonds, dried apricots, carob, and licorice; these may be prepared at home but are also sold in the market, sometimes offered free to children by costumed vendors playing cymbals and calling out. Various soups are also used to rehydrate. Larger quantities of meat may be consumed during Ramadan. Rice, vegetables, salads, falafel, and hummos are also consumed. Of key importance is the preparation of additional food for distribution to the poor and one's neighbors: Like for like, the same amount of food eaten by a house must go to the needy. Christians are included in Ramadan as well: It is a cultural signpost, a holiday also. Christian and Muslim alike anticipate the delicate sweet pastry making that occurs, such as the fragile pastry *barazek na'mine,* flavored with sesame seed. Only in Ramadan are *katayif* sold; they appear on the first day of Ramadan. These resemble pancakes, but only the batter base is cooked, and the top is filled either with sweetened, unsalted goat cheese or sugar, crushed walnuts, and cinnamon.

men but non-gender-specific coffee shops have proliferated in the newer areas of urban centers. These do tend to have a generational attraction, favored as they are by a younger clientele. Located in the souks of urban centers are cake and sweet shops, *mahal 'hilewayet,* selling baklava, cookies, and kanafeh; some focus on one particular sweet.

Special Occasions

Celebratory traditions vary regionally and in terms of religious observance in Palestine. Traditionally, lamb would be at the core of the celebration, with its many metaphorical resonances, but it can turn up in celebrations for many things, from recovery from an illness through to the acquisition of a new car. The appearance of lamb as a trope for sacrifice is most clearly seen in the feasts of Adha and Easter.

Small pancakes stuffed with cheese, folded over to make sealed packets and fried. These qatayef pancakes are only made during the Muslim holy month of Ramadan as a special treat. (Paul Cowan | Dreamstime.com)

Eid al-Adha, the Feast of Sacrifice, which comes at the end of March, commemorates Abraham's obedience in his willingness to sacrifice Ishmael (rather than his brother Isaac, as in the Hebrew Bible), with the substitution of a lamb for Ishmael, and is marked with religious observance based on the sacrifice of an animal. But the consumption of lamb at times of religious celebration is not limited to the Muslim community: To celebrate Easter, stuffed lamb and lamb ribs are eaten by the Christian Orthodox community. Both Easter and Eid al-Adha are marked by the consumption of round semolina date- or walnut-filled ka'ek, with wreath-shaped ka'ek bi ajwah (date cake) intended to resemble Christ's crown of thorns. Food as metaphor

further exists in the traditional stuffed kubeh that is popular at Easter, symbolizing as it does the spear that pierced Christ's side. Palm Sunday, the Annunciation, and the Transfiguration are points in the Christian calendar when fish may be consumed in Orthodox families.

Religious veneration is offered through food on various days in the Palestinian Christian year: For the feast of the Virgin Mary on August 28, semolina is combined with fenugreek seeds to make *hilbeh.* December sees the Saint's Day, the Feast of St. Barbara, and the making of *burbara,* a pudding based on wheat because, reputedly, after her imprisonment, St. Barbara would eat only wheat or gave wheat to the poor. Wheat is soaked overnight to soften it, after which it is boiled. Aniseed, sugar, and raisins are combined with it. This is then decorated with pomegranate seeds, almonds, and nuts. The dish is then left out all night in the hope that St. Barbara would visit the house and try a mouthful with three fingers. Children would, then, look for this indentation on the burbara on the morning of St. Barbara's Day. September's Feast of the Cross comes with anise cookies and an eggplant and pomegranate dish, while Epiphany is marked with macaroons and sweet *zalabieh,* deep-fried balls of batter, which are then dropped into orange blossom syrup.

Secular celebrations are also marked through the presence of other sweet stuffs: *Knafeh* (a sweet made with cheese and shredded phyllo pastry) is traditionally associated with the New Year. Dishes with white sauces and gravies can signal the New Year. Birth and death are ritualized in food. A pudding made from spiced ground rice and sugar, sprinkled with almonds, and called *mughli* is made when a baby is born, to thank the guests for coming and to stimulate the flow of milk from the nursing mother. Even the baby cutting its first tooth can be celebrated with bowls of *snounieh,* sweetened wheat. After circumcision baklava will be eaten. Mourning can be marked through a number of food devices: Unsweetened Arab coffee accompanied by dates may be served in Muslim households, while Christians use a *rahmeh,* a special bun, to accompany such coffee, functioning as a memory of the loved one and as a metaphorical blessing on the deceased's soul.

Diet and Health

Various herbs and spices in Palestinian food are associated with health and well-being. Maramiyyeh (sage), *babunej* (chamomile), and za'atar (thyme) are all herbs that have medical applications to alleviate discomfort associated with stomach pains, colds, and so on. A number of medical practices are centered around the use of fenugreek, *hilbeh*. Hilbeh paste functions as a poultice for boils. An infusion of hilbeh leaves is sipped to ease digestive complaints such as inflammations and cramps. Stomach complaints are also addressed through the misnomer "white coffee," or *qahwa beyda,* an infusion of sweetened orange blossom water or rose water in hot water. This lacks any coffee—hence the whiteness alluded to in its name. Plants such as hilbeh have found their way into pharmaceutically produced capsules that are retailed to address glucose imbalance in older diabetic patients. Hilbeh seeds, when infused, are thought to ease menstrual pain and increase lactation in breast-feeding mothers. Cumin is noted as preventing flatulence, while za'atar, in its incarnations as both thyme and the dried mixture, is used in an infusion as a sore throat medicine, while combined with olive oil and rubbed on joints it is used to alleviate rheumatism. This same combination kept in a house augurs good fortune. An interesting submythology adheres to za'atar: The dried powdered leaves, when consumed, will guarantee safety from serpents for 40 days.

Fiona Ross

Further Reading

Baramki, G. "Winter Traditions in Palestine." *This Week in Palestine,* Edition No. 106, February 2007.

Bsisu, May. S. *The Arab Table.* New York: William Morrow, 2005.

Dabdoub Nasser, Christiane. *Classic Palestinian Cookery.* London: Saqi Books, 2001.

Dabdoub Nasser, Christiane. "Revisiting Our Table." *This Week in Palestine* 98 (June 2006).

Heine, Peter. *Food Culture in the Near East, Middle East, and North Africa.* Westport, CT: Greenwood Press, 2004.

Institute for Middle East Understanding. "Cuisine." 2006. http://imeu.net/news/article00258.shtml.

Oleibo, A. "Tamarind, Tomatoes and Dried Yoghurt: The Aesthetics of the Palestinian Cuisine." *This Week in Palestine* 98 (June 2006).

Shihab, Aziz. *A Taste of Palestine: Menus and Memories.* San Antonio, TX: Corona, 1993.

Smith, Maggie. "In Gaza, Eating under Siege." *The Atlantic,* August 19, 2009. http://imeu.net/news/article0017247.shtml.

Syria

Overview

Syria is bordered by Turkey on the north, Iraq on the east, Jordan on the south, and Israel, Lebanon, and the Mediterranean Sea on the west. The primary agricultural region is a strip about 100 miles wide: a coastal plain around Latakia, the Jebel Ansarieh Mountains just inland, and, east of the Jebel Ansarieh and the mountains that form the Lebanese border, a corridor of farmland irrigated from wells and rivers that mostly originate in Lebanon. The northern city of Aleppo gets its water from the Turkish highlands, as does a secondary agricultural area extending east from Aleppo to the Iraqi border. The country has been investing in projects to expand agriculture in the east, particularly in the Euphrates Valley. The rest of the country consists of sparse grassland and the rocky Syrian Desert, which extends eastward into Iraq and south through Jordan to the deserts of the Arabian Peninsula. Outside of scattered oases, the arid region is inhabited by a small population of sheep- and goat-herding nomads.

Syria's 18 million people are about equally divided between urban and rural. The population is 76 percent Sunnite Muslim, 10 percent Christians (largely the Nestorians of the northeast, along with Greek Orthodox, Armenians, and other eastern churches), and 14 percent Shiites, including two Shiite offshoots, the Druze in the south and the Alawites of the Jebel Ansarieh.

🍽 Food Culture Snapshot

Ma'an and Maysim Hamwi and their children, Yusuf and Lamya, live in Damascus, in an apartment block built in the 1970s on former farmland within walking distance of the ancient walled city. Ma'an is a clerk in a government agency. They are typical of the urban middle class. The Hamwis buy their food from various shops in the neighborhood: a butcher, a bread bakery, a pastry shop, a dairy goods shop, one specializing in dry foods (grain, flour, beans, nuts, and dried fruit), and one selling syrups, preserves, and canned goods. They buy their fruits and vegetables in a produce market, Damascus's traditional wandering street vendors with their colorful cries (e.g., "Bride of the frying pan," indicating eggplant) having become somewhat rare.

Maysim herself is of part Turkish ancestry, and Ma'an's late mother grew up next to a Turkish family, so the Hamwis' cookery is a little more Turkish than most. One of Ma'an's mother's specialties was *oturtma,* a Turkish dish belonging to the vast Near Eastern repertoire of lamb, tomato, and eggplant stews. The name means "settled," which is close to the sense of the name of a Damascus specialty called *mnazzli,* "lowered, cooked down."

Major Foodstuffs

The Syrian diet is based on much the same vegetables as in any Mediterranean country, particularly tomatoes, onions, eggplant, zucchini, turnips, and potatoes, but including less common ones such as cardoon (*kangar*) and kohlrabi (*karamb*) and some specifically Middle Eastern vegetables, such as grape leaves for stuffing and mallow (*molukhiyyi*), a coarse green that cooks up with a slightly sticky texture. Other greens include lettuce, cabbage, spinach, and Swiss chard. Some produce vendors sell gathered foods such as '*akkub,* a sort of rugged wild thistle cooked much like artichokes.

The main meats are lamb and chicken, and to a lesser degree goat, but more of Syrians' protein comes from dairy products and pulses, particularly chickpeas and lentils, than from meat. People living in the villages rely even more on dairy products and pulses. Fish is rarely eaten in Syria except on the Mediterranean coast and is not a major food even there.

Wheat and rice are the chief grains. Pita bread (called simply *khubz,* "bread") is eaten at most meals, even when rice is served. Wheat is also consumed as *burghul* (bulgur): Wheat grains are boiled until the starch gelatinizes and then dried and crushed, making a product that can be made ready to eat simply by boiling or even soaking in water. Bulgur soaked in yogurt and then sun-dried makes *kishk,* a sort of instant soup mix with a tart, slightly musty flavor. Wheat is also used in sweet and savory pastries.

The leading cooking fats are olive oil, butter, and lamb fat. The olive does not flourish away from the coast, so in the inland cities it is partly replaced by other fats. Lamb fat comes from sheep varieties bred to deposit their body fat in their tails (*liyyeh*), which look as a result somewhat like beaver tails. This fat has a low melting point, giving it a pleasant mouth feel, so bits of tail fat are often threaded between the chunks of meat in shish kebab or used as a stuffing for meatballs to produce a spurt of hot lamb fat in the mouth. A bit of tail fat is traditionally added to the butter in baklava to give a subtle gamy tang.

Milk, principally from sheep and goats, is rarely consumed fresh except in ice cream. Mostly it's

Groats seller at the Hamidiyyah souq (marketplace) in Damascus, Syria. Groats are hulled cereal grains used in many staple dishes. (Shutterstock)

soured into yogurt (*laban*). Yogurt can be strained to make *labni,* an even more noticeably sour product with the consistency of a soft cheese. Both yogurt and labni keep better than milk in the absence of refrigeration. Fresh milk is curdled to make cheese, mostly consumed as *jibni baida* (white cheese), which is stored in brine like feta. The curd can also be boiled to make a sort of mozzarella called *musanara,* and this can also be twisted into *mudaffara,* which resembles Armenian string cheese. A sort of cheese called *qarish* is made by boiling yogurt until it curdles and then straining out the solids.

Butter is nearly always clarified of its solids and whey to produce pure butterfat (*samni*), mostly used in making sweets. A product called *qaymaq* is made by simmering whole milk so that a skin of rich cream rises to the surface, being skimmed off as it forms to make a very rich product comparable to English clotted cream. It can be eaten by itself or used as a filling for pastries. Other dairy products include *shanklish,* which is dried balls of yogurt or qarish cultured with mold to produce something a little like blue cheese, and *ayran,* a tart drink made by diluting yogurt with water.

Cooking

City people use gas or electric ranges, though villagers may still cook on a wood-fired range made of clay or stone. In the western part of the country, bread is baked in European-type brick ovens, but the *tannur,* the ancient Mesopotamian clay oven, survives in the east. This is essentially a clay jar two or three feet high with an opening at the bottom for feeding a fire. Flatbreads are cooked by slapping them onto the inside of the neck of the jar, where they cook very quickly in the high heat.

The usual cooking utensils of a home kitchen are much the same as in Europe, with the notable exception of the *siniyya.* This is a round baking pan about 16 inches in diameter with sides about an inch high. It's used for baking baklava-type pastries and a variety of homey stews. The siniyya owes its existence to the fact that traditional kitchens did not have ovens, so dishes to be baked were sent to the village bakery, where enough heat would remain in the oven's bricks after the day's bread baking to cook them. The siniyya's flat shape made it possible to fit a number of these pans into one of these ovens at a single time. Occasionally, one will still see children even in big cities balancing siniyyas on their heads on the way to a local bakery. These days, city people more often use the siniyya in the oven of a home range. By its nature, cooking in a siniyya exposes a large amount of the food's surface to heated air, so stews baked in one develop a special traditional flavor because of evaporation and a slight browning of the vegetables, including tomatoes.

Traditional kitchens may have a large stone or marble mortar (*jorn*) and a pestle (*mdaqqa*) about the size of a baseball bat, which are used for making *kibbi,* a versatile paste of meat, bulgur, and onions. Making kibbi in the jorn is a laborious process taking an hour or two. The Hamwis own a food processor, which reduces the process to a matter of minutes.

Typical Meals

A usual breakfast for city people would be flatbread (plain or perhaps topped with *zaatar,* a mixture of wild thyme, sesame seeds, and tart ground sumac berries) and cheese—white cheese or qarish—along with a handful of olives. Some city people have a Continental breakfast of croissants, an imported soft cheese, and the rather syrupy local fruit preserves (*mrabba*). Turkish coffee is usually served with breakfast. Farmers might start the day with a hearty soup made from kishk or lentils.

When possible, people prefer to eat lunch at home. Those who can't because their workplace is at the other end of town may go out to a shish kebab restaurant. On weekends, people will have a simple lunch—say, roast chicken or stuffed eggplant accompanied by pilaf and salad. Lunch is accompanied by water or ayran, or sometimes a soft drink.

A typical dinner would be lentil soup followed by lamb stewed with a vegetable, accompanied by plain pilaf (*rizz mfalfal*) or pilaf garnished with toasted vermicelli (*rizz bi-sha'riyyi*). Tomato and cucumber salad is likely to appear on the side. Rural people eat the same sort of dinner so far as their budget allows. Coffee and fresh fruit end the meal. The famous Middle Eastern pastries are not usually served with a meal but consumed as snacks during the day.

Two features of Syrian food survive from medieval cookery, though in an altered form. In the Middle Ages, most Arab stews contained a sour fruit juice such as lemon, pomegranate, or even rhubarb juice, and all were flavored with complex spice mixtures. Both practices are still known, but in many cases the fruit juice has been replaced by tomato juice and the spice mixtures reduced to cinnamon and allspice, or even allspice alone. On the table, salt and allspice appear instead of salt and pepper.

Kibbi is one of the most versatile Syrian foods. The meat, bulgur, and onion paste can be rolled into meatballs and grilled on a skewer, baked in a siniyya with a filling of fried onions and lamb fat, made into tangerine-sized, torpedo-shaped meatballs with the same filling and then deep-fried, or made into meat-stuffed flying-saucer disks and grilled, fried, or even poached.

In the 16th century, most Arab countries entered a period of economic stagnation, partly because the region's middleman trade declined after the European voyages of exploration to the Far East. Aleppo, however, continued to have a vigorous economy. One sign of this is that some of its caravanserais (*khans*), which served as hotels and warehouses for traveling merchants in the Middle Ages, are still in service as warehouses, while in other countries caravanserais have mostly been converted to other uses such as museums.

As a result, Aleppo has long been the most prosperous city in Syria, and it has developed an opulent and distinctive cuisine. It often uses pomegranate juice or tamarind in place of lemon juice, making for particularly aromatic stews. The medieval tradition of cooking meat with fruits such as quinces is still quite lively. Unlike the rest of Syria, which is not particularly fond of red pepper, Aleppo uses large quantities of a medium-hot dried pepper known throughout the area as Aleppo pepper. To Syrians from other parts of the country, the Aleppines seem to substitute this crushed pepper wherever possible for fresh herbs such as parsley or mint. The city has long had a substantial Armenian population, and until the mid-20th century it was home to an ancient Jewish colony; both groups had their own culinary specialties.

The proverbial expression is *Halab, ahl il-mahashi wal-kibab* (Aleppo, the people of stuffed vegetables and varieties of kibbi). Aleppo cooks stuff cabbage leaves the way grape leaves are stuffed elsewhere in Syria (and with red pepper in the filling). They even stuff laboriously hollowed-out carrots. As for kibbi, Aleppo kebab shops regularly offer *kibbit banjan,* which is kibbi meatballs alternating on the skewer with slices of eggplant. The most famous version is *kibbi halabiyyi:* stuffed disks of kibbi poached in a lemony sauce. Among sweets, a local specialty is *halawat jibn,* a stretchy sweet dough kneaded with butter and cheese, which can be eaten as is or rolled around a filling of qaymaq or ground nuts.

Bedouin in the Syrian desert baking bread in the sand. (Styve | Dreamstime.com)

Mhammara

Serves 6–8 as an appetizer

This is Aleppo's best-known dish. It shows the city's characteristic use of medium-hot crushed pepper (*filfil halabi*) and pomegranate molasses (*dibs rumman* or *rob-e anar*), a concentrate of tart pomegranate juice. Both ingredients are available at Middle Eastern markets, as are pine nuts. Do not use the sweetened pomegranate syrup called grenadine, which is only for making cocktails.

3 tbsp breadcrumbs

3 tbsp hot water

1½ tbsp pomegranate molasses, or substitute ¼ c unsweetened pomegranate juice and omit the water

1 tbsp olive oil

3 tbsp Aleppo pepper, or substitute 1 tbsp crushed red pepper and 2 tbsp sweet paprika

½ tsp cumin

1 c crushed walnuts

Salt

¼ c pine nuts

2 oz (¼ c) vegetable oil

3 loaves pita bread, each layer separated, cut into 8 wedge shapes and toasted until stiff, or substitute crackers

Mix the breadcrumbs with the hot water, and stir in the pomegranate molasses, olive oil, Aleppo pepper, and cumin. Add the walnuts, and process into a slightly coarse puree in a blender or food processor. It should have about the thickness of mashed potatoes; add a bit of water or breadcrumbs as needed. Season with salt to taste.

Put the pine nuts and oil in a frying pan and toast over medium heat, shaking often to prevent scorching, until the nuts are golden and fragrant. Drain and sprinkle lightly with salt.

Mound the mhammara on a serving dish and sprinkle with the pine nuts. To eat, scoop up with the pita bread croutons.

The other great city of Syria is Damascus. Before World War I, it was a center of administration under the Ottoman Empire. As a result, its food has a distinct Turkish tinge, even though Damascus is farther from Turkey than Aleppo is. It is known for making the best baklava-type pastries in the Arab world.

The Turkish dishes known in Damascus include *jazzmazz* (fried meatballs; in Turkish, *cızbız*), *tirli* (mixed vegetables fried and then stewed with garlic and tomato juice; Turkish *türlü*), and *bashmishkat.*

This last dish, though it has a Turkish name (*başmış kat,* "pressed layer"), is not known in Turkey itself, so it may be a creation of the Damascus Turks. It requires a particular thin layer of muscle from the lamb's shoulder blade, which is flattened, stuffed with a filling of rice and fried meat, sewn up like a baseball, and cooked in a lamb and tomato stew.

Mnazzlit Ahmar wa-Aswad

In Lebanon and elsewhere in Syria, *mnazzli* is a stew of lamb, eggplant, and tomatoes. Damascus makes several varieties, including a meatless one of kohlrabi, so it distinguishes its tomato and eggplant version by calling it "mnazzli of red and black." Some people toast the eggplant in a pan rather than frying it in fat, so that it develops a flavor that faintly recalls roasted corn. Despite the foreign ingredients of tomato and allspice, this stew has a rather medieval flavor.

If mnazzli is made with olive oil instead of butter, it is called *mqalli.*

2 oz (½ stick) butter

1¼ to 1½ lb eggplant

1 lb ground lamb

1 tsp salt

½ tsp allspice

⅛ tsp cinnamon

12 cloves garlic, peeled and coarsely chopped

4 lb tomatoes

1½ c chopped cilantro

Water or tomato juice

Melt the butter and skim the solids off the surface. Separate the clear butterfat from the liquid underneath and transfer it to a saucepan.

Slice the eggplant ⅛ to ¼ inch thick. In a frying pan, fry the slices without butter until softened and brown in patches and beginning to become translucent, a minute or so on a side. Set aside.

Mix the meat, salt, allspice, and cinnamon and roll into meatballs ¾ to 1 inch in diameter. Place the meatballs in the pan with the clarified butter and fry over medium-high heat until they are stiff and turning brown. Add the garlic and continue frying, stirring often, until the garlic is softened and off-white.

Slice the tomatoes and add to the pan of meatballs, then add the eggplant and cilantro. Bring the contents to a boil, reduce the heat to medium, and cover the saucepan for 10 minutes. Remove the lid; the tomatoes should have given up their liquid. If the liquid level is not enough to cover everything, add a little water or tomato juice. Reduce the temperature, cover the pan, and simmer for 1 hour.

Add salt to taste. Serve with rice pilaf.

The cooking around Latakia on the Mediterranean coast resembles Lebanese food, with its free use of olive oil and lemon juice. The northeastern area of the country, like neighboring northern Iraq, makes lots of hearty soups and stews and often cooks disks of kibbi by poaching them in a vegetable stew.

Nomad food revolves around yogurt and flatbread, but for special occasions the Bedouin roast a whole lamb (*quzi*) stuffed with rice. They are famous for making an elaborate ceremony of roasting, grinding, and boiling coffee to honor a guest. They like to flavor their coffee with cardamom, and the closer a city is to the desert, the more likely settled people are to do the same. Coffee is an essential part of hospitality in all parts of society, and throughout Syria visitors are typically welcomed with Turkish coffee and a sweet. When finished with their coffee, guests politely say, "Qahwi daimi," that is, "May there always be coffee (in your house)."

Eating Out

In big cities such as Damascus and Aleppo, it is possible to find restaurants serving French or Italian food, and even hamburgers. However, most public eateries serve traditional roast meat dishes such as shish kebab (*lahm mishwi*) and *shawerma* (thin-sliced meat arranged on a vertical spit; browned portions are sliced off for serving as they are done). The meat may come with rizz bi-sha'riyyi, turnip pickles, and a tomato-cucumber salad, or it may be sold in pita bread with garlicky tahini sauce. These places also offer dips such as *hummus bi-tahini* and baba ghanoush and various salads, including tabbouleh.

Except in the most westernized segment of society, women rarely go to restaurants unaccompanied. Many restaurants have two sections—the regular section, serving men, and a separate room (*'ailat*), often on the second floor, serving families. Coffeehouses are even more of a male preserve. They serve much the same function that bars do in Europe or America, or teahouses in Iran and Central Asia: as a place for male socializing. They serve Turkish coffee and a variety of pastries.

Special Occasions

The chief religious celebrations of the Muslim majority are Eid al-Adha (the Feast of the Sacrifice), which falls on the last day of the Meccan pilgrimage, and Eid al-Fitr (the Feast of the Fast Breaking) at the end of the month of Ramadan. Eid al-Adha is the day when Muslims around the world, as well as those on the pilgrimage, sacrifice sheep (or other animals) in remembrance of Abraham's faithful willingness to sacrifice his son at the command of God, who allowed him to sacrifice a sheep in his son's place. It is a festive time of year, when stores are filled with decorations to welcome home the pilgrims who will soon return from Mecca. On Eid al-Adha, people dine and make sociable visits to family and friends.

Some people do slaughter their own sheep for the occasion, but most arrange with a butcher shop for some quantity of meat. Those who can afford to buy meat are expected to distribute some of it to families who can't. Naturally, Eid al-Adha spotlights meat dishes. Because the Islamic calendar is based entirely on the phases of the moon, Eid al-Adha can fall at any time of year, so on the whole the dishes served are those of the season rather than dishes unique to the Eid.

One of the principal religious obligations of Islam is abstaining from food and drink during the daylight hours of the month of Ramadan. From sunset to sunrise, in contrast, the faithful are permitted to eat and drink whatever they wish. They tend to avoid salty foods, which would make them thirstier during the following day. At the end of Ramadan, Eid al-Fitr is a day of feasting and socializing. In distinction from Eid al-Adha, it emphasizes pastries and other sweets rather than meat dishes.

The Shiites observe Ashura, the 10th day of the month of Muharram, with bitter mourning for the seventh-century martyrdom of the imam Husain ibn Ali. *Ashura* is also the name of a dish associated with this day; it consists of boiled whole wheat enriched with raisins and nuts. Grains and other seeds symbolize rebirth and/or the afterlife, and a similar dish is served among Christians at Easter.

Happy occasions such as weddings and births are celebrated with sweet foods—puddings and pastries. By the same token, sweet foods are considered inappropriate at sad occasions. After a funeral, guests are always poured bitter coffee.

Diet and Health

The Syrian diet is rich in fresh vegetables and notably in nuts, which figure in the fillings of both pastries and stuffed vegetables, so vitamin deficiency is not a serious problem. It is also rich in other healthful ingredients such as yogurt and garlic. However, it is low in fish and relatively high in saturated fats such as butter and lamb fat. This poses the danger of cardiovascular problems for sedentary city dwellers. At all levels of society, grain foods are a very important part of diet. Many urban men consume more simple than complex carbohydrates, because of the social institution of the coffeehouse and its tempting variety of baklavas.

Traditional medicinal concepts were derived from ancient Greek and Persian medicine; most complaints were analyzed as due to an imbalance of the bodily humors. Medical treatments aimed to correct this supposed imbalance. All foods were held to have medicinal qualities, so medieval doctors often prescribed particular dishes—they even gave recipes, which cookbook writers eagerly plagiarized. These theories no longer exert much influence on diet, and Syrian doctors now use modern medicines and techniques. Folk remedies survive, however. Tea and yogurt are often recommended to those suffering from diarrhea, and mothers brew bitter medicinal teas for sick children.

Charles Perry

Further Reading

Heine, Peter. *Food Culture in the Near East, Middle East, and North Africa.* Westport, CT: Greenwood Press, 2004.

Malouf, Greg, Lucy Malouf, Anthony Bourdain, and Matt Harvey. *Saha: Chefs Journey through Lebanon.* Berkeley, CA: Periplus, 2007.

Saleh, Nada. *Seductive Flavors of the Levant.* London: Robson Books, 2001.

Shoup, John A. *Culture and Customs of Syria.* Westport, CT: Greenwood Press, 2008.

Turkey

Overview

Turkey connects the southeastern tip of Europe with Asia and the Middle East; it has a population of 75 million that is predominantly Muslim. To the north of the country lies the Black Sea and to the south is the Mediterranean. The Aegean Sea lying to the west between Greece and Turkey connects to the Black Sea via the straits of the Dardanelles and Bosporus and the inland Sea of Marmara. The straits define the geological boundary between Europe and Asia: The European part of Turkey is called Thrace, and the Asian part is called Anatolia (Asia Minor). The present-day capital is Ankara, but the largest city is Istanbul, previously capital of the Byzantine and Ottoman empires. The country has nine neighbors: Georgia, Armenia, Azerbaijan, and Iran to the east; Iraq and Syria to the southeast; the island of Cyprus to the south; and Greece and Bulgaria to the west and northwest.

The literature on Turkish food culture generally begins with a reference to its Central Asian Turkic origins and continues with the legacy of the Seljuk and Ottoman empires. However, Turkey's cuisine is also heir to ancient Anatolian culture, whose roots lie in the Neolithic period, when farming began in this region, and which was subsequently shaped by a series of civilizations, including the Hittites, Urartians, Phrygians, Lydians, Greeks, Romans, and Byzantines. Persian and Arab influences have also been significant. The Turks came to Anatolia in the 11th century and continued to move westward, settling in the Balkans and pushing their way deep into Europe, reaching the gates of Vienna in the 16th century. The Ottoman Empire also extended southward to the Middle East and Africa. Consequently, today's Turkish food culture has a very varied and complex historical legacy, fostered by bountiful geography. Central Asian, Iranian, Middle Eastern, Mediterranean, and Balkan traditions echo in rituals, celebrations, cooking techniques, and eating habits, while recent archaeological studies reveal that some crops, harvesting and food-preparation methods, cooking techniques, and dishes have remained unaltered since Neolithic times. Stone mortars found in Çatalhöyük, a Neolithic settlement dating back to 7500 B.C., are almost identical with the ones still in use in the vicinity.

Turkey also hosts many ethnic cuisines including Circassian, Georgian, Armenian, Jewish, and Greek, but regionality rather than ethnicity dominates the kitchen. In the eastern city of Malatya, for example, people of Turkish, Armenian, Kurdish, and Arabic origin share the same foodways, such as the local specialty of stuffed cherry leaves, and their culinary culture is very different from that of a Kurd of southeastern Anatolia or an Armenian of Istanbul. Even within the Sephardic Jewish cuisine there is great regional diversity. There are also examples of localized communities with cuisines very different from those around them, as in the case of Tatar Turks in the central Turkish city of Eskişehir. Likewise, Circassian communities tend to keep their distinct cuisine intact wherever they live.

🍽 Food Culture Snapshot

Zeynep and her husband, Mehmet Yılmaz, live in Ankara, the capital of Turkey. They have two children, one

Famous Turkish appetiser imam bayaldi, baked stuffed eggplant, with turkish pide, or flatbread. The name literally means "the priest fainted", apparently due to the dish being so delicious. (iStockPhoto)

Early each morning the family begins the day by putting the kettle on for the tea. The janitor of the block of flats where they live leaves a fresh loaf of bread at the door, along with the daily newspaper. Breakfast is almost always the same: white cheese, yellow cheese, black olives, jam, honey, butter, and some sliced tomatoes accompanied by bread and glasses of tea. Zeynep also likes to have a dip of olive oil on the table. Mehmet usually buys cheese from a charcuterie, as he likes to sample it before making a selection. Zeynep laments that the taste of greenhouse tomatoes is not as good as traditional field-grown varieties. Recently she joined a nonprofit seed-exchange Internet group and started to grow heirloom tomatoes on their balcony. If it is a Sunday, Mehmet walks across the road to a nearby *bakkal,* a small grocery store, to buy extra newspapers and *sucuk,* spicy cured sausage. He also buys a couple of crusty *simit,* sesame-covered bread rings, from a street seller to accompany an extra Sunday treat of fried eggs with sucuk.

Zeynep, who is now retired, does the shopping. She buys fresh vegetables and fruits from the neighborhood market held twice weekly but makes an extra journey to the district where they used to live, to the butcher she has been accustomed to since they were first married, to buy meat and sometimes ready-made meatballs. However, many of their friends who have moved to new homes in the suburbs now buy packaged meat from supermarkets. When there is an urgent need or if a better selection is desired, she also shops from the *manav,* the pricier greengrocer. About twice weekly she buys freshly rolled *yufka,* thin pastry sheets similar to phyllo dough, to prepare *börek,* layered pastries. Since Mehmet comes from Gaziantep, the baklava capital of Turkey, he frequently brings a box of baklava from his favorite sweet shop. He also likes to buy a selection of meze (appetizers) from a good charcuterie if friends are invited for a meal accompanied by *rakı* (anise-flavored spirits) or wine. Until recently they used to buy thick yogurt from the street yogurt seller. Nowadays, Zeynep and Mehmet cannot resist regularly driving out of town to one of the large supermarkets to stock up on staples.

On the rare occasions when they go out to eat, the family usually opts for fish restaurants, since Zeynep has at last won her battle against Mehmet's preference

working in Istanbul, the other a university student still living at home. They met years ago in eastern Turkey, where Mehmet was working as an engineer and Zeynep as a teacher. Mehmet, originally from the southeastern agricultural city of Gaziantep, still receives an annual supply of homemade tomato paste, cracked wheat, dried vegetables, and so on from his family. Zeynep is from the small town of Ayvalık on the North Aegean coast and is still not reconciled to her husband's taste for meat and hot spices, as she comes from the land of olive oil and fresh greens. Her parents were migrants from Crete. The family usually spends their summer vacation in Ayvalık, where they get their year's supply of cured black and green olives and tins of olive oil from local producers.

for kebab restaurants, on the grounds of healthier eating. This once-sleepy town in Central Anatolia now has numerous fish restaurants, and many people argue that the best fish is to be had there because freshly caught fish from the Black Sea is transported to Ankara within hours.

Major Foodstuffs

Turkey is an important agricultural producer with a strong food industry. Climatic conditions vary widely from region to region. Except for high mountainous terrain the land is generally suitable for a wide range of agriculture and animal husbandry. There are some tropical microclimatic spots in unexpected corners of the country, such as the town of Rize on the northeastern Black Sea coast, where tea is a major crop, followed by kiwis and tangerines. The central and southeastern regions are the granaries of Turkey, while maize is the principal cereal grown in Thrace and the Black Sea coastal region. Rice is grown in the inland Black Sea region and northern central Turkey, and the Aegean is a major center of grape and fig cultivation. Turkey is the foremost world producer of hazelnuts, raisins, dried figs, dried apricots, cherries, and quinces. Turkey's Mediterranean region, especially the environs of Antalya, is the center of greenhouse production in Turkey, with year-round cultivation of fresh tomatoes, cucumbers, peppers, and other salad greens. A large range of other crops are grown in this region, including bananas and citrus fruits. Turkey's wide climatic diversity means that a very extensive range of different vegetables and fruits are grown in different parts of the country.

Wheat is the most important cereal, grown predominantly in central and southeastern Anatolia. Other cereals such as millet, barley, oats, and rye have mostly given way to wheat, while barley is on the rise again for beer production. Wheat is widely consumed as bulgur, parboiled and dried cracked wheat. Bulgur comes in many varieties and grades, fine for meatballs, coarse for pilafs, and so on. The earliest evidence of wheat agriculture is recorded in Anatolia and Upper Mesopotamia, in contemporary southeastern Turkey, and both wild species and the early cultivated wheat species einkorn (*Triticum monococcum*) and emmer (*Triticum dicoccum*) are still found in the region. Einkorn and in some regions emmer are known as *siyez,* apparently from the Hittite word *zez* for wheat. A regional wheat product is parched unripe wheat grains known as *firik.* Maize is grown mostly in the Black Sea region and Thrace. In the former region dried corn and cornmeal are major staples. Rice is popular throughout the country, as an ideal Turkish meal cannot be considered complete without rice pilaf. Bread of all sorts is also an indispensable staple food. Yufka, leaves of paper-thin pastry, is freshly produced in almost every neighborhood in cities to be baked into savory börek, a layered pastry dish with meat, cheese, or spinach fillings. *Yufka ekmeği* is unleavened flatbread dried for winter consumption.

Legumes constitute another major part of local diets. Lentils and chickpeas are among the most ancient Anatolian crops. Both appear in many dishes like soups, pilafs, casseroles, and stews. Roasted chickpeas are a popular snack called *leblebi.* Dried beans, such as black-eyed peas and fava beans, have always been an indispensable part of Turkish cuisine, although the *Phaseolus* species introduced following the Columbian Exchange is the main type grown today.

Vegetables of all sorts constitute an important part of the daily diet in Turkey. King of vegetables in Turkish cuisine is the eggplant, a native of India that arrived in Anatolia in the medieval period. It is cooked in many forms, usually fried and then braised with other ingredients, or char-grilled in the skin. It is also pickled and made into a sweet preserve. Famous eggplant dishes include *musakka* (sautéed eggplant, green peppers, onions, and ground meat, though not layered like its Greek cousin), *imam bayıldı* ("imam fainted"—braised eggplant stuffed with onions and tomatoes), *karnıyarık* ("split belly"—similar to imam bayıldı though with ground meat), and *hünkar beğendi* ("sultan's delight"— eggplant puree with cheese). Among other popular vegetables are zucchini, peppers, green beans, peas, and okra. A regional favorite of Istanbul and the Aegean region is artichokes, whose hearts are used to make several elaborate dishes. The use of garlic and onions is abundant. Root vegetables like celery, carrots, Jerusalem artichokes, beets, and potatoes dominate during the winter, along with leeks, cabbage, and cauliflower. Tomato is used abundantly in many dishes; when reduced to a sauce it lends a tang to all braised dishes. The concentrated tomato paste *salça* is a basic condiment that goes into most hot dishes.

Green leafy vegetables like spinach, chard, purslane, and wild purslane are very popular, the latter two also consumed raw as a salad. Anatolian foraging culture is deep-rooted, and local wild greens are consumed in all regions. Though there is a common perception that wild greens are a feature of Aegean cuisine, all regions have a wide variety and profound knowledge of using wild greens and herbs, as both food and folk medicine. Wild greens that can also be found in local markets include nettle, sorrel, mallow, borage, knotweed, *rumex* (a type of sorrel), mustard greens, wild chicory, wild fennel, wild asparagus, wild rhubarb, cardoons, poppy leaves, pennyroyal, arum, smilax, and wild lily shoots. Many vegetables and greens are dried for winter consumption.

Dairy products are also a major part of Turkish cuisine, as animal husbandry plays a prominent role in food production. Yogurt is a staple product for both rural and urban families throughout the country, consumed plain, as an accompaniment to dishes, or as a cooking ingredient in a wide range of dishes, from soups (*yayla çorbası*) to desserts (*yoğurt tatlısı*). Milk is drunk cold or hot, especially for breakfast. It is also used in soups, some savory dishes, and a large number of *sütlü tatlılar*, milk puddings. *Peynir*, cheese, ranges from fresh curd cheese to matured varieties. The most popular cheese is *beyaz peynir*, white cheese in brine. Other major cheeses include *kaşar*, hard yellow cheese; *lor* and *çökelek*, both types of curd; and *tulum* (cheese cured in goat- or sheepskin). *Kaymak*, clotted cream, is either served with honey at breakfast or added as a topping to desserts.

Butter is one of the principal cooking fats and in the past was clarified to prevent it from going rancid. This custom has now largely died out with the introduction of refrigerators. Other widely used cooking fats include sunflower oil and corn oil, and more recently hazelnut and peanut oils have become available. The once-popular sesame oil has totally vanished from the food scene, but sesame paste, *tahin*, is as popular as ever. Likewise, poppy oil consumption declined after the restrictions imposed on poppy cultivation (it is the source of illegal opium), but the much-loved poppy seed paste is used abundantly in the poppy-growing city of Afyon. Turkey is the second-largest producer of the opium poppy, which is cultivated under strict control.

Olive oil is the major type used in the Aegean region, and it is becoming increasingly popular in other parts of the country. Turkey is the fourth or fifth (depending on the year) olive oil–producing country in the world, and the second in cured olives after Spain. Olive oil is the essential ingredient in a large category of dishes known as *zeytinyağlı* (literally, "with olive oil"), the generic name for a vegetable or legume dish cooked with olive oil and eaten cold or at room temperature. These dishes were favored particularly by the Christian communities of the Ottoman Empire during the long Lenten fasts. Their cooling effect makes these dishes very popular during hot summer months.

All sugar in Turkey is made from sugar beets. Sugar beet production was introduced in the early years of Turkish Republic, and the establishment of sugar factories was like a manifesto of economic independence.

Meat is important in Turkish cuisine; some think meat dishes predominate. This is partially true, but in reality, for the majority of the population, meat is hard to afford. Still, it is not easy to be a vegetarian in Turkey as it is customary to put at least a handful of cubed or minced meat into most hot vegetable or pulse dishes. Meat is also consumed in the form of *kebap* (meaning roasted meats), which can be grilled or oven baked, or slow cooked in a pot. Another very popular category is *köfte*, meatballs of all varieties, and almost every town claims a specialty of its own. The meat of preference is lamb or mutton, although beef is now very common. Goat and kid remain a regional and seasonal specialty. Pork is forbidden for Muslims and Jews, so pork

Market, Kas, Mediterranean coast. (Corel)

products are very rare, with only very few farms catering to Christians and those who do not observe the religious ban. Poultry, mainly chicken, is also widely consumed and very popular. Game is restricted to regional cuisines and is not a part of the urban culinary scene. Meat is also preserved in various ways, dried, cured, or dry fried. Preserved meats like *pastırma* (cured dried beef coated with a spicy paste), sucuk (spicy cured sausage), and *kavurma* (potted meat) are consumed on their own or as a lavish ingredient upgrading various dishes from baked beans to fried eggs, or as a topping for *pide*, thin, pizzalike flatbreads.

Offal is still much appreciated, though getting rarer. There are specialized eateries for offal dishes. *Kelle* (lamb's head), *paça* (trotters), *ciğer* (liver), *işkembe* (tripe), *beyin* (brain), *böbrek* (kidneys), and *koç yumurtası* (lamb's testicles) are admired by

enthusiasts. Lamb's intestines are grilled as a popular street food called *kokoreç* and are stuffed to make the regional specialty *bumbar.*

Eggs are used in many dishes. Whether scrambled with tomatoes, green peppers, and sometimes onion to make the dish known as *menemen* or *şakaşuka*; fried with spinach, minced meat, or cured meats; or poached and served with garlic and yogurt sauce (*çılbır*), eggs constitute a quick meal. It is very common to consume wild greens scrambled with eggs in rural areas.

Sea fish and other seafood are mostly confined to coastal areas, although freshwater fish features in regional cuisines. The Black Sea region is renowned for *hamsi,* fresh anchovies. Istanbulites claim that fish caught in the Bosporus Strait are the finest of all. Sea bass, red mullet, bream, sole, turbot, bonito, mackerel, swordfish, and sardines are the most popular types. Mussels, squid, octopus, and shrimp are among the most widely consumed types of seafood.

Herbs and spices are very important in Turkish cuisine; however, they are used sparingly, to enhance the flavor of the dish, never to mask or to dominate. Parsley, dill, and mint are the major herbs used fresh, and dried mint and thyme are at hand in every kitchen. Dried purple basil (*reyhan*), dried tarragon, basil, and bay leaf are mainly used in regional cuisines. Chili flakes, paprika, black pepper, sumac, allspice, cumin, cinnamon, and cloves are the most common spices. Nigella seeds (the seeds of the plant known in the West as love-in-a-mist) and sesame seeds are sprinkled on buns and breads. Rarer flavorings are *mahlep* (the kernel of the *mahaleb* cherry) and *damla sakızı* (the resin of the mastic tree), which are added to breads, savory buns, and sweet cookies. The latter is also added to ice creams along with *salep* (the powdered root of flowers in the *Orchis* genus). Pomegranate concentrate is used as a souring agent. Pickles usually appear as a condiment on the table. Cabbage, green chilies, green tomatoes, cucumbers, carrots, unripe melons, and eggplants stuffed with chopped vegetables are most commonly pickled.

Fruit is abundant in Turkey, and white mulberries, black mulberries, strawberries, cherries, loquats, apricots, peaches, cherries, sour cherries, plums, damsons (a kind of plum), pears, apples, melons, watermelons, grapes, figs, quinces, pomegranates, persimmons, medlars, jujubes, bananas, oranges, grapefruits, and tangerines are consumed fresh seasonally. Many fruits are dried and consumed as snacks or stewed into compotes; mulberries, figs, grapes (as well as raisins), apricots, and prunes are among the most popular. The pulp of fruits such as apricots, plums, mulberries, and grapes is dried in sheets known as *pestil* (fruit leather). The juice of many fruits, above all grapes, is made into *pekmez*, molasses, which is still a very popular sweetener. Strings of nuts dipped several times in grape must boiled with starch make a sweet delicacy called *cevizli sucuk*, literally, "walnut sausage." Walnuts, pistachios, almonds, and pine nuts are much liked in both sweet and savory dishes. Hazelnuts and peanuts are used more in regional cooking or consumed

as snacks along with sunflower and melon or pumpkin seeds.

Water is served with meals. Turkey is very rich in spring and mineral waters, and many people pride themselves on being able to differentiate between water from different springs. After water, ayran (diluted salted yogurt) is the most popular beverage. Packaged fruit juices of all kinds have become popular in recent years, replacing the traditional *sherbets* made of various fruits, flowers, or spices. Fermented turnip juice, *şalgam suyu,* is a popular accompaniment to kebap. Despite having a history of only one and a half centuries, tea has become a national drink, brewed strong and served in tulip-shaped glasses. Herbal teas of all sorts are consumed widely, with linden flower, sage, and thyme being the most popular. Turkish coffee is served in-between meals or after lunch. It is made with finely ground coffee boiled and served unfiltered in a small cup in which the solids settle. In winter a sweet hot milk drink called *salep,* made from ground orchid root and sprinkled with cinnamon or ginger, and a thick drink known as *boza,* made from fermented grain, are popular.

The national alcoholic drink is rakı, anise-flavored grape spirit. Beer is very popular, and the selection of local wines keeps increasing every year. Wine producers have been giving emphasis to reviving native grape varieties recently. Anatolia is home to one of the oldest wine cultures in the world, a complete set of legislation being dedicated to vineyards and wine making back in the Hittite period (ca. 1650–1100 B.C.).

Cooking

Turkish cuisine involves many preparation and cooking techniques that range from simple to very labor-intensive. Most cooking is done over a burner. Many Turkish dishes start by sautéing onion in butter or olive oil. For hot dishes salça (tomato paste) and minced or cubed meat are also fried briefly. Other ingredients and water are added, and cooking is completed by simply braising and reducing the cooking juices. This method mingles and concentrates flavors, and the tasty cooking juice is mopped up with bread. Cold olive oil–based dishes are also cooked using the same technique but omitting the tomato paste and meat and reducing the cooking liquid almost completely. *Kavurma,* pan-frying meat and vegetables in their own juices with a little fat or oil, is another common method. Others include boiling, deep-frying or shallow frying, oven baking, embedding in hot embers, and grilling.

The traditional oven, the *tandır,* is a large earthenware pot sunk into the ground. Most towns still keep the tradition of stone-lined wood-burning communal ovens, called *taş fırın.* In the past it was common to take dishes that required baking to the local bakery, but nowadays most urban households possess a gas-fired or electric oven. One important utensil related to the oven is the earthen pot called *güveç.* A vegetable stew baked in the pot is called by the same name, *güveç.* Rural households have a trio of special equipment for preparing and cooking flatbreads and pastry: *hamur tahtası,* a low circular wooden table; *oklava,* a long, slim rolling pin; and *sac,* a domed tin griddle.

Some dishes involve skills that require experience and patience. *Sarma,* wrapped vine, chard, cabbage, or wild green leaves filled with meat or rice; *dolma,* vegetables such as bell peppers, red peppers, eggplants, squash, and tomatoes with a similar filling; and *mantı,* tiny pasta dumplings with a minced meat and onion filling, are among the most demanding examples.

Sauces are not common as the reduced cooking liquid serves as a sauce of its own. Some dishes, particularly soups, are perked up with a drizzle of butter sizzled with crushed dried mint and paprika. Cold garlic yogurt is a popular accompaniment for many hot vegetable dishes like meat-stuffed dolma or wrapped sarma. Garlic yogurt sauce is poured on mantı or on poached eggs, in the case of *çılbır,* and then drizzled with hot sizzling paprika butter.

Preparing foodstuffs for winter is a very important activity even in urban households. Most households prepare their own jams, preserves, pickles, and grape leaves in brine during the summer months. Many urban families still have connections with their native villages and return to the countryside

Kadayif, or Kanafeh, is a very fine vermicelli-like pastry used to make sweet pastries and desserts. Kanafeh is also found in the Balkans and is a feature of Lebanese, Turkish, Greek, and Levantine cuisine. (iStockPhoto)

to help with the harvest and winter preparations. Communal labor sharing is a common practice. Tomato paste and red pepper paste are among the essential end-of-summer preparations. Vegetables of all kinds are dried for winter. Hollowed-out eggplant, squash, bell peppers, and red peppers are dried to be used in stuffed dishes. Vegetables like okra, green beans, and wild greens are also dried. Another widespread dried preparation is *tarhana,* a fermented mixture of grains or flour and yogurt, and in some cases tomatoes and peppers, used as a ready soup mix, either crumbled or in the form of flattened patties to be reconstituted to a grainy soup.

Typical Meals

First thing in the morning tea is brewed. Breakfast is always accompanied by tea served in tulip-shaped glasses. Breakfast consists of fresh bread, black and green olives, beyaz peynir (white cheese in brine), *kaşar peyniri* (yellow cheese), *reçel* (homemade fruit preserves), honey, and butter. Usually fresh tomato and cucumber slices and fresh green peppers accompany the cheese. For a more elaborate table, kaymak (clotted cream) is served along with honey and jams. The most popular fruit preserves are *vişne* (sour cherries), *kayısı* (apricot), *çilek* (strawberry), *incir* (fig), and *gül* (rose). Sunday breakfast would also include fried eggs with sucuk (cured spicy garlic sausage) or pastırma (cured pressed beef). Breakfast in rural areas could be just a bowl of soup or flat unleavened bread rolled up with some wild greens, spring onions, or salty cheese.

For the midmorning break some people take tea with simit (bread rings sprinkled with sesame seed). This is called *kuşluk,* literally meaning "a bite fit for a bird." Others take Turkish coffee, traditionally served with a single piece of Turkish delight (*lokum*)— fruit-flavored jellies, though they come in many different flavors, sometimes studded with nuts.

Lunch is around noon and usually taken at a local eatery catering to working people. Students have a set lunch provided by their school canteens. Lunch usually consists of soup; pilaf made with either rice or bulgur; and a stew of beans, chickpeas, or lentils, or a meat and vegetable stew. A dried fruit compote or yogurt may accompany the main dish, sometimes replaced by a salad or *cacık,* a cold dish of yogurt mixed with diced cucumbers. Dessert may follow the meal or be eaten separately as an afternoon treat in a pudding shop or patisserie. Lunch for peasants working in the fields is often a wrap of flatbread with salty cheese, spring onions, and wild greens, usually accompanied by a jug of ayran, a diluted yogurt drink.

A midafternoon snack is known as *ikindi,* after the time of the afternoon prayer. Schoolchildren are sometimes served *ikindi kahvaltısı,* an afternoon "breakfast" that can be a mini-replica of breakfast, or *poğaça,* a savory bun, or börek. Housewives take this opportunity to arrange gatherings called *gün,* meaning "day," at which they take turns inviting friends. Dinner normally consists of soup, a meat and vegetable dish, rice or bulgur pilaf, a cold vegetable dish made with olive oil, and a salad, followed by dessert. Tea is again drunk after the dinner, and later at night fruit can be shared while watching TV.

Eating Out

Turkey has a deep-rooted tradition of public kitchens called *imaret,* established as institutions of charity. During the Ottoman times, imarets became an inseparable part of the urban landscape in most cities, offering free food for the needy. The institution is still functioning to a certain extent. Many eateries are formed around bazaars, another typical feature of Ottoman cities. Today, in many shopping and business areas, there are little eateries called *esnaf lokantası,* mainly catering to shop owners and shoppers, and often serving only lunch. The food on offer is mostly a choice of soups and a wide range of hot *tencere yemeği* (ready-braised hot dishes) laid out warm for the customers to choose from. The range includes legume/vegetable and meat stews, eggplant dishes, stuffed vegetables with minced meat, chicken stew or a slow-cooked meat dish, and rice pilaf. For dessert, *hoşaf,* dried fruit compote, is almost always present and can also be sipped alongside the meal as a palate cleanser. Depending on the season, pumpkin or quince desserts topped with walnuts or clotted cream and a milk dessert like rice pudding (*sütlaç*) are available.

For those who do not have the time to sit down for a full meal, another ubiquitous feature of modern Turkish cities is the *büfe,* sandwich bar, which offers toasted sandwiches with cheese or sucuk, spicy cured meat sausage, and *döner,* meat slices piled on a large vertical spit, roasted, and shaved into slivers. These places offer a variety of freshly squeezed fruit juices or *limonata* (lemonade).

In addition, a variety of specialized eateries offer one kind of food only. A *köfteci* is a place to have meatballs, often served accompanied by assorted pickles and *piyaz,* a bean and onion salad. The *pideci* serves pide, which is thin, oblong flatbread topped with cheese, meat, spinach, or eggs, or a mixture of these. The *işkembeci* sells *işkembe çorbası,* tripe soup, and is usually open overnight, as tripe soup is considered to be an ideal hangover remedy. The *çorbacı* is a soup (*çorba*) restaurant, which again remains open until late at night. The *börekçi* has a variety of börek (layered pastries), often served chopped up on small plates to be eaten quickly on the spot. The *muhallebici* specializes in milk puddings. Curiously, many milk-pudding shops also sell chicken soup and rice pilaf with chicken as a by-product of the signature pudding of the place, *tavuk göğsü kazandibi,* a milk pudding made of pounded chicken breast and caramelized on the bottom. Pastries of many varieties soaked in syrup are also sold in specialist shops, the favorite being baklava, a multilayered pastry filled with pistachios, walnuts, or cream. Others include *tel kadayıf* (pastry threads stuffed with nuts), *ekmek kadayıf* (rusks topped with clotted cream), *künefe* (pastry threads stuffed with cheese and served hot), *tulumba tatlısı* (fritters made of batter squeezed from a syringe), *lokma* (ball-shaped fritters), *revani* (cake made with semolina), and *şekerpare* (domed cookies).

A *kebapçı* can range from a modest eatery to an upmarket restaurant specializing in a wide range of grilled meat dishes. A kebapçı may also offer *lahmacun,* thin, round flatbread with minced meat topping; *çiğ köfte,* spicy raw meatballs; or *içli köfte,* fried or boiled fist-sized balls of bulgur filled with minced meat and chopped walnuts. Traditional eateries almost never serve alcoholic drinks, with a few exceptions in major cities.

Though prohibited by Islam, alcoholic drinks are widely enjoyed, especially in large cities and coastal regions. Drinking is considered a social occasion enjoyed at a table for long hours, the most typical location being a *meyhane.* The meyhane typically offers a selection of small platters of meze to be shared. The range of the meze on offer varies greatly from region to region; wild greens and seafood feature in the Aegean region, and hot and spicy spreads and dips in the southeast, with the greatest diversity found in Istanbul. The national drink is rakı. The essential basic mezes are white cheese and melon. Others include *ezme,* crushed tomato spread; *haydari,* yogurt and herb dip; *fava,* broad bean paste; *humus,* chickpea paste with tahini; *tarama,* salted carp roe; *lakerda,* salted bonito; *çiroz,* dried mackerel; *midye dolması,* mussels stuffed with rice; *Arnavut ciğer,* Albanian-style fried liver; fried eggplant; char-grilled eggplant salad; roasted red peppers; grape leaves stuffed with rice; octopus salad; and so on. Although a typical meze table spread is generally conceived as an array of cold dishes, there are also hot appetizers, which generally include fried börek, *kalamar tava* (fried calamari), and *midye tava* (fried mussels). It is possible to continue drinking through a main course, which can be either fish or an assortment of grilled meats. A meyhane dinner often concludes with a plate of fruit and Turkish coffee.

When eating out for recreation, Turkish families always prefer places serving dishes that cannot be prepared at home, such as specialties requiring a wood-fired oven or a special cooking technique. However, a modern Western restaurant culture has also developed in major cities. White Russian immigrants escaping the revolution had a major impact on Turkish restaurant culture as they established European-style dining venues, mainly in Istanbul and in the new capital, Ankara. International eating venues ranging from fast-food chains to coffee joints are common in many towns and cities. The Turkish response to this has been the recent phenomenon called *simit sarayı,* sesame-ring palaces, offering varied ways to consume the ubiquitous simit, the sesame ring bun. High-end restaurants that used to serve French cuisine seem to have switched to Italian or even to sushi. There is a recent trend of discovering lost local values, like reviving Ottoman court cuisine and the quest for regional foodways. Some young Turkish chefs are keen on experimenting to create a connection between the historical and the contemporary. Places to pass the time between meals are mainly the *kahve,* the coffeehouse, where men traditionally congregate, or the more family-friendly *çay bahçesi,* or tea garden.

Special Occasions

Turkey has a strong tradition of celebrations, whether religious, seasonal, or related to life transitions. Certain foods mark each such occasion. Life transitions are often marked by eating special foods. The engagement, *nişan,* can be celebrated like a small-scale wedding. Sugary cookies like *kurabiye* or *çörek* can be sent to the house of the bride to symbolize a commitment on the part of the groom. A box of chocolate has in many places taken the place of traditional sweets. Before the wedding there is a series of events, especially in rural areas. The houses of the groom and the bride hold different all-male and all-female gatherings. The bathing ritual at the *hamam* (Turkish bath) gets transformed into a party with lots of food and drinks served. The *kına gecesi* (henna night), held the night before the wedding, is an all-female event, involving the dyeing of the hands and feet with henna. Sherbets and sweets are essential at these events. The wedding ceremony is called *düğün* and is a big feast for all. Weddings usually take place in the summer and often after the harvest in rural areas.

At most celebrations and traditional weddings, four main dishes are important: soup, meat, rice, and dessert. Soup is preferably *düğün çorbası* (wedding soup—a meat-and-vegetable-based soup thickened with egg yolk and lemon), the meat can be kavurma or spit-roasted or oven-baked lamb. Rice pilaf can be prepared with chicken or meat stock. *Helva* (sesame paste, but there are also other varieties) or baklava is favored as a sweet. The meat and grain dish used to be *keşkek,* a long slow-cooked wheatberry and meat stew, cooked to a porridge-like consistency. This tradition still prevails in some rural areas.

Births are celebrated by *lohusa şerbeti,* the puerperal sherbet, a very sweet pinkish-red-colored warm drink. Strongly flavored with cinnamon and cloves, almonds or pine nuts are floated on top. The first tooth of the baby is celebrated by *diş buğdayı,* literally translated as "tooth wheat," which is boiled wheat berries tossed with sugar, sprinkled with cinnamon, and sometimes topped with a handful of crushed walnuts.

The *sünnet düğünü,* circumcision feast, is another important occasion. The father takes particular pride in this feast and uses the chance to show off his wealth. As well as abundant food there is entertainment for the children, such as the traditional shadow theater Karagöz. Vendors of sweets that are children's favorites like *pamuk helva* (cotton candy), *elma şekeri* (sugar-glazed apples), *kağıt helva* (wafer disks), *horoz şekeri* (rooster-shaped lollypops), and *macun* (assorted flavored sugar paste twirled on a stick) cheer up the crowd.

Death is commonly associated with helva, a generic name for many sweets but in this case made of semolina or wheat flour. Semolina or flour and some pine nuts are slowly pan-roasted in butter; syrup is added and stirred till the mixture reaches the desired consistency. It is important to take turns and recall all the deceased loved ones while stirring the helva. No cooking is done in the bereaved house; instead, abundant food is brought in by neighbors and relatives for the family and all those paying their condolences. Prayers are held on the evening of the 40th day following the death, and *mevlut şekeri* (a paper cone filled an assortment of *akide şekeri,* pulled sugar, topped with a plump lokum, Turkish delight) is distributed to the guests. *Lokma* (fried fritters soaked in syrup) is another sweet often distributed in memory of the deceased person.

Seasonal transitions are also celebrated. Nevruz on March 24 and Hıdrellez on May 6 are two rituals celebrated to welcome the spring. White dishes or milk-based dishes wish for a bright future at Nevruz and greens for a fresh beginning at Hıdrellez, which used to be the day when the first lamb of the season was spit-roasted. Both celebrations take place in the open air like a picnic, preferably near the seashore. Spring onions and boiled eggs are essentials of the picnic meal.

Religious festivals follow the Islamic lunar calendar. Ramadan, the month when most Muslims fast from sunrise to sunset, is a time of the year when eating becomes a focus of life. Certain foods mark Ramadan. Bakeries start making a special type of pide, leavened bread in flattened circles, which people line up to buy before sunset. Dinner following the fast is known as *iftar.* The fast is generally broken with dates or olives, and dinner continues with a soup and *iftariyelik,* a breakfast-like assortment of small bites including pastırma, followed by a main meat dish and rice pilaf, and then börek. The custom of having fried eggs before the meat dish has almost vanished. The foremost dessert of Ramadan is *güllaç,* a sweet prepared with paper-thin starch wafers, milk, and rose water. Ramadan is followed by a holiday that in Turkey is called *Şeker Bayramı,* meaning "the feast of candy." Gifts of candies are given to children, and sweets are served to guests. The other Islamic holiday is Kurban Bayramı, the feast of sacrifice, three lunar months after Ramadan. Distributing the meat of the sacrificed lamb to needy families is an important part of this feast. The month of Muharrem, which is the first month of Islamic calendar, is the time for *aşure,* a pudding of wheat berries, beans, chickpeas, dried fruit, and nuts.

Turkish coffee in a *zarf.* Taken from the Arabic word meaning container, the *zarf* gained popularity in Turkey as the serving of coffee became complex and ritualistic. (Shutterstock)

Diet and Health

The relation between food and health was central to Ottoman medicine both as a preventive measure and as a method of treatment. Ottoman medicine was based on Islamic medicine, which also followed the theories of the Greeks Hippocrates and Galen. Based on Galenic theory, as well as further knowledge developed by the Islamic physician İbn'i Sina (Avicenna) and the Andalusian botanist and pharmacist İbn-i Baytar, Ottoman medicine simply posited a direct causal connection between food and health. According to the system of thought, the human body has four humors or a combination of them, namely, blood, phlegm, yellow bile, and black bile, relating to the four elements of air, water, fire, and earth. Each represented qualities like hot, cold, moist, and dry. All foodstuffs carry these qualities, and one has to take care as to which combination of foods is to be consumed for one's health. This approach also gives much importance to seasonality, specifying what kinds of food have to be consumed to restore one's health.

This thought system is nowadays not known, but its influences still prevail. Turkish cuisine attaches much importance to seasonality and a balanced meal. Many dishes are automatically associated with seasons. A typical meal has a balanced distribution of proteins and carbohydrates and is accompanied by vegetables or wild greens. Two major healthy food items in Turkish cuisine are bulgur and yogurt. Bulgur is parboiled, dried, and cracked wheat berries, and this process enables the nutrients in the grain to be more easily absorbed. Dried fruit and nut snacks contribute to a healthy diet, along with the popular combination of *tahin-pekmez,* sesame paste and grape molasses.

Aylin Öney Tan

Further Reading

Algar, Ayla Esen. *The Complete Book of Turkish Cooking.* New York: Kegan Paul International, 1985.

Bilgin, Arif, and Samancı Özge, eds. *Turkish Cuisine.* Ankara, Turkey: Ministry of Culture and Tourism Publications, 2008.

Halıcı, Nevin. *Nevin Halıcı's Turkish Cookbook.* London: Dorling Kindersley, 1989.

Halıcı, Nevin. *Sufi Cuisine.* London: Saqi Books, 2005.

Heine, Peter. *Food Culture in the Near East, Middle East, and North Africa.* Westport, CT: Greenwood Press, 2004.

Peterson, Joan, and David Peterson. *Eat Smart in Turkey.* Madison, WI: Ginkgo Press, 1996.

Şavkay, Tuğrul, ed. *Timeless Tastes: Turkish Culinary Culture.* Istanbul, Turkey: Vehbi Koç Vakfı, 1996.

Turkish Cultural Foundation. Turkish Cuisine. http://www.turkishcusine.org/english.

Yemen and Oman

Overview

The Sultanate of Oman and the Republic of Yemen are on the southeastern coast of the Arabian Peninsula. Oman, about the size of Kansas, is a hereditary sultanate with an elected advisory council, and Yemen, midway in size between California and Texas, is a presidential republic.

From 1507 through 1742, Oman was occupied by the Portuguese. After Omanis drove out the Portuguese, they built up the country until in the 1800s, it was the most powerful country in the Arabian Peninsula. However, things deteriorated. The ruler from 1932 to 1970, Sultan Said bin Taimur, was suspicious of the outside world to the point of paranoia, and he did his best to isolate the country from outside, especially Western, influences. He restricted travel within the country, and Omanis who managed to leave were seldom allowed to return. Worried that his people might rebel against him, he even abolished schools. Although he had sent his son, Qaboos bin Said, to school and university in Britain, once Qaboos returned, Said kept him under house arrest, fearing that he might try to take over. In 1964, oil was discovered in Oman. In 1970, unhappy Omanis rose up against Said bin Taimur and, with British help, established Qaboos bin Said as Sultan. Qaboos built schools, hospitals, and other infrastructure to bring the country up to modern Western standards and also developed a tourism industry. Oman has little arable land but produces fruits and vegetables such as bananas, dates, melons, and tomatoes and raises camels, cattle, and goats. Unlike the rest of the peninsula, it receives rainfall in the summer from the monsoons.

Yemen has the most history of unrest on the Arabian Peninsula. It was part of the Ottoman Empire from the 1500s until the British gained control of part of the country in the 1800s. North Yemen and South Yemen were established in 1904. These two countries went through various changes of name and uprisings, including driving the British out of South Yemen in 1967. In 1984, oil was discovered in Yemen, and reunification talks began. Unification occurred in 1990. Yemen has not yet built itself up to the point reached by other countries on the peninsula. Yemen is the only country on the Arabian Peninsula that opposed the 1991 Gulf War against Iraq, leading to poor relations with the United States and other countries. In 2000, terrorists attacked the USS *Cole,* docked off the Yemeni town of Aden. The relationship between Yemen and the United States continues to be tense.

The kidnappings of several tourists over the years have hampered Yemen's efforts to develop a tourist industry. Yemen has good agricultural land and raises a large amount of the products its inhabitants use, including apricots, bananas, dates, eggplant, figs, grapes, mangoes, melons, okra, onions, and tomatoes, plus barley, millet, sorghum, wheat, chickens and eggs, cattle, goats, and sheep. Yemen also produces and exports honey, a major ingredient in many Arab desserts. Anticipating modern trends, Yemenis value local food highly.

Yemen's most famous agricultural product is coffee, considered by many the finest in the world. Although coffee originated in Ethiopia, scholars believe that it was first cultivated in Yemen and that the beans were first roasted there. The word *mocha* comes from *al-Makhâ,* the Yemeni port from which coffee was exported. Until the 18th century, Yemen dominated the world coffee trade; then, Dutch coffee enthusiasts obtained coffee beans to grow in Indonesia (hence the slang term *java*), and other countries developed coffee crops. Yemen no longer ranks even among the top 10 world coffee producers.

Oman and Yemen were famous in ancient times for their frankincense trees, and they supplied incense and myrrh to the Roman Empire at its height. Although their foods have some similarities with those of the other countries on the peninsula, geography has created some differences as well. They are more accessible from the sea coast than from land. Many of their food influences have come from India, Iran, and western Africa, leading to Omani and Yemeni foods being hotter and spicier than those of the other parts of the peninsula, and to the use of Indian breads.

🍽 Food Culture Snapshot

Khadija lives in a small village in Yemen. Every morning, she and her two daughters bake rounds of flatbread for the family's meals that day. They grind the sorghum that they prefer for bread and mix it with water, yeast, and salt. The oven is a *tannur,* a traditional clay oven shaped like a truncated cone. It takes practice to slap the bread quickly onto the inner sides of the tannur and remove one's hand before it gets uncomfortably warm. A grate rests on the open top to hold pots where Khadija boils rice, vegetables, and meat. A small hole in the oven's side allows her to insert fuel (charcoal or wood). A charcoal brazier, for warming the coffeepot, sits in a corner. The kitchen windows are closed, to keep dust out, making the kitchen almost unbearably warm in the summer. The windows are high in the wall, so men passing the house cannot look in at the women.

Coffee farmer picking ripe cherry beans for harvesting on the island of St. Helena, Yemen. (Darrinhenry | Dreamstime.com)

Both Oman and Yemen have modern supermarkets in the major cities, but residents also shop for food in traditional *suqs* (markets). Rural areas have smaller food shops and also *suqs* with merchants specializing in different kinds of foods and spices. In Yemen, men usually do the shopping.

Major Foodstuffs

Meals in these two countries are usually simple, but marinades and spices are used to add flavor. Most meals include meat, mostly chicken, fish, or mutton, as well as rice, vegetables, soups, and salads. Curried vegetables reflect the Indian influence. Oman grows limes that are dried (*loomi*) and used throughout the Middle East. Grated into powder or pierced and added to a stew, they give a tangy, musky taste. Food in Yemen is hotter than that in the rest of the peninsula, with liberal use of chilies and hot peppers. A typical Yemeni condiment is *zhug,* a spicy bread dip and relish often added to salads and main dishes. Yemeni cooking is particularly differentiated from the remainder of the peninsula by the use of the spice fenugreek. Another popular condiment is *hilbeh* or *hulba* (regional variations of the same name, with regional variations in the ingredients). It includes fenugreek, hot chilies, coriander, garlic, onions, tomatoes, cayenne pepper, salt, and black pepper. Sorghum and millet are the two most popular grains for bread.

Zhug

This spicy mixture is popular in Yemen as a dip or a flavoring for stews. Yemenis believe it aids health and long life.

3 cardamom pods

1 tsp black peppercorns

1 tsp caraway seeds

4 hot chilies

1 c parsley

1 c fresh cilantro

6 cloves garlic

1 tsp ground cumin

½ tsp salt

½ tsp pepper

2 tbsp olive oil

With a blender or food processor, grind the first three ingredients. Add the remaining ingredients and blend into a coarse puree. Store the zhug in the refrigerator.

Between meals, especially in the afternoon, many Yemeni men (and some women) chew the leaves of a plant called *qat,* not swallowing, but keeping a ball of it in their cheek. Qat contains an amphetamine-like chemical, which is a mild stimulant and appetite suppressant. It may cause insomnia, is addictive, and, worse, may be carcinogenic and cause other health problems. In Saudi Arabia, the United States, and other countries, growing and using qat is illegal. Use of qat has increased greatly in Yemen since 1970. Because it is popular and easy to grow, it is one of Yemen's major agricultural products. Some Yemenis are concerned about the effects of qat, both in terms of lost human productivity and because growing the plant uses water resources and acreage that could better be used for growing other crops the country needs. Farmers have increased qat production using land where coffee formerly grew, so coffee production has dropped.

Cooking

Because oil was found later in this area, it is not as developed as the other parts of the peninsula and so has fewer new houses and apartment buildings. Although many kitchens in the big cities have modern appliances, the kitchen of an older house has one or more tannurs, used as both oven and cooktop. In some areas, kitchens are roofed, semi-enclosed areas in the courtyards of houses, allowing the cooks better ventilation. An older house may have a traditional food-cooling system, based on evaporative cooling. A niche in the wall, with doors into the kitchen and holes in the outside walls, contains a stone or clay jar of water. Wind blowing through the holes evaporates water, cooling the air and any food that is in the niche. Traditionally, Yemenis used cooking pots made of iron and also shallow pots carved of soapstone. Now they are just as likely to use modern pots and pans.

Typical Meals

Most Omanis and Yemenis still eat in the traditional Arab style, with food served on communal platters placed on a cloth on the floor or ground. People serve themselves using pieces of flatbread as scoops or taking small pieces of meat or balls of rice with their fingers. As elsewhere in the Muslim world, they use only their right hands. In Yemen, even soup is presented in a single bowl; diners drink it from a common ladle. Omanis serve soup in glasses. Men eat first, and then women and children eat. They often eat the main part of the meal in relative silence, then move to another room for dessert, coffee, and conversation. All meals include dates, flatbreads, *laban* (a yogurt drink), and usually rice.

Breakfast includes stewed or fried beans, fried eggs with onion and tomatoes, or bread dipped in laban. Yemenis drink coffee with ginger or other spices in the early morning, then switch to *qishr,* a tea made from ground coffee husks, ground ginger, and sometimes cinnamon, cardamom, and/or sugar.

The main meal is usually the midday meal. It begins with a salad or raw vegetables, such as onions, radishes, or eggplant. On special occasions, Yemenis begin their meal with *bint al-sahn,* a dish made of a stack of very thin flatbreads with *samna* (clarified butter) between the layers, baked and served with honey and more samna. The main course includes vegetables, possibly spiced or curried, and rice with meat, fish, or chicken. Kebabs are popular. Another popular Yemeni dish is a stew called *saltah.* The cook simmers lamb, lentils, onions, potatoes, salt, cilantro leaves, and water together. When the stew is cooked, she adds hulba. Soups usually contain vegetables, meat, and lentils. With their long coastlines, both countries have an abundance of fish and shrimp. Omanis enjoy shark.

Bint al-Sahn

Serves 8–16

1 packet active dry yeast (0.25 oz), dissolved in ½ c warm water with 1 tsp sugar

4 c flour

1 tsp salt

5 eggs, beaten

¾ c samna (clarified butter), divided

For Serving

Melted samna or butter

Warm honey

1. Dissolve yeast in the warm water with the sugar.

2. Sift the flour and salt into a large mixing bowl.

3. Make a well in the center of the flour mixture. Pour eggs and the yeast mixture into the flour mixture.

4. Blend well, and turn out onto a board.

5. Slowly knead in ¼ cup of the samna. Continue kneading until dough is smooth and elastic.

6. Divide the dough into 12 balls.

7. Place a dough ball on a lightly floured board and form into a very thin round shape, about 8 inches across, using the heel of your hand or a rolling pin. If you haven't shaped such things by hand before, a rolling pin will work much better. Don't obsess about making perfect rounds.

8. Brush a baking sheet with samna.

9. Place the completed round on the baking tray, and brush well with melted samna.

10. Make 5 more rounds. After completing each round, place on top of the previous round, press the edges with fingertips, and brush well with samna.

11. Make a second stack of 6 more rounds. Brush the last round with the samna.

12. Let rest in a warm place for 45 minutes.

13. Preheat oven to 350°F.

14. Bake for 25–30 minutes until light brown. Don't overbake.

15. Serve with samna or butter and warm honey.

At the end of a meal, Yemenis take whatever food is left over, put it into a pot with sauce, and mix and heat it to create a stew, which they then eat with bread. Many Yemeni desserts include local honey. Popular desserts in Oman include *halwa* and *lokhemat,* fried pastry balls drizzled with lime and cardamom syrup. Coffee spiced with cardamom ends the meal in Oman. As in other Arab countries, Omanis and Yemenis drink large amounts of sweet tea, often spiced with mint, ginger, lemon, or cinnamon.

The evening meal is a lighter meal, similar to breakfast, or smaller amounts of the foods eaten at midday. For snacks, people in this area eat things like flatbread with hummus, falafel, kebabs, *shawarma* (similar to gyros), boiled potatoes, boiled eggs, fried fish, fruit, juice, or pastries.

Breads in Oman and Yemen include not only Arab breads such as *khubz* and *mardouf* (made with

A man sells fenugreek at a street market in front of Nakhl Fort in Oman. (Styve | Dreamstime.com)

dates) but also Indian breads such as chapatis, *parathas,* and *pooris* (flatbreads made in a tandoor oven, or fried and puffed). One of Yemen's specialties is *kutma.* It includes equal parts of wheat and sorghum flour and is made into a roll that is thicker than most flatbreads. *Lahuh,* a thin sourdough bread, is made with sorghum. Yemenis also eat samosas (Indian filled pastries, both savory and sweet), although they have developed some with Arab-style fillings such as cheese and mint.

Eating Out

Restaurants offer a variety of foreign cuisines, including European, Indian, and Oriental. American fast-food chains like Burger King, KFC, and McDonald's have franchises in the larger cities. As in the other peninsula countries, restaurants have segregated areas: an area for families, an area for men only, and sometimes an area for women only.

While Yemen is a dry country, non-Muslims may bring two bottles of alcoholic beverages into the country. They must consume these on private property. In Oman, alcohol is sold (to visitors only) in large hotels and is expensive. As with the other Arabian Peninsula countries, the natives of the country are Muslims and not allowed to drink. Visitors to the country should not offer liquor to Muslims.

Special Occasions

In Oman, a variation on the tradition of breaking the Ramadan fast with dates, obviously modern, is to freeze dates and break the fast with cold dates. Omanis also make *suh,* which is dates mixed with samna, sesame seeds and aniseed, cardamom, cumin, and/or fennel, a candy that they give as gifts during Ramadan. Other traditional Omani Ramadan foods are *sakhana,* a porridge made of dates, milk, molasses, and wheat, and *fattah,* a mixture of meats, vegetables, and bread. Omanis enjoy drinking laban, a yogurt-based drink, to break the fast, or perhaps lemonade with mint and rose water, watermelon juice with rose syrup, or tamarind juice with rose water. In Yemen, qishr is traditional for breaking the fast.

A popular dish for the Eid al-Fitr is *shuwa,* a labor-intensive dish that several families make together. A whole cow or goat is marinated in spices—cardamom, cinnamon, cloves, cumin, garlic, *loomi* (dried limes), red pepper, and turmeric—and date paste. This is wrapped in mats made of banana or palm leaves, buried in an underground pit oven lined with hot charcoal, and sealed so the smoke cannot escape. After 24 to 48 hours it is removed and served with rice.

In Oman, modern weddings for the more affluent include a party for the women at a hotel or wedding hall. As in other parts of the peninsula, the wedding party starts in the late evening and goes on until early morning. Buffets include items like flatbread, cheese, hummus, baba ghanoush, stuffed grape leaves, and other meze (little appetizer plates). When the groom comes to claim his bride at the end of the party, they cut the cake. Old-style weddings are simpler. Each family holds a party at its own house, with traditional foods including whole roasted sheep on platters of rice.

In Yemen, at the conclusion of the marriage contract, the father of the bridegroom throws raisins on the carpet. Male guests try to pick up as many raisins, representing future happiness in the marriage, as possible. The actual Yemeni wedding feast, with men and women in separate groups, features sheep and perhaps a calf. After the meal, the men chew qat or smoke water pipes.

Diet and Health

Modern medicine has come to Oman and Yemen relatively recently. Traditional medicine included herbs, spices, and honey. Yemeni honey has a reputation for curing all ills, from sore throats to ulcers to insomnia. Both countries now have modern hospitals. Obesity is less of a problem in these two countries than in the rest of the peninsula, partly because Western influences have not been around so long and partly because of the use of qat, an appetite suppressant, in Yemen.

Christine Crawford-Oppenheimer

Further Reading

Alford, Jeffrey, and Naomi Duguid. *Flatbreads and Flavors: A Baker's Atlas.* New York: Morrow, 1995.

al-Taie, Lamees Abdullah. *Al-Azaf: The Omani Cookbook.* Ruwi, Oman: Oman Bookshop, 1995.

Dorr, Marcia S. *A Taste of Oman: Traditional Omani Food—Authentic Recipes and How to Prepare Them.* Muttrah, Oman: Mazoon, 1992.

Heine, Peter. *Food Culture in the Near East, Middle East, and North Africa.* Westport, CT: Greenwood Press, 2004.

Levi, Zion. *The Yemenite Cookbook.* New York: Seaver Books, 1988.

About the Editor and Contributors

Ken Albala, Editor, is professor of history at the University of the Pacific in Stockton, California. He also teaches in the gastronomy program at Boston University. Albala is the author of many books, including *Eating Right in the Renaissance* (University of California Press, 2002), *Food in Early Modern Europe* (Greenwood Press, 2003), *Cooking in Europe 1250–1650* (Greenwood Press, 2005), *The Banquet: Dining in the Great Courts of Late Renaissance Europe* (University of Illinois Press, 2007), *Beans: A History* (Berg Publishers, 2007; winner of the 2008 International Association of Culinary Professionals Jane Grigson Award), and *Pancake* (Reaktion Press, 2008). He has co-edited two works, *The Business of Food* and *Human Cuisine.* He is also editor of three food series with 29 volumes in print, including the Food Cultures Around the World series for Greenwood Press. Albala is also co-editor of the journal *Food Culture and Society.* He is currently researching a history of theological controversies surrounding fasting in the Reformation Era and is editing two collected volumes of essays, one on the Renaissance and the other entitled *The Lord's Supper.* He has also coauthored a cookbook for Penguin/Perigee entitled *The Lost Art of Real Cooking,* which was released in July 2010.

Julia Abramson has visited France on a regular basis for more than 25 years to study, research, travel, and eat. She has published essays on aspects of food culture from vegetable carving to gastronomic writing and is the author of the book *Food Culture in France.* Abramson teaches French literature and culture and food studies at the University of Oklahoma, Norman.

M. Shahrim Al-Karim is a senior lecturer of food service and hospitality management at the Universiti Putra Malaysia. His research interests include food and culture, culinary tourism, food habits, and consumer behavior. He received a BS in hotel and restaurant management from New York University; an MBA from Universiti Teknologi MARA, Malaysia; and a PhD in hospitality and tourism from Oklahoma State University, United States.

E. N. Anderson is professor emeritus of the Department of Anthropology, University of California, Riverside.

Laura P. Appell-Warren holds a doctorate in psychological anthropology from Harvard University. Her primary focus of research has been the study of personhood; however, she has also studied the effects of social change on children's play. She has done research among the Bulusu' of East Kalimantan, Indonesia, and among the Rungus Momogon, a Dusunic-speaking peoples, of Sabah, Malyasia. In addition, she has traveled widely throughout Arctic Canada. She is the editor of *The Iban Diaries of Monica Freeman 1949–1951: Including Ethnographic Drawings, Sketches, Paintings, Photographs and Letters* and is author of the forthcoming volume entitled *Personhood: An Examination of the History and Use of an Anthropological Concept.* In addition to her current research on cradleboard use among Native North Americans, she is a teacher of anthropology at St. Mark's School in Southborough, Massachusetts.

Heather Arndt-Anderson is a Portland, Oregon, native who draws culinary inspiration from many world cuisines but prefers cooking from her own backyard. She is a part-time natural resources consultant and a full-time radical homemaker; in her (rare) spare time she writes the food blog *Voodoo & Sauce.*

Michael Ashkenazi is a scholar, writer, and consultant who has been researching and writing about Japanese food since 1990. In addition to books and articles on Japanese society, including its food culture, he has written numerous scholarly and professional articles and papers on various subjects including theoretical and methodological issues in anthropology, organized violence, space exploration, migration, religion and ritual, resettling ex-combatants, and small arms. He has taught at higher-education institutions in Japan, Canada, Israel, and the United Kingdom, directing graduate and undergraduate students. He is currently senior researcher and project leader at the Bonn International Center for Conversion in Germany, with responsibility for the areas of small arms and reintegration of ex-combatants. He has conducted field research in East and Southeast Asia, East and West Africa, the Middle East, and Latin America.

Babette Audant went to Prague after college, where she quickly gave up teaching English in order to cook at a classical French restaurant. After graduating from the Culinary Institute of America, she worked as a chef in New York City for eight years, working at Rainbow Room, Beacon Bar & Grill, and other top-rated restaurants. She is a lecturer at City University of New York Kingsborough's Department of Tourism and Hospitality, and a doctoral candidate in geography at the City University of New York Graduate Center. Her research focuses on public markets and food policy in New York City.

Gabriela Villagran Backman, MA (English and Hispanic literature), was born in Sweden and raised in Mexico and the United States; she currently lives in Stockholm, Sweden. She is an independent researcher, interested in food studies, cultural heritage, writing cookbooks, red wine, and the Internet.

Carolyn Bánfalvi is a writer based in Budapest. She is the author of *Food Wine Budapest* (Little Bookroom) and *The Food and Wine Lover's Guide to Hungary: With Budapest Restaurants and Trips to the Wine Country* (Park Kiado). She contributes to numerous international food and travel publications and leads food and wine tours through Taste Hungary, her culinary tour company.

Peter Barrett is a painter who writes a food blog and is also the Food & Drink writer for *Chronogram Magazine* in New York's Hudson Valley.

Cynthia D. Bertelsen is an independent culinary scholar, nutritionist, freelance food writer, and food columnist. She lived in Haiti for three years and worked on a food-consumption study for a farming-systems project in Jacmel, Haiti. She writes a food history blog, *Gherkins & Tomatoes,* found at http://gherkinstoma toes.com.

Megan K. Blake is a senior lecturer in geography at the University of Sheffield. She has published research that examines the intersections between place and social practices. While her previous work focused on entrepreneurship and innovation, her recent work has examined food practices and family life.

Janet Boileau is a culinary historian who holds a master of arts degree in gastronomy from Le Cordon Bleu Paris and a doctorate in history from the University of Adelaide.

Andrea Broomfield is associate professor of English at Johnson County Community College in Overland Park, Kansas, and author of *Food and Cooking in Victorian England: A History.*

Cynthia Clampitt is a culinary historian, world traveler, and award-winning author. In 2010, she was elected to the Society of Women Geographers.

Neil L. Coletta is assistant director of food, wine, and the arts and lecturer in the MLA in gastronomy program at Boston University. His current research includes food and aesthetics and experimental pedagogy in the field of food studies.

Paul Crask is a travel writer and the author of two travel guides: *Dominica* (2008) and *Grenada, Carriacou and Petite Martinique* (2009).

Christine Crawford-Oppenheimer is the information services librarian and archivist at the Culinary Institute of America. She grew up in Ras Tanura, Saudi Arabia.

Anita Verna Crofts is on the faculty at the University of Washington's Department of Communication, where she serves as an associate director of the master of communication in digital media program. In addition, she holds an appointment at the University of Washington's Department of Global Health, where she collaborates with partner institutions in Sudan, Namibia, and India on trainings that address leadership, management, and policy development, with her contributions targeted at the concept of storytelling as a leadership and evidence tool. Anita is an intrepid chowhound and publishes on gastroethnographic topics related to the intersection of food and identity. She hosts the blog *Sneeze!* at her Web site www.pepperforthebeast.com.

Liza Debevec is a research fellow at the Scientific Research Centre of the Slovene Academy of sciences and arts in Ljubljana, Slovenia. She has a PhD in social anthropology from the University of St. Andrews, United Kingdom. Her research interests are West Africa and Burkina Faso, food studies, Islam, gender, identity, and practice of everyday life.

Jonathan Deutsch is associate professor of culinary arts at Kingsborough Community College, City University of New York, and Public Health, City University of New York Graduate Center. He is the author or editor of five books including, with Sarah Billingsley, *Culinary Improvisation* (Pearson, 2010) and, with Annie Hauck-Lawson, *Gastropolis: Food and New York City* (Columbia University Press, 2009).

Deborah Duchon is a nutritional anthropologist in Atlanta, Georgia.

Nathalie Dupree is the author of 10 cookbooks, many of which are about the American South, for which she has won two James Beard Awards. She has hosted over 300 television shows on the Public Broadcasting Service, The Food Network, and TLC. She lives with her husband, Jack Bass, who has authored 9 books about the American South and helped with her contribution to *Food Cultures of the World.*

Pamela Elder has worked in food public relations and online culinary education and is a freelance writer in the San Francisco Bay area.

Rachel Finn is a freelance writer whose work has appeared in various print and online publications. She is the founder and director of Roots Cuisine, a nonprofit organization dedicated to promoting the foodways of the African diaspora around the globe.

Richard Foss has been a food writer and culinary historian since 1986, when he started as a restaurant critic for the *Los Angeles Reader*. His book on the history of rum is slated for publication in 2011, to be followed by a book on the history of beachside dining in Los Angeles. He is also a science fiction and fantasy author, an instructor in culinary history and Elizabethan theater at the University of California, Los Angeles, Extension, and is on the board of the Culinary Historians of Southern California.

Nancy G. Freeman is a food writer and art historian living in Berkeley, California, with a passion for food history. She has written about cuisines ranging from Ethiopia to the Philippines to the American South.

Ramin Ganeshram is a veteran journalist and professional chef trained at the Institute of Culinary Education in New York City, where she has also worked as a recreational chef instructor. Ganeshram also holds a master's degree in journalism from Columbia University. For eight years she worked as a feature writer/stringer for the *New York Times* regional sections, and she spent another eight years as a food columnist and feature writer for *Newsday*. She is the author of *Sweet Hands: Island Cooking from Trinidad and Tobago* (Hippocrene NY, 2006; 2nd expanded edition, 2010) and *Stir It Up* (Scholastic, 2011). In addition to contributing to a variety of food publications including *Saveur, Gourmet, Bon Appetit,* and epicurious.com, Ganeshram has written articles on food, culture, and travel for *Islands* (as contributing editor), *National Geographic Traveler,*

Forbes Traveler, Forbes Four Seasons, and many others. Currently, Ganeshram teaches food writing for New York University's School of Continuing Professional Studies.

Hanna Garth is a doctoral candidate in the Department of Anthropology at the University of California, Los Angeles. She is currently working on a dissertation on household food practices in Santiago de Cuba. Previously, she has conducted research on food culture, health, and nutrition in Cuba, Chile, and the Philippines.

Mary Gee is a medical sociology doctoral student at the University of California, San Francisco. Her current research interests include herbalism and Asian and Asian American foodways, especially with regards to multigenerational differences. Since 1995, she has actively worked with local and national eating disorders research and policy and advocacy organizations as well as for a program evaluation research consulting firm.

Che Ann Abdul Ghani holds a bachelor's degree in English and a master's degree in linguistics. She has a keen interest in studying language and language use in gastronomy. She is currently attached to the English Department at Universiti Putra Malaysia. Her research interests range from the use of language in context (pragmatics) to language use in multidisciplinary areas, namely, disciplines related to the social sciences. She also carries out work in translation and editing.

Maja Godina-Golija is research adviser at the Institute of Slovenian Ethnology, Scientific Research Centre of Slovenian Academy of Science and Arts, Ljubljana, Slovenia.

Annie Goldberg is a graduate student studying gastronomy at Boston University.

Darra Goldstein is Frances Christopher Oakley Third Century Professor of Russian at Williams College and the founding editor-in-chief of *Gastronomica: The Journal of Food and Culture.*

Keiko Goto, PhD, is associate professor at the Department of Nutrition and Food Sciences, California State University, Chico. Dr. Goto has more than 15 years of work experience in the field of nutrition and has worked as a practitioner and researcher in various developing countries. Dr. Goto's current research areas include food and culture, child and adolescent nutrition, sustainable food systems, and international nutrition.

Carla Guerrón Montero is a cultural and applied anthropologist trained in Latin America and the United States. She is currently associate professor of anthropology in the Department of Anthropology at the University of Delaware. Dr. Guerrón Montero's areas of expertise include gender, ethnicity, and identity; processes of globalization/nationalism, and particularly tourism; and social justice and human rights.

Mary Gunderson calls her practice paleocuisineology, where food and cooking bring cultures alive. Through many media, including the sites HistoryCooks.com and MaryGunderson.com, she writes and speaks about South and North American food history and contemporary creative living and wellness. She wrote and published the award-winning book *The Food Journal of Lewis and Clark: Recipes for an Expedition* (History Cooks, 2003) and has authored six food-history books for kids.

Liora Gvion is a senior lecturer at the Kibbutzim College of Education and also teaches at the Faculty of Agriculture, Food and Environment at the Institute of Biochemistry, Food Science and Nutrition Hebrew University of Jerusalem.

Cherie Y. Hamilton is a cookbook author and specialist on the food cultures and cuisines of the Portuguese-speaking countries in Europe, South America, Africa, and Asia.

Jessica B. Harris teaches English at Queens College/City University of New York and is director of the Institute for the Study of Culinary Cultures at Dillard University.

Melanie Haupt is a doctoral candidate in English at the University of Texas at Austin. Her dissertation, "Starting from Scratch: Reading Women's Cooking Communities," explores women's use of cookbooks and recipes in the formation and reification of real and virtual communities.

Ursula Heinzelmann is an independent scholar and culinary historian, twice awarded the prestigious Sophie Coe Prize. A trained chef, sommelier, and ex-restaurateur, she now works as a freelance wine and food writer and journalist based in Berlin, Germany.

Jennifer Hostetter is an independent food consultant specializing in writing, research, and editing. She has degrees in history and culinary arts and holds a master's degree in food culture and communications from the University of Gastronomic Sciences in Italy. She also served as editorial assistant for this encyclopedia.

Kelila Jaffe is a doctoral candidate in the Food Studies Program at New York University. Originally from Sonoma, California, and the daughter of a professional chef, she has pursued anthropological and archaeological foodways research since her entry into academia. She received a BA with distinction in anthropology from the University of Pennsylvania, before attending the University of Auckland, where she earned an MA with honors in anthropology, concentrating in archaeology. Her research interests include past foodways, domestication, and zooarchaeology, and she has conducted fieldwork in Fiji, New Zealand, and Hawaii.

Zilkia Janer is associate professor of global studies at Hofstra University in New York. She is the author of *Puerto Rican Nation-Building Literature: Impossible Romance* (2005) and *Latino Food Culture* (2008).

Brelyn Johnson is a graduate of the master's program in food studies at New York University.

Kate Johnston is currently based in Italy, where she is an independent cultural food researcher and writer and a daily ethnographer of people's food habits. She has a degree in anthropology from Macquarie University in Sydney, Australia, and a recent master's degree in food culture and communication from the University of Gastronomic Sciences, Italy. She was also editorial assistant for this encyclopedia.

Desiree Koh was born and raised in Singapore. A writer focusing on travel, hospitality, sports, fitness, business, and, of course, food, Koh's explorations across the globe always begin at the market, as she believes that the sight, scent, and savoring of native produce and cuisine are the key to the city's heart. The first and only female in Major League Eating's Asia debut, Koh retired from competition to better focus on each nibble and sip of fine, hopefully slow food.

Bruce Kraig is emeritus professor of history at Roosevelt University in Chicago and adjunct faculty at the Culinary School of Kendall College, Chicago. He has published and edited widely in the field of American and world food history. Kraig is also the founding president of the Culinary Historians of Chicago and the Greater Midwest Foodways Alliance.

R. J. Krajewski is the research services librarian at Simmons College, where among other things he facilitates discovery of food-culture research, especially through the lens of race, class, and gender. His own engagement with food is seasonally and locally rooted, starting in his own small, urban homestead, much like his Polish and German ancestors.

Erin Laverty is a freelance food writer and researcher based in Brooklyn, New York. She holds a master's degree in food studies from New York University.

Robert A. Leonard has a PhD in theoretical linguistics from Columbia. He studies the way people create and communicate meaning, including through food. He was born in Brooklyn and trained as a cook and *panaderia-reposteria* manager in the Caribbean; his doctoral studies led him to eight years of fieldwork in language, culture, and food in Africa and Southeast Asia. In the arts, as an undergraduate he cofounded and led the rock group Sha Na Na and with them opened for their friend Jimi Hendrix at the Woodstock Festival. Leonard is probably one of a very few people who have worked with both the Grateful Dead and the Federal Bureau of Investigation, which in recent years recruited him to teach the emerging science of forensic linguistics at Quantico.

Jane Levi is an independent consultant and writer based in London, England. She is currently working on her PhD at the London Consortium, examining food in utopias, funded by her work on post-trade financial policy in the City of London.

Yrsa Lindqvist is a European ethnologist working as the leading archivist at the Folk Culture Archive in Helsinki. Her research about food and eating habits in the late 1990s, combined with earlier collections at the archive, resulted in 2009 in the publication *Mat, Måltid, Minne. Hundraår av finlandssvensk matkulur.* The book analyzes the changes in housekeeping and attitudes toward food. She has also contributed to other publications focusing on identity questions and has worked as a junior researcher at the Academy of Finland.

William G. Lockwood is professor emeritus of cultural anthropology at the University of Michigan. His central interest is ethnicity and interethnic relations. He has conducted long-term field research in Bosnia-Herzegovina and the Croatian community in Austria and also among Roma and with a variety of ethnic groups in America, including Arabs, Finns, and Bosnians. He has long held a special interest in how food functions in ethnic group maintenance and in reflecting intra- and intergroup relations.

Yvonne R. Lockwood is curator emeritus of folklife at the Michigan State University Museum. Her formal training is in folklore, history, and Slavic languages and literatures. Research in Bosnia, Austria, and the United States, especially the Great Lakes region, has resulted in numerous publications, exhibitions, festival presentations, and workshops focused on her primary interests of foodways and ethnic traditions.

Janet Long-Solís, an anthropologist and archaeologist, is a research associate at the Institute of Historical Research at the National University of Mexico. She has published several books and articles on the chili pepper, the history of Mexican food, and the exchange of food products between Europe and the Americas in the 16th century.

Kristina Lupp has a background in professional cooking and has worked in Toronto and Florence. She is currently pursuing a master of arts in gastronomy at the University of Adelaide.

Máirtín Mac Con Iomaire is a lecturer in culinary arts in the Dublin Institute of Technology. Máirtín is well known as a chef, culinary historian, food writer, broadcaster, and ballad singer. He lives in Dublin with his wife and two daughters. He was the first Irish chef to be awarded a PhD, for his oral history of Dublin restaurants.

Glenn R. Mack is a food historian with extensive culinary training in Uzbekistan, Russia, Italy, and the United States. He cofounded the Culinary Academy of Austin and the Historic Foodways Group of Austin and currently serves as president of Le Cordon Bleu College of Culinary Arts Atlanta.

Andrea MacRae is a lecturer in the Le Cordon Bleu Graduate Program in Gastronomy at the University of Adelaide, Australia.

Giorgos Maltezakis earned his PhD in anthropology with research in cooperation with the Institute Studiorium Humanitatis of the Ljubljana Graduate School of the Humanities. His dissertation was on consumerism, the global market, and food, which was an ethnographic approach to the perception of food in Greece and Slovenia.

Bertie Mandelblatt is assistant professor at the University of Toronto, cross-appointed to the departments of Historical Studies and Geography. Her research concerns the early-modern French Atlantic, with a focus on commodity exchanges at the local and global scales: Her two current projects are the history of food provisioning in the Franco-Caribbean and the transatlantic circulation of French rum and molasses, both in the 17th and 18th centuries.

Marty Martindale is a freelance writer living in Largo, Florida.

Laura Mason is a writer and food historian with a special interest in local, regional, and traditional foods in the United Kingdom and elsewhere. Her career has explored many dimensions of food and food production, including cooking for a living, unraveling the history of sugar confectionery, and trying to work out how many traditional and typically British foods relate to culture and landscape. Her publications include *Taste of Britain* (with Catherine Brown; HarperCollins, 2006), *The Food Culture of Great Britain* (Greenwood, 2004), and *The National Trust Farmhouse Cookbook* (National Trust, 2009).

Anton Masterovoy is a PhD candidate at the Graduate Center, City University of New York. He is working on his dissertation, titled "Eating Soviet: Food and Culture in USSR, 1917–1991."

Anne Engammare McBride, a Swiss native, food writer, and editor, is the director of the Experimental Cuisine Collective and a food studies PhD candidate at New York University. Her most recent book is *Culinary Careers: How to Get Your Dream Job in Food,* coauthored with Rick Smilow.

Michael R. McDonald is associate professor of anthropology at Florida Gulf Coast University. He is the author of *Food Culture in Central America.*

Naomi M. McPherson is associate professor of cultural anthropology and graduate program coordinator at the University of British Columbia, Okanagan Campus. Since 1981, she has accumulated over three years of field research with the Bariai of West New Britain, Papua New Guinea.

Katrina Meynink is an Australia-based freelance food writer and researcher. She has a master's degree in gastronomy through Le Cordon Bleu and the University of Adelaide under a scholarship from the James Beard Foundation. She is currently completing her first cookbook.

Barbara J. Michael is a sociocultural anthropologist whose research focuses on social organization, economics, decision making, and gender. Her geographic focus is on the Middle East and East Africa, where she has done research with the pastoral nomadic Hawazma Baggara and on traditional medicine in Yemen and is working on a video about men's cafes as a social institution. She teaches anthropology at the University of North Carolina Wilmington and has also worked as a consultant for several United Nations agencies.

Diana Mincyte is a fellow at the Rachel Carson Center at the Ludwig Maximilian University-Munich and visiting assistant professor in the Department of Advertising at the University of Illinois, Urbana-Champaign. Mincyte examines topics at the interface of food, the environment, risk society, and global inequalities. Her book investigates raw-milk politics in the European Union to consider the production risk society and its institutions in post-Socialist states.

Rebecca Moore is a doctoral student studying the history of biotechnology at the University of Toronto in Ontario, Canada.

Nawal Nasrallah, a native of Iraq, was a professor of English and comparative literature at the universities of Baghdad and Mosul until 1990. As an independent scholar, she wrote the award-winning *Delights from the Garden of Eden: A Cookbook and a History of the Iraqi Cuisine* and *Annals of the Caliphs' Kitchens* (an English translation of Ibn Sayyar al-Warraq's 10th-century Baghdadi cookbook).

Henry Notaker graduated from the University of Oslo with a degree in literature and worked for many years as a foreign correspondent and host of arts and letters shows on Norwegian national television. He has written several books about food history, and with *Food Culture in Scandinavia* he won the Gourmand World Cookbook Award for best culinary history in 2009. His last book is a bibliography of early-modern culinary literature, *Printed Cookbooks in Europe 1470–1700.* He is a member of the editorial board of the journal *Food and History.*

Kelly O'Leary is a graduate student at Boston University in gastronomy and food studies and executive chef at the Bayridge University Residence and Cultural Center.

Fabio Parasecoli is associate professor and coordinator of food studies at the New School in New York City. He is author of *Food Culture in Italy* (2004) and *Bite Me: Food and Popular Culture* (2008).

Susan Ji-Young Park is the program director and head of curriculum development at École de Cuisine Pasadena (www.ecolecuisine.com); project leader for Green Algeria, a national environmental initiative; and a writer for LAWEEKLY'S Squid Ink. She has written curriculum for cooking classes at Los Angeles Unified School District, Sur La Table, Whole Foods Market, Central Market, and Le Cordon Bleu North America. She and her husband, Chef Farid Zadi, have co-written recipes for *Gourmet Magazine* and the *Los Angeles Times.* The couple are currently writing several cookbooks on North African, French, and Korean cuisines.

Rosemary Parkinson is author of *Culinaria: The Caribbean, Nyam Jamaica,* and *Barbados Bu'n-Bu'n,* and she contributes culinary travel stories to Caribbean magazines.

Charles Perry majored in Middle East languages at Princeton University, the University of California, Berkeley, and the Middle East Centre for Arab Studies, Shimlan, Lebanon. From 1968 to 1976 he was a copy editor and staff writer at *Rolling Stone* magazine in San Francisco, before leaving to work as a freelance writer specializing in food. From 1990 to 2008, he was a staff writer in the food section of the *Los Angeles Times.* He has published widely on the history of Middle Eastern food and was a major contributor to the *Oxford Companion to Food* (1999).

Irina Petrosian is a native of Armenia and a professional journalist who has written for Russian, Armenian, and U.S.-based newspapers. She is the coauthor of

Armenian Food: Fact, Fiction, and Folklore and holds degrees in journalism from Moscow State University and Indiana University.

Suzanne Piscopo is a nutrition, family, and consumer studies lecturer at the University of Malta in Malta. She is mainly involved in the training of home economics and primary-level teachers, as well as in nutrition and consumer-education projects in different settings. Suzanne is a registered public health nutritionist, and her research interests focus on socioecological determinants of food intake, nutrition interventions, and health promotion. She has also written a series of short stories for children about food. Suzanne enjoys teaching and learning about the history and culture of food and is known to creatively experiment with the ingredients at hand when cooking the evening meal together with her husband, Michael.

Theresa Preston-Werner is an advanced graduate student in anthropology at Northwestern University.

Meg Ragland is a culinary history researcher and librarian. She lives in Boston, Massachusetts.

Carol Selva Rajah is an award-winning chef and food writer currently based in Sydney, Australia. She has written 10 cookbooks on Malaysian and Southeast Asian cuisine. Her book *The Food of India* won the gold award for the Best Hardcover Recipe Book at the prestigious Jacob's Creek World Food Media Awards.

Birgit Ricquier is pursuing a PhD in linguistics at the Université Libre de Bruxelles and the Royal Museum for Central Africa, Tervuren, Belgium, with a fellowship from the Fonds de la Recherche Scientifique (FNRS). The topic of her PhD project is "A Comparative Linguistic Approach to the History of Culinary Practice in Bantu-Speaking Africa." She has spent several months in central Africa, including one month in the Democratic Republic of the Congo as a member of the Boyekoli Ebale Congo 2010 Expedition and two months of research focused on food cultures in Congo.

Amy Riolo is an award-winning author, lecturer, cooking instructor, and consultant. She is the author of *Arabian Delights: Recipes and Princely Entertaining Ideas from the Arabian Peninsula, Nile Style: Egyptian Cuisine and Culture,* and *The Mediterranean Diabetes Cookbook.* Amy has lived, worked, and traveled extensively through Egypt and enjoys fusing cuisine, culture, and history into all aspects of her work. Please see www.amyriolo.com, www.baltimoreegypt.org, and diningwithdiplomats.blogspot.com for more information and further reading.

Owen Roberts is a journalist, communications instructor, and director of research communications for the University of Guelph in Guelph, Ontario, Canada. He holds a doctorate of education from Texas Tech University and Texas A&M University.

Fiona Ross is a gastrodetective whose headquarters is the Bodleian Library in Oxford, United Kingdom. She spends her time there investigating the eating foibles of the famous and infamous. Her cookery book *Dining with Destiny* is the result: When you want to know what Lenin lunched on or what JFK ate by the poolside, *Dining with Destiny* has the answer.

Signe Rousseau (née Hansen) is Danish by birth but a long-term resident of southern Africa and is a researcher and part-time lecturer at the University of Cape Town. Following an MA in the Department of English and a PhD (on food media and celebrity chefs) in the Centre for Film and Media Studies, she now teaches critical literacy and professional communication in the School of Management Studies (Faculty of Commerce).

Kathleen Ryan is a consulting scholar in the African Section of the University of Pennsylvania Museum of Archaeology and Anthropology, Philadelphia. She has carried out research in Kenya since 1990, when she began a study of Maasai cattle herders in Kajiado District.

Helen Saberi was Alan Davidson's principal assistant in the completion of the *Oxford Companion to Food*. She is the author of *Noshe Djan: Afghan Food and Cookery;* coauthor of *Trifle* with Alan Davidson; and coauthor of *The Road to Vindaloo* with David Burnett; her latest book is *Tea: A Global History.*

Cari Sánchez holds a master of arts in gastronomy from the University of Adelaide/Le Cordon Bleu in South Australia. Her dissertation explores the global spread of the Argentine *asado*. She currently lives in Jacksonville, Florida, where she writes the food and travel blog *viCARIous* and is the marketing manager for a craft brewery.

Peter Scholliers teaches history at the Vrije Universiteit Brussel and is currently head of the research group "Social and Cultural Food Studies" (FOST). He studies the history of food in Europe in the 19th and 20th centuries. He co-edits the journal *Food and History* and is involved in various ways in the Institut Européen d'Histoire et des Cultures de l'Alimentation (Tours, France). Recently, he published *Food Culture in Belgium* (Greenwood, 2008). More information can be found at http://www.vub.ac.be/FOST/fost_in_english/.

Colleen Taylor Sen is the author of *Food Culture in India; Curry: A Global History; Pakoras, Paneer, Pappadums: A Guide to Indian Restaurant Menus,* and many articles on the food of the Indian Subcontinent. She is a regular participant in the Oxford Food Symposium.

Roger Serunyigo was born and lives in Kampala, Uganda. He graduated from Makerere University with a degree in urban and regional planning, has worked in telecommunications, and is now a professional basketball player for the Uganda National Team. He also coaches a women's basketball team (The Magic Stormers).

Dorette Snover is a chef and author. Influenced by French heritage and the food traditions of the Pennsylvania Dutch country, Chef Snover teaches exploration of the world via a culinary map at her school, C'est si Bon! in Chapel Hill. While the stock simmers, she is writing a novel about a French bread apprentice.

Celia Sorhaindo is a freelance photographer and writer. She was the editor of the 2008 and 2009 *Dominica Food and Drink Guide* magazine and content manager for the Dominica section of the magazine *Caribbean Homes & Lifestyle.*

Lyra Spang is a PhD candidate in the Department of Anthropology and the Food Studies Program at Indiana University. She has written about food, sex, and symbolism; the role of place in defining organic; and the importance of social relationships in small-scale food business in Belize. She grew up on a farm in southern Belize and is a proud promoter of that country's unique and diverse culinary heritage.

Lois Stanford is an agricultural anthropologist in the Department of Anthropology at New Mexico State University. In her research, she has examined the globalization of food systems both in Mexico and in the U.S. Southwest. Her current research focuses on the critical role of food heritage and plant conservation in constructing and maintaining traditional foodways and cultural identity in New Mexico. In collaboration with local food groups, she is currently developing a community food assessment project in the Mesilla Valley in southern New Mexico.

Aliza Stark is a senior faculty member at the Agriculture, Food, and Environment Institute of Biochemistry, Food Science, and Nutrition at the Hebrew University of Jerusalem.

Maria "Ging" Gutierrez Steinberg is a marketing manager for a New York City–based specialty food company and a food writer. She has a master's degree in food studies from New York University and is a graduate of Le Cordon Bleu. Her articles have appeared in various publications in Asia and the United States.

Anita Stewart is a cookbook author and Canadian culinary activist from Elora, Ontario, Canada.

Emily Stone has written about Guatemalan cuisine in the *Radcliffe Culinary Times,* and she is at work on a nonfiction book about chocolate in Central America. She currently teaches journalism and creative writing at Sun Yat-sen University in Guangzhou, China.

Asele Surina is a Russian native and former journalist who now works as a translator and interpreter. Since 1999 she has worked at the Institute of Classical Archaeology at the University of Texas on joint projects with an archaeological museum in Crimea, Ukraine.

Aylin Öney Tan is an architect by training and studied conservation of historic structures in Turkey, Italy, and the United Kingdom. Eventually, her passion for food and travel led her to write on food. Since 2003, she has had a weekly food column in *Cumhuriyet,* a prestigious national daily, and contributes to various food magazines. She was a jury member of the Slow Food Award 2000–2003, with her nominees receiving awards. She contributes to the Terra Madre and Presidia projects as the leader of the Ankara Convivium. She won the Sophie Coe Award on food history in 2008 for her article "Poppy: Potent yet Frail," presented previously at the Oxford Symposium on Food and Cookery where she's become a regular presenter. Currently, she is the curator of the Culinary Culture Section of Princess Islands' City Museum. She is happy to unite her expertise in archaeology and art history from her previous career with her unbounded interest in food culture.

Nicole Tarulevicz teaches at the School of Asian Languages and Studies at the University of Tasmania.

Karen Lau Taylor is a freelance food writer and consultant whose food curriculum vitae includes a master's degree in food studies from New York University, an advanced certificate from the Wine and Spirits Education Trust, and a gig as pastry cook at a five-star hotel after completing L'Academie de Cuisine's pastry arts program. She is working toward a master's degree in public health while she continues to write, teach, test recipes, eat, and drink from her home in Alexandria, Virginia.

Thy Tran is trained as a professional chef. She established Wandering Spoon to provide cooking classes, culinary consultation, and educational programming for culinary academies and nonprofit organizations throughout Northern California. Currently, she is a chef instructor at the International Culinary Schools at the Art Institute of California–San Francisco and Tante Marie's. She is also the founder and director of the Asian Culinary Forum. She co-authored *The Essentials of Asian Cooking, Taste of the World,* and the award-winning guide, *Kitchen Companion.*

Leena Trivedi-Grenier is a Bay-area food writer, cooking teacher, and social media consultant. Her writings have appeared in *The Business of Food: Encyclopedia of the Food and Drink Industry, Culinary Trends* magazine, and the *Cultural Arts Resources for Teachers and Students* newsletter and will be featured in several upcoming titles by Greenwood Press. She also runs a food/travel/gastronomy blog called *Leena Eats This Blog* (www.leenaeats.com).

Karin Vaneker graduated from the AKI Academy of Visual Arts in Enschede, the Netherlands. She later attended Sint-Lukas Hoger Instituut voor Schone Kunsten in Brussels, Belgium. She has written for numerous Dutch newspapers and magazines, specializing in trends and the cultural and other histories of ingredients and cuisines, and has published several books. Furthermore, Vaneker has worked for museums and curated an exhibition about New World taro (L. *Xanthosoma* spp.). At present she is researching its potential in domestic cuisines and gastronomy.

Penny Van Esterik is professor of anthropology at York University, Toronto, where she teaches nutritional anthropology, advocacy anthropology, and feminist theory. She does fieldwork in Southeast Asia and has developed materials on breast-feeding and women's work and infant and young child feeding.

Richard Wilk is professor of anthropology and gender studies at Indiana University, where he directs the Food Studies Program. With a PhD in anthropology from the University of Arizona, he has taught at the University of California,

Berkeley; University of California, Santa Cruz; New Mexico State University; and University College London and has held fellowships at Gothenburg University and the University of London. His publications include more than 125 papers and book chapters, a textbook in economic anthropology, and several edited volumes. His most recent books are *Home Cooking in the Global Village* (Berg Publishers), *Off the Edge: Experiments in Cultural Analysis* (with Orvar Lofgren; Museum Tusculanum Press), *Fast Food/Slow Food* (Altamira Press), and *Time, Consumption, and Everyday Life* (with Elizabeth Shove and Frank Trentmann; Berg Publishers).

Chelsie Yount is a PhD student of anthropology at Northwestern University in Evanston, Illinois. She lived in Senegal in 2005 and again in 2008, when performing ethnographic research for her master's thesis at the École des Hautes Études en Sciences Sociales in Paris, on the topic of Senegalese food and eating habits.

Marcia Zoladz is a cook, food writer, and food-history researcher with her own Web site, Cozinha da Marcia (Marcia's Kitchen; www.cozinhadamarcia.com.br). She is a regular participant and contributor at the Oxford Symposium on Food and History and has published three books in Brazil, Germany, and Holland—*Cozinha Portuguesa* (Portuguese cooking), *Muito Prazer* (Easy recipes), and *Brigadeiros e Bolinhas* (Sweet and savory Brazilian finger foods).

Index